THE GUINNESS
RECORD OF THE

WORLD
CUP

1930-94

THE GUINNESS RECORD OF THE

WORLD CUP

1930-94

JACK ROLLIN

GUINNESS PUBLISHING

CONTENTS

HOW IT ALL BEGAN

The idea of a World Cup first emerged in 1904 when FIFA was formed, but it was not until 1930 that it became reality and the tournament has since matured into the symbol of world soccer supremacy. In the 60 years that have followed, both the membership of FIFA and the competition itself have grown in stature. Long-forgotten has been the simple idea of a knock-out tournament; the World Cup has become a business operation, with television and sponsorship considerations taking precedence over all other aspects.

But it began modestly enough. The Federation Internationale de Football Association (FIFA) was founded on 21 May 1904 in Paris by representatives of seven European countries: France, Belgium, Denmark, the Netherlands, Spain, Sweden and Switzerland. Included in the statutes of what was to become the governing body of world football was a clause to the effect that FIFA alone would have the right to organise a world championship.

Membership gradually increased. Germany joined shortly afterwards; Austria, England and Italy the following year. By the end of the First World War, there were 25 countries affiliated including Scotland and Wales, admitted in 1910, and Northern Ireland a year later, plus Argentina, Brazil and Chile as well as the USA from the Americas.

In 1921 Jules Rimet, a French lawyer, became President of FIFA and the possibility of a World Cup came closer, though it took years of lengthy persuasion on his part to convince others to accept the concept. His efforts were assisted in a practical way by Uruguay coming over from South America to win the Olympic Games football tournaments in Europe in 1924 and 1928. In May 1929 it was agreed that a World Cup competition would be held the following year.

FIFA's membership then stood at 41, though England, Northern Ireland, Wales and Scotland had left the organisation for a second time and were ineligible for the inaugural competition. The four had originally withdrawn after refusing to be associated with either Austria, Germany or Hungary (members of the axis nations in the First World War) and they quit for a second time over broken time-payments to amateurs.

Although there had not been universal approval among the members, FIFA's meeting in 1926 had brought a strong plea from Henri Delaunay, secretary of the French Federation, that an international football tournament at the highest level could no longer be confined to the Olympics because of professionalism. At the 1928 Congress however, the proposals put forward by Delaunay were carried with over 80 percent of the members in favour of the project.

Six countries — Italy, Holland, Hungary, Sweden, Spain and Uruguay — applied to stage the finals. But Sweden had even voted against the idea! Uruguay was the obvious choice. They had proved their playing ability with two Olympic gold medals, the country was celebrating its independence centenary in 1930 and they promised to underwrite the costs of the competing countries.

It was only then that enthusiasm began to wane. Few European countries could afford to send a team to South America, since the players would be away from home for at least two months, travelling to and from the venue by boat. Had it not been for the intervention of Rimet himself, France would not have entered, and neither would Belgium but for their FIFA representative Rudolphe Seeldrayers. Rumania and Yugoslavia were the only other European acceptors. King Carol of Rumania actually picked his team and succeeded in obtaining time off

Jules Rimet, the man who gave his name to the first World Cup trophy. A Frenchman, he was President of FIFA from 1921 to 1954. (POPPERFOTO)

work for the players who were chosen to undertake the journey.

All four European teams travelled together and South America dominated the overall entry. Uruguay had also guaranteed a new ground and work on the Centenario Stadium in Montevideo was started in February. It remained unfinished at the beginning of the tournament on 13 July, despite day and night construction, because of intermittent heavy rain. Opening matches were played either at the Pocitos or Parque Central stadia until the main stadium was available.

The trophy which was presented to the winners of the World Cup was a gold cup designed by Abel Lafleur, a French sculptor; appropriately it was named after Jules Rimet himself. After Brazil's three successes in 1958, 1962 and 1970 they were allowed to retain it. It was replaced by the FIFA World Cup, designed by the Italian sculptor Silvio Gazamiga, made of solid gold 36 cm high and insured for £1.8 million.

FIFA's membership now stands at 166 countries, distributed in six Confederations and there is a waiting list of other nations eager to join the world-wide organisation. The World Cup every four years has to attempt to satisfy the clamour of all of them to have a reasonable chance of progressing to the final stage. The increase from 16 to 24 teams in the final tournament has eased the problem but by no means solved it.

It would be naive to pretend that the finalists represent all of the most outstanding of contemporary teams. The system does not allow for this eventuality. Indeed it would be difficult to conceive of a tournament on a world-wide scale that could improve on the present one, without alienating a huge chunk of the member nations. But it remains the game's pinnacle and a target for all the countries to aim at.

Lorenzo
Fernandez, Pedro
Cea and Hector
Scarone celebrate
Uruguay's World
Cup victory in
Montevideo.
(HULTON DEUTSCH)

URUGUAY

1930

Uruguay proved to be worthy champions and despite the disappointment of the the small European entry, this first tournament was a success with only one serious reservation: the bitterness between the supporters of the two finalists, Uruguay and Argentina. The repercussions of this reverberated back from Montevideo to Buenos Aires across the River Plate and resulted in the Argentine FA severing connections with the hosts.

The first hint of trouble came two days after the competition had started on July 13, when the Uruguayan crowd supported the French team against Argentina. Argentine supporters had arrived in ten boats and were searched for weapons both at the docks and before entering the ground. All the visiting teams were guarded by soldiers with fixed bayonets!

Argentina's delegation almost returned home as a result of this incident, in a match which ended in a bizarre manner. Referee Almeida Rego blew for time a full five minutes too early, as France appeared likely to score an equaliser. The crowd invaded the pitch and after protests from the French, the remaining minutes were then completed.

Controversy followed Argentina. The Bolivian referee Ulysses Saucedo awarded five penalties in their game with Mexico and police had to step in to stop fighting between players in the fracas with Chile, instigated by Argentine centre-half Luisito Monti, a belligerent if commanding figure.

The United States team, nicknamed the 'shot-putters' by the French, included five ex-Scottish professionals and an Englishman. They won their group well and were fancied in the semi-final with Argentina. But they lost one player with a broken leg after ten minutes, their goalkeeper was badly injured by half-time and another received a kick in the mouth. They lost 6-1.

Uruguay reached the final without being over-extended. They also had a 6-1 semi-final win, over Yugoslavia. Their strength was built around the half-back line of Jose Andrade, Lorenzo Fernandez and Alvaro Gestido, known as 'la costilla metallica' — the iron curtain. The nucleus of the side which had won the 1924 and 1928 Olympics was formidable.

Although Pablo Dorado scored for Uruguay after 12 minutes, Argentina led 2-1 at half-time through goals by Peucelle and Stabile, the latter effort claimed as off-side by the Uruguayans. After the break, the home crowd saw Uruguay's territorial domination and slight technical superiority turned into goals. Pedro Cea scored an opportunist equaliser and Iriarte made it 3-2. In the dying moments Castro put a truer finish on the score with a splendid long-range drive.

Though the game had been played in a good spirit, in Buenos Aires the locals took it badly. There were public demonstrations and anti-Uruguayan outbursts in the press. It proved that national prestige meant as much as the game itself.

Jose Leandro Andrade, Uruguay's outstanding right-half in their 1924 and 1928 Olympic winning teams and in their successful 1930 World Cup side.
(PRESSENS BILD)

The two captains, Nasazzi (left) of
Uruguay and Ferreyra (right) of
Argentina, shake hands before the
1930 final in Montevideo, watched
by Belgian referee Langenus.
(HULTON DEUTSCH)

Final Tournament URUGUAY
GROUP 1

13.7.30 France (3) 4, Mexico (0) 1 MONTEVIDEO
France: Thepot, Mattler, Capelle, Villaplane, Pinel, Chantrel, Liberati, Delfour, Maschinot (2), Laurent (1), Langiller (1)
Mexico: Bonfiglio, Gutierrez R, Rosas M, Rosas F, Sanchez, Amezcua, Perez, Carreno (1), Mejia, Ruiz, Lopez
Referee: Lombardi (Uruguay)

15.7.30 Argentina (0) 1, France (0) 0 MONTEVIDEO
Argentina: Bossio, Della Torre, Muttis, Suarez, Monti (1), Evaristo J, Perinetti, Varallo, Ferreyra, Gierro, Evaristo M
France: Thepot, Mattler, Capelle, Villaplane, Pinel, Chantrel, Liberati, Delfour, Maschinot, Laurent, Langiller
Referee: Rego (Brazil)

16.7.30 Chile (1) 3, Mexico (0) 0 MONTEVIDEO
Chile: Cortes, Morales, Porier, Torres A, Saavedra, Helgueta, Ojeda, Subiabre (2), Villalobos, Vidal (1), Scheuerberger
Mexico: Sota, Gutierrez R, Rosas M, Rosas F, Sanchez, Amezcua, Perez, Carreno, Ruiz, Gayon, Lopez
Referee: Christophe (Belgium)

19.7.30 Chile (0) 1, France (0) 0 MONTEVIDEO
Chile: Cortes, Ciaparro, Morales, Torres A, Saavedra, Torres C, Ojeda, Subiabre (1), Villalobos, Vidal, Scheuerberger
France: Thepot, Mattler, Capelle, Chantrel, Delmer, Villaplane, Liberati, Delfour, Pinel, Veinante, Langiller
Referee: Tejada (Uruguay)

19.7.30 Argentina (3) 6, Mexico (1) 3 MONTEVIDEO
Argentina: Bossio, Della Torre, Paternoster, Cividini, Zumelzu (2 pens), Orlandini, Peucelle, Varallo (1), Stabile (3), Demaria, Spadaro
Mexico: Bonfiglio, Gutierrez R, Gutierrez F, Rosas M (2 pens), Sanchez, Rodriguez, Rosas F, Lopez (1), Gayon, Carreno, Olivares
Referee: Saucedo (Bolivia)

22.7.30 Argentina (2) 3, Chile (1) 1 MONTEVIDEO
Argentina: Bossio, Della Torre, Paternoster, Evaristo J, Monti, Orlandini, Peucelle, Varallo, Stabile (2), Ferreyra, Evaristo M (1)
Chile: Cortes, Ciaparro, Morales, Torres A, Saavedra, Torres C, Avellane, Subiabre (1), Villalobos, Vidal, Aquilera
Referee: Langenus (Belgium)

	P	W	D	L	F	A	Pts
Argentina	3	3	0	0	10	4	6
Chile	3	2	0	1	5	3	4
France	3	1	0	2	4	3	2
Mexico	3	0	0	3	4	13	0

GROUP 2

14.7.30 Yugoslavia (2) 2, Brazil (0) 1 MONTEVIDEO
Yugoslavia: Jaksic, Ivkovic, Mihailovic, Arsenijevic, Stefanovic, Dokic, Tirnanic (1), Marjanovic (1), Beck, Vujadinovic, Sekulic
Brazil: Joel, Brilhante, Italia, Hermogenes, Fausto, Fernando, Poly, Nilo, Araken, Preguinho (1), Moderato
Referee: Tejada (Uruguay)

17.7.30 Yugoslavia (0) 4, Bolivia (0) 0 MONTEVIDEO
Yugoslavia: Jaksic, Ivkovic, Mihailovic, Arsenijevic, Stefanovic, Dokic, Tirnanic (1), Beck (2), Vujadinovic (1), Marjanovic (1), Najdanovic
Bolivia: Bermudez, Durandal, Ciavarria, Argote, Lara, Valderrama, Gomez, Bustamante, Mendez, Alborta, Fernandez
Referee: Mateucci (Mexico)

20.7.30 Brazil (1) 4, Bolivia (0) 0 MONTEVIDEO
Brazil: Velloso, Ze Luiz, Italia, Hermogenes, Fausto, Fernando, Benedito, Russinho, Leite, Preguinho (2), Moderato (2)
Bolivia: Bermudez, Durandal, Ciavarria, Sainz, Lara, Valderrama, Ortiz, Bustamante, Mendez, Alborta, Fernandez
Referee: Balway (France)

	P	W	D	L	F	A	Pts
Yugoslavia	2	2	0	0	6	1	4
Brazil	2	1	0	1	5	2	2
Bolivia	2	0	0	2	0	8	0

GROUP 3

14.7.30 Rumania (1) 3, Peru (0) 1 MONTEVIDEO
Rumania: Lapusneanu, Steiner, Burger, Rafinski, Vogl, Fieraru, Covaci, Desu, Wetzer, Staucin (2), Barbu (1)
Peru: Valdiviso, De Las Casas, Soria, Galindo, Garcia, Valle, Flores, Villanueva, Denegri, Neira, Souza (1)
Referee: Warken (Chile)

18.7.30 Uruguay (0) 1, Peru (0) 0 MONTEVIDEO
Uruguay: Ballesteros, Nasazzi, Tejera, Andrade, Fernandez, Gestido, Urdinaran, Castro (1), Petrone, Cea, Iriarte
Peru: Pardon, De Las Casas, Maquillon, Denegri, Galindo, Astengo, Lavalle, Flores, Villanueva, Neira, Souza
Referee: Langenus (Belgium)

21.7.30 Uruguay (3) 4, Rumania (0) 0 MONTEVIDEO
Uruguay: Ballesteros, Nasazzi, Mascheroni, Andrade, Fernandez, Gestido, Dorado (1), Scarone (1), Anselmo (1), Cea (1), Iriarte
Rumania: Lapusneanu, Burger, Tacu, Robi, Vogl, Fieraru, Covaci, Desu, Wetzer, Rafinski, Barbu
Referee: Rego (Brazil)

	P	W	D	L	F	A	Pts
Uruguay	2	2	0	0	5	0	4
Rumania	2	1	0	1	3	5	2
Peru	2	0	0	2	1	4	0

GROUP 4

13.7.30 USA (2) 3, Belgium (0) 0 MONTEVIDEO
USA: Douglas, Wood, Moorhouse, Gallacher, Tracey, Brown, Gonzalvez, Florie, Patenaude (1), Auld, McGhee (2)
Belgium: Badjou, Nouwens, Hoydonckx, Braine, Hellemans, Declercq, Diddens, Moeschal, Adams, Voorhoof, Versijp
Referee: Macias (Argentina)

17.7.30 USA (2) 3, Paraguay (0) 0 MONTEVIDEO
USA: Douglas, Wood, Moorhouse, Gallacher, Tracey, Brown, Gonzalvez, Florie (1), Patenaude (2), Auld, McGhee
Paraguay: Denis, Olmedo, Miracca, Etcheverrey, Diaz, Aguirre, Nessi, Dominquez, Gonzales, Gaceres, Pena
Referee: Macias (Argentina)

20.7.30 Paraguay (1) 1, Belgium (0) 0 MONTEVIDEO
Paraguay: Benitez P, Olmedo, Flores, Benitez S, Diaz, Garcete, Nessi, Romero, Gonzales, Gaceres, Pena (1)
Belgium: Badjou, Dedeken, Hoydonckx, Braine, Hellemans, Moeschal, Versijp, Delbeke, Adams, Nouwens, Diddens
Referee: Vallarino (Uruguay)

	P	W	D	L	F	A	Pts
USA	2	2	0	0	6	0	4
Paraguay	2	1	0	1	1	3	2
Belgium	2	0	0	2	0	4	0

SEMI FINALS

26.7.30 Argentina (1) 6, USA (0) 1 MONTEVIDEO
Argentina: Botasso, Della Torre, Paternoster, Evaristo J, Monti (2), Orlandini, Peucelle, Scopelli (2), Stabile (2), Ferreyra, Evaristo M
USA: Douglas, Wood, Moorhouse, Gallacher, Tracey, Brown (1), Gonzalvez, Florie, Patenaude, Auld, McGhee
Referee: Langenus (Belgium)

27.7.30 Uruguay (3) 6, Yugoslavia (1) 1 MONTEVIDEO
Uruguay: Ballesteros, Nasazzi, Mascheroni, Andrade, Fernandez, Gestido, Dorado, Scarone, Anselmo (2), Cea (3), Iriarte (1)
Yugoslavia: Jaksic, Ivkovic, Mihailovic, Arsenijevic, Stefanovic, Dokic, Tirnanic, Marjanovic, Beck, Vujadinovic, Sekulic (1)
Referee: Rego (Brazil)

FINAL

30.7.30 Uruguay (1) 4, Argentina (2) 2 MONTEVIDEO
Uruguay: Ballesteros, Nasazzi, Mascheroni, Andrade, Gestido, Fernandez, Dorado (1), Scarone, Castro (1), Cea (1), Iriarte (1)
Argentina: Botasso, Della Torre, Paternoster, Evaristo J, Monti, Suarez, Peucelle (1), Varallo, Stabile (1), Ferreyra, Evaristo M
Referee: Langenus (Belgium)

The Italian team
raise their arms in
the fascist salute
prior to the 1934
final against
Czechoslovakia.
(HULTON DEUTSCH)

ITALY

1934

Apart from the doubtful political aspect, Italy was a good choice as the host nation. Dictator Mussolini was determined to make as much capital out of the competition as possible, but it had needed eight meetings of FIFA to agree to the Italian venue.

Thirty-two countries originally entered and were geographically grouped in 12 sections of a qualifying tournament. England, still outside FIFA, and Uruguay, piqued by the lack of interest in their own series and worried by domestic matters, did not enter. Even Italy had to play a qualifying game, against Greece.

The 16 finalists were paired in a knock-out round, eight seeded against weaker opposition, the matches held in eight different cities. Italy were the favourites, largely because it was agreed that Austria's 'wunderteam' was over-the-hill. The Italian manager Vittorio Pozzo was shrewd and had a talented team. He had succeeded in blending the natural strength and team work he had so admired when he had visited England, with the individual ability of the Latins.

Two factors stood out — the individual performances of several players and the increase of violence on the field as national pride and international disagreement came to the fore.

Czechoslovakia had a resourceful and adept goalkeeper in Frantisek Planicka, and Spain a custodian of equal ability in the legendary Ricardo Zamora. The latter played in what was then the most disgraceful of all World Cup matches, Italy's violent clash with Spain in Florence. The result was a 1-1 draw, but when the replay took place the following day, seven injured Spaniards and four Italians were non-starters!

Italy won the replay 1-0 and had a similar result in the semi-final against Austria, the goal being scrambled in off a post by the Argentine-born Enrico Guaita, one of three

from that country of Italian parentage, including Monti from the 1930 final. The Italians' star forward was Giuseppe Meazza, but in the final the Czechs' neat, short-passing game surprised the hosts. The stadium in Rome was not full, but Mussolini was among the 55,000. Twenty minutes from the end of an undistinguished match, the crowd was stunned when Puc put Czechoslovakia ahead following a corner, much to the delight of visiting supporters who had travelled to Rome from Prague by road and rail.

Possibly through over-eagerness the Czechs then missed two further chances, one hitting a post. The Italians switched their forwards in a desperate bid to save the game. Eight minutes from time the Argentine Raimondo Orsi hit a swerving shot of speculative origin to equalise.

Only in extra time did the Italians display the tactical skill and strategy for which they were renowned and Angelo Schiavio scored the winner. For the Italian regime, it represented everything they had hoped for.

Qualifying Tournament
32 entries
Argentina, Austria, Belgium, Brazil, Bulgaria, Chile, Cuba, Czechoslovakia, Egypt, Estonia, France, Germany, Greece, Haiti, Holland, Hungary, Rep of Ireland, Italy, Lithuania, Luxembourg, Mexico, Palestine, Peru, Poland, Portugal, Rumania, Spain, Sweden, Switzerland, Turkey, USA, Yugoslavia

A preliminary qualification round in ten regional groups had been prepared. This was adapted according to the entries and increased to twelve groups. Each group produced one qualifier with the exception of groups 8, 10, 11 and 12 where the first two progressed. However there were one or two complications.

In Group 10, Switzerland qualified after successfully protesting that Rumania had fielded an ineligible player against them. Rumania's qualification was thus under threat. Meanwhile in Group 1, Cuba had won two and drawn one of three games in Haiti and went on to play three games in Mexico which they lost. Since the USA had not played, it was agreed that an extra qualifying game would be completed between them and Mexico. At the same time there would be a possibility that the USA could compete in the finals in any case, because of the likely loss of a qualifier from Group 10. So the extra game was arranged in Rome, three days before the final tournament began. But Rumania appealed against the decision involving their alleged ineligible player and found it upheld in their favour. They were then awarded a place in the finals. The USA and Mexico played off for another place.

Many of the preliminary groups had seeded teams in them. Italy in Group 7 needed to play just one home game with Greece to qualify, presumably so as not to risk them losing over two matches and thus not appearing in their own tournament!

In Group 8, Austria merely had to play Bulgaria at home while their opponents were forced to play Hungary home and away. Moreover, though the Bulgaria v Hungary scores cancelled each other out, the 6-1 defeat in Vienna put Bulgaria out of the finals.

In Groups 10 and 11, each of the three teams had one home game; in Group 12 Germany and France each played away in Luxembourg. In Group 5, Sweden played Estonia at home and Lithuania away, while in Group 9 Poland, having lost at home to Czechoslovakia, withdrew before the return match. In Group 11, Belgium qualified on goal average over the Republic of Ireland.

Group 1 (USA, Cuba, Mexico, Haiti)
Haiti v Cuba 1 - 3, 1 - 1, 0 - 6
Mexico v Cuba 3 - 2, 5 - 0, 4 - 1
Extra qualifying match (in Rome): USA v Mexico 4 - 2
USA qualified

Group 2 (Brazil, Peru)
Brazil qualified (Peru withdrew)

Group 3 (Argentina, Chile)
Chile qualified (Argentina withdrew)

Group 4 (Egypt, Palestine; Turkey withdrew)
Egypt v Palestine 7 - 1, 4 - 1
Egypt qualified

Group 5 (Sweden, Estonia, Lithuania)
Sweden v Estonia 6 - 2; Lithuania v Sweden 0 - 2
Sweden qualified

Group 6 (Spain, Portugal)
Spain v Portugal 9 - 0, 2 - 1
Spain qualified

Group 7 (Italy, Greece)
Italy v Greece 4 - 0
Italy qualified

Group 8 (Austria, Hungary, Bulgaria)
Bulgaria v Hungary 1 - 4; Austria v Bulgaria 6 - 1; Hungary v Bulgaria 4 - 1
Austria and Hungary qualified

Group 9 (Czechoslovakia, Poland)
Poland v Czechoslovakia 1 - 2. Poland withdrew before return match.
Czechoslovakia qualified.

Group 10 (Yugoslavia, Switzerland, Rumania)
Yugoslavia v Switzerland 2 - 2; Switzerland v Rumania 2 - 2; Rumania v Yugoslavia 2 - 1
Switzerland and Rumania qualified

Group 11 (Holland, Belgium, Rep of Ireland)
Rep of Ireland v Belgium 4 - 4; Holland v Rep of Ireland 5 - 2; Belgium v Holland 2 - 4
Holland and Belgium qualified (Belgium on goal average)

Group 12 (Germany, France, Luxembourg)
Luxembourg v Germany 1 - 9; Luxembourg v France 1 - 6
Germany and France qualified

Final Tournament ITALY
Preliminary round
27.5.34 Italy (3) 7, USA (0) 1 ROME
Italy: Combi, Rosetta, Allemandi, Pizzioli, Monti, Bertolini, Guaita, Meazza (1), Schiavio (3), Ferrari (1), Orsi (2)
USA: Hjulian, Czerkiewicz, Moorhouse, Pietras, Gonzalvez, Florie, Ryan, Nilson, Donelli (1), Dick, MacLean
Referee: Mercet (Switzerland)

27.5.34 Czechoslovakia (0) 2, Rumania (1) 1 TRIESTE
Czechoslovakia: Planicka, Zenizek, Ctyroky, Kostalek, Cambal, Krcil, Junek, Silny, Sobotka, Nejedly (1), Puc (1)
Rumannia: Zambori, Vogl, Albu, Deheleanu, Cotormani, Moravet, Bindea, Covaci, Sepi, Bodola, Dobai (1)
Referee: Langenus (Belgium)

27.5.34 Spain (3) 3, Brazil (0) 1 GENOA
Spain: Zamora, Ciriaco, Quincoces, Cilaurren, Muquerza, Marculeta, Lafuente, Iraragorri (1 pen), Langara (2), Lecue, Gorostiza
Brazil: Pedrosa, Sylvio, Luz, Tinoco, Martim, Armandinho, Canalli, Luizinho, Waldemar, Patesko, Leonidas (1)
Referee: Birlem (Germany)

27.5.34 Switzerland (2) 3, Holland (1) 2 MILAN
Switzerland: Sechehaye, Minelli, Weiler II, Guinchard, Jaccard, Hufschmid, Von Kanel, Passello, Kielholz (2), Abegglen (1), Bossi
Netherlands: Van der Meulen, Weber, Van Run, Pellikaan, Anderiesen, Van Heel, Wels, Vente (1), Bakhuijs, Smit (1), Van Nellen
Referee: Eklind (Sweden)

27.5.34 Sweden (1) 3, Argentina (1) 2 BOLOGNA
Sweden: Rydberg, Axelsson, Andersson S, Carlsson, Rosen, Andersson E, Dunker, Gustavsson, Jonasson (2), Keller, Kroon (1)
Argentina: Freschi, Pedevilla, Belis (1), Nehin, Sosa-Ubrieta, Lopez, Rua, Wilde, De Vincenzi, Galateo (1), Iraneta
Referee: Braun (Austria)

27.5.34 Germany (1) 5, Belgium (2) 2 FLORENCE
Germany: Kress, Haringer, Schwartz, Janes, Szepan, Zielinski, Lehner, Hohmann, Conen (3), Siffling, Kobierski (2)
Belgium: Van De Weyer, Smellinckx, Joachim, Peeraer, Welkenhuyzen, Klaessens, Devries, Voorhoof (2), Capelle, Gimmonprez, Herremans
Referee: Mattea (Italy)

27.5.34 Austria (1) 3, France (1) 2 (aet, 1 - 1 at 90 mins) TURIN
Austria: Platzer, Cisar, Sesta, Wagner, Smistik, Urbanek, Zischek, Bican (1), Sindelar (1), Schall(1), Viertel
France: Thepot, Mairesse, Mattler, Delfour, Verriest (1 pen), Llense, Keller, Alcazar, Nicolas (1), Rio, Aston
Referee: Van Moorsel (Netherlands)

27.5.34 Hungary (2) 4, Egypt (2) 2 NAPLES
Hungary: Szabo A, Futo, Sternberg, Palotas, Szucs, Lazar, Markos, Vincze (1), Teleki (1), Toldi (2), Szabo F
Egypt: Moustafa Kemal, Ali Caf, Hamitu, El Far, Refaat, Rayab, Latif, Fawzi (2), Muktar, Masoud Kemal, Hassan
Referee: Barlassina (Italy)

QUARTER FINALS
31.5.34 Germany (0) 2, Sweden (0) 1 MILAN
Germany: Kress, Haringer, Busch, Gramlich, Szepan, Zielinski, Lehner, Hohmann (2), Conen, Siffling, Kobierski

Sweden: Rydberg, Axelsson, Andersson S, Carlsson, Rosen, Andersson E, Dunker (1), Gustavsson, Jonasson, Keller, Kroon
Referee: Barlassina (Italy)

31.5.34 Czechoslovakia (1) 3, Switzerland (1) 2 TURIN
Czechoslovakia: Planicka, Zenizek, Ctyroky, Kostalek, Cambal, Krcil, Junek, Svoboda (1), Sobotka (1), Nejedly (1), Puc
Switzerland: Sechehaye, Minelli, Weiler II, Guinchard, Jaccard, Hufschmid, Von Kanel, Jaeggi IV, Kielholz (1), Abegglen III (1), Jack
Referee: Beranek (Austria)

31.5.34 Austria (1) 2, Hungary (0) 1 BOLOGNA
Austria: Platzer, Cisar, Sesta, Wagner, Smistik, Urbanek, Zischek (1), Bican, Sindelar, Horvath (1), Viertel
Hungary: Szabo A, Vago, Sternberg, Palotas, Szucs, Szalay, Markos, Avar, Sarosi (1 pen), Toldi, Kemeny
Referee: Mattea (Italy)

31.5.34 Italy (0) 1, Spain (1) 1 (aet, 1 - 1 at 90 mins) FLORENCE
Italy: Combi, Monzeglio, Allemandi, Pizziolo, Monti, Castellazzi, Guaita, Meazza, Schiavio, Ferrari (1), Orsi
Spain: Zamora, Ciriaco, Quincoces, Cillaurren, Muquerza, Lecue, Lafuente, Iraragorri, Langara, Regueiro (1), Gorostiza
Referee: Baert (Belgium)

Quarter Final replay
1.6.34 Italy (1) 1, Spain (0) 0 FLORENCE
Italy: Combi, Monzeglio, Allemandi, Ferraris IV, Monti, Bertolini, Guaita, Meazza (1), Borel II, Demaria, Orsi
Spain: Nogues, Zabalo, Quincoces, Cillaurren, Muquerza, Lecue, Ventolra, Regueiro, Campanal, Chacha, Bosch
Referee: Mercet (Switzerland)

SEMI FINALS
3.6.34 Czechoslovakia (1) 3, Germany (0) 1 ROME
Czechoslovakia: Planicka, Ctyroky, Burger, Kostalek, Kambal, Krcil (1), Junek, Svoboda, Sobotka, Nejedly (2), Puc
Germany: Kress, Busch, Haringer, Zielinski, Szepan, Bender, Lehner, Conen, Noack (1), Kobierski
Referee: Barlassina (Italy)

3.6.34 Italy (1) 1, Austria (0) 0 MILAN
Italy: Combi, Monzeglio, Allemandi, Ferraris IV, Monti, Bertolini, Guaita (1), Meazza, Schiavio, Ferrari, Orsi
Austria: Platzer, Cisar, Sesta, Wagner, Smistik, Urbanek, Zischek, Bican, Sindelar, Schall, Viertel
Referee: Carraro (Italy)

Match for third place
6.6.34 Germany (3) 3, Austria (1) 2 NAPLES
Germany: Jakob, Janes, Busch, Zielinski, Munzenberg, Bender, Lehner (2), Siffling, Conen (1), Szepan, Heidemann
Austria: Platzer, Cisar, Sesta (1), Wagner, Smistik, Urbanek, Zischek, Braun, Bican, Horvath (1), Viertel
Referee: Carraro (Italy)

FINAL
10.6.34 Italy (0) 2, Czechoslovakia (0) 1 (aet, 1-1 at 90 mins) ROME
Italy: Combi, Monzeglio, Allemandi, Ferraris IV, Monti, Bertolini, Guaita, Meazza, Schiavio (1), Ferrari, Orsi (1)
Czechoslovakia: Planicka, Zenizek, Ctyroky, Kostalek, Cambal, Krcil, Junek, Svoboda, Sobotka, Nejedly, Puc (1)
Referee: Eklind (Sweden)

Pozzo brandishes the Jules Rimet trophy after Italy's second successive World Cup victory, surrounded by delighted players and officials. (HULTON DEUTSCH)

FRANCE

1938

The Italians retained the World Cup four years after staging the tournament, overcoming Hungary in an entertaining final, while the war clouds were gathering in Europe. The sound of hostilities had already been heard in two of the countries who qualified and the atmosphere was charged with apprehension.

As a gesture to FIFA President Jules Rimet, it had been agreed to hold the 1938 competition in France. There was a record entry of 36 but of this number, Austria found themselves overrun by Germany after qualifying and Spain was embroiled in a civil war. The 1930 finalists Uruguay and Argentina did not enter, the former because of continuing domestic problems, the latter after withdrawing a late application for entry. England received an invitation to compete, but again declined. As holders, Italy were exempted from the qualifying competition.

In the Preliminary Round, Austria's withdrawal gave Sweden a walk-over in the knock-out system retained from the previous series. The highest scoring match involved Brazil and Poland, the Brazilians winning 6-5 after extra time. Both sides had an ace marksman who scored four times: Brazil's Leonidas da Silva and Poland's Ernest Willimowski.

Italy, with only two survivors from 1934 — the captain Meazza and Ferrari — but several members of their 1936 Olympic Games gold medal side, struggled to beat Norway 2-1 after the extra period. Czechoslovakia, who had been Italy's final victims four years earlier, were involved in a second round battle with Brazil in Bordeaux. Brazil had Procopio and Machado sent off along with the Czechs' Riha. Czechoslovakia also lost Nejedly with a broken leg and goalkeeper Planicka with a broken arm. The sides were level 1-1 after extra time. The teams showed 15 changes for the replay which passed

Italy's cultured right-back Alfredo Foni executes an overhead kick to clear his lines in the 1938 final against Hungary. (HULTON DEUTSCH)

off without incident, with Brazil winning 2-1.

The Brazilians were so confident they left out Leonidas and Tim for the semi-final with Italy in Marseilles, in order to save them for the final. But Colaussi put the Italians ahead and when Domingos da Guia pulled down Italy's crack centre-forward Silvio Piola, Meazza scored from the spot in a 2-1 win.

In the other semi-final, Hungary cleverly cut off the supply to Sweden's Gustav Wetterstrom, who had scored four times against Cuba, and won easily 5-1. But in the final, Italy swept aside the delicate Hungarians.

Colaussi scored after six minutes, but Hungary's persistence with short-passing produced an equaliser. Back came Italy with more goals from Colaussi and Piola before half-time. Afterwards, the Hungarians gained a hold in midfield and made it 3-2, before Piola drove in another ten minutes from the end.

Then Meazza's fascist salute said it all.

Qualifying Tournament

36 entries
Europe (25): Austria, Belgium, Bulgaria, Czechoslovakia, Egypt, Estonia, Finland, France, Germany, Greece, Holland, Hungary, Republic of Ireland, Italy, Latvia, Lithuania, Luxembourg, Norway, Palestine, Poland, Portugal, Rumania, Sweden, Switzerland, Yugoslavia
North and Central America (5): Costa Rica, Cuba, Mexico, El Salvador, USA
South America (4): Argentina, Brazil, Colombia, Surinam
Asia (2): Dutch East Indies, Japan

Spain had also entered but because of the civil war could not compete. Argentina's entry was late, but accepted — then they withdrew! For the first time both holders (Italy) and hosts (France) were exempted from the qualifying competition.

Europe had eight groups, each producing one qualifier with the exception of groups 1, 2 and 8 where the first two progressed. Final places in France were to be distributed as follows: Europe (11 + France, Italy), North and Central America (1), South America (1), Asia (1).

In Group 2 there was a sub-division of two teams playing against each other in the four-team section. In Group 4 Switzerland and Portugal met in one match played in a neutral country, while in Group 5, Hungary played the winners of Palestine v Greece in one game. In Group 1 teams played each other just once.

Austria, who also met the winners of Latvia and Lithuania in one match and qualified, were drawn to play Sweden in the finals in Lyons on 5 June, but on 12 April the organisers were informed that Germany's annexation of Austria had left the country without an independent team which reduced the number of finalists to 15.

Group 1 (Germany, Sweden, Estonia, Finland)
Sweden v Finland 4 - 0; Sweden v Estonia 7 - 2; Finland v Germany 0 - 2; Finland v Estonia 0 - 1; Germany v Estonia 4 -1; Germany v Sweden 5 - 0
Germany and Sweden qualified

Group 2 (Poland, Norway, Yugoslavia, Rep of Ireland)
Poland v Yugoslavia 4 - 0; Yugoslavia v Poland 1 - 0; Norway v Rep of Ireland 3 - 2; Rep of Ireland v Norway 3 - 3
Poland and Norway qualified

Group 3 (Rumania, Egypt)
Rumania qualified (Egypt withdrew)

Group 4 (Switzerland, Portugal)
Switzerland v Portugal 2 - 1 (in Milan)
Switzerland qualified

Group 5 (Hungary, Greece, Palestine)
Palestine v Greece 1 - 3; Greece v Palestine 1 - 0
Hungary v Greece 11 - 1
Hungary qualified

Group 6 (Czechoslovakia, Bulgaria)
Bulgaria v Czechoslavakia 1 - 1, 0 - 6
Czechoslovakia qualified

Group 7 (Austria, Latvia, Lithuania)
Latvia v Lithuania 4 - 2; Lithuania v Latvia 1 - 5; Austria v Latvia 2 - 1
Austria qualified

Group 8 (Belgium, Holland, Luxembourg)
Holland v Luxembourg 4 - 0; Luxembourg v Belgium 2 - 3; Belgium v Holland 1-1
Holland and Belgium qualified

Group 9 (Dutch East Indies, Japan)
Dutch East Indies qualified (Japan withdrew)

Group 10 (Brazil, Argentina)
Brazil qualified (Argentina withdrew)

Group 11 (USA)
USA withdrew

Group 12 (Colombia, Costa Rica, Cuba, Mexico, El Salvador, Surinam)
All teams except Cuba withdrew
Cuba qualified

Final Tournament FRANCE

Preliminary round

4.6.38 Switzerland (1) 1, Germany (1) 1 (aet, 1-1 at 90 mins) PARIS
Switzerland: Huber, Minelli, Lehmann, Springer, Vernati, Lortscher, Amado, Walaschek, Bickel, Abegglen III (1), Aeby
Germany: Raftl, Janes, Schmaus, Kupfer, Mock, Ritzinger, Lehner, Gellesch, Gauchel (1), Hahnemann, Pesser
Referee: Langenus (Belgium)

4.6.38 Hungary (4) 6, Dutch East Indies (0) 0 REIMS
Hungary: Hada, Koranyi, Biro, Lazar, Turai, Balogh, Sas, Zsengeller (2), Sarosi (2), Toldi (1), Kohut (1)
Dutch East Indies: Mo Heng, Hu Kon, Samuels, Nawir, Meng, Anwar, Hang Djin, Soedarmadji, Sommers, Pattiwael, Taihutti
Referee: Conrie (France)

5.6.38 France (2) 3, Belgium (1) 1 PARIS
France: Dilorto, Cazenave, Mattler, Bastien, Jordan, Diagne, Aston, Nicolas (2), Delfour, Vienante (1), Heisserer
Belgium: Badjou, Paverick, Sayes, Van Alphen, Stynen, De Winter, Van de Wouwer, Voorhoof, Isemborghs (1), Braine, Byle
Referee: Wuthrich (Switzerland)

5.6.38 Brazil (2) 6, Poland (1) 5 (aet, 4 - 4 at 90 mins) STRASBOURG
Brazil: Batatais, Domingos, Machado, Procopio, Martim, Afonsinho, Lopes, Romeu (1), Leonidas (4), Peracio (1), Hercules
Poland: Madesjski, Szczepaniak, Galecki, Gora, Nyc, Dytko, Piece L, Piontek (1), Szerfke, Willimowski (4), Wodarz
Referee: Eklind (Sweden)

5.6.38 Czechoslovakia (0) 3, Holland (0) 0 (aet, 0 - 0 at 90 mins) LE HAVRE
Czechoslovakia: Planicka, Burger, Daucik, Kostalek (1), Boucek (1), Kopecky, Riha, Simunek, Zeman, Nejedly (1), Puc
Holland: Van Male, Weber, Caldenhove, Paauwe, Anderiesen, Van Heel, Wels, Van de Veen, Smit, Vente, De Harder
Referee: Leclerq (France)

5.6.38 Italy (1) 2, Norway (0) 1 (aet, 1 - 1 at 90 mins) MARSEILLES
Italy: Olivieri, Monzeglio, Rava, Serantoni, Andreolo, Locatelli, Pasinati, Meazza, Piola (1), Ferrari (1), Ferraris II
Norway: Johansen H, Johannesen R, Holmsen, Henriksen, Eriksen, Homberg, Frantzen, Kvammen, Brunyldsen, Isaksen, Brustad (1)
Referee: Beranek (Austria)

5.6.38 Cuba (1) 3, Rumania (1) 3 (aet, 2-2 at 90 mins) TOULOUSE
Cuba: Carvajales, Barquin, Chorens, Arias, Rodriguez, Bergas, Maquina (1), Fernandez, Sosorro, Tunes (1), Sosa (1)
Rumania: Pavlovici, Burger, Chiroiu, Vintila, Rasinaru, Rafinski, Bindea, Covaci (1), Baratki (1), Bodola, Dobai (1)
Referee: Scarpi (Italy)

Replays

9.6.38 Switzerland (1) 4, Germany (2) 2 PARIS
Switzerland: Huber, Minelli, Lehmann, Springer, Vernati, Lortscher (o. g.), Amado, Abegglen III (2), Bickel (1), Walaschek (1), Aeby
Germany: Raftl, Janes, Streitle, Kupfer, Goldbrunner, Skoumal, Lehner, Stroh, Hahnemann (1), Szepan, Neumer
Referee: Eklind (Sweden)

9.6.38 Cuba (1) 2, Rumania (1) 1 TOULOUSE
Cuba: Ayra, Barquin, Chorens, Arias, Rodriguez, Berges, Maquina (1), Fernandez, Socorro (1), Tunas, Sosa
Rumania: Sadowski, Burger, Felecan, Barbulescu, Racinaru, Rafinski, Bogden, Moldoveanu, Baratki, Pranzler, Dobai (1)
Referee: Birlem (Germany)

QUARTER FINALS

12.6.38 Sweden (4) 8, Cuba (0) 0 ANTIBES
Sweden: Abrahamsson, Eriksson, Kallgren, Almgren, Jacobsson, Svanstrom, Wetterstrom (4), Keller (1), Andersson H (1), Jonasson (1), Nyberg (1)
Cuba: Carvajales, Barquin, Chorens, Arias, Rodriguez, Berges, Ferrer, Fernandez, Socorro, Tunas, Alonzo
Referee: Krist (Czechoslovakia)

12.6.38 Hungary (1) 2, Switzerland (0) 0 LILLE
Hungary: Szabo, Koranyi, Biro, Szalay, Turai, Lazar, Sas, Vincze, Sarosi, Zsengeller (2), Kohut
Switzerland: Huber, Stelzer, Lehmann, Springer, Vernati, Lortscher, Amado, Walashek, Bickel, Abegglen III, Grassi
Referee: Barlasina (Italy)

12.6.38 Italy (1) 3, France (1) 1 PARIS
Italy: Olivieri, Foni, Rava, Serantoni, Andreolo, Locatelli, Biavati, Meazza, Piola (2), Ferrari, Colaussi (1)
France: Dilorto, Cazenave, Mattler, Bastien, Jordan, Diagne, Aston, Heisserer (1), Nicolas, Delfour, Veinante
Referee: Baert (Belgium)

12.6.38 Brazil (1) 1, Czechoslovakia (1) 1 (aet, 1 - 1 at 90 mins) BORDEAUX
Brazil: Walter, Domingos, Machado, Procopio, Martim, Afonsinho, Lopes, Romeu (1), Leonidas (1), Peracio, Hercules
Czechoslovakia: Planicka, Burger, Daucik, Kostalek, Boucek, Kopecky, Riha, Simunek, Ludl, Nejedly (1 pen), Puc
Referee: Hertzka (Hungary)

Replay

14.6.38 Brazil (0) 2, Czechoslovakia (1) 1 BORDEAUX
Brazil: Walter, Jau, Nariz, Brito, Brandao, Argemiro, Roberto (1), Luizinho, Leonidas (1), Tim, Patesko
Czechoslovakia: Burkert, Burger, Daucik, Kostalek, Boucek, Ludl, Horak, Senecky, Kreutz, Kopecky (1), Rulc
Referee: Capdeville (France)

SEMI FINALS

16.6.38 Italy (0) 2, Brazil (0) 1 MARSEILLES
Italy: Olivieri, Foni, Rava, Serantoni, Andreolo, Locatelli, Biavati, Meazza (1 pen), Piola, Ferrari, Colaussi (1)
Brazil: Walter, Domingos, Machado, Procopio, Martim, Afonsinho, Lopes, Luizinho, Peracio, Romeu (1), Patesko
Referee: Wuthrich (Switzerland)

16.6.38 Hungary (3) 5, Sweden (1) 1 PARIS
Hungary: Szabo, Koranyi, Biro, Szalay, Turai, Lazar, Sas, Zsengeller (3), Sarosi (1), Toldi, Titkos (1)
Sweden: Abrahamsson, Eriksson, Kallgren, Almgren, Jacobsson, Svanstrom, Wetterstrom, Keller, Andersson H, Jonasson, Nyberg (1)
Referee: Leclerq (France)

Match for third place

19.6.38 Brazil (1) 4, Sweden (2) 2 BORDEAUX
Brazil: Batatais, Domingos, Machado, Procopio, Brandao, Afonsinho, Roberto, Romeu (1), Leonidas (2) Peracio (1), Patesko
Sweden: Abrahamsson, Eriksson, Nilsson, Almgren, Linderholm, Svanstrom, Persson, Andersson H, Jonasson (1), Andersson A, Nyberg (1)
Referee: Langenus (Belgium)

FINAL

19.6.38 Italy (3) 4, Hungary (1) 2 PARIS
Italy: Olivieri, Foni, Rava, Serantoni, Andreolo, Locatelli, Biavati, Meazza, Piola (2), Ferrari, Colaussi (2)
Hungary: Szabo, Polgar, Biro, Szalay, Szucs, Lazar, Sas, Vincze, Sarosi (1), Zsengeller, Titkos (1)
Referee: Capdeville (France)

Second World War

Zurich, the headquarters of FIFA in neutral Switzerland, managed to keep its office open throughout the war under Dr Ivo Schricker. Although the 1940 Congress planned for Luxembourg was postponed indefinitely, some meetings of the continental members of the executive committee were held. Resources were non-existent and without a full complement attending , no resolutions were passed, although in 1941 Germany put forward the idea that charging by players challenging for the ball should be made legal...

Italy had won the World Cup in 1938, and the Jules Rimet Trophy itself was the subject of considerable wartime mystery. Most of the sports officials in the Italian government were by definition Mussolini supporters, including the brothers Francesco and Giovanni Mauro, secretary Ottorino Barassi and the Head of Italian Sport, Consule-Generale Giorgio Vaccaro.

Yet all of them put sport above politics and for security decided not to trust each other too much. Thus General Vaccaro and Giovanni Mauro smuggled the trophy from the safe of the Italian bank in Rome. But Dr Barassi, fearing the Nazis would still confiscate the gold statuette, decided to find a safer hiding place for it. Thus the World Cup spent most of the war in a shoe box under his bed!

BRAZIL

1950

Brazil was chosen as the venue for the fourth World Cup. The entire South American continent had been unaffected by the ravages of war but overall only 31 teams entered including the British associations for the first time, all four having rejoined FIFA in 1946.

The Home Championship was used as part of the qualification, with two places guaranteed in the finals. But when England beat Scotland 1-0 at Hampden Park to win the title, the Scots carried out their threat not to go to Brazil unless they were champions.

Travel requirements in this vast country called upon teams to make enormous journeys. France, originally eliminated, were invited to take part when Turkey withdrew, but declined on learning their tour itinerary. India withdrew when informed by FIFA that they would not be allowed to play barefooted! Thus only 13 teams competed in the finals, the competition unsatisfactorily split in four groups — Uruguay had just one opponent in their section — plus a final pool with no knock-out matches at all.

Brazil, firm favourites, won their group, dropping only one point — to Switzerland in Sao Paulo, when they purposely included many local players. One of their goals looked suspect; the ball appeared to have gone out of play before being crossed. By the final pool the Brazilians were showing irresistible form, their individual brilliance dove-tailing as a team in a relaxed, but masterful manner.

(Main photo) England's most humiliating moment: USA centre-forward Larry Gaetjens beats Bert Williams with the only goal of the game in Belo Horizonte, 13 June 1950. (GSL) (Inset) Barbosa, the Brazilian goalkeeper, scrambles the ball away from the feet of Hans Jeppson, Sweden's centre-forward. It was one of few anxious moments for Brazil who won this final pool game 7-1.(JR)

Sweden became the overall 'giant-killers' beating Italy 3-2. Coached by George Raynor, it was an ironic triumph for the Swedes who had lost many of their 1948 Olympic stars to Italian clubs. Yet the real shock was England losing to the hotch-potch USA. This humiliating defeat was sealed after 37 minutes; left-half Walter Bahr crossed into the goalmouth, goalkeeper Bert Williams failed to gather cleanly and the oncoming Larry Gaetjens deflected the ball in with his head. England had been unimpressive in beating Chile 2-0, but it was a scintillating performance compared with this shattering shambles.

In the final pool Ademir scored four as Brazil slaughtered Sweden 7-1; Uruguay, after taking eight goals off Bolivia, were held 2-2 by Spain who had topped England's group. The firecrackers were already heralding a Brazilian success. A samba 'Brazil the Victors' was recorded. Spain were crushed 6-1 by the rampant Brazilians. Uruguay's 3-2 win over Sweden left Brazil needing a point for the title.

Brazil were 10-1 on favourites and put Uruguay's well-organised defence under constant pressure. When Friaca gave them the lead just after the interval, Brazil looked safe. However, with nothing to lose Uruguay made every pass count. Spurred on by the industrious Rodriguez Andrade and fine distribution by Obdulio Varela, they took control. Slender schemer Juan Schiaffino hit Chico Ghiggia's cross first time for the equaliser and 11 minutes from time, Ghiggia drove in low for the winner inside Barbosa's near post.

Qualifying Tournament
32 entries
Europe and Near East (19): Austria, Belgium, England, Finland, France, Northern Ireland, Republic of Ireland, Israel, Italy, Luxembourg, Portugal, Scotland, Spain, Sweden, Switzerland, Syria, Turkey, Wales, Yugoslavia
South America (8): Argentina, Bolivia, Brazil, Chile, Ecuador, Paraguay, Peru, Uruguay
North and Central America (3): Cuba, Mexico, USA
Asia (3): Burma, India, Philippines

Europe and the Near East had six groups. In four of these one seeded team met the winners of another tie. In another, the Home International Championship was used to determine the first British entry into the World Cup. Two representatives were guaranteed final places from this group, one each from the other five.

There were two groups from South America, each with two final places plus one representative from North and Central America and Asia. Final places in Brazil were to be distributed as follows: Europe and Near East (7 + Italy), South America (4 + Brazil), North and Central America (2), Asia (I).

The knock-out principle was abandoned completely for the finals. For the first time the winners of four groups were required to play in a final section. There were four seeded teams: Brazil as hosts, Italy as holders, England as the British champions and Argentina representing South America. But withdrawals ruined these arrangements.

Europe
Group 1 (Austria, Turkey, Syria)
Turkey v Syria 7 - 0
Austria withdrew; Syria refused to play the return game with Turkey, who withdrew. Portugal were offered a place in finals but declined.

Group 2 (Yugoslavia, Israel, France)
Yugoslavia v Israel 6 - 0; Israel v Yugoslavia 2 - 5; France v Yugoslavia 1 - 1; Yugoslavia v France 1 - 1
Play-off (in Florence): Yugoslavia v France 3 - 2
Yugoslavia qualified

Group 3 (Switzerland, Luxembourg, Belgium)
Belgium withdrew
Switzerland v Luxembourg 5 - 2, 3 - 2
Switzerland qualified

Group 4 (Sweden, Rep of Ireland, Finland)
Sweden v Rep of Ireland 3 - 1; Rep of Ireland v Finland 3 - 0; Finland v Rep of Ireland 1 - 1; Rep of Ireland v Sweden 1 - 3
Sweden qualified

Group 5 (England, Scotland, Northern Ireland, Wales)
Northern Ireland v Scotland 2 - 8; Wales v England 1 - 4; Scotland v Wales 2 - 0; England v Northern Ireland 9 - 2; Wales v Northern Ireland 0 - 0; Scotland v England 0 - 1

	P	W	D	L	F	A	Pts
England	3	3	0	0	14	3	6
Scotland	3	2	0	1	10	3	4
Wales	3	0	1	2	1	6	1
Northern Ireland	3	0	1	2	4	17	1

England qualified with Scotland, who refused a final place as did France, who were invited to replace them

Group 6 (Spain, Portugal)
Spain v Portugal 5 - 1, 2 - 2
Spain qualified

South America
Group 7 (Chile, Bolivia, Argentina)
Chile and Bolivia qualified (Argentina withdrew)

Group 8 (Uruguay, Paraguay, Ecuador and Peru)
Uruguay and Paraguay qualified (Ecuador and Peru withdrew)

Asia
Group 9 (Burma, India, Philippines)
All withdrew

North and Central America
Group 10 (USA, Mexico, Cuba) (In Mexico City)
USA v Mexico 0 - 6; Mexico v USA 6 - 2; Cuba v USA 1 - 1; USA v Cuba 5 - 2; Cuba v Mexico 0 - 3; Mexico v Cuba 2 - 0

	P	W	D	L	F	A	Pts
Mexico	4	4	0	0	17	2	8
USA	4	1	1	2	8	15	3
Cuba	4	0	1	3	3	11	1

USA and Mexico qualified

Final Tournament BRAZIL
GROUP 1
24.6.50 Brazil (1) 4 , Mexico (0) 0 RIO DE JANEIRO
Brazil: Barbosa, Augusto, Juvenal, Ely, Danilo, Bigode, Maneca, Ademir (2), Baltazar (1), Jair (1), Friaca
Mexico: Carbajal, Zetter, Montemajor, Ruiz, Ochoa, Roca, Septien, Ortiz, Casarin, Perez, Velasquez
Referee: Reader (England)

25.6.50 Yugoslavia (3) 3, Switzerland (0) 0 BELO HORIZONTE
Yugoslavia: Mrkusic, Horvat, Stankovic, Cajkovski I, Jovanovic, Djajic, Ognanov (1), Mitic, Tomasevic (2), Bobek, Vukas
Switzerland: Stuber, Lusenti, Quinche, Bocquet, Eggimann, Neury, Bickel, Antenen, Tamini, Bader, Fatton
Referee: Galeati (Italy)

28.6.50 Brazil (2) 2, Switzerland (1) 2 SAO PAULO
Brazil: Barbosa, Augusto, Juvenal, Bauer, Rui, Noronha, Alfredo II (1), Maneca, Baltazar (1), Ademir, Friaca
Switzerland: Stuber, Neury, Bocquet, Lusenti, Eggimann, Quinche, Tamini, Bickel, Friedlander, Bader, Fatton (2)
Referee: Azon (Spain)

28.6.50 Yugoslavia (2) 4, Mexico (0) 1 PORTO ALEGRE
Yugoslavia: Mrkusic, Horvat, Stankovic, Cajkovski I, Jovanovic, Djajic, Mihailovic, Mitic, Tomasevic (1), Bobek (1), Cajovski II (2)
Mexico: Carbajal, Gutierrez, Ruiz, Gomez, Ochoa, Ortiz, Flores, Naranjo, Casarin (1), Perez, Velasquez
Referee: Leafe (England)

1.7.50 Brazil (1) 2, Yugoslavia (0) 0 RIO DE JANEIRO
Brazil: Barbosa, Augusto, Juvenal, Bauer, Danilo, Bigode, Maneca, Zizinho (1), Ademir (1), Jair, Chico
Yugoslavia: Mrkusic, Horvat, Brokela, Cajkovski I, Jovanovic, Djajic, Vukas, Mitic, Tomasevic, Bobek, Cajkovski II
Referee: Griffiths (Wales)

2.7.50 Switerland (2) 2, Mexico (0) 1 PORTO ALEGRE
Switzerland: Hug, Neury, Bocquet, Lusenti, Eggimann, Quinche, Tamini, Antenen, Freidlander, Bader (1), Fatton (1)
Mexico: Carbajal, Gutierrez, Gomez, Roca, Ortiz, Guevara, Flores, Ochoa, Casarin, Borbolla, Velasquez (1)
Referee: Eklind (Sweden)

	P	W	D	L	F	A	Pts
Brazil	3	2	1	0	8	2	5
Yugoslavia	3	2	0	1	7	3	4
Switzerland	3	1	1	1	4	6	3
Mexico	3	0	0	3	2	10	0

GROUP 2

24.6.50 England (1) 2, Chile (0) 0 RIO DE JANEIRO
England: Williams, Ramsey, Aston, Wright, Hughes, Dickinson, Finney, Mortensen, Bentley, Mannion (1), Mullen
Chile: Livingstone, Farias, Roldon, Alvarez, Busquets, Carvalho, Prieto, Cremaschi, Robledo, Munoz, Diaz
Referee: Van de Meer (Netherlands)

25.6.50 Spain (0) 3, USA (1) 1 CURITIBA
Spain: Eizaguirre, Antunez, Alonso, Gonzalvo III, Gonazalvo II, Puchades, Basora (2), Hernandez, Zarra (1), Igoa, Gainza
USA: Borghi, Keough, Marca, McIlvenny, Colombo, Bahr, Craddock, Souza J (1), Gaetjens, Pariani, Valentini
Referee: Viana (Brazil)

29.6.50 USA (1) 1 England (0) 0 BELO HORIZONTE
USA: Borghi, Keough, Marca, McIlvenny, Colombo, Bahr, Wallace, Pariani, Gaetjens (1), Souza J, Souza E
England: Williams, Ramsey, Aston, Wright, Hughes, Dickinson, Finney, Mortensen, Bentley, Mannion, Mullen
Referee: Dattilo (Italy)

29.6.50 Spain (2) 2, Chile (0) 0 RIO DE JANEIRO
Spain: Ramallets, Alonso, Parra, Gonzalvo III, Gonzalvo II, Puchades, Basora (1), Igoa, Zarra (1), Panizo, Gainza
Chile: Livingstone, Farias, Roldon, Alvarez, Busqueta, Carvalho, Prieto, Cremaschi, Robledo, Munoz, Diaz
Referee: De Gama (Brazil)

2.7.50 Spain (0) 1, England (0) 0 RIO DE JANEIRO
Spain: Ramallets, Alonso, Parra, Gonzalvo III, Gonazalvo II, Puchades, Basora, Igoa, Zarra (1), Panizo, Gainza
England: Williams, Ramsey, Eckersley, Wright, Hughes, Dickinson, Matthews, Mortensen, Milburn, Baily, Finney
Referee: Galeati (Italy)

2.7.50 Chile (2) 5, USA (0) 2 RECIFE
Chile: Livingstone, Machuca, Roldon, Alvarez, Busquets, Farias, Munoz, Cremaschi (3), Robledo (1), Prieto (1), Ibanez
USA: Borghi, Keough, Marca, McIlvenny, Colombo, Bahr, Wallace, Pariani (1), Gaetjens, Souza J (1 pen), Souza E
Referee: Gardelli (Brazil)

	P	W	D	L	F	A	Pts
Spain	3	3	0	0	6	1	6
England	3	1	0	2	2	2	2
Chile	3	1	0	2	5	6	2
USA	3	1	0	2	4	8	2

GROUP 3

25.6.50 Sweden (2) 3, Italy (1) 2 SAO PAULO
Sweden: Svensson, Samuelsson, Nilsson E, Andersson (1), Nordahl K, Gaerd, Sundqvist, Palmer, Jeppson (2), Skoglund, Nilsson S
Italy: Sentimenti IV, Giovannini, Furiassi, Annovazzi, Parola, Magli, Muccinelli (1), Boniperti, Capello, Campatelli, Carapellese (1)
Referee: Lutz (Switerland)

29.6.50 Sweden (2) 2, Paraguay (0) 2 CURITIBA
Sweden: Svensson, Samuelsson, Nilsson E, Andersson, Nordahl K, Gaerd, Jonsson, Palmer (1), Jeppson, Skoglund, Sundqvist (1)
Paraguay: Vargas, Gonzalito, Cespedes, Gavilan, Lequizamon, Cantero, Avalos, Lopez A (1), Saquir, Lopez F (1), Unzain
Referee: Mitchell (Scotland)

2.7.50 Italy (1) 2, Paraguay (0) 0 SAO PAULO
Italy: Moro, Blason, Furiassi, Fattori, Remondini, Mari, Muccinelli (1), Amadei, Capello, Carapellese (1)
Paraguay: Vargas, Gonzales, Cespedes, Gavilan, Lequizamon, Cantero, Avalos, Loprez A, Saquir, Lopez F, Unzain
Referee: Ellis (England)

	P	W	D	L	F	A	Pts
Sweden	2	1	1	0	5	4	3
Italy	2	1	0	1	4	3	2
Paraguay	2	0	1	1	2	4	1

GROUP 4

2.7.50 Uruguay (4) 8, Bolivia (0) 0 BELO HORIZONTE
Uruguay: Maspoli, Gonzales M, Tejera, Gonzales J, Varela, Andrade, Ghiggia (1), Perez, Miquez (2), Schiaffino (4), Vidal (1)
Bolivia: Gutierrez I, Acha, Bustamante, Greco, Valencia, Ferrel, Algranez, Ugarte, Caparelli, Gutierrez II, Maldonado
Referee: Reader (England)

FINAL POOL

9.7.50 Brazil (3) 7, Sweden (0) 1 RIO DE JANEIRO
Brazil: Barbosa, Augusto, Juvenal, Bauer, Danilo, Bigode, Maneca (1), Zizinho, Ademir (4), Jair, Chico (2)
Sweden: Svensson, Samuelsson, Nilsson E, Andersson (1 pen), Nordahl K, Gaerd, Sundqvist, Palmer, Jeppson, Skoglund, Nilsson S
Referee: Ellis (England)

9.7.50 Uruguay (1) 2, Spain (2) 2 SAO PAULO
Uruguay: Maspoli, Gonzales M, Tejera, Gonzales J, Varela (1), Andrade, Ghiggia (1), Perez, Miquez, Schiaffino, Vidal
Spain: Ramallets, Alonso, Gonzalvo II, Gonzalvo III, Parra, Puchades, Basora (2), Igoa, Zarra, Molowny, Gainza
Referee: Griffiths (Wales)

13.7.50 Brazil (3) 6, Spain (0) 1 RIO DE JANEIRO
Brazil: Barbosa, Augusto, Juvenal, Bauer, Danilo, Bigode, Friaca, Zizinho (1), Ademir (2), Jair (1), Chico (2)
Spain: Ramallets, Alonso, Gonzalvo II, Gonzalvo III, Parra, Puchades, Basora, Igoa (1), Zarra, Panizo, Gainza
Referee: Leafe (England)

13.7.50 Uruguay (1) 3, Sweden (2) 2 SAO PAULO
Uruguay: Paz, Gonzales M, Tejera, Gambetta, Varela, Andrade, Ghiggia, Perez (1), Miquez, Schiaffino (2), Vidal
Sweden: Svensson, Samuelsson, Nilsson E, Andersson, Johansson, Gaerd, Sunqvist, Palmer (1), Jeppson (1), Jonsson, Nilsson S
Referee: Galeati (Italy)

16.7.50 Sweden (2) 3, Spain (0) 1 SAO PAULO
Sweden: Svensson, Samuelsson, Nilsson E, Andersson, Johansson, Gaerd, Jonsson, Mellberg (1), Rydell, Palmer (1), Sundqvist (1)
Spain: Eizaguirre, Alonso, Asensi, Silva, Parra, Puchades, Basora, Hernandez, Zarra (1), Paniza, Juncosa
Referee: Van de Meer (Netherlands)

16.7.50 Uruguay (0) 2, Brazil (0) 1 RIO DE JANEIRO
Uruguay: Maspoli, Gonzales M, Tejera, Gambetta, Varela, Andrade, Ghiggia (1), Perez, Miquez, Schiaffino (1), Moran
Brazil: Barbosa, Augusto, Juvenal, Bauer, Danilo, Bogode, Friaca (1), Zizinho, Ademir, Jair, Chico
Referee: Reader (England)

	P	W	D	L	F	A	Pts
Uruguay	3	2	1	0	7	5	5
Brazil	3	2	0	1	14	4	4
Sweden	3	1	0	2	6	11	2
Spain	3	0	1	2	4	11	1

SWITZERLAND

1954

The tournament in Switzerland produced another beaten favourite in the final, the most disgraceful scenes in the history of the competition and the finest exhibition of World Cup football. By coincidence, Hungary were involved in all three.

Yet it was West Germany, only re-admitted by FIFA four years earlier, following banishment after the Second World War, who upset the form book in an eccentrically-organised tournament. There were two seeded teams in each of the four groups and they did not play each other. The unseeded Germans cheekily exploited the system to their advantage.

Although designed to reduce the risk of shock results, the scheme back-fired in Group 2. Hungary swamped the luckless South Koreans 9-0 and West Germany beat seeded Turkey 4-1. Gambling that they could defeat the Turks in a play-off if level on points, the German team manager, Sepp Herberger, cunningly fielded six reserves against Hungary. As it was, the Hungarians won 8-3. However Ferenc Puskas suffered a badly injured ankle.

Goalscoring generally reached new heights as a result of positive ideas, at least half a dozen teams possessing players of outstanding ability, the peculiarities of the system and some weak competitors.

(Main photo) Before the match deteriorated into the 'Battle of Berne', both Hungary and Brazil played some delightful football. Left to right: Castilho (Brazil's goalkeeper, on one knee); Hungary's Nandor Hidegkuti; Didi and Bauer (6), both of Brazil. (HULTON DEUTSCH)
(Inset, above) Stanley Matthews (7) watches Uruguay's Roque Maspoli punch clear from England centre-forward Nat Lofthouse. (POPPERFOTO)
(Inset, below) Maspoli is on all fours as Tom Finney (second from left) and the sprawling Lofthouse try to force the ball home. Uruguay's Andrade is far left. England lost 4-2 in Basle, but gave an improved performance. (POPPERFOTO)

The Germans duly won their play-off, beating Turkey 7-2 and there were other surprise unseatings of seeds. In Group 1, France lost to Yugoslavia and in Group 4, Italy were forced to play-off with Switzerland and found themselves beaten 4-1. England improved after an error-ridden 4-4 draw with Belgium to beat the Swiss 2-0 on one of the few hot days.

Scotland were trounced 7-0 by Uruguay and then lost by the only goal of the game to Austria. Brazil, after a comfortable win over Mexico, were held by the Yugoslavs and found themselves drawn against Hungary in the quarter-finals.

They met in what became known as the infamously belligerent Battle of Berne. A hotly disputed penalty which put the Hungarians 3-1 ahead really ignited an already smouldering match. English referee Arthur Ellis sent off the Brazilian Nilton Santos and Hungary's Joszef Boszik for fighting and later dismissed a second Brazilian, Humberto. Hungary eventually won 4-2 but fights continued in the dressing-room afterwards.

The goals flowed freely in Lausanne. Switzerland scored five against Austria, but still lost. They were 3-0 up in 20 minutes but went in at half-time losing 5-4. They also missed a penalty and were beaten 7-5. The Germans clinically disposed of Yugoslavia, and Uruguay beat a much improved England side 4-2.

In the semi-final at Lausanne played in torrential rain, Hungary and Uruguay put on a classic. The anticipated blood bath did not materialise and the ring of coal-scuttle helmeted soldiers surrounding the pitch proved unnecessary. Hungary won 4-2 in extra time, Sandor Kocsis heading two superbly taken goals to finish off the gallant South Americans, who thus suffered their first ever defeat in the World Cup.

The West German machine was now operating in top gear and ran through the erratic but attractive Austrians, the brothers Walter scoring twice each in a 6-1 win which drove them into the final and another meeting with Hungary.

Hungary's manager Gustav Sebes gambled on bringing back Puskas, declared fit after a morning test. It rained heavily again but the Hungarians seemed home and dry, especially when Puskas pounced on a deflection after six minutes and Zoltan Czibor capitalised on a defensive mistake two minutes later.

Creditably the Germans refused to be rattled. They swung the ball about cleverly, using their fast raiding wingers to good effect, and aided by the slippery conditions they put the Hungarians out of their stride. They were helped considerably by a goal scored one minute after Hungary's second, Max Morlock netting from another deflection. On 18 minutes they were level, Helmut Rahn driving in a left-wing corner when Gyula Grosics failed to clear.

Hungary came back to hit the woodwork twice, but Toni Turek was inspired in the German goal and eventually his team counter-attacked. Six minutes from time a defensive error enabled Rahn to plant his second goal, only for Puskas to immediately equalise, the effort ruled out by English referee Bill Ling after Welsh linesman Mervyn Griffiths controversially waved offside. Germany won 3-2 on merit, but Hungary were probably the finest team in Europe. Moreover, it provided a memorable final.

Qualifying Tournament

38 entries

Europe and Near East (28): Austria, Belgium, Bulgaria, Czechoslovakia, Egypt, England, Finland, France, West Germany, Greece, Hungary, Republic of Ireland, Northern Ireland, Israel, Italy, Luxembourg, Norway, Poland, Portugal, Rumania, Saar, Scotland, Spain, Sweden, Switzerland, Turkey, Wales, Yugoslavia

North and Central America (3): Haiti, Mexico, USA

South America (4): Brazil, Chile, Paraguay, Uruguay

Asia (3): China, Japan, South Korea

In addition to the misguided system that produced two seeded teams in each group of four for the finals, these 'seeds' were determined before the qualifying tournament. Thus when Spain, one of the seeded teams, were eliminated by Turkey, the victors automatically became the 'seed'. It was to have far-reaching consequences as the tournament unfolded. Again the Home International Championship produced two places. Final places in Switzerland were to be distributed as follows: Europe and Near East (11 + Switzerland), North and Central America (1), South America (1 + Uruguay), Asia (1)

Europe

Group 1 (West Germany, Saar, Norway)

Norway v Saar 2 -3 ; Saar v Norway 0 - 0; West Germany v Saar 3 - 0; Saar v West Germany 1 -3 ; Norway v West Germany 1 - 1; West Germany v Norway 5 - 1

	P	W	D	L	F	A	Pts
West Germany	4	3	1	0	12	3	7
Saar	4	1	1	2	4	8	3
Norway	4	0	2	2	4	9	2

West Germany qualified

Group 2 (Belgium, Sweden, Finland)

Finland v Belgium 2 - 4; Belgium v Finland 2 - 2; Sweden v Belgium 2 - 3; Belgium v Sweden 2 - 0; Finland v Sweden 3 - 3; Sweden v Finland 4 - 0

	P	W	D	L	F	A	Pts
Belgium	4	3	1	0	11	6	7
Sweden	4	1	1	2	9	8	3
Finland	4	0	2	2	7	13	2

Belgium qualified

Group 3 (England, Scotland, Northern Ireland, Wales)

Northern Ireland v Scotland 1 - 3; Wales v England 1 - 4; Scotland v Wales 3 - 3; England v Northern Ireland 3 - 1; Wales v Northern Ireland 1 - 2; Scotland v England 2 - 4

	P	W	D	L	F	A	Pts
England	3	3	0	0	11	4	6
Scotland	3	1	1	1	8	8	3
Northern Ireland	3	1	0	2	4	7	2
Wales	3	0	1	2	5	9	1

England and Scotland qualified

Group 4 (France, Rep of Ireland, Luxembourg)

Luxembourg v France 1 - 6; France v Luxembourg 8 - 0; Rep of Ireland v Luxembourg 0 - 1; Rep of Ireland v France 3 - 5; France v Rep of Ireland 1 - 0

	P	W	D	L	F	A	Pts
France	4	4	0	0	20	4	8
Rep of Ireland	4	2	0	2	8	6	4
Luxembourg	4	0	0	4	1	19	0

France qualified

Group 5 (Austria, Portugal)
Austria v Portugal 9 - 1, 0 - 0
Austria qualified

Group 6 (Turkey, Spain)
Spain v Turkey 4 - 1, 0 - 1
Play-off (in Rome): Turkey v Spain 2 - 2 (Turkey won toss up)
Turkey qualified

Group 7 (Hungary, Poland)
Hungary qualified (Poland withdrew)

Group 8 (Czechoslovakia, Rumania, Bulgaria)
Czechoslovakia v Rumania 2 - 0; Rumania v Czechoslovakia 0 - 1; Bulgaria
v Czechoslovakia 1 - 2; Czechoslovakia v Bulgaria 0 - 0; Rumania v Bulgaria
3 - 1; Bulgaria v Rumania 1 - 2

	P	W	D	L	F	A	Pts
Czechoslovakia	4	3	1	0	5	1	7
Rumania	4	2	0	2	5	5	4
Bulgaria	4	0	1	3	3	7	1

Czechoslovakia qualified

Group 9 (Italy, Egypt)
Egypt v Italy 1 - 2, 1 - 5
Italy qualified

Group 10 (Yugoslavia, Greece, Israel)
Israel v Yugoslavia 0 - 1; Yugoslavia v Israel 1 - 0; Yugoslavia v Greece 1 - 0;
Greece v Yugoslavia 0 - 1; Israel v Greece 0 - 2; Greece v Israel 1 - 0

	P	W	D	L	F	A	Pts
Yugoslavia	4	4	0	0	4	0	8
Greece	4	2	0	2	3	2	4
Israel	4	0	0	4	0	5	0

Yugoslavia qualified

North and Central America
Group 11 (Mexico, USA, Haiti)
Mexico v Haiti 8 - 0; Haiti v Mexico 0 - 4; Mexico v USA 3 - 1;
USA v Mexico 0 - 4; USA v Haiti 3 - 0; Haiti v USA 2 - 3

	P	W	D	L	F	A	Pts
Mexico	4	4	0	0	19	1	8
USA	4	2	0	2	7	9	4
Haiti	4	0	0	4	2	18	0

Mexico qualified

South America
Group 12 (Brazil, Paraguay, Chile)
Paraguay v Chile 4 - 0; Chile v Paraguay 1 - 3; Chile v Brazil 0 - 2; Brazil
v Chile 1 - 0; Brazil v Paraguay 4 - 1; Paraguay v Brazil 0 - 1

	P	W	D	L	F	A	Pts
Brazil	4	4	0	0	8	1	8
Paraguay	4	2	0	2	8	6	4
Chile	4	0	0	4	1	10	0

Brazil qualified

Asia
Group 13 (South Korea, Japan, China)
China withdrew

Japan v South Korea (in Tokyo) 1 - 5, 2 - 2
South Korea qualified

Final Tournament SWITZERLAND
GROUP 1
16.6.54 Yugoslavia (1) 1, France (0) 0 LAUSANNE
Yugoslavia: Beara, Stankovic, Crnkovic, Cajkovski, Horvat, Boskov,
Milutinovic, Mitic, Vukas, Bobek, Zebec
France: Remetter, Gianessi, Kaelbel, Penverne, Jonquet, Marcel, Kopa,
Glovacki, Strappe, Dereuddre, Vincent
Referee: Griffiths (Wales)

16.6.54 Brazil (4) 5, Mexico (0) 0 GENEVA
Brazil: Castilho, Santos D, Santos N, Brandaozinho, Pinheiro, Bauer,
Julinho (1), Didi (1), Baltazar (1), Pinga (2), Rodriguez
Mexico: Mota, Lopez, Gomez, Cardenas, Romo, Avalos, Torres, Naranjo,
Lamadrid, Balcazar, Arellano
Referee: Wyssling (Switzerland)

19.6.54 France (1) 3, Mexico (0) 2 GENEVA
France: Remetter, Gianessi, Marche, Marcel, Kaelbel, Mahjoub, Kopa
(1 pen), Dereuddre, Strappe, Ben Tifour, Vincent (1)
Mexico: Carbajal, Lopez, Romo, Cardenas (o. g.), Avalos, Martinez, Torres,
Naranjo (1), Lamadrid, Balcazar (1), Arellano
Referee: Asensi (Spain)

19.6.54 Brazil (0) 1, Yugoslavia (0) 1 (aet, 1 - 1 at 90 mins) LAUSANNE
Brazil: Castilho, Santos D, Santos N, Brandaozinho, Pinheiro, Bauer,
Julinho, Didi (1), Baltazar, Pinga, Rodriguez
Yugoslavia: Beara, Stankovic, Crnkovic, Cajkovski, Horvat, Boskov,
Milutinovic, Mitic, Zebec (1), Vukas, Dvornik
Referee: Faultless (Scotland)

	P	W	D	L	F	A	Pts
Brazil	2	1	1	0	6	1	3
Yugoslavia	2	1	1	1	2	1	3
France	2	1	0	1	3	3	2
Mexico	2	0	0	2	2	8	0

GROUP 2
17.6.54 Hungary (4) 9, South Korea (0) 0 ZURICH
Hungary: Grosics, Buzanszky, Lantos (1), Bozsik, Lorant, Szojka, Budai,
Kocsis (3), Palotas (2), Puskas (2), Czibor (1)
South Korea: Hong, Kyu Park, Kang, Min, Yae Seung Park, Chu, Chung, Kap
Park, Sung, Woo, Yung Keun Choi
Referee: Vincenti (France)

17.6.54 West Germany (1) 4, Turkey (1) 1 BERNE
West Germany: Turek, Laband, Kohlmeyer, Eckel, Posipal, Mai, Klodt (1),
Morlock (1), Walter O (1), Walter F, Schafer (1)
Turkey: Turgay, Ridvan, Basri, Mustafa, Cetin, Rober, Erol, Suat (1), Feridun,
Burhan, Lefter
Referee: Da Costa (Portugal)

20.6.54 Hungary (3) 8, West Germany (1) 3 BASLE
Hungary: Grosics, Buzanszky, Lantos, Bozsik, Lorant, Zakarias, Toth (1),
Kocsis (4), Hidegkuti (2), Puskas (1), Czibor
West Germany: Kwaitkowski, Bauer, Kohlmeyer, Posipal, Liebrich, Mebus,
Rahn (1), Eckel, Walter F, Pfaff (1), Hermann (1)
Referee: Ling (England)

20.6.54 Turkey (4) 7, South Korea (0) 0 GENEVA
Turkey: Turgay, Ridvan, Basri, Mustafa, Cetin, Rober, Erol (1), Suat (2),
Necmettin, Lefter (1), Burhan (3)
South Korea: Hong, Kyu Park, Kang, Han, Chong Kap Lee, Kim, Yung Keun
Choi, Soo Nam Lee, Gi Choo Lee, Woo, Chung
Referee: Marino (Uruguay)

	P	W	D	L	F	A	Pts
Hungary	2	2	0	0	17	3	4
West Germany	2	1	0	1	7	9	2
Turkey	2	1	0	1	8	4	2
South Korea	2	0	0	2	0	16	0

Play off for 2nd place
23.6.54 West Germany (3) 7, Turkey (1) 2 ZURICH
West Germany: Turek, Laband, Bauer, Eckel, Posipal, Mai, Klodt, Morlock
(3), Walter O (1), Walter F (1), Schafer (2)
Turkey: Sukru, Ridvan, Basri, Naci, Cetin, Rober, Erol, Mustafa (1),
Necmettin, Coskun, Lefter (1)
Referee: Vincenti (France)

GROUP 3
16.6.54 Austria (1) 1, Scotland (0) 0 ZURICH
Austria: Schmied, Hanappi, Barschandt, Ocwirk, Happel, Koller, Korner R,
Schleger, Dienst, Probst (1), Korner A
Scotland: Martin, Cunningham, Aird, Docherty, Davidson, Cowie,
McKenzie, Fernie, Mochan, Brown, Ormond
Referee: Franken (Belgium)

16.6.54 Uruguay (0) 2, Czechoslovakia (0) 0 BERNE
Uruguay: Maspoli, Santamaria, Martinez, Andrade, Varela, Cruz, Abbadie, Ambrois, Miquez (1), Schiaffino (1),Borges
Czechoslovakia: Reimann, Safranek, Novak, Trnka, Hledlik, Hertl, Hlavacek, Hemele, Kacany, Pazicky, Peser
Referee: Ellis (England)

19.6.54 Austria (4) 5, Czechoslovakia (0) 0 ZURICH
Austria: Schmied, Hanappi, Barschandt, Ocwirk, Happel, Koller, Korner R, Wagner, Stojaspal (2), Probst (3), Korner A
Czechoslovakia: Stacho, Safranek, Novak, Trnka, Pluskal, Hertl, Hlavacek, Hemele, Kacany, Pazicky, Krauss
Referee: Stafanovic (Yugoslavia)

19.6.54 Uruguay (2) 7, Scotland (0) 0 BASLE
Uruguay: Maspoli, Santamaria, Martinez, Andrade, Varela, Cruz, Abbadie (2), Ambrois, Miguez (2), Schiaffino, Borges (3)
Scotland: Martin, Cunningham, Aird, Docherty, Davidson, Cowie, McKenzie, Fernie, Mochan, Brown, Ormond
Referee: Orlandini (Italy)

	P	W	D	L	F	A	Pts
Uruguay	2	2	0	0	9	0	4
Austria	2	2	0	0	6	0	4
Czechoslovakia	2	0	0	2	0	7	0
Scotland	2	0	0	2	0	8	0

GROUP 4

17. 6. 54 England (2) 4, Belgium (1) 4 (aet, 3 - 3 at 90 mins) BASLE
England: Merrick, Staniforth, Byrne, Wright, Owen, Dickinson (o.g), Matthews, Broadis (2), Lofthouse (2), Taylor, Finney
Belgium: Gernaey, Dries, Van Brandt, Huysmans, Carre, Mees, Van den Bosch P, Houf, Coppens (1), Anoul (2), Mermans
Referee: Schmetzer (West Germany)

17.6.54 Switzerland (1) 2, Italy (1) 1 LAUSANNE
Switzerland: Parlier, Neury, Kernen, Fluckiger, Bocquet, Casali I, Ballaman (1), Vonlanthen, Hugi II (1), Meier, Fatton
Italy: Ghezzi, Vincenzi, Giacomazzi, Neri, Tognon, Nesti, Muccinelli, Boniperti (1), Galli, Pandolfini, Lorenz
Referee: Viana (Brazil)

20.6.54 England (1) 2, Switzerland (0) 0 BERNE
England: Merrick, Staniforth, Byrne, McGarry, Wright, Dickinson, Finney, Broadis, Wilshaw (1), Taylor, Mullen (1)
Switzerland: Parlier, Neury, Kernen, Eggimann, Bocquet, Bigler, Antenen, Vonlanthen, Meier, Ballaman, Fatton
Referee: Zsolt (Hungary)

26.6.54 Italy (1) 4, Belgium (0) 1 LUGANO
Italy: Ghezzi, Magnini, Giacomazzi, Neri, Tognon, Nesti, Frignani (1), Cappello, Galli, Pandolfini (1 pen), Lorenzi (1)
Belgium: Gernaey, Dries, Van Brandt, Huysmans, Carre, Mees, Mermans, Van den Bosch H, Coppens, Anoul (1), Van Den Bosch P
Referee: Steiner (Austria)

	P	W	D	L	F	A	Pts
England	2	1	1	0	6	4	3
Switzerland	2	1	0	1	2	3	2
Italy	2	1	0	1	5	3	2
Belgium	2	0	1	1	5	8	1

Play off for 2nd place
23.6.54 Switzerland (1) 4, Italy (0) 1 BASLE
Switzerland: Parlier, Neury, Kernen, Eggimann, Bocquet, Casali, Antenen, Vonlanthen, Hugi II (2), Ballaman (1), Fatton (1)
Italy: Viola, Magnini, Giacomazzi, Mari, Tognon, Nesti (1), Muccinelli, Pandolfini, Lorenzi, Segato, Frignani
Referee: Griffiths (Wales)

QUARTER FINALS
26.6.54 Austria (5) 7, Switzerland (4) 5 LAUSANNE
Austria: Schmied, Hanappi (o. g.), Barschandt, Ocwirk (1), Happel, Koller, Korner R, Wagner (3), Stojaspal, Probst (1), Korner A (2)
Switzerland: Parlier, Neury, Kernen, Eggimann, Bocquet, Casali, Antenen, Vonlanthen, Hugi II (2), Ballaman (2), Fatton
Referee: Faultless (Scotland)

26.6.54 Uruguay (2) 4, England (1) 2 BASLE
Uruguay: Maspoli, Santamaria, Martinez, Andrade, Varela (1), Cruz, Abbadie, Ambrois (1), Miguez (1), Schiaffino (1), Borges (1)
England: Merrick, Staniforth, Byrne, McGarry, Wright, Dickinson, Matthews, Broadis, Lofthouse (1), Wilshaw, Finney (1)
Referee: Steiner (Austria)

27.6.54 West Germany (1) 2, Yugoslavia (0) 0 GENEVA
West Germany: Turek, Laband, Kohlmeyer, Eckel, Liebrich, Mai, Rahn (1), Morlock, Walter O, Walter F, Schafer
Yugoslavia: Beara, Stankovic, Crnkovic, Cajkovski, Horvat (o. g.), Boskov, Milutinovic, Mitic, Vukas, Bobek, Zebec
Referee: Zsolt (Hungary)

27.6.54 Hungary (2) 4, Brazil (1) 2 BERNE
Hungary: Grosics, Buzanszky, Lantos (1 pen), Bozsik, Lorant, Zakarias, Toth M, Kocsis (2), Hidegkuti (1), Czibor, Toth J
Brazil: Castilho, Santos D (1 pen), Santos N, Brandaozinho, Pinheiro, Bauer, Julinho (1), Didi, Indio, Humberto, Maurinho
Referee: Ellis (England)

SEMI FINALS
30.6.54 West Germany (1) 6, Austria (0) 1 BASLE
West Germany: Turek, Posipal, Kohlmeyer, Eckel, Liebrich, Mai, Rahn, Morlock (1), Walter O (2), Walter F (2 pens), Schafer (1)
Austria: Zeman, Hanappi, Schleger, Ocwirk, Happel, Koller, Korner R, Wagner, Stojaspal, Probst (1), Korner A
Referee: Orlandini (Italy)

30.6.54 Hungary (1) 4, Uruguay (0) 2 (aet, 2 - 2 at 90 mins) LAUSANNE
Hungary: Grosics, Buzanszky, Lantos, Bozsik, Lorant, Zakarias, Budai, Kocsis (2), Palotas, Hidegkuti (1), Czibor (1)
Uruguay: Maspoli, Santamaria, Martinez, Andrade, Carballo, Cruz, Souto, Ambrois, Schiaffino, Hohberg (2), Borges
Referee: Griffiths (Wales)

Match for third place
3.7.54 Austria (1) 3, Uruguay (1) 1 ZURICH
Austria: Schmied, Hanappi, Barschandt, Ocwirk (1), Kollmann, Koller, Korner R, Wagner, Dienst, Stojaspal (1 pen), Probst
Uruguay: Maspoli, Santamaria, Martinez, Andrade, Carballo, Cruz (o. g.), Abbadie, Hohberg (1), Mendez, Schiaffino, Borges
Referee: Wyssling (Switzerland)

FINAL
4.7.54 West Germany (2) 3, Hungary (2) 2 BERNE
West Germany: Turek, Posipal, Kohlmeyer, Eckel, Liebrich, Mai, Rahn (2), Morlock (1), Walter O, Walter F, Schafer
Hungary: Grosics, Buzanszky, Lantos, Bozsik, Lorant, Zakarias, Czibor (1), Kocsis, Hidegkuti (1), Puskas (1), Toth J
Referee: Ling (England)

SWEDEN

1958

Though England, Northern Ireland, Scotland and Wales all reached the finals in Sweden, it was George Raynor, the English-born manager of the host nation, who almost achieved the impossible with a team packed with ageing exiles brought back from Italy.

Against any country other than Brazil, who had been perfecting a 4-2-4 system, the Swedes might have succeeded. But by stealing the ball, rather than tackling for it, and plundering opposing defences, the Brazilians emerged as the first team to win the competition outside their own continent.

It was the most truly representative series staged to date, 46 of the 53 original entries played in 89 qualifying games, watched by four million spectators. For the first time, no team other than the host nation and holders had a bye to the finals and when no opponent could be found for politically isolated Israel, Wales made the most of their second-chance ballot success as promising runners-up in the preliminary round.

Though Scotland again disappointed, Wales, Northern Ireland and England — despite the Munich air disaster the previous February in which they lost Roger Byrne, Duncan Edwards and Tommy Taylor — were not disgraced. There were several other pleasing features about the competition. In the cooler atmosphere of Scandinavia, there was a refreshing absence of some of the unpleasantness which had marred earlier tournaments.

The French tandem of Just Fontaine (with 13 goals, the leading marksman) and Raymond Kopa impressed, but was overshadowed by a Brazilian trio: a teenage prodigy called Pele, a devastating right-winger in Garrincha, and Didi, an inside-forward of rare delicacy.

There were four groups, with each comprising a team from South America, Eastern Europe, Britain and Western Europe. Teams level on points had to play-off. Northern Ireland, under the shrewd guidance of manager Peter Doherty, had problems finding a suitable centre-forward but showed typical spirit and considerable skill until hit hard by injuries. They defeated Czechoslovakia 2-1 in a play-off to go through with West Germany, who had drawn 2-2 with the Irish.

Yugoslavia went through on merit in Group 2 after beating the talented French 3-2 while in Group 3, Wales edged out Hungary 2-1 in a play-off, the beaten finalists of four years earlier clearly over-the-hill as a team. But in Group 4 England put up a splendid performance against Brazil, drawing 0-0 thanks chiefly to some superb handling by goalkeeper Colin McDonald. Alas, forward weaknesses proved costly when the USSR beat them by the only goal in a play-off.

With the system requiring so many play-offs, it was 48 hours and further action for the victors. Gallant Wales defended magnificently against Brazil and only went down by a single goal. Had John Charles been fit to play in the game, it might have been even more interesting. But Northern Ireland, ravaged by injuries, conceded four goals to the ebullient French.

The USSR became the third play-off winner to lose; Sweden scoring twice in the second half to eliminate them. The other successful quarter-final side was West Germany, who needed all their guile to overcome Yugoslavia in Malmo, which they did with a first-half Helmut Rahn goal.

The Brazilians took full advantage of an injury to a key French defender in the semi-final, when the score was still 1-1, to win 5-2 in a match of free-flowing attack at both ends. In the other game, Sweden, spurred on by a growing enthusiasm from their followers, beat West Germany 3-1 but it was a close run thing.

(Above) England inside-forward Johnny Haynes finds his attempt at goal blocked by Brazilian goalkeeper Gylmar. (PRESSENS BILD)

Brazil's talented squad spent most of the 1958 tournament scoring goals and enjoying the aftermath. Here Vava is injured scoring against the USSR (left) but is prevented from falling to the ground by his colleagues. (PRESSENS BILD)

The Germans took the lead, and when Nils Liedholm, 36, started the move which led to Sweden's equaliser, he clearly handled the ball. In the second half, the German left-back Juskowiak, who had been tormented by Kurt Hamrin on the Swedish right-wing, was sent off for retaliation. Gunnar Gren, 37, and Hamrin added further goals for Sweden.

In the final it rained and appeared to give the hosts a better chance. Indeed they went ahead when the intrepid Liedholm contrived an opening for himself after only four minutes. Undeterred, Brazil kept their heads as well as they had lost them in 1954 and, playing with even more style than the 1950 side, were soon in control. It took them just three minutes to draw level. Garrincha, the 'Little Bird' flying on the wing who had only been put into the side following a deputation of players to coach Vicente Feola, destroyed Sweden's left flank.

His acceleration and swerving runs led to crosses and Vava supplied the finish, equalising then putting Brazil ahead. After the break Pele, memorably, and Zagalo made it 4-1 before Sweden, shut down on the wings, managed a goal through Agne Simonsson. But Pele had the last word with a header to make it 5-2. It had been a remarkable triumph for instinctive innovation in a 4-2-4 formation which was to be adapted elsewhere as the shield of the unskilled.

French forward Raymond Kopa leaps high in the air (left) but Brazilian goalkeeper Gylmar fists the ball away from danger. Injury-hit France lost this semi-final 5-2. (PRESSENS BILD)

(Below) England held Brazil to a goalless draw in Gothenburg, thanks to some splendid goalkeeping by Colin McDonald, seen here gathering the ball safely. (AP)

Qualifying Tournament

53 entries

Europe (29): Austria, Belgium, Bulgaria, Czechoslovakia, Denmark, England, Finland, France, East Germany, West Germany, Greece, Holland, Hungary, Iceland, Rep of Ireland, Northern Ireland, Italy, Luxembourg, Norway, Poland, Portugal, Rumania, Scotland, Spain, Sweden, Switzerland, USSR, Wales, Yugoslavia

South America (9): Argentina, Bolivia, Brazil, Chile, Colombia, Paraguay, Peru, Uruguay, Venezuela

North and Central America (6): Canada, Costa Rica, Curacao, Guatemala, Mexico, USA

Asia/Africa (9): China, Cyprus, Egypt, Indonesia, Israel, Sudan, Syria, Taiwan, Turkey

This qualifying competition proved to be the most satisfactory to date, with the exception of the Asia/Africa group. The original plan there was for the winners of the four groups to meet for one place in the finals. Only two groups actually managed to record games. The others were beset by withdrawals caused by politics. Thus Israel were left without an opponent. FIFA decided that as no other country apart from the hosts and holders had failed to play at least two matches in order to reach the finals, Israel would have to meet one of the originally eliminated teams. This was achieved by a lottery.

Final places in Sweden were to be distributed as follows: Europe (9 + West Germany, Sweden); South America (3), North and Central America (1), Asia/Africa (1).

Europe

Group 1 (England, Rep of Ireland, Denmark)

Rep of Ireland v Denmark 2 - 1; England v Denmark 5 - 2; England v Rep of Ireland 5 - 1; Denmark v England 1 - 4; Rep of Ireland v England 1 - 1; Denmark v Rep of Ireland 0 - 2

	P	W	D	L	F	A	Pts
England	4	3	1	0	15	5	7
Rep of Ireland	4	2	1	1	6	7	5
Denmark	4	0	0	4	4	13	0

England qualified

Group 2 (France, Belgium, Iceland)

France v Belgium 6 - 3; France v Iceland 8 - 0; Belgium v Iceland 8 - 3; Iceland v France 1 - 5; Iceland v Belgium 2 - 5; Belgium v France 0 - 0

	P	W	D	L	F	A	Pts
France	4	3	1	0	19	4	7
Belgium	4	2	1	1	16	11	5
Iceland	4	0	0	4	6	26	0

France qualified

Group 3 (Hungary, Bulgaria, Norway)

Norway v Bulgaria 1 -2 ; Norway v Hungary 2 - 1, Hungary v Bulgaria 4 - 1;
Bulgaria v Hungary 1 - 2; Bulgaria v Norway 7 - 0; Hungary v Norway 5 - 0

	P	W	D	L	F	A	Pts
Hungary	4	3	0	1	12	4	6
Bulgaria	4	2	0	2	11	7	4
Norway	4	1	0	3	3	15	2

Hungary qualified

Group 4 (Czechoslovakia, Wales, East Germany)

Wales v Czechoslovakia 1 - 0; East Germany v Wales 2 - 1; Czechoslovakia v Wales 2 - 0;East Germany v Czechoslovakia 1 - 4

	P	W	D	L	F	A	Pts
Czechoslovakia	4	3	0	1	9	3	6
Wales	4	2	0	2	6	5	4
East Germany	4	1	0	3	5	12	2

Czechoslovakia qualified

Group 5 (Austria, Holland, Luxembourg)

Austria v Luxembourg 7 - 0; Holland v Luxembourg 4 - 1;
Austria v Holland 3 - 2; Luxembourg v Holland (in Rotterdam) 2 -5;
Holland v Austria 1 - 1; Luxembourg v Austria 0 - 3

	P	W	D	L	F	A	Pts
Austria	4	3	1	0	14	3	7
Holland	4	2	1	1	12	7	5
Luxembourg	4	0	0	4	3	19	0

Austria qualified

Group 6 (USSR, Poland, Finland)

USSR v Poland 3 - 0; Finland v Poland 1 - 3; USSR v Finland 2 - 1;
Finland v USSR 0 - 10; Poland v USSR 2 - 1; Poland v Finland 4 - 0

	P	W	D	L	F	A	Pts
USSR	4	3	0	1	16	3	6
Poland	4	3	0	1	9	5	6
Finland	4	0	0	4	2	19	0

Play-off (in Leipzig): USSR v Poland 2 - 0
USSR qualified

Group 7 (Yugoslavia, Rumania, Greece)

Greece v Yugoslavia 0 - 0; Greece v Rumania 1 - 2; Rumania v Yugoslavia 1 - 1; Rumania v Greece 3 - 0; Yugoslavia v Greece 4 - 1
Yugoslavia v Rumania 2 - 0

	P	W	D	L	F	A	Pts
Yugoslavia	4	2	2	0	7	2	6
Rumania	4	2	1	1	6	4	5
Greece	4	0	1	3	2	9	1

Yugoslavia qualified

Group 8 (Northern Ireland, Italy, Portugal)

Portugal v Northern Ireland 1 - 1; Italy v Northern Ireland 1 - 0; Northern Ireland v Portugal 3 - 0; Portugal v Italy 3 - 0; Italy v Portugal 3 - 0; Northern Ireland v Italy 2 - 1

	P	W	D	L	F	A	Pts
Northern Ireland	4	2	1	1	6	3	5
Italy	4	2	0	2	5	5	4
Portugal	4	1	1	2	4	7	2

Northern Ireland qualified

Group 9 (Scotland, Spain, Switzerland)

Spain v Switzerland 2 - 2; Scotland v Spain 4 - 2; Switzerland v Scotland; 1 - 2; Spain v Scotland 4 -1 ; Scotland v Switzerland 3 - 2
Switzerland v Spain 1 - 4

	P	W	D	L	F	A	Pts
Scotland	4	3	0	1	10	9	6
Spain	4	2	1	1	12	8	5
Switzerland	4	0	1	3	6	11	1

Scotland qualified

South America

Group 1 (Brazil, Peru, Venezuela)

Venezuela withdrew
Peru v Brazil 1 - 1, 0 - 1
Brazil qualified

Group 2 (Argentina, Bolivia, Chile)

Chile v Bolivia 2 - 1; Bolivia v Chile 3 - 0; Bolivia v Argentina 2-0;
Chile v Argentina 0 - 2; Argentina v Chile 4 - 0; Argentina v Bolivia 4 - 0

	P	W	D	L	F	A	Pts
Argentina	4	3	0	1	10	2	6
Bolivia	4	2	0	2	6	6	4
Chile	4	1	0	3	2	10	2

Argentina qualified

Group 3 (Paraguay, Uruguay, Colombia)

Colombia v Uruguay 1 - 1; Colombia v Paraguay 2 - 3; Uruguay v Colombia 1 - 0; Paraguay v Colombia 3 - 0; Paraguay v Uruguay 5 - 0;
Uruguay v Paraguay 2 - 0

	P	W	D	L	F	A	Pts
Paraguay	4	3	0	1	11	4	6
Uruguay	4	2	1	1	4	6	5
Colombia	4	0	1	3	3	8	1

Paraguay qualified

North and Central America

Sub-Group 1 (Costa Rica, Curacao, Guatemala)

Guatemala v Costa Rica 2 - 6; Costa Rica v Guatemala 3 - 1 (match abandoned, awarded to Costa Rica); Costa Rica v Curacao 4 - 0; Guatemala v Curacao 1 - 3; Curacao v Costa Rica 1 - 2; Curacao v Guatemala not played

	P	W	D	L	F	A	Pts
Costa Rica	4	4	0	0	15	4	8
Curacao	3	1	0	2	4	7	2
Guatemala	3	0	0	3	4	12	0

Sub-Group 2 (Mexico, Canada, USA)

Mexico v USA 6 - 0; USA V Mexico 2 - 7; Canada v USA 5 - 1; Mexico v Canada 3 - 0; Canada v Mexico 0 - 2 (in Mexico City); USA v Canada 2 - 3

	P	W	D	L	F	A	Pts
Mexico	4	4	0	0	18	2	8
Canada	4	2	0	2	8	8	4
USA	4	0	0	4	5	21	0

Final round

Mexico v Costa Rica 2 - 0, 1 - 1
Mexico qualified

Asia/Africa

Sub-Group 1 (Indonesia, China, Taiwan)

Taiwan withdrew
Indonesia v China 2 - 0, 3 - 4
Play-off (in Rangoon): Indonesia v China 0 - 0
(Indonesia won on scoring more goals in previous matches)

Sub-Group 2 (Israel, Turkey)

Turkey withdrew

Sub-group 3 (Egypt, Cyprus)

Cyprus withdrew

Sub-Group 4 (Sudan, Syria

Sudan v Syria 1 - 0, 1 - 1

Second round

Israel walked over (Indonesia withdrew); Sudan walked over
(Egypt withdrew)

Final round

Israel walked over (Sudan withdrew); Wales won draw among all second-placed teams to play Israel, Belgium and Uruguay declined
Israel v Wales 0 - 2, 0 - 2
Wales qualified

Final Tournament SWEDEN
GROUP 1

8.6.58 West Germany (2) 3, Argentina (1) 1 MALMO
West Germany: Herkenrath, Stollenwerk, Juskowiak, Eckel, Erhardt, Szymaniak, Rahn (2), Walter F, Seeler (1), Schmidt, Schafer
Argentina: Carrizo, Dellacha, Vairo, Lombardo, Rossi, Varacka, Corbatta (1), Prado, Menendez, Rojas, Cruz
Referee: Leafe (England)

8.6.58 Northern Ireland (1) 1, Czechoslovakia (0) 0 HALMSTAD
Northern Ireland: Gregg, Keith, McMichael, Blanchflower, Cunningham, Peacock, Bingham, Cush (1), Dougan, McIlroy, McParland
Czechoslovakia: Dolejsi, Mraz, Novak, Pluskal, Cadek, Masopust, Hovorka, Dvorak, Borovicka, Hertl, Krauss
Referee: Seipelt (Austria)

11.6.58 West Germany (0) 2, Czechoslovakia (2) 2 HALSINGBORG
West Germany: Herkenrath, Stollenwerk, Juskowiak, Schnellinger, Erhardt, Szymaniak, Rahn (1), Walter F, Seeler, Schafer (1), Klodt
Czechoslovakia: Dolejsi, Mraz, Novak, Pluskal, Popluhar, Masopust, Hovorka, Dvorak (1 pen), Molnar, Farajsl, Zikan (1)
Referee: Ellis (England)

11.6.58 Argentina (1) 3, Northern Ireland (1) 1 HALMSTAD
Argentina: Carrizo, Dellacha, Vairo, Lombardo, Rossi, Varacka, Corbatta (1 pen), Avio (1), Menendez (1), Labruna, Boggio
Northern Ireland: Gregg, Keith, McMichael, Blanchflower, Cunningham, Peacock, Bingham, Cush, Coyle, McIlroy, McParland (1)
Referee: Ahlner (Sweden)

15.6.58 West Germany (1) 2, Northern Ireland (1) 2 MALMO
West Germany: Herkenrath, Stollenwerk, Juskowiak, Eckel, Erhardt, Szymaniak, Rahn (1), Walter F, Seeler (1), Schafer, Klodt
Northern Ireland: Gregg, Keith, McMichael, Blanchflower, Cunningham, Peacock, Bingham, Cush, Casey, McIlroy, McParland (2)
Referee: Campos (Portugal)

15.6.58 Czechoslovakia (3) 6, Argentina (0) 1 HALSINGBORG
Czechoslovakia: Dolejsi, Mraz, Novak, Dvorak (1), Popluhar, Masopust, Hovorka (1), Borovicka, Molnar, Farajsl (2), Zikan (2)
Argentina: Carrizo, Dellacha, Vairo, Lombardo, Rossi, Varacka, Corbatta (1), Avio, Menendez, Labruna, Cruz
Referee: Ellis (England)

	P	W	D	L	F	A	Pts
West Germany	3	1	2	0	7	5	4
Northern Ireland	3	1	1	1	4	5	3
Czechoslovakia	3	1	1	1	8	4	3
Argentina	3	1	0	2	5	10	2

Play off for 2nd place

17.6.58 Northern Ireland (1) 2, Czechoslovakia (1) 1 (aet, 1 - 1 at 90 mins) MALMO
Northern Ireland: Uprichard, Keith, McMichael, Blanchflower, Cunningham, Peacock, Bingham, Cush, Scott, McIlroy, McParland (2)
Czechoslovakia: Dolejsi, Mraz, Novak, Bubernik, Popluhar, Masopust, Dvorak, Molnar, Farajsl, Borovicka, Zikan (1)
Referee: Guigue (France)

GROUP 2

8.6.58 Yugoslavia (1) 1, Scotland (0) 1 VASTERAS
Yugoslavia: Beara, Sijakovic, Crnkovic, Krstic, Zebec, Boskov, Petakovic (1), Veselinovic, Milutinovic, Sekularac, Rajkov
Scotland: Younger, Caldow, Hewie, Turnbull, Evans, Cowie, Leggat, Murray (1), Mudie, Collins, Imlach
Referee: Wyssling (Switzerland)

8.6.58 France (2) 7, Paraguay (2) 3 NORRKOPING
France: Remetter, Kaelbel, Lerond, Penverne, Jonquet, Marcel, Wisnieski (1), Fontaine (3), Kopa (1), Piantoni (1), Vincent (1)
Paraguay: Mageregger, Miranda, Arevalo, Villalba, Lezcano, Achucarro, Aguero, Parodi, Romero (1), Re, Amarilla (2, 1 pen)
Referee: Gardeazabal (Spain)

11.6.58 Paraguay (2) 3, Scotland (1) 2 NORRKOPING
Paraguay: Aguilar, Arevalo, Echague, Villalba, Lezcano, Achucarro, Aguero (1), Parodi, Romero (1), Re (1), Amarilla
Scotland: Younger, Parker, Caldow, Turnbull, Evans, Cowie, Leggat, Collins (1), Mudie (1), Robertson, Fernie
Referee: Orlandini (Italy)

11.6.58 Yugoslavia (1) 3, France (1) 2 VASTERAS
Yugoslavia: Beara, Tomic, Crnkovic, Krstic, Zebec, Boskov, Petakovic (1), Veselinovic (2), Milutinovic, Sekularac, Rajkov
France: Remetter, Kaelbel, Marche, Penverne, Jonquet, Lerond, Wisnieski, Fontaine (2), Kopa, Piantoni, Vincent
Referee: Griffiths (Wales)

15.6.58 France (2) 2, Scotland (0) 1 OREBRO
France: Abbes, Kaelbel, Lerond, Penverne, Jonquet, Marcel, Wisnieski, Fontaine (1), Kopa (1), Piantoni, Vincent
Scotland: Brown, Caldow, Hewie, Turnbull, Evans, Mackay, Collins, Murray, Mudie, Baird (1), Imlach
Referee: Brozzi (Argentina)

15.6.58 Paraguay (1) 3, Yugoslavia (2) 3 ESKISTUNA
Paraguay: Aguilar, Arevalo, Echague, Villalba, Lezcano, Achucarro, Aguero (1), Parodi (1), Romero (1), Re, Amarilla
Yugoslavia: Beara, Tomic, Crnkovic, Krstic, Zebec, Boskov, Petakovic, Veselinovic (1), Ogjanovi (2), Sekularac, Rajkov
Referee: Macko (Czechoslovakia)

	P	W	D	L	F	A	Pts
France	3	2	0	1	11	7	4
Yugoslavia	3	1	2	0	7	6	4
Paraguay	3	1	1	1	9	12	3
Scotland	3	0	1	2	4	6	1

GROUP 3

8.6.58 Sweden (1) 3, Mexico (0) 0 STOCKHOLM
Sweden: Svensson, Bergmark, Axbom, Liedholm (1 pen), Gustavsson, Parling, Hamrin, Mellberg, Simonsson (2), Gren, Skoglund
Mexico: Carbajal, Del Muro, Villegas, Portugal, Romo, Flores, Hernandez, Reyes, Calderon, Gutierrez, Sesma
Referee: Latyschev (USSR)

8.6.58 Hungary (1) 1, Wales (1) 1 SANDVIKEN
Hungary: Grosics, Matrai, Sarosi, Bozsik (1), Sipos, Berendi, Sandor, Hidegkuti, Tichy, Bundzsak, Fenyvesi
Wales: Kelsey, Williams, Hopkins, Sullivan, Charles M, Bowen, Webster, Medwin, Charles J (1), Allchurch, Jones
Referee: Codesal (Uruguay)

11.6.58 Mexico (1) 1, Wales (1) 1 STOCKHOLM
Mexico: Carbajal, Del Muro, Gutierrez, Cardenas, Romo, Flores, Belmonte (1), Reyes, Blanco, Gonzalez, Sesma
Wales: Kelsey, Williams, Hopkins, Baker, Charles M, Bowen, Webster, Medwin, Charles J, Allchurch (1), Jones
Referee: Lemesic (Yugoslavia)

12.6.58 Sweden (2) 2, Hungary (0) 1 STOCKHOLM
Sweden: Svensson, Bergmark, Axbom, Liedholm, Gustavsson, Parling, Hamrin (2), Mellberg, Simonsson, Gren, Skoglund
Hungary: Grosics, Matrai, Sarosi, Szojka, Sipos, Berendi, Sandor, Bundzsak, Bozsik, Tichy (1), Fenyvesi
Referee: Mowat (Scotland)

15.6.58 Sweden (0) 0, Wales (0) 0 STOCKHOLM
Sweden: Svensson, Bergmark, Axbom, Borjesson, Gustavsson, Parling, Berndtsson, Selmosson, Kallgren, Lofgren, Skoglund
Wales: Kelsey, Williams, Hopkins, Sullivan, Charles M, Bowen, Vernon, Hewitt, Charles J, Allchurch, Jones
Referee: Van Nuffel (Belgium)

15.6.58 Hungary (1) 4, Mexico (0) 0 SANDVIKEN
Hungary: Ilku, Matrai, Sarosi, Szojka, Sipos, Kotasz, Budai, Bencsics, Hidegkuti, Tichy (2), Sandor (1)
Mexico: Carbajal, Del Muro, Gutierrez, Cardenas, Sepulveda, Flores, Belmonte, Reyes, Blanco, Gonzalez (o. g.), Sesma
Referee: Eriksson (Finland)

	P	W	D	L	F	A	Pts
Sweden	3	2	1	0	5	1	5
Wales	3	0	3	0	2	2	3
Hungary	3	1	1	1	6	3	3
Mexico	3	0	1	2	1	8	1

Play off for 2nd place
17.6.58 Wales (0) 2, Hungary (1) 1 STOCKHOLM
Wales: Kelsey, Williams, Hopkins, Sullivan, Charles M, Bowen, Medwin (1), Hewitt, Charles J, Allchurch (1), Jones
Hungary: Grosics, Matrai, Sarosi, Bozsik, Sipos, Kostasz, Budai, Bencsics, Tichy (1), Bundzsak, Fenyvesi
Referee: Latyschev (USSR)

GROUP 4
8.6.58 USSR (1) 2, England (0) 2 GOTHENBURG
USSR: Yashin, Kessarov, Kusnezov, Voinov, Krischevsky, Zarev, Ivanov A, Ivanov V (1), Simonian (1), Salnikov, Iljin
England: McDonald, Howe, Banks, Clamp, Wright, Slater, Douglas, Robson, Kevan (1), Haynes, Finney (1 pen)
Referee: Zsolt (Hungary)

8.6.58 Brazil (1) 3, Austria (0) 0 UDEVALLA
Brazil: Gylmar, De Sordi, Santos N (1), Dino, Bellini, Orlando, Joel, Didi, Mazzola (2), Dida, Zagalo
Austria: Szanwald, Halla, Svoboda, Hanappi, Happel, Koller, Horak, Senekowitsch, Buzek, Korner A, Schleger
Referee: Guigue (France)

11.6.58 Brazil (0) 0, England (0) 0 GOTHENBURG
Brazil: Gylmar, De Sordi, Santos N, Dino, Bellini, Orlando, Joel, Didi, Mazzola, Vava, Zagalo
England: McDonald, Howe, Banks, Clamp, Wright, Slater, Douglas, Robson, Kevan, Haynes, A'Court
Referee: Dusch (West Germany)

11.6.58 USSR (1) 2, Austria (0) 0 BORAS
USSR: Yashin, Kessarov, Kusnezov, Voinov, Krischevsky, Zarev, Ivanov A, Ivanov V (1), Simonian, Salnikov, Iljin (1)
Austria: Schmied, Kozliczek E, Svoboda, Hanappi, Stotz, Koller, Horak, Kozliczek P, Buzek, Korner A, Senekowitsch
Referee: Jorgensen (Denmark)

15.6.58 Brazil (1) 2, USSR (0) 0 GOTHENBURG
Brazil: Gylmar, De Sordi, Santos N, Zito, Bellini, Orlando, Garrincha, Didi, Vava (2), Pele, Zagalo
USSR: Yashin, Kessarov, Kusnezov, Voinov, Krischevsky, Zarev, Ivanov A, Ivanov V, Simonjan, Netto, Iljin
Referee: Guigue (France)

15.6.58 England (0) 2, Austria (1) 2 BORAS
England: McDonald, Howe, Banks, Clamp, Wright, Slater, Douglas, Robson, Kevan (1), Haynes, A'Court
Austria: Szanwald, Kollmann, Svoboda, Hanappi, Happel, Koller (1), Kozliczek E, Kozliczek P, Buzek, Korner A (1), Senekowitsch
Referee: Asmussen (Denmark)

	P	W	D	L	F	A	Pts
Brazil	3	2	1	0	5	0	5
USSR	3	1	1	1	4	4	3
England	3	0	3	0	4	4	3
Austria	3	0	1	2	2	7	1

Play off for 2nd place
17.6.58 USSR (0) 1, England (0) 0 GOTHENBURG
USSR: Yashin, Kessarov, Kusnezov, Voinov, Krischevsky, Zarev, Apuchtin, Ivanov V, Simonian, Falin, Iljin (1)
England: McDonald, Howe, Banks, Clayton, Wright, Slater, Brabrook, Broadbent, Kevan, Haynes, A'Court
Referee: Dusch (West Germany)

QUARTER FINALS
19.6.58 West Germany (1) 1, Yugoslavia (0) 0 MALMO
West Germany: Herkenrath, Stollenwerk, Juskowiak, Eckel, Erhardt, Szymaniak, Rahn (1), Walter F, Seeler, Schmidt, Schafer
Yugoslavia: Krivokuca, Sijakovic, Crnkovic, Boskov, Zebec, Krstic, Petakovic, Ogjanovic, Milutinovic, Veselinovic, Rajkov
Referee: Wyssling (Switzerland)

19.6.58 France (1) 4, Northern Ireland (0) 0 NORRKOPING
France: Abbes, Kaelbel, Lerond, Penverne, Jonquet, Marcel, Wisnieski (1), Fontaine (2), Kopa, Piantoni (1), Vincent
Northern Ireland: Gregg, Keith, McMichael, Blanchflower, Cunningham, Cush, Bingham, Casey, Scott, McIlroy, McParland
Referee: Gardeazabal (Spain)

19.6.58 Sweden (0) 2, USSR (0) 0 STOCKHOLM
Sweden: Svensson, Bergmark, Axbom, Borjesson, Gustavsson, Parling, Hamrin, Gren, Simonsson (1), Liedholm, Skoglund
USSR: Yashin, Kessarov, Kuznezov, Voinov, Krischevsky, Zarev, Ivanov A, Ivanov V, Simonian, Salnikov, Iljin
Referee: Leafe (England)

19.6.58 Brazil (0) 1, Wales (0) 0 GOTHENBURG
Brazil: Gylmar, De Sordi, Santos N, Zito, Bellini, Orlando, Garrincha, Didi, Mazzola, Pele (1), Zagalo
Wales: Kelsey, Williams, Hopkins, Sullivan, Charles M, Bowen, Medwin, Hewitt, Webster, Allchurch, Jones
Referee: Seipelt (Austria)

SEMI FINALS
24.6.58 Sweden (1) 3, West Germany (1) 1 GOTHENBURG
Sweden: Svensson, Bergmark, Axbom, Borjesson, Gustavsson, Parling, Hamrin (1), Gren (1), Simonsson, Liedholm, Skoglund (1)
West Germany: Herkenrath, Stollenwerk, Juskowiak, Eckel, Erhardt, Szymaniak, Rahn, Walter F, Seeler, Schafer (1), Cieslarczyk
Referee: Zsolt (Hungary)

24.6.58 Brazil (2) 5, France (1) 2 STOCKHOLM
Brazil: Gylmar, De Sordi, Santos N, Zito, Bellini, Orlando, Garrincha, Didi (1), Vava (1), Pele (3), Zagalo
France: Abbes, Kaelbel, Lerond, Penverne, Jonquet, Marcel, Wisnieski (1), Fontaine (1), Kopa, Piantoni (1), Vincent
Referee: Griffiths (Wales)

Match for third place
28.6.58 France (3) 6, West Germany (1) 3 GOTHENBURG
France: Abbes, Kaelbel, Lerond, Penverne, Lafond, Marcel, Wisnieski, Douis (1), Kopa (1 pen), Fontaine (4), Vincent
West Germany: Kwiatkowski, Stollenwerk, Erhardt, Schnellinger, Wewers, Szymaniak, Rahn (1), Sturm, Kelbassa, Schafer (1), Cieslarczyk (1)
Referee: Brozzi (Argentina)

FINAL
29.6.58 Brazil (2) 5, Sweden (1) 2 STOCKHOLM
Brazil: Gylmar, Santos D, Santos N, Zito, Bellini, Orlando, Garrincha, Didi, Vava (2), Pele (2), Zagalo (1)
Sweden: Svensson, Bergmark, Axbom, Borjesson, Gustavsson, Parling, Hamrin, Gren, Simonsson (1), Liedholm (1), Skoglund
Referee: Guigue (France)

CHILE
1962

Chile held the tournament despite being devastated by earthquakes a year previously. A new stadium in Santiago had been completed in December, another more modest ground was located at the coastal town of Vina del Mar, while Rancagua and Arica completed the four sites. However, apart from Chile's matches, which were the best attended of all, only Brazil's group attracted crowds of more than four figures. High admission charges did not help.

Brazil retained their title in a singularly uninspired series, stifled by defensive-minded football and pock-marked by some of the crudest, if effective tactics ever seen in international competition. The opening matches produced some serious injuries, several as the result of reckless tackling. An appeal for restraint by FIFA to the competing nations and Yugoslavia's withdrawal from the tournament of a player sent off after being involved with a Russian who suffered a broken leg, did not altogether restore calm.

Chile, who surprised and surpassed themselves, ultimately taking third place, were unfortunately involved in the debacle which became known as the 'Battle of Santiago'. Italy's Ferrini was sent off by English referee Ken Aston for a foul. Then Chile's outside-left Leonel Sanchez, son of a professional boxer, broke the nose of the Italian Humberto Maschio with a flawless left hook clearly seen by television and film audiences, but missed by the linesman standing only feet away. Italian defender Mario David was not so lucky to escape, as his retaliatory kick at Sanchez ended in dismissal, though years later Sanchez admitted he had not been touched.

Garrincha of Brazil caused England endless problems. Here Ray Wilson manages to get a toe to the ball on the edge of the penalty area. (POPPERFOTO)

The Chilean team acknowledge the cheers of the home crowd after beating Yugoslavia to clinch third place. (ALLSPORT)

While the Italians had failed to stamp the right kind of authority on the matches themselves, their *catenaccio* defensive system led to others copying this negative trend. Even Brazil did not operate as smoothly as before, despite retaining nine of their 1958 side; they used a more cautious 4-3-3 pattern, with winger Zagalo dropping back.

Goal difference counted in the group games and merely added to the safety-first measures employed. However, there were the usual shocks. Uruguay and the physical Argentines were eliminated after being expected to do well. England overcame Argentina 3-1 after losing 2-1 to Hungary, and a goalless draw with Bulgaria saw them reach the last eight.

The USSR and Yugoslavia had come through in Group 1, though the normally efficient Lev Yashin had a nightmare game in goal against Colombia in a 4-4 draw which stunned the Russians. Unbeaten West Germany and Chile progressed in Group 2 while Brazil and Czechoslovakia, who shared a goalless draw in Group 3, also reached the quarter-finals. But it was to be Pele's last appearance in the tournament after suffering a pulled muscle.

In Santiago, Yugoslavia's single-goal victory over West Germany was clinched by Radakovic with four minutes remaining. It buried the memory of two quarter-final defeats in previous tournaments against the Germans. England had to bow to Brazil, or rather Garrincha, who was behind all three goals in their 3-1 win.

Czechoslovakia owed much to their half-back line of Pluskal, Popluhar and Masopust and the goalkeeping of Schroif in the 1-0 win over Hungary, whose 6-1 group win over Bulgaria had given Florian Albert the only hat-trick of the tournament. Then in the other quarter-final, Russia's Yashin had another poor day which allowed Sanchez and Eladio Rojas to score for a now rampant Chile in a 2-1 win.

This brought the Chileans a semi-final with Brazil and inevitable trouble. One player from each side was sent off, but Garrincha was given permission to play in the final after Brazil's 4-2 win. He and Vava had each scored twice. In the all-Eastern bloc game between Czechoslovakia and Yugoslavia, the Czechs' finishing was clinical in a 3-1 success, though their opponents had enjoyed more of the play.

There was some consolation for Chile as they took third place, much to the delight of the local supporters, with a 1-0 win over Yugoslavia. But considerable interest surrounded the final in which the Brazilians were again parading their 'Pele-substitute' Amarildo, whose two goals on his first appearance in the tournament had beaten Spain 2-1.

Yet it was the Czechs who opened the scoring, Scherer splitting the Brazilian defence for Masopust to run in. Brazil equalised through Amarildo who squeezed the ball inside Schroif's near post from a ludicrously acute angle. Amarildo centred for Zito to head Brazil into a second-half lead, and 13 minutes from the end, Schroif erred again. He flapped at a high cross and allowed Vava to slot in the third Brazilian goal.

For Brazil it was a worthy victory, without the flamboyance achieved in Sweden. But it was the least remembered of the World Cups and did not bode well for the future, as the game withdrew into itself defensively, faced with the fear of defeat.

Qualifying Tournament
56 entries

Eastern Hemisphere (Africa, Asia, Europe) (39): Africa — Egypt, Ethiopia, Ghana, Morocco, Nigeria, Sudan, Tunisia; Asia — Indonesia, Japan, South Korea; Europe — Belgium, Bulgaria, Cyprus, Czechoslovakia, England, Finland, France, East Germany, West Germany, Greece, Holland, Hungary, Republic of Ireland, Northern Ireland, Israel, Italy, Luxembourg, Norway, Poland, Portugal, Rumania, Scotland, Spain, Sweden, Switzerland, Turkey, USSR, Wales, Yugoslavia

Western Hemisphere (North, Central and South America) (17): North — Canada, Mexico, USA; Central — Costa Rica, Guatemala, Honduras, Netherlands Antilles, Surinam;

South America — Argentina, Bolivia, Brazil, Chile, Colombia, Ecuador, Paraguay, Peru, Uruguay.

Ten groups in Europe included provision for play-offs against the winners from sub-groups of Asia, Africa and the Near East. With hosts and holders from South America, that continent was awarded places in the final tournament for just over half its entry of nine. The original scheme was for the final competition to be held in nine different towns and cities, but ultimately only four were used.

Final places in Chile were to be distributed as follows: Europe (10)*, South America (3 + Brazil, Chile), North/Central America (1), Asia/Africa (0)*.

*Play-off between Yugoslavia and South Korea gave Europe a further final place.

Europe/Africa/Asia
Group 1 (Switzerland, Sweden, Belgium)
Sweden v Belgium 2 - 0; Belgium v Switzerland 2 - 4; Switzerland v Belgium 2 - 1; Sweden v Switzerland 4 - 0; Belgium v Sweden 0 -2 ; Switzerland v Sweden 3 - 2

	P	W	D	L	F	A	Pts
Sweden	4	3	0	1	10	3	6
Switzerland	4	3	0	1	9	9	6
Belgium	4	0	0	4	3	10	0

Play-off (in Berlin): Switzerland v Sweden 2 - 1
Switzerland qualified

Group 2 (Bulgaria, France, Finland)
Finland v France 1 - 2; France v Bulgaria 3 - 0; Finland v Bulgaria 0 - 2; France v Finland 5 - 1; Bulgaria v Finland 3 - 1; Bulgaria v France 1 - 0

	P	W	D	L	F	A	Pts
Bulgaria	4	3	0	1	6	4	6
France	4	3	0	1	10	3	6
Finland	4	0	0	4	3	12	0

Play-off (in Milan): Bulgaria v France 1 - 0
Bulgaria qualified

Group 3 (West Germany, Northern Ireland, Greece)
Northern Ireland v West Germany 3 - 4; Greece v West Germany 0 - 3 ; Greece v Northern Ireland 2 - 1; West Germany v Northern Ireland 2 - 1; Northern Ireland v Greece 2 - 0; West Germany v Greece 2 - 1

	P	W	D	L	F	A	Pts
West Germany	4	4	0	0	11	5	5
Northern Ireland	4	1	0	3	7	8	2
Greece	4	1	0	3	3	8	2

West Germany qualified

Group 4 (Hungary, Holland, East Germany)
Hungary v East Germany 2 - 0; Holland v Hungary 0 - 3; East Germany v Holland 1 - 1; East Germany v Hungary 2 - 3; Hungary v Holland 3 - 3; Holland v East Germany not played

	P	W	D	L	F	A	Pts
Hungary	4	3	1	0	11	5	7
Holland	3	0	2	1	4	7	2
East Germany	3	0	1	2	3	6	1

Hungary qualified

Group 5 (USSR, Turkey, Norway)
Norway v Turkey 0 - 1; USSR v Turkey 1 - 0; USSR v Norway 5 - 2; Norway v USSR 0 - 3; Turkey v Norway 2 - 1; Turkey v USSR 1 - 2

	P	W	D	L	F	A	Pts
USSR	4	4	0	0	11	3	8
Turkey	4	2	0	2	4	4	4
Norway	4	0	0	4	3	11	0

USSR qualified

Group 6 (England, Portugal, Luxembourg)
Luxembourg v England 0 - 9; Portugal v Luxembourg 6 - 0; Portugal v England 1 - 1; England v Luxembourg 4 - 1; Luxembourg v Portugal 4 - 2; England v Portugal 2 - 0

	P	W	D	L	F	A	Pts
England	4	3	1	0	16	2	7
Portugal	4	1	1	2	9	7	3
Luxembourg	4	1	0	3	5	21	2

England qualified

Group 7
Sub-Group A (Cyprus, Israel, Ethiopia)

First Round
Cyprus v Israel 1 - 1, 1 - 6

Second Round
Israel v Ethiopia (in Tel Aviv) 1 - 0, 3 - 2

Sub-Group B (Italy, Rumania)
Rumania withdrew

Israel v Italy 2 - 4, 0 - 6
Italy qualified

Group 8 (Czechoslovakia, Scotland, Rep of Ireland)
Scotland v Rep of Ireland 4 - 1; Rep of Ireland v Scotland 0 - 3; Czechoslovakia v Scotland 4 - 0; Scotland v Czechoslovakia 3 - 2; Rep of Ireland v Czechoslovakia 1 - 3; Czechoslovakia v Rep of Ireland 7 - 1

	P	W	D	L	F	A	Pts
Czechoslovakia	4	3	0	1	16	5	6
Scotland	4	3	0	1	10	7	6
Rep of Ireland	4	0	0	4	3	17	0

Play-off (in Brussels): Czechoslovakia v Scotland 4 - 2
Czechoslovakia qualified

Group 9 (Spain, Wales)
Wales v Spain 1 - 2, 1 - 1

Sub-Group 1 (Sudan and Egypt)
Both withdrew

Sub-Group 2 (Morocco, Tunisia)
Morocco v Tunisia 2 - 1, 1 - 2
Play-off (in Palermo): Morocco v Tunisia 1 - 1
(Morocco won on toss-up)

Sub-Group 3 (Ghana, Nigeria)
Ghana v Nigeria 4 - 1, 2 - 2

Sub-Group final
Ghana v Morocco 0 - 0, 0 - 1

Group final
Morocco v Spain 0 - 1, 2 - 3
Spain qualified

Group 10 (Yugoslavia, Poland)
Yugoslavia v Poland 2 - 1, 1 - 1

Sub-Group 1 (South Korea, Indonesia, Japan)
Indonesia withdrew
South Korea v Japan 2 - 1, 2 - 0

Group final
Yugoslavia v South Korea 5 - 1, 3 - 1
Yugoslavia qualified

South America
Group 11 (Argentina, Ecuador)
Ecuador v Argentina 3 - 6, 0 - 5
Argentina qualified

Group 12 (Uruguay, Bolivia)
Bolivia v Uruguay 1 - 1, 1 - 2
Uruguay qualified

Group 13 (Colombia, Peru)
Colombia v Peru 1 - 0, 1 - 1
Colombia qualified

Group 14 (Paraguay)
Play-off with North and Central American group winners

North and Central America
Sub-Group 1 (USA, Canada, Mexico)
Canada withdrew
USA v Mexico 3 - 3, 0 - 3

Sub-Group 2 (Costa Rica, Guatemala, Honduras)
Costa Rica v Guatemala 3 - 2; Guatemala v Costa Rica 4 -4; Honduras v Costa Rica 2 - 1; Costa Rica v Honduras 5 - 0; Honduras v Guatemala 1 - 1; Guatemala v Honduras 0 - 2 (abandoned)

	P	W	D	L	F	A	Pts
Costa Rica	4	2	1	1	13	8	5
Honduras	3	1	1	1	3	7	3
Guatemala	3	0	2	1	7	8	2

Play-off (in Guatemala): Honduras v Costa Rica 0 - 1

Sub-Group 3 (Surinam, Netherlands Antilles)
Surinam v Netherlands Antilles 1 - 2, 0 - 0

Final round

Costa Rica v Mexico 1 - 0; Costa Rica v Netherlands Antilles 6 - 0; Mexico v Netherlands Antilles 7 - 0; Mexico v Costa Rica 4 - 1; Netherlands Antilles v Costa Rica 2 - 0; Netherlands Antilles v Mexico 0 - 0

	P	W	D	L	F	A	Pts
Mexico	4	2	1	1	11	2	5
Costa Rica	4	2	0	2	8	6	4
N'lands/Antilles	4	1	1	2	2	13	3

Mexico v Paraguay 1 - 0, 0 - 0
Mexico qualified

Final Tournament CHILE
GROUP 1

30.5.62 Uruguay (0) 2, Colombia (1) 1 ARICA
Uruguay: Sosa, Troche, Alvarez E W, Mendez, Goncalvez, Alvarez E, Cubilla (1), Rocha, Langon, Sasia (1), Perez
Colombia: Sanchez C, Gonzalez J, Lopez, Echeverri, Zuluaga (1), Silva, Aceros, Coll, Klinger, Gamboa, Arias
Referee: Dorogi (Hungary)

31.5.62 USSR (0) 2, Yugoslavia (0) 0 ARICA
USSR: Yashin, Dubinski, Maslonkin, Ostrovsky, Voronin, Netto, Metreveli, Ivanov V (1), Ponedelnik (1), Kanevski, Meschki
Yugoslavia: Soskic, Durkovic, Jusufi, Matus, Markovic, Popovic, Mujic, Sekularac, Jerkovic, Galic, Skoblar
Referee: Dusch (West Germany)

2.6.62 Yugoslavia (2) 3, Uruguay (1) 1 ARICA
Yugoslavia: Soskic, Durkovic, Radakovic, Markovic, Jusufi, Popovic, Melic, Sekularac, Jerkovic (1), Galic (1), Skoblar (1)
Uruguay: Sosa, Troche, Alvarez E W, Mendez, Goncalvez, Alvarez E, Rocha, Bergara, Cabrera (1), Sasia, Perez
Referee: Galba (Czechoslovakia)

3.6.62 USSR (3) 4, Colombia (1) 4 ARICA
USSR: Yashin, Tschokeli, Ostrovsky, Voronin, Maslonkin, Netto, Chislenko (1), Ivanov V (2), Ponedelnik (1), Kanevski, Meschki
Colombia: Sanchez C, Alzate, Gonzalez J, Echeverri, Lopez, Serrano, Aceros (1), Coll (1), Klinger (1), Rada (1), Gonzalez H
Referee Filho (Brazil)

6.6.62 USSR (1) 2, Uruguay (0) 1 ARICA
USSR: Yashin, Tschokeli, Voronin, Netto, Ostrovsky, Maslonkin, Chislenko, Ivanov V (1), Ponedelnik, Mamykin (1), Chusainov
Uruguay: Sosa, Mendez, Alvarez E W, Goncalvez, Alvarez E, Troche, Cubilla, Cortes, Cabrera, Sasia (1), Perez
Referee: Jonni (Italy)

7.6.62 Yugoslavia (2) 5, Colombia (0) 0 ARICA
Yugoslavia: Soskic, Durkovic, Jusufi, Radakovic, Markovic, Popovic, Ankovic, Sekularc, Jerkovic (3), Galic (1), Melic (1)
Colombia: Sanchez C, Alzate, Gonzalez J, Echeverri, Lopez, Serrano, Aceros, Coll, Klinger, Rada, Gonzalez H
Referee: Robles (Chile)

	P	W	D	L	F	A	Pts
USSR	3	2	1	0	8	5	5
Yugoslavia	3	2	0	1	8	3	4
Uruguay	3	1	0	2	4	6	2
Colombia	3	0	1	2	5	11	1

GROUP 2

30.5.62 Chile (1) 3, Switzerland (1) 1 SANTIAGO
Chile: Escuti, Eyzaguirre, Sanchez R, Navarro, Contreras, Rojas, Ramirez (1), Toro, Landa, Fouilloux, Sanchez L (2)
Switzerland: Elsener, Grobety, Morf, Weber, Schneiter, Tacchella, Antenen, Allemann, Wuthrich (1), Eschmann, Pottier
Referee: Aston (England)

31.5.62 West Germany (0) 0, Italy (0) 0 SANTIAGO
West Germany: Fahrian, Nowak, Schnellinger, Schulz, Erhardt, Szymaniak, Sturm, Haller, Seeler, Brulls, Schafer
Italy: Buffon, Losi, Robotti, Salvadore, Maldini, Radice, Ferrini, Rivera, Altafini, Sivori, Menichelli
Referee: Davidson (Scotland)

2.6.62 Chile (0) 2, Italy (0) 0 SANTIAGO
Chile: Escuti, Eyzaguirre, Sanchez R, Navarro, Contreras, Rojas, Ramirez (1), Toro (1), Landa, Fouilloux, Sanchez L
Italy: Mattrel, David, Robotti, Salvadore, Janich, Tumburus, Mora, Maschio, Altafini, Ferrini, Menichelli
Referee: Aston (England)

3.6.62 West Germany (1) 2, Switzerland (0) 1 SANTIAGO
West Germany: Fahrian, Nowak, Schnellinger, Schulz, Erhardt, Szymaniak, Koslowski, Haller, Seeler (1), Schafer, Brulls (1)
Switzerland: Elsener, Schneiter (1), Tacchella, Grobety, Wuthrich, Weber, Antenen, Vonlanthen, Eschmann, Allemann, Durr
Referee: Horn (Netherlands)

6.6.62 West Germany (1) 2, Chile (0) 0 SANTIAGO
West Germany: Fahrian, Nowak, Schnellinger, Schulz, Erhardt, Giesemann, Kraus, Szymaniak (1 pen) Seeler (1), Schafer, Brulls
Chile: Escuti, Eyzaguirre, Navarro, Contreras, Sanchez R, Rojas, Moreno, Tobar, Landa, Sanchez L, Ramirez
Referee: Davidson (Scotland)

7.6.62 Italy (1) 3, Switzerland (0) 0 SANTIAGO
Italy: Buffon, Losi, Radice, Salvadore, Maldini, Robotti, Mora (1), Bulgarelli (1), Sormani, Sivori, Pascutti (1)
Switzerland: Elsener, Schneiter, Tacchella, Groberty, Meier, Weber, Antenen, Vonlanthen, Wuthrich, Allemann, Durr
Referee: Latyschev (USSR)

	P	W	D	L	F	A	Pts
West Germany	3	2	1	0	4	1	5
Chile	3	2	0	1	5	3	4
Italy	3	1	1	1	3	2	3
Switzerland	3	0	0	3	2	8	0

GROUP 3

30.5.62 Brazil (0) 2, Mexico (0) 0 VINA DEL MAR
Brazil: Gylmar, Santos D, Santos N, Zito, Mauro, Zozimo, Garrincha, Didi, Vava, Pele (1), Zagalo (1)
Mexico: Carbajal, Del Muro, Villegas, Cardenas, Sepulveda, Najera, Del Aguila, Reyes, Hernandez H, Jasso, Diaz
Referee: Dienst (Switzerland)

31.5.62 Czechoslovakia (0) 1, Spain (0) 0 VINA DEL MAR
Czechoslovakia: Schroif, Lala, Novak, Pluskal, Popluhar, Masopust, Stibranyi (1), Scherer, Kvasnak, Adamec, Jelinek
Spain: Carmelo, Rivilla, Reija, Segarra, Santamaria, Garay, Del Sol, Martinez, Suarez, Puskas, Gento
Referee: Steiner (Austria)

2.6.62 Brazil (0) 0, Czechoslovakia (0) 0 VINA DEL MAR
Brazil: Gylmar, Santos D, Santos N, Zito, Mauro, Zozimo, Garrincha, Didi, Vava, Pele, Zagalo
Czechoslovakia: Schroif, Lala, Novak, Pluskal, Popluhar, Masopust, Stibranyi, Scherer, Kvasnak, Adamec, Jelinek
Referee: Schwinte (France)

3.6.62 Spain (0) 1, Mexico (0) 0 VINA DEL MAR
Spain: Carmelo, Rodriguez, Gracia, Verges, Santamaria, Pachin, Del Sol, Peiro (1), Puskas, Suarez, Gento
Mexico: Carbajal, Del Muro, Jauregui, Cardenas, Sepulveda, Jasso, Najera, Del Aguila, Reyes, Hernandez H, Diaz
Referee: Tesanic (Yugoslavia)

6.6.62 Brazil (0) 2, Spain (1) 1 VINA DEL MAR
Brazil: Gylmar, Santos D, Santos N, Zito, Mauro, Zozimo, Garrincha, Didi, Vava, Amarildo (2), Zagalo
Spain: Araquistain, Rodriguez, Gracia, Verges, Echeverria, Pachin, Collar, Adelardo (1), Puskas, Peiro, Gento
Referee: Bustamante (Chile)

7.6.62 Mexico (2) 3, Czechoslovakia (1) 1 VINA DEL MAR
Mexico: Carbajal, Del Muro, Sepulveda, Jauregui, Cardenas, Najera, Del Aguila (1), Hernandez A, Hernandez H (1 pen), Reyes, Diaz (1)
Czechoslovakia: Schroif, Lala, Novak, Pluskal, Popluhar, Masopust, Stibranyi, Scherer, Kvasnak, Adamec, Masek (1)
Referee: Dienst (Switzerland)

	P	W	D	L	F	A	Pts
Brazil	3	2	1	0	4	1	5
Czechoslovakia	3	1	1	1	2	3	3
Mexico	3	1	0	2	3	4	2
Spain	3	1	0	2	2	3	2

GROUP 4

30.5.62 Argentina (1) 1, Bulgaria (0) 0 RANCAGUA
Argentina: Roma, Navarro, Marzolini, Sainz, Sacchi, Paez, Facundo (1), Rossi, Pagani, Sanfilippo, Belen
Bulgaria: Naidenov, Rakarov, Dimitrov, Kitov, Kostov D, Rovatchev, Diev, Velitschkov, Iljev, Yakimov, Kolev
Referee: Gardeazabal (Spain)

31.5.62 Hungary (1) 2, England (0) 1 RANCAGUA
Hungary: Grosics, Matrai, Meszoly, Sarosi, Solymosi, Sipos, Sandor, Rakosi, Tichy (1), Albert (1), Fenyvesi
England: Springett, Armfield, Wilson, Moore, Norman, Flowers (1 pen), Douglas, Greaves, Hitchens, Haynes, Charlton R
Referee: Horn (Netherlands)

2.6.62 England (2) 3, Argentina (0) 1 RANCAGUA
England: Springett, Armfield, Wilson, Moore, Norman, Flowers (1 pen), Douglas, Greaves, Peacock (1), Haynes, Charlton R (1)
Argentina: Roma, Cap, Marzolini, Sacchi, Navarro, Paez, Oleniak, Rattin, Sosa, Sanfilippo (1), Belen
Referee: Latyschev (USSR)

3.6.62 Hungary (4) 6, Bulgaria (0) 1 RANCAGUA
Hungary: Ilku, Matrai, Sarosi, Solymosi (1), Meszoly, Sipos, Sandor, Gorocs, Albert (3), Tichy (2), Fenyvesi
Bulgaria: Naidenov, Rakarov, Kitov, Kostov D, Dimitrov, Kovatchev, Sokolov (1), Velitschkov, Asparoukhov, Kolev, Dermendjiev
Referee: Gardeazabal (Spain)

6.6.62 Hungary (0) 0, Argentina (0) 0 RANCAGUA
Hungary: Grosics, Matrai, Sarosi, Solymosi, Meszoly, Sipos, Kuharszky, Gorocs, Monostori, Tichy, Rakosi
Argentina: Dominguez, Sainz, Marzolini, Delgado, Cap, Sacchi, Facundo, Pando, Pagani, Oleniak, Gonzalez
Referee: Yakasaki (Peru)

7.6.62 England (0) 0, Bulgaria (0) 0 RANCAGUA
England: Springett, Armfield, Wilson, Moore, Norman, Flowers, Douglas, Greaves, Peacock, Haynes, Charlton R
Bulgaria: Naidenov, Pentshev, Jetchev, Kostov D, Dimitrov, Kovatchev, Kostov A, Velitschkov, Sokolov, Kolev, Dermendjiev
Referee: Blavier (Belgium)

	P	W	D	L	F	A	Pts
Hungary	3	2	1	0	8	2	5
England	3	1	1	1	4	3	3
Argentina	3	1	1	1	2	3	3
Bulgaria	3	0	1	2	1	7	1

QUARTER FINALS

10.6.62 Yugoslavia (0) 1, West Germany (0) 0 SANTIAGO
Yugoslavia: Soskic, Durkovic, Jusufi, Radakovic (1), Markovic, Popovic, Kovacevic, Sekularac, Jerkovic, Galic, Skoblar
West Germany: Fahrian, Nowak, Schnellinger, Schulz, Erhardt, Giesemann, Brulls, Haller, Seeler, Szymaniak, Schafer
Referee: Yamasaki (Peru)

10.6.62 Chile (2) 2, USSR (1) 1 ARICA
Chile: Escuti, Eyzaguirre, Navarro, Contreras, Sanchez R, Rojas (1), Ramirez, Toro, Landa, Tobar, Sanchez L (1)
USSR: Yashin, Tschokeli, Ostrovsky, Voronin, Maslonkin, Netto, Chislenko (1), Ivanov, Ponedelnik, Mamykin, Meschki
Referee: Horn (Netherlands)

10.6.62 Brazil (1) 3, England (1) 1 VINA DEL MAR
Brazil: Gylmar, Santos D, Santos N, Zito, Mauro, Zozimo, Garrincha (2), Didi, Vava (1), Amarildo, Zagalo
England: Springett, Armfield, Wilson, Moore, Norman, Flowers, Douglas, Greaves, Hitchens (1), Haynes, Charlton R
Referee: Schwinte (France)

10.6.62 Czechoslovakia (1) 1, Hungary (0) 0 RANCAGUA
Czechoslovakia: Schroif, Lala, Novak, Pluskal, Popluhar, Masopust, Pospichal, Scherer (1), Kadraba, Kvasnak, Jelinek
Hungary: Grosics, Matrai, Sarosi, Solymosi, Meszoly, Sipos, Sandor, Rakosi, Tichy, Albert, Fenyvesi
Referee: Latyschev (USSR)

SEMI FINALS

13.6.62 Czechoslovakia (0) 3, Yugoslavia (0) 1 VINA DEL MAR
Czechoslovakia: Schroif, Lala, Novak, Pluskal, Popluhar, Masopust, Pospichal, Scherer (2, 1 pen), Kvasnak, Kadraba (1), Jelinek
Yugoslavia: Soskic, Durkovic, Jusufi, Radakovic, Markovic, Popovic, Sijakovic, Sekularac, Jerkovic (1), Galic, Skoblar
Referee: Dienst (Switzerland)

13.6.62 Brazil (2) 4, Chile (1) 2 SANTIAGO
Brazil: Gylmar, Santos D, Santos N, Zito, Mauro, Zozimo, Garrincha (2), Didi, Vava (2), Amarildo, Zagalo
Chile: Escuti, Eyzaguirre, Rodriguez, Contreras, Sanchez R, Rojas, Ramirez, Toro (1), Landa, Tobar, Sanchez L (1 pen)
Referee: Yamasaki (Peru)

Match for third place

16.6.62 Chile (0) 1, Yugoslavia (0) 0 SANTIAGO
Chile: Godoy, Eyzaguirre, Rodriguez, Cruz, Sanchez R, Rojas (1), Ramirez, Toro, Campos, Tobar, Sanchez L
Yugoslavia: Soskic, Durkovic, Svinjarevic, Radakovic, Markovic, Popovic, Kovacevic, Sekularac, Jerkovic, Galic, Skoblar
Referee: Gardeazabal (Spain)

FINAL

17.6.62 Brazil (1) 3, Czechoslovakia (1) 1 SANTIAGO
Brazil: Gylmar, Santos D, Santos N, Zito (1), Mauro, Zozimo, Garrincha, Didi, Vava (1), Amarildo (1), Zagalo
Czechoslovakia: Schroif, Tichy, Novak, Pluskal, Popluhar, Masopust (1), Pospichal, Scherer, Kadraba, Kvasnak, Jelinek
Referee: Latyschev (USSR)

ENGLAND

1966

Alf Ramsey's wingless Wembley wonders deserved their extra-time win over West Germany, who had prolonged their agony with a dramatic last-minute equaliser, but Geoff Hurst's hat-trick was a controversial treble for England. The first was a header from a free-kick quickly taken while Dienst, the referee, was admonishing an opponent; the second hit the bar and came down so fast that the official had to consult his Russian linesman, Bakhramov, who was badly positioned 10 yards from the goal-line; the third, in the dying minutes, came with three spectators running inside the opposite touchline.

In a tournament of cynical tackling, with players apparently fouling in rotation, five men were sent off: two Argentines, two Uruguayans and a Russian. Four of the dismissals were against the often provocative West Germans; the other culprit, Argentine captain Antonio Rattin, was sent off by a German referee for 'violence of the tongue'.

Yet England showed only flashes in their group games, being easily contained by a defensive Uruguay and beating a poor Mexican side and an injury-hit French team, both by two clear goals. In Group 2, Argentina and West Germany also settled for no goals to ensure that the top two places would not be unrealistic.

However, Group 3 appeared to be the strongest overall. Hungary and Portugal had looked attractive in pre-World Cup games, Bulgaria were tough and Brazil still had Pele; moreover a fit Pele. But he was singled out for roughing-up treatment in the opening game with Bulgaria. Brazil won by two free-kicks, one from Garrincha, who had lost his speed, the other from Pele.

Martin Peters (16) scores England's second goal in the 1966 final against West Germany. (POPPERFOTO)

The Portuguese combination of Mario Coluna's midfield scheming, the giant Jose Torres up front and the athleticism of Eusebio proved too much for Hungary, for whom goalkeeping appeared a lost art. But the Mighty Magyars did better against a Brazil lacking Pele, who had suffered a right knee injury against Bulgaria. Facing elimination, the ten-man Brazilian selection committee brought in nine new players against Portugal, then watched 'old-boy' Pele, not quite fit, get kicked out of the cup. Vicente had him limping after half an hour, Morais finished him off just before the interval.

Still, the real shock came in Group 4, where the unknown North Koreans humiliated Italy. Reduced by injury to ten men after 35 minutes, the Italians fell behind to a goal from Pak Doo Ik just three minutes before half-time and never recovered. The North Koreans progressed behind the USSR, who topped the section.

In the quarter-final at Wembley, Argentina's spoiling tactics upset referee Rudolf Kreitlein more than the England players. His notebook was beginning to curl up at the edges in the sun. Someone had to go. Captain Rattin argued over every decision and once too often; Kreitlein ordered him off. Unfortunately it took eight minutes to persuade him to leave. Incredibly Argentina dominated the game, until tiring. Then in the 78th minute, Hurst headed in at the near post from Peters' cross.

(Top left) Eusebio climbs above a North Korean defender during Portugal's 5-3 quarter-final win over the Asians who shocked an unsuspecting western world in 1966. (POPPERFOTO)

(Top right) The most controversial goal in a World Cup final. Geoff Hurst's shot hits the bar and bounces behind the German goalkeeper Hans Tilkowski. (ALLSPORT)
(Main photo) Both sides appeal, and some look towards the Russian linesman Bakhramov; his verdict was that the ball had crossed the line and the referee awarded a goal. (ALLSPORT)

(Left) West Germany's Uwe Seeler appears pole-axed by this tackle from the Uruguayan defender Manicera. The Germans won 4-0 in a controversial game at Hillsborough, Sheffield.
(HULTON DEUTSCH)

At Hillsborough there was more grief for the South American continent. Uruguay hit the bar against West Germany and then had a strong claim for a penalty, when Karl-Heinz Schnellinger handled under the crossbar, turned down by English referee Jim Finney. The West Germans, sensing they could provoke the Uruguayans into retaliation, achieved their objective. Four goals down at the end with nine men said it all for Uruguay.

At Roker Park, had the goalkeepers changed places, Hungary would probably have beaten the Russians, but the sensation was reserved for Goodison Park where the Koreans had the audacity to score three times before Portugal and Eusebio woke up. Eusebio eventually scored four himself including two penalties and the Portuguese won 5-3.

England had played all their games at Wembley and — surprise, surprise — they also met Portugal there in the semi-final. The Portuguese had apparently decided beforehand to atone for their previous sins, leaving out their hatchet men. However there was much speculation that England's more-than-combative midfield player Nobby Stiles would be taking care of Eusebio.

Reality was something else. Eusebio was insignificant, there was scarcely an infringement and England appeared to coast through with a Charlton effort from a rebound and another driven in just inside the penalty area. Eusebio did manage to convert a penalty for Banks' first back-breaking effort.

The war of attrition which masqueraded as the other semi-final between heavyweights West Germany and the USSR at Goodison Park, finally went to the West Germans by the same 2-1 scoreline, the Russians having Igor Chislenko sent off and another handicapped by injury.

For the final, the Germans rightly or wrongly decided to allow Franz Beckenbauer to shadow Charlton. But they led after Helmut Haller snapped up Ray Wilson's one error of the tournament in the 12th minute. Seven minutes later England were level, Bobby Moore's free-kick being headed in by Hurst. But it was not until the 78th minute that England regained the lead, Peters stabbing the ball in following a corner and a blocked shot from Hurst.

In the dying seconds Wolfgang Weber equalised. A dubious free-kick bounced agonisingly around, hit a defender, was prodded at by Siggi Held, appeared to be handled by Schnellinger and was finally knocked over the line by Weber. Extra time gave England the victory their preparation, dedication, spirit and teamwork had deserved.

Qualifying Tournament

71 entries

Europe (32): Albania, Austria, Belgium, Bulgaria, Cyprus, Czechoslovakia, Denmark, England, Finland, France, East Germany, West Germany, Greece, Holland, Hungary, Republic of Ireland, Northern Ireland, Israel, Italy, Luxembourg, Norway, Poland, Portugal, Rumania, Scotland, Spain, Sweden, Switzerland, Turkey, USSR, Wales, Yugoslavia

South America (10): Argentina, Bolivia, Brazil, Chile, Colombia, Ecuador, Paraguay, Peru, Uruguay, Venezuela

North, Central America and Caribbean (9): Costa Rica, Cuba, Honduras, Jamaica, Mexico, Netherlands Antilles, Surinam, Trinidad, USA

Africa, Asia, Australia (20): Algeria, Australia, Cameroon, Egypt, Ethiopia, Gabon, Ghana, Guinea, Liberia, Libya, Mali, Morocco, Nigeria, North Korea, Senegal, South Africa, South Korea, Sudan, Syria, Tunisia.

The mass withdrawal of all 16 African countries plus the suspension of South Africa by FIFA for violating anti-discrimination codes in the FIFA charter, left only three teams in the sprawling Africa, Asia and Australia zone. A tournament in Cambodia was boycotted by South Korea on the pretext that they preferred to concentrate on the 1968 Olympics, leaving only North Korea and Australia to contest a place in the finals.

In Europe, the draw was made geographically group by group, but with only one team from a particular region in each section. This was not entirely satisfactory though, as there were five groups of four teams and another three of three but only two teams in Group 9 following the withdrawal of Syria. Israel were included in Group 1.

Final places in England were to be distributed as follows: Europe (9 + England), South America (3 + Brazil), North/Central America and Caribbean (1), Asia (1). For the first time since holders and hosts had been exempted to the finals, Brazil and England were offically drawn in the qualifying stages but given a group of their own without opposition.

Europe

Group 1 (Bulgaria, Belgium, Israel)

Belgium v Israel 1 - 0; Bulgaria v Israel 4 - 0; Bulgaria v Belgium 3 - 0; Belgium v Bulgaria 5 - 0: Israel v Belgium 0 - 5; Israel v Bulgaria 1 - 2

	P	W	D	L	F	A	Pts
Belgium	4	3	0	1	11	3	6
Bulgaria	4	3	0	1	9	6	6
Israel	4	0	0	4	1	12	0

Play-off (in Florence): Bulgaria v Belgium 2 - 1

Bulgaria qualified

Group 2 (West Germany, Sweden, Cyprus)

West Germany v Sweden 1 - 1; West Germany v Cyprus 5 - 0; Sweden v Cyprus 3 - 0; Sweden v West Germany 1 - 2; Cyprus v Sweden 0 - 5; Cyprus v West Germany 0 - 6

	P	W	D	L	F	A	Pts
West Germany	4	3	1	0	14	2	7
Sweden	4	2	1	1	10	3	5
Cyprus	4	0	0	4	0	19	0

West Germany qualified

Group 3 (France, Norway, Yugoslavia, Luxembourg)

Yugoslavia v Luxembourg 3 - 1; Luxembourg v France 0 - 2; Luxembourg v Norway 0 - 2; France v Norway 1 - 0; Yugoslavia v France 1 - 0; Norway v Luxembourg 4 - 2; Norway v Yugoslavia 3 - 0; Norway v France 0 - 1; Luxembourg v Yugoslavia 2 - 5; France v Yugoslavia 1 - 0; France v Luxembourg 4 - 1; Yugoslavia v Norway 1 - 1

	P	W	D	L	F	A	Pts
France	6	5	0	1	9	2	10
Norway	6	3	1	2	10	5	7
Yugoslavia	6	3	1	2	10	8	7
Luxembourg	6	0	0	6	6	20	0

France qualified

Group 4 (Portugal, Czechoslovakia, Rumania, Turkey)

Portugal v Turkey 5 - 1; Turkey v Portugal 0 - 1; Czechoslovakia v Portugal 0 - 1; Rumania v Turkey 3 - 0; Rumania v Czechoslovakia 1 - 0; Portugal v Rumania 2 - 1; Czechoslovakia v Rumania 3 - 1; Turkey v Czechoslovakia 0 - 6; Turkey v Rumania 2 - 1; Portugal v Czechoslovakia 0 - 0; Czechoslovakia v Turkey 3 - 1; Rumania v Portugal 2 - 0

	P	W	D	L	F	A	Pts
Portugal	6	4	1	1	9	4	9
Czechoslovakia	6	3	1	2	12	4	7
Rumania	6	3	0	3	9	7	6
Turkey	6	1	0	5	4	19	2

Portugal qualified

Group 5 (Switzerland, Northern Ireland, Holland, Albania)

Holland v Albania, 2- 0; Northern Ireland v Switzerland 1 - 0; Albania v Holland 0 - 2; Switzerland v Northern Ireland 2 -1; Northern Ireland v Holland 2 - 1; Holland v Northern Ireland 0 - 0; Albania v Switzerland 0 - 2; Switzerland v Albania 1 - 0; Northern Ireland v Albania 4 - 1; Holland v Switzerland 0 - 0; Switzerland v Holland 2 - 1; Albania v Northern Ireland 1 - 1

	P	W	D	L	F	A	Pts
Switzerland	6	4	1	1	7	3	9
Northern Ireland	6	3	2	1	9	5	8
Holland	6	2	2	2	6	4	6
Albania	6	0	1	5	2	12	1

Switzerland qualified

Group 6 (Hungary, East Germany, Austria)

Austria v East Germany 1 - 1; East Germany v Hungary 1 - 1; Austria v Hungary 0 - 1; Hungary v Austria 3 - 0; Hungary v East Germany 3 - 2; East Germany v Austria 1 - 0

	P	W	D	L	F	A	Pts
Hungary	4	3	1	0	8	3	7
East Germany	4	1	2	1	5	5	4
Austria	4	0	1	3	1	6	1

Hungary qualified

Group 7 (USSR, Wales, Greece, Denmark)

Denmark v Wales 1 - 0; Greece v Denmark 4 - 2; Greece v Wales 2 - 0; Wales v Greece 4 - 1; USSR v Greece 3 - 1; USSR v Wales 2 - 1; USSR v Denmark 6 - 0; Greece v USSR 1 - 4; Denmark v USSR 1 - 3; Denmark v Greece 1 - 1; Wales v USSR 2 - 1; Wales v Denmark 4 - 2

	P	W	D	L	F	A	Pts
USSR	6	5	0	1	19	6	10
Wales	6	3	0	3	11	9	6
Greece	6	2	1	3	10	14	5
Denmark	6	1	1	4	7	18	3

USSR qualified

Group 8 (Italy, Scotland, Poland, Finland)

Scotland v Finland 3 - 1; Italy v Finland 6 - 1; Poland v Italy 0 - 0; Poland v Scotland 1 - 1; Finland v Scotland 1 - 2; Finland v Italy 0 - 2; Finland v Poland 2 - 0; Scotland v Poland 1 - 2; Poland v Finland 7 - 0; Italy v Poland 6 - 1; Scotland v Italy 1 - 0; Italy v Scotland 3 - 0

	P	W	D	L	F	A	Pts
Italy	6	4	1	1	17	3	9
Scotland	6	3	1	2	8	8	7
Poland	6	2	2	2	11	10	6
Finland	6	1	0	5	5	20	2

Italy qualified

Group 9 (Spain, Rep of Ireland, Syria (withdrew))

Rep of Ireland v Spain 1 - 0; Spain v Rep of Ireland 4 - 1; Play-off (in Paris): Spain v Rep of Ireland 1 - 0

Spain qualified

Group 10 (England)

England qualified

South America

Group 11 (Uruguay, Peru, Venezuela)

Peru v Venezuela 1 - 0; Uruguay v Venezuela 5 - 0; Venezuela v Uruguay 1 - 3; Venezuela v Peru 3 - 6; Peru v Uruguay 0 - 1; Uruguay v Peru 2 - 1

	P	W	D	L	F	A	Pts
Uruguay	4	4	0	0	11	2	8
Peru	4	2	0	2	8	6	4
Venezuela	4	0	0	4	4	15	0

Uruguay qualified

Group 12 (Chile, Ecuador, Colombia)

Colombia v Ecuador 0 - 1; Ecuador v Colombia 2 - 0; Chile v Colombia 7 - 2; Colombia v Chile 2 - 0; Ecuador v Chile 2 - 2; Chile v Ecuador 3 - 1

	P	W	D	L	F	A	Pts
Chile	4	2	1	1	12	7	5
Ecuador	4	2	1	1	6	5	5
Colombia	4	1	0	3	4	10	2

Play-off (in Lima): Chile v Ecuador 2 - 1

Chile qualified

Group 13 (Argentina, Paraguay, Bolivia)

Paraguay v Bolivia 2 - 0; Argentina v Paraguay 3 - 0; Paraguay v Argentina 0 - 0; Argentina v Bolivia 4 - 1; Bolivia v Paraguay 2 - 1; Bolivia v Argentina 1 - 2

	P	W	D	L	F	A	Pts
Argentina	4	3	1	0	9	2	7
Paraguay	4	1	1	2	3	5	3
Bolivia	4	1	0	3	4	9	2

Argentina qualified

Group 14 (Brazil)

Brazil qualified

North and Central America

Group 15

Sub-Group 1 (Jamaica, Netherlands Antilles, Cuba)

Jamaica v Cuba 1 - 0; Cuba v Netherlands Antilles 1 - 1; Jamaica v Netherlands Antilles 2 - 0; Netherlands Antilles v Cuba 1 - 0; Netherlands Antilles v Jamaica 0 - 0; Cuba v Jamaica 2 - 1

	P	W	D	L	F	A	Pts
Jamaica	4	2	1	1	4	2	5
Netherlands Antilles	4	1	2	1	2	3	4
Cuba	4	1	1	2	3	4	3

Sub-Group 2 (Costa Rica, Surinam, Trinidad)

Trinidad v Surinam 4 - 1; Costa Rica v Surinam 1 - 0; Costa Rica v Trinidad 4 - 0; Surinam v Costa Rica 1 - 3; Trinidad v Costa Rica, 0 - l; Surinam v Trinidad 6 - 1

	P	W	D	L	F	A	Pts
Costa Rica	4	4	0	0	9	1	8
Surinam	4	1	0	3	8	9	2
Trinidad	4	1	0	3	5	12	2

Sub-Group 3 (Mexico, USA, Honduras)

Honduras v Mexico 0 - 1; Mexico v Honduras 3 - 0; USA v Mexico 2 - 2; Mexico v USA 2 - 0; Honduras v USA 0 - 1; USA v Honduras 1 - 1

	P	W	D	L	F	A	Pts
Mexico	4	3	1	0	8	2	7
USA	4	1	2	1	4	5	4
Honduras	4	0	1	3	1	6	1

Final round

Costa Rica v Mexico 0 - 0; Jamaica v Mexico 2 - 3; Mexico v Jamaica 8 - 0; Costa Rica v Jamaica 7 - 0; Mexico v Costa Rica 1 - 0; Jamaica v Costa Rica 1 -1

	P	W	D	L	F	A	Pts
Mexico	4	3	1	0	12	2	7
Costa Rica	4	1	2	1	8	2	4
Jamaica	4	0	1	3	3	19	1

Mexico qualified

Asia/Africa

Group 16 (Australia, North Korea, South Korea)

(In Cambodia)
South Korea withdrew
North Korea v Australia 6 - 1, 3 - 1
North Korea qualified

Final Tournament ENGLAND
GROUP 1

11.7.66 England (0) 0, Uruguay (0) 0 WEMBLEY
England: Banks, Cohen, Wilson, Stiles, Charlton J, Moore, Ball, Greaves, Hunt, Charlton R, Connelly
Uruguay: Mazurkiewicz, Troche, Manicera, Ubinas, Goncalvez, Caetano, Cortes, Viera, Silva, Rocha, Perez
Referee: Zsolt (Hungary)

13.7.66 France (0) 1, Mexico (0) 1 WEMBLEY
France: Aubour, Djorkaeff, Artelesa, Budzinski, De Michele, Bonnel, Bosquier, Combin, Herbin, Gondet, Hausser (1)
Mexico: Calderon, Chaires, Nunez, Hernandez, Pena, Mercado, Diaz, Reyes, Fragoso, Padilla, Borja (1)
Referee: Ashkenasi (Israel)

15.7.66 Uruguay (2) 2, France (1) 1 WHITE CITY
Uruguay: Mazurkiewicz, Troche, Manicera, Ubinas, Goncalvez, Caetano, Cortes (1), Viera, Sasia, Rocha (1), Perez
France: Aubour, Djorkaeff, Artelesa, Budzinski, Bosquier, Bonnel, Simon, Herbet, De Bourgoing (1 pen), Gondet, Hausser
Referee: Galba (Czechoslovakia)

16.7.66 England (1) 2, Mexico (0) 0 WEMBLEY
England: Banks, Cohen, Wilson, Stiles, Charlton J, Moore, Paine, Greaves, Hunt (1), Charlton R (1), Peters
Mexico: Calderon, Chaires, Pena, Del Muro, Juaregui, Diaz, Padilla, Borja, Nunez, Reyes, Hernandez
Referee: Lo Bello (Italy)

19.7.66 Uruguay (0) 0, Mexico (0) 0 WEMBLEY
Uruguay: Mazurkiewicz, Troche, Manicera, Ubinas, Goncalvez, Caetano, Cortes, Viera, Sasia, Rocha, Perez
Mexico: Carbajal, Chaires, Pena, Nunez, Hernandez, Diaz, Mercado, Reyes, Cisneros, Borja, Padilla
Referee: Loow (Sweden)

20.7.66 England (1) 2, France (0) 0 WEMBLEY
England: Banks, Cohen, Wilson, Stiles, Charlton J, Moore, Callaghan, Greaves, Hunt (2), Charlton R, Peters
France: Aubour, Djorkaeff, Artelesa, Budzinski, Bosquier, Bonnel, Simon, Herbet, Gondet, Herbin, Hausser
Referee: Yamasaki (Peru)

	P	W	D	L	F	A	Pts
England	3	2	1	0	4	0	5
Uruguay	3	1	2	0	2	1	4
Mexico	3	0	2	1	1	3	2
France	3	0	1	2	2	5	1

GROUP 2

12.7.66 West Germany (3) 5, Switzerland (0) 0 HILLSBOROUGH
West Germany: Tilkowski, Hottges, Weber, Schulz, Schnellinger, Beckenbauer (2), Haller (2, 1 pen), Brulls, Seeler, Overath, Held (1)
Switzerland: Elsener, Grobety, Schneiter, Tacchella, Fuhrer, Bani, Durr, Odermatt, Kunzli, Hosp, Schindelholz
Referee: Phillips (Scotland)

13.7.66 Argentina (0) 2, Spain (0) 1 VILLA PARK
Argentina: Roma, Ferreiro, Perfumo, Albrecht, Marzolini, Solari, Rattin, Gonzalez, Artime (2), Onega (x), Mas
Spain: Iribar, Sanchis, Gallego, Zoco, Eladio, Pirri (1), Suarez, Del Sol, Ufarte, Peiro, Gento
Referee: Rumentschev (Bulgaria)

15.7.66 Spain (0) 2, Switzerland (1) 1 HILLSBOROUGH
Spain: Iribar, Sanchis (1), Gallego, Zoco, Reija, Pirri, Del Sol, Amancio (1), Peiro, Suarez, Gento
Switzerland: Elsener, Fuhrer, Brodmann, Leimgruber, Stierli, Bani, Armbruster, Gottardi, Hosp, Kuhn, Quentin (1)
Referee: Bakhramov (USSR)

16.7.66 West Germany (0) 0, Argentina (0) 0 VILLA PARK
West Germany: Tilkowski, Hottges, Weber, Schulz, Schnellinger, Beckenbauer, Haller, Brulls, Seeler, Overath, Held
Argentina: Roma, Ferreiro, Perfumo, Albrecht, Marzolini, Solari, Rattin, Gonzalez, Artime, Onega, Mas
Referee: Zecevic (Yugoslavia)

19.7.66 Argentina (0) 2, Switzerland (0) 0 HILLSBOROUGH
Argentina: Roma, Ferreiro, Perfumo, Calics, Marzolini, Solari, Rattin, Gonzalez, Artime (1), Onega (1), Mas
Switzerland: Eichmann, Fuhrer, Bani, Brodmann, Stierli, Armbruster, Kuhn, Gottardi, Kunzli, Hosp, Quentin
Referee: Campos (Portugal)

20.7.66 West Germany (1) 2, Spain (1) 1 VILLA PARK
West Germany: Tilkowski, Hottges, Weber, Schulz, Schnellinger, Beckenbauer, Overath, Kramer, Seeler (1), Held, Emmerich (1)
Spain: Iribar, Sanchis, Gallego, Zoco, Reija, Glaria, Fuste (1), Amancio, Adelardo, Marcelino, Lapetra
Referee: Marques (Brazil)

	P	W	D	L	F	A	Pts
West Germany	3	2	1	0	7	1	5
Argentina	3	2	1	0	4	1	5
Spain	3	1	0	2	4	5	2
Switzerland	3	0	0	3	1	9	0

GROUP 3

12.7.66 Brazil (1) 2, Bulgaria (0) 0 GOODISON PARK
Brazil: Gylmar, Santos D, Bellini, Altair, Paulo Henrique, Denilson, Lima, Garrincha (1), Alcindo, Pele (1), Jairzinho
Bulgaria: Naidenov, Chalamanov, Penev, Vutzov, Gaganelov, Kitov, Jetchev, Dermendjiev, Asparoukhov, Yakimov, Kolev
Referee: Tschenscher (West Germany)

13.7.66 Portugal (1) 3, Hungary (0) 1 OLD TRAFFORD
Portugal: Carvalho, Morais, Baptista, Vicente, Hilairo, Graca, Coluna, Jose Augusto (2), Eusebio, Torres (1), Simoes
Hungary: Szentmihalyi, Kaposzta, Matrai, Meszoly, Sovari, Nagy I, Sipos, Bene (1), Albert, Farkas, Rakosi
Referee: Callaghan (Wales)

15.7.66 Hungary (1) 3, Brazil (1) 1 GOODISON PARK
Hungary: Gelei, Matrai, Kaposzta, Meszoly (1 pen), Sipos, Szepesi, Mathesz, Rakosi, Bene (1), Albert, Farkas (1)
Brazil: Gylmar, Santos D, Bellini, Altair, Paulo Henrique, Gerson, Lima, Garrincha, Alcindo, Tostao (1), Jairzinho
Referee: Dagnall (England)

16.7 66 Portugal (2) 3, Bulgaria (0) 0 OLD TRAFFORD
Portugal: Pereira, Festa, Germano, Vicente, Hilario, Graca, Coluna, Jose Augusto, Eusebio (1), Torres (1), Simoes
Bulgaria: Naidenov, Chalamanov, Vutzov (o. g.), Gaganelov, Penev, Jetchev, Yakimov, Dermendjiev, Jekov, Asparoukhov, Kostov
Referee: Codesal (Uruguay)

17.7.66 Portugal (2) 3, Brazil (0) 0 GOODISON PARK
Portugal: Pereira, Morais, Baptista, Vicente, Hilairo, Graca, Coluna, Jose Augusto, Eusebio (2), Torres, Simoes (1)
Brazil: Manga, Fidelis, Brito, Orlando, Rildo (1), Denilson, Lima, Jairzinho, Silva, Pele, Parana
Referee: McCabe (England)

20.7.66 Hungary (2) 3, Bulgaria (1) 1 OLD TRAFFORD
Hungary: Gelei, Matrai, Kaposzta, Meszoly (1), Sipos, Szepesi, Mathesz, Rakosi, Bene (1), Albert, Farkas
Bulgaria: Simeonov, Penev, Largov, Vutzov, Gaganelov, Jetchev, Davidov (o. g.), Yakimov, Asparoukhov (1), Kolev, Kostov
Referee: Goicoechea (Argentina)

	P	W	D	L	F	A	Pts
Portugal	3	3	0	0	9	2	6
Hungary	3	2	0	1	7	5	4
Brazil	3	1	0	2	4	6	2
Bulgaria	3	0	0	3	1	8	0

GROUP 4

12.7.66 USSR (2) 3, North Korea (0) 0 AYRESOME PARK
USSR: Kavazashvili, Ponomarev, Shesternev, Khurtsilava, Ostrovksky, Sabo, Sichinava, Chislenko, Banischevski (1), Khusainov, Malofeyev (2)
North Korea: Chan Myung, Li Sup, Yung Kyoo, Bong Chil, Zoong Sun, Seung Hwi, Bong Zin, Doo Ik, Ryong Woon, Seung Il, Seung Zin
Referee: Gardeazabal (Spain)

13.7.66 Italy (1) 2, Chile (0) 0 ROKER PARK
Italy: Albertosi, Burgnich, Rosato, Salvadore, Facchetti, Bulgarelli, Lodetti, Perani, Mazzola (1), Rivera, Barison (1)
Chile: Olivares, Eyzaguirre, Cruz, Figueroa, Villanueva, Prieto, Marcos, Fouilloux, Araya, Tobar, Sanchez L
Referee: Dienst (Switzerland)

13.7.66 North Korea (0) 1, Chile (1) 1 AYRESOME PARK
North Korea: Chan Myung, Li Sup, Yung Kyoo, Zoong Sun, Yoon Kyung, Seung Zin (1), Seung Hwi, Bong Zin, Doo Ik, Dong Woon, Seung Il
Chile: Olivares, Valentini, Cruz, Figueroa, Villanueva, Prieto, Marcos (1 pen), Araya, Landa, Fouilloux, Sanchez L
Referee: Kandil (Egypt)

16.7.66 USSR (0) 1, Italy (0) 0 ROKER PARK
USSR: Yashin, Ponomarev, Shesternev, Khurtsilava, Danilov, Sabo, Voronin, Chislenko (1), Malofeyev, Banischevski, Khusainov
Italy: Albertosi, Burgnich, Rosato, Salvadore, Facchetti, Lodetti, Leoncini, Meroni, Mazzola, Bulgarelli, Pascutti
Referee: Kreitlein (West Germany)

19.7.66 North Korea (1) 1, Italy (0) 0 AYRESOME PARK
North Korea: Chang Myung, Zoong Sun, Yung Kyoo, Yung Won, Yoon Kyung, Seung Hwi, Bong Zin, Doo Ik (1), Seung Zin, Bong Hwan, Seung Kook
Italy: Albertosi, Landini, Guarneri, Janich, Facchetti, Bulgarelli, Fogli, Perani, Mazzola, Rivera, Barison
Referee: Schwinte (France)

20.7.66 USSR (1) 2, Chile (1) 1 ROKER PARK
USSR: Kavazashvili, Getmanov, Shesternev, Kornejev, Ostrovsky, Voronin, Afonin, Metreveli, Serebrannikov, Markarov, Porkujan (2)
Chile: Olivares, Valentini, Cruz, Figueroa, Villanueva, Marcos (1), Prieto, Araya, Landa, Yavar, Sanchez L
Referee: Adair (Northern Ireland)

	P	W	D	L	F	A	Pts
USSR	3	3	0	0	6	1	6
North Korea	3	1	1	1	2	4	3
Italy	3	1	0	2	2	2	2
Chile	3	0	1	2	2	5	1

QUARTER FINALS
23.7.66 England (0) 1, Argentina (0) 0 WEMBLEY
England: Banks, Cohen, Wilson, Stiles, Charlton J, Moore, Ball, Hunt, Hurst (1), Charlton R, Peters
Argentina: Roma, Ferreiro, Perfumo, Albrecht, Marzolini, Solari, Rattin, Gonzalez, Artime, Onega, Mas
Referee: Kreitlein (West Germany)

23.7.66 West Germany (1) 4, Uruguay (0) 0 HILLSBOROUGH
West Germany: Tilkowski, Hottges, Weber, Schulz, Schnellinger, Haller (2), Beckenbauer (1), Overath, Seeler (1), Emmerich, Held
Uruguay: Mazurkiewicz, Troche, Ubinas, Caetano, Manicera, Rocha, Goncalvez, Salva, Cortes, Silva, Perez
Referee: Finney (England)

23.7.66 Portugal (2) 5, North Korea (3) 3 GOODISON PARK
Portugal: Pereira, Morais, Baptista, Vicente, Hilario, Graca, Coluna, Jose Augusto (1), Eusebio (4, 2 pens), Torres, Simoes
North Korea: Chan Myung, Zoong Sun, Yung Kyoo, Yung Won, Yoon Kyung, Seung Zin, Seung Hwi, Bong Zin, Doo Ik, Dong Woon (1), Seung Kook (2)
Referee: Ashkenasi (Israel)

23.7.66 USSR (1) 2, Hungary (0) 1 ROKER PARK
USSR: Yashin, Ponomarev, Shesternev, Danilov, Voronin, Sabo, Khusainov, Chislenko (1), Banischevski, Malofeyev, Porkujan (1)
Hungary: Gelei, Kaposzta, Matrai, Meszoly, Szepesi, Nagy I, Sipos, Bene (1), Albert, Farkas, Rakosi
Referee: Gardeazabal (Spain)

SEMI FINALS
25.7.66 West Germany (1) 2, USSR (0) 1 GOODISON PARK
West Germany: Tilkowski, Lutz, Weber, Schulz, Schnellinger, Beckenbauer (1), Overath, Seeler, Haller (1), Held, Emmerich
USSR: Yashin, Ponomarev, Shesternev, Danilov, Voronin, Sabo, Khusainov, Chislenko, Banischevski, Malofeyev, Porkujan (1)
Referee: Lo Bello (Italy)

26.7.66 England (1) 2, Portugal (0) 1 WEMBLEY
England: Banks, Cohen, Wilson, Stiles, Charlton J, Moore, Ball, Hunt, Hurst, Charlton R (2), Peters
Portugal: Pereira, Festa, Baptista, Jose Carlos, Hilario, Graca, Coluna, Jose Augusto, Eusebio (1 pen), Torres, Simoes
Referee: Schwinte (France)

Match for third place
28.7.66 Portugal (1) 2, USSR (1) 1 WEMBLEY
Portugal: Pereira, Festa, Baptista, Jose Carlos, Hilario, Graca, Coluna, Jose Augusto, Eusebio (1 pen), Torres (1), Simoes
USSR: Yashin, Ponomarev, Korneev, Khurtsilava, Danilov, Voronin, Sichinava, Serebrannikov, Banischevski, Malofeyev (1), Metreveli
Referee: Dagnall (England)

FINAL
30.7.66 England (1) 4, West Germany (1) 2 (aet, 2-2 at 90 mins) WEMBLEY
England: Banks, Cohen, Wilson, Stiles, Charlton J, Moore, Ball, Hunt, Hurst (3), Charlton R, Peters (1)
West Germany: Tilkowski, Hottges, Weber (1), Schulz, Schnellinger, Haller (1), Beckenbauer, Overath, Seeler, Emmerich, Held
Referee: Dienst (Switzerland)

MEXICO
1970

Pele powers in a header to put Brazil 1-0 up against Italy in the 1970 final in Mexico City. Brazil won 4-1 in a masterly display of individual skill and flair.
(PRESSENS BILD)

Fears that the choice of Mexico as the venue would produce untold problems relating to heat and altitude as well as fan the flames of violence on the field were dispelled. Skill, thought and officials who threatened to use the the red and yellow disciplinary cards to advantage, contributed to a memorable tournament.

Its winners were Brazil, easily the most gifted team, if possessing certain weaknesses. As usual, their off-the-field preparations were faultless. A meticulous four months' training was rewarded with a vintage victory. They succeeded not only through this single-minded devotion to detail, but because of outstanding performances by several brilliant individuals, whose ability overcame the shortcomings of colleagues.

Brazil had even had a change of manager after the qualifying stage, Joao Saldanha giving way to Zagalo who had collected two winners medals as a player. He inherited a goalkeeper in Felix who was shaky, and had to struggle to keep his four-man zonal defence operating the system at all, when they were not giving the ball away.

But moving foward, either in swift counter-attacks or with breathtaking passing movements, simply transformed Brazil into a flexible, potent striking force. There was the deceptively languid Gerson controlling the midfield; the industry of Clodoaldo; the explosive dead-ball shooting of Rivelino; Jairzinho's penetration on the flank and the unselfishness of Tostao, forbidden to head the ball because of an operation for a detached retina. Above all there was Pele, restored to full vigour and at the peak of his illustrious career.

A rash of yellow cards in the opening goalless draw between Mexico and the USSR set the pattern for improved behaviour and the competition did not produce one dismissal. These two teams progressed to

51

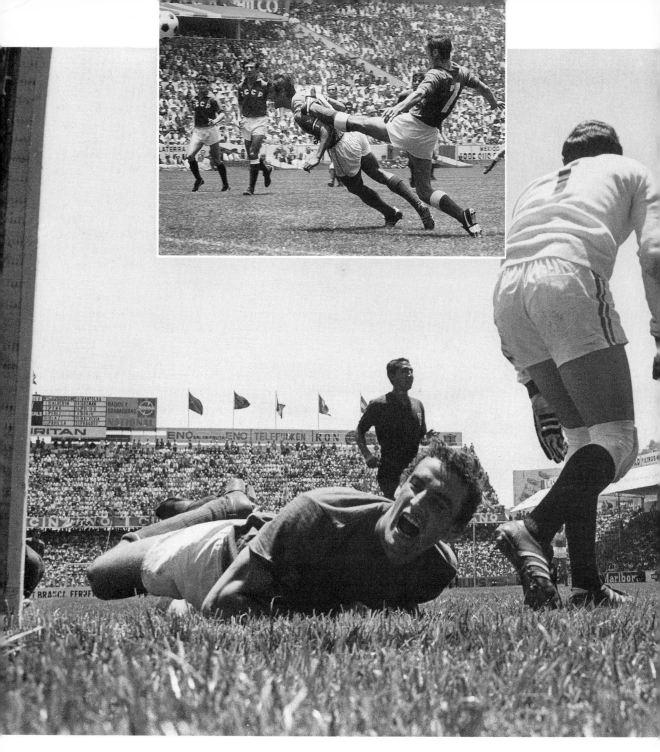

the quarter-finals as did Italy and Uruguay in Group 2, though neither impressed. Italy scored only one goal, an error by the Swedish goalkeeper.

Group 3 was well contested with Brazil winning all three games, though runners-up England pressed them fiercely in Guadalajara. The only goal came from an unselfish pass from Pele for the onrushing Jairzinho, but England still moved on. Yet the most entertaining group was the one in which West Germany and Peru emerged in front of Bulgaria and Morocco.

The Germans paired the veteran Uwe Seeler with the lethal poacher Gerd Muller and with substitutes allowed for the first time in the competition, switched wingers to telling effect during the games. Overall, some imaginative free-kicks added to the spectators' delight and the cavalier approach of Peru was another pleasing aspect.

In the quarter-finals, Uruguay survived a gruelling extra-time encounter with the USSR to emerge 1-0 winners in Mexico City, but it was the other three matches that had the drama and the goals.

England met West Germany in Leon, a repeat of the 1966 World Cup final at Wembley. Again it went to extra time, but with an entirely different narrative. Alan Mullery from six yards and Martin Peters running in at the far post had given England a deserved half-time lead. But in the 57th minute, Helmut Schoen the West Germany manager put on Grabowski as a fresh winger to run at a tiring defence. Beckenbauer rounded Mullery and reduced the scoreline to 2-1. Ramsey replied by taking off Charlton and bringing on Colin Bell.

Nine minutes from the end Seeler scored with a back header from an acute angle to force extra time. Inevitably, with the Germans once more underestimated but on top, it was Muller who stole in to hook the winner from close range. Ramsey's always cautious approach had proved his downfall.

The Guadalajara meeting between Brazil and Peru provided another feast of fast, entertaining fare, Brazil winning 4-2, while in Toluca, Italy hit the hosts Mexico with three goals in a 12-minute spell in the second half to win 4-1.

But the real heart-stopping affair was the semi-final involving the Italians and Germans in Mexico City. Roberto Boninsegna scored for Italy after eight minutes and they held the lead until the last minute when Schnellinger equalised with a volley. The Germans were handicapped, with Beckenbauer bravely playing on despite a dislocated shoulder, as they had used both substitutes.

Both teams were exhausted and it was a question of which side made more mistakes. Muller forced one over the line, Burgnich equalised. Riva restored Italy's lead only for Muller to head the Germans level at 3-3. Equality lasted only two minutes. Gianni Rivera drove in the winner in the 112th minute.

(Top left) The opening game in any World Cup tournament invariably ends in a goalless draw. 1970 was no exception. Horatio Lopez (Mexico) has his head menaced by USSR forward Gennadi Logofet (7). (PRESSENS BILD)

(Left) Down but not out: Luigi Riva shouts in delight after scoring Italy's fourth goal against Mexico. Italy won their quarter-final tie 4-1. (PRESSENS BILD)

(Below) Contrasting moods: Roberto Boninsegna (20) leaps for joy, Muller (13) despairs as Italy score against the Germans. (PRESSENS BILD)

In the other semi-final in Guadalajara, Uruguay gave a fine account of themselves in the first half against Brazil, taking the lead through a half-hit angled shot from Luis Cubilla that made Felix look vulnerable. But Clodoaldo equalised right on half-time and in the second half it was all Brazil, though they did not score again until the 76th minute through Jairzinho and then in the last minute through Rivelino.

Thus the *catenaccio* of Italy faced Brazil's improvisation in the final and it stayed goalless only until the 17th minute when a teasing cross from Rivelino was headed powerfully in by Pele. Sheer carelessness gave Boninsegna an equaliser 20 minutes later and it was not until the 65th minute that Brazil regained the lead. Gerson's strong, long-range, left-foot drive finally broke down Italian resistance and Pele again laid on goals for Jairzinho six minutes later and for Carlos Alberto with three minutes remaining. Brazil had won the Jules Rimet Trophy for the third time and were allowed to keep it. But it was the end of an era.

Qualifying Tournament

70 entries

Europe (30): Austria, Belgium, Bulgaria, Cyprus, Czechoslovakia, Denmark, England, Finland, France, East Germany, West Germany, Greece, Holland, Hungary, Republic of Ireland, Northern Ireland, Italy, Luxembourg, Norway, Poland, Portugal, Rumania, Scotland, Spain, Sweden, Switzerland, Turkey, USSR, Wales, Yugoslavia

South America (10): Argentina, Bolivia, Brazil, Chile, Colombia, Ecuador, Paraguay, Peru, Uruguay, Venezuela

Concacaf (12): Bermuda, Canada, Costa Rica, Guatemala, Haiti, Honduras, Jamaica, Netherlands Antilles, El Salvador, Surinam, Trinidad, USA

Asia/Oceania (7): Australia, Israel, Japan, New Zealand, North Korea, Rhodesia, South Korea

Africa (11): Algeria, Cameroon, Ethiopia, Ghana, Libya, Morocco, Nigeria, Senegal, Sudan, Tunisia, Zambia

Finding a niche in the World Cup qualifying stages was becoming a problem politically for Israel. They were moved into the Asia/Oceania zone only to discover North Korea unwilling to meet them. Moreover although Rhodesia's entry had been accepted,they had a government which was not recognised; it was impossible for other countries to travel to Rhodesia or receive a team from that country. However Australia finally agreed to meet them on neutral territory over two matches in Mozambique.

Again England as holders and Mexico as hosts were included in the qualifying draw without having to play; again given a group of their own.

Final places in Mexico were to be distributed as follows:
Europe (8 + England), South America (3), Concacaf (1 + Mexico), Asia/Oceania (1), Africa (1)

Europe

Group 1 (Rumania, Greece, Switzerland, Portugal)
Switzerland v Greece 1 - 0; Portugal v Rumania 3 - 0; Rumania v Switzerland 2 - 0; Greece v Portugal 4 - 2; Portugal v Switzerland 0 - 2; Greece v Rumania 2 - 2; Portugal v Greece 2 - 2; Switzerland v Rumania 0 - 1; Rumania v Portugal 1 - 0; Greece v Switzerland 4 - 1; Switzerland v Portugal 1 - 1; Rumania v Greece 1 - 1

	P	W	D	L	F	A	Pts
Rumania	6	3	2	1	7	6	8
Greece	6	2	3	1	13	9	7
Switzerland	6	2	1	3	5	8	5
Portugal	6	1	2	3	8	10	4

Rumania qualified

Group 2 (Hungary, Czechoslovakia, Denmark, Rep of Ireland)
Denmark v Czechoslovakia 0 - 3; Czechoslovakia v Denmark 1 - 0; Rep of Ireland v Czechoslovakia 1 - 2; Hungary v Czechoslovakia 2 - 0; Rep of Ireland v Denmark 1 - 1 (after abandoned game after 51 minutes at 1 - 1 due to fog); Rep of Ireland v Hungary 1 - 2; Denmark v Hungary 3 - 2; Czechoslovakia v Hungary 3 - 3; Czechoslovakia v Rep of Ireland 3 - 0; Denmark v Rep of Ireland 2 - 0; Hungary v Denmark 3 - 0; Hungary v Rep of Ireland 4 - 0

	P	W	D	L	F	A	Pts
Hungary	6	4	1	1	16	7	9
Czechoslovakia	6	4	1	1	12	6	9
Denmark	6	2	1	3	6	10	5
Rep of Ireland	6	0	1	5	3	14	1

Play-off (in Marseilles): Czechoslovakia v Hungary 4 - 1
Czechoslovakia qualified

Group 3 (Italy, East Germany, Wales)
Wales v Italy 0 - 1; East Germany v Italy 2 - 2; East Germany v Wales 2 - 1; Wales v East Germany 1 - 3; Italy v Wales 4 - 1; Italy v East Germany 3 - 0

	P	W	D	L	F	A	Pts
Italy	4	3	1	0	10	3	7
East Germany	4	2	1	1	7	7	5
Wales	4	0	0	4	3	10	0

Italy qualified

Group 4 (USSR, Northern Ireland, Turkey)
Northern Ireland v Turkey 4 - 1; Turkey v Northern Ireland 0 - 3; Northern Ireland v USSR 0 - 0; USSR v Turkey 3 - 0; USSR v Northern Ireland 2 - 0; Turkey v USSR 1 - 3

	P	W	D	L	F	A	Pts
USSR	4	3	1	0	8	1	7
Northern Ireland	4	2	1	1	7	3	5
Turkey	4	0	0	4	2	13	0

USSR qualified

Group 5 (Sweden, France, Norway)
Sweden v Norway 5 - 0; France v Norway 0 - 1; Norway v Sweden 2 - 5; Norway v France 1 - 3; Sweden v France 2 - 0; France v Sweden 3 - 0

	P	W	D	L	F	A	Pts
Sweden	4	3	0	1	12	5	6
France	4	2	0	2	6	4	4
Norway	4	1	0	3	4	13	2

Sweden qualified

Group 6 (Belgium, Yugoslavia, Spain, Finland)
Finland v Belgium 1 - 2; Yugoslavia v Finland 9 - 1; Belgium v Finland 6 - 1; Belgium v Yugoslavia 3 - 0; Yugoslavia v Spain 0 - 0; Spain v Belgium 1 - 1; Belgium v Spain 2 - 1; Finland v Yugoslavia 1 - 5; Finland v Spain 2 - 0; Spain v Finland 6 - 0; Yugoslavia v Belgium 4 - 0

	P	W	D	L	F	A	Pts
Belgium	6	4	1	1	14	8	9
Yugoslavia	6	3	1	2	19	7	7
Spain	6	2	2	2	10	6	6
Finland	6	1	0	5	6	28	2

Belgium qualified

Group 7 (West Germany, Scotland, Austria, Cyprus)
Austria v Cyprus 7 - 1; Austria v West Germany 0 - 2; Scotland v Austria 2 - 1; Cyprus v West Germany 0 - 1; Cyprus v Scotland 0 - 5; Scotland v West Germany 1 - 1; Cyprus v Austria 1 - 2; West Germany v Austria 1 - 0; Scotland v Cyprus 8 - 0; West Germany v Cyprus 12 - 0; West Germany v Scotland 3 - 2; Austria v Scotland 2 - 0

	P	W	D	L	F	A	Pts
West Germany	6	5	1	0	20	3	11
Scotland	6	3	1	2	18	7	7
Austria	6	3	0	3	12	7	6
Cyprus	6	0	0	6	2	35	0

West Germany qualified

Group 8 (Bulgaria, Poland, Holland, Luxembourg)
Luxembourg v Holland 0 - 2; Bulgaria v Holland 2 - 0; Holland v Luxembourg 4 - 0; Poland v Luxembourg 8 - 1; Bulgaria v Luxembourg 2 - 1; Holland v Poland 1 - 0; Bulgaria v Poland 4 - 1; Poland v Holland 2 - 1; Luxembourg v Poland 1 - 5; Holland v Bulgaria 1 - 1; Poland v Bulgaria 3 - 0; Luxembourg v Bulgaria 1 - 3

	P	W	D	L	F	A	Pts
Bulgaria	6	4	1	1	12	7	9
Poland	6	4	0	2	19	8	8
Holland	6	3	1	2	9	5	7
Luxembourg	6	0	0	6	4	24	0

Bulgaria qualified

Group 9 (England)
England qualified as holders

South America
Group 10 (Peru, Bolivia, Argentina)
Bolivia v Argentina 3 - 1; Peru v Argentina 1 - 0; Bolivia v Peru 2 - 1; Peru v Bolivia 3 - 0; Argentina v Bolivia 1 - 0; Argentina v Peru 2 - 2

	P	W	D	L	F	A	Pts
Peru	4	2	1	1	7	5	5
Bolivia	4	2	0	2	5	6	4
Argentina	4	1	1	2	4	6	3

Peru qualified

Group 11(Brazil, Paraguay, Colombia, Venezuela)
Colombia v Venezuela 3 - 0; Venezuela v Colombia 1 - 1; Colombia v Brazil 0 - 2; Venezuela v Paraguay 0 - 2; Colombia v Paraguay 0 - 1; Venezuela v Brazil 0 - 5; Paraguay v Brazil 0 - 3; Brazil v Colombia 6 - 2; Paraguay v Venezuela 1 - 0; Brazil v Venezuela 6 - 0; Paraguay v Colombia 2 - 1; Brazil v Paraguay 1 - 0

	P	W	D	L	F	A	Pts
Brazil	6	6	0	0	23	2	12
Paraguay	6	4	0	2	6	5	8
Colombia	6	1	1	4	7	12	3
Venezuela	6	0	1	5	1	18	1

Brazil qualified

Group 12 (Uruguay, Chile, Ecuador)
Ecuador v Uruguay 0 - 2; Chile v Uruguay 0 - 0; Uruguay v Ecuador 1 - 0; Chile v Ecuador 4 - 1; Ecuador v Chile 1 - 1; Uruguay v Chile 2 - 0

	P	W	D	L	F	A	Pts
Uruguay	4	3	1	0	5	0	7
Chile	4	1	2	1	5	4	4
Ecuador	4	0	1	3	2	8	1

Uruguay qualified

Concacaf
Group 13 (Honduras, Costa Rica, Jamaica, Haiti, Guatemala, Trinidad, El Salvador, Surinam, Netherlands Antilles, USA, Canada, Bermuda)

Sub-Group A
Costa Rica v Jamaica 3 - 0; Jamaica v Costa Rica 1 - 3; Honduras v Jamaica 3 - 1; Jamaica v Honduras 0 - 2; Honduras v Costa Rica 1 - 0; Costa Rica v Honduras 1 - 1

	P	W	D	L	F	A	Pts
Honduras	4	3	1	0	7	2	7
Costa Rica	4	2	1	1	7	3	5
Jamaica	4	0	0	4	2	11	0

Sub-Group B
Guatemala v Trinidad 4 - 0; Trinidad v Guatemala 0 - 0; Trinidad v Haiti 0 - 4; Haiti v Trinidad 2 - 4; Haiti v Guatemala 2 - 0; Guatemala v Haiti 1 - 1

	P	W	D	L	F	A	Pts
Haiti	4	2	1	1	9	5	5
Guatemala	4	1	2	1	5	3	4
Trinidad	4	1	1	2	4	10	3

Sub-Group C
Surinam v Netherlands Antilles 6 - 0; El Salvador v Surinam 6 - 0; Netherlands Antilles v Surinam 2 - 0; El Salvador v Netherlands Antilles 1 - 0; Netherlands Antilles v El Salvador 1 - 2; Surinam v El Salvador 4 - 1

	P	W	D	L	F	A	Pts
El Salvador	4	3	0	1	10	5	6
Surinam	4	2	0	2	10	9	4
N'lands/ Antilles	4	1	0	3	3	9	2

Sub-Group D
Canada v Bermuda 4 - 0; Canada v USA 4 - 2; Bermuda v Canada 0 - 0; USA v Canada 1 - 0; USA v Bermuda 6 - 2; Bermuda v USA 0 - 2

	P	W	D	L	F	A	Pts
USA	4	3	0	1	11	6	6
Canada	4	2	1	1	8	3	5
Bermuda	4	0	1	3	2	12	1

2nd Round
Haiti v USA 2 - 0, 1 - 0; Honduras v El Salvador 1 - 0, 0 - 3
Play-off (in Mexico City): El Salvador v Honduras 3 - 2

3rd Round
Haiti v El Salvador 1 - 2, 3 - 0
Play-off (in Kingston): El Salvador v Haiti 1 - 0
El Salvador qualified

Group 14 (Mexico)
Mexico qualified as hosts

Oceania
Group 15 (Australia, South Korea, Japan, Rhodesia, Israel, New Zealand)
Sub-Group A (in Seoul)
Australia v Japan 3 - 1; South Korea v Japan 2 - 2; Australia v South Korea 2 - 1; Japan v Australia 1 - 1; South Korea v Japan 2 - 0; South Korea v Australia 1 - 1

	P	W	D	L	F	A	Pts
Australia	4	2	2	0	7	4	6
South Korea	4	1	2	1	6	5	4
Japan	4	0	2	2	4	8	2

Sub-Group B (in Tel Aviv)
North Korea eliminated for refusing to play Israel
Israel v New Zealand 4 - 0, 2 - 0

2nd Round (in Lourenco Marques)
Australia v Rhodesia 1 - 1, 0 - 0
Play-off: Australia v Rhodesia 3 - 1

Final Round
Israel v Australia 1 - 0, 1 - 1
Israel qualified

Africa
Group 16 (Algeria, Tunisia, Nigeria, Cameroon, Ghana (bye), Morocco, Senegal, Libya, Ethiopia, Zambia, Sudan)
Morocco v Senegal 1 - 0, 1 - 2; Play-off (in Las Palmas): Morocco v Senegal 2 - 0; Algeria v Tunisia 1 - 2, 0 - 0; Libya v Ethiopia 2 - 0, 1 - 5; Zambia v Sudan 4 - 2, 2 - 4 (Sudan winners by scoring more goals in second match); Nigeria v Cameroon 1 - 1, 3 - 2

2nd Round
Tunisia v Morocco 0 - 0, 0 - 0; Play-off: Morocco v Tunisia 2 - 2 (Morocco won on toss of coin); Ethiopia v Sudan 1 - 1, 1 - 3; Nigeria v Ghana 2 - 1, 1 - 1

Final Round
Nigeria v Sudan 2 - 2; Morocco v Nigeria 2 - 1; Sudan v Nigeria 3 - 3; Sudan v Morocco 0 - 0; Morocco v Sudan 3 - 0; Nigeria v Morocco 2 - 0

	P	W	D	L	F	A	Pts
Morocco	4	2	1	1	5	3	5
Nigeria	4	1	2	1	8	7	4
Sudan	4	0	3	1	5	8	3

Morocco qualified

Final Tournament MEXICO
GROUP 1

31.5.70 Mexico (0) 0, USSR (0) 0 MEXICO CITY
Mexico: Calderon, Pena, Perez, Hernandez, Lopez, Vantolra, Guzman, Pulido, Velarde (Manguia), Valdivia, Fragoso
USSR: Kavazashvili, Kaplichny Lovchev, Logofet, Shesternev, Asatiani, Muntian, Serebrannikov (Puzach), Nodia (Khmelnitski) Byshovets, Evryushikhin
Referee: Tchenscher (West Germany)

3.6.70 Belgium (1) 3, El Salvador (0) 0 MEXICO CITY
Belgium: Piot, Heylens, Thissen, Dewalque, Dockx, Semmeling (Polleunis), Van Moer (2), Devrindt, Van Himst, Puis, Lambert (1 pen)
El Salvador: Magana, Rivas, Mariona, Osorio, Quintanilla, Rodriguez Lindo (Sermeno), Vasquez, Martinez, Cabezas, Aparicio, Manzano (Mendes C)
Referee: Radulescu (Rumania)

6.6.70 USSR (1) 4, Belgium (0) 1 MEXICO CITY
USSR: Kavazashvili, Dzodzuashvili (Kiselev), Afonin, Shesternev, Khurtsilava, Kaplichny (Lovchev), Asatiani (1), Muntian, Byshovets (2), Evryushikhin, Khmelnitski (1)
Belgium: Piot, Heylens, Thissen, Dewalque, Jeck, Dockx, Semmeling, Van Moer, Van Himst, Puis, Lambert (1)
Referee: Scheurer (Switzerland)

7.6.70 Mexico (1) 4, El Salvador (0) 0 MEXICO CITY
Mexico: Calderon, Vantolra, Pena, Guzman, Perez, Gonzalez, Munguia, Valdivia (2), Borja (Lopez then Basaguren (1)), Fragoso (1), Padilla
El Salvador: Magana, Rivas, Mariona, Osorio, Mendez C (Monge), Quintanilla, Rodriguez Lindo, Vasquez, Martinez, Cabezas, Aparicio (Mendez S)
Referee: Kandil (Egypt)

10.6.70 USSR (0) 2, El Salvador (0) 0 MEXICO CITY
USSR: Kavazashvili, Dzodzuashvili, Khurtsilava, Shesternev, Afonin, Kiselev (Asatiani), Serebrannikov, Muntian, Pusach (Evryushikhin), Byshovets (2), Khmelnitski
El Salvador: Magana, Rivas, Mariona, Castro, Osorio, Vasquez, Portillo, Cabezas (Aparicio), Rodriguez Lindo (Sermeno), Mendez S, Monge
Referee: Hormazabal (Chile)

11.6.70 Mexico (1) 1, Belgium (0) 0 MEXICO CITY
Mexico: Calderon, Vantolra, Guzman, Pena (1 pen), Perez, Pulido, Gonzalez, Munguia, Padilla, Valdivia (Basaguren), Fragosa
Belgium: Piot, Heylens, Thissen, Dewalque, Jeck, Dockx, Semmeling, Van Moer, Van Himst, Puis, Polleunis (Devrindt)
Referee: Coerezza (Argentina)

	P	W	D	L	F	A	Pts
USSR	3	2	1	0	6	1	5
Mexico	3	2	1	0	5	0	5
Belgium	3	1	0	2	4	5	2
El Salvador	3	0	0	3	0	9	0

GROUP 2

2.6.70 Uruguay (1) 2, Israel (0) 0 PUEBLA
Uruguay: Mazurkiewicz, Ubinas, Ancheta, Matosas, Mujica (1), Montero Castillo, Rocha (Cortes), Maneiro (1), Cubilla, Esparrago, Losado
Israel: Vissoker, Schwager, Rosen, Rosenthal, Primo, Spiegel, Shum, Spiegler, Talbi (Bar), Faygenbaum, Rom (Vollach)
Referee: Davidson (Scotland)

3.6.70 Italy (1) 1, Sweden (0) 0 TOLUCA
Italy: Albertosi, Burgnich, Facchetti, Cera, Niccolai (Rosato), Bertini, Riva, Domenghini (1), Mazzola, Di Sisti, Boninsegna
Sweden: Hellstrom, Axelsson, Nordqvist, Grip, Svensson, Bo Larsson (Nicklasson), Eriksson (Ejderstedt), Kindvall, Grahn, Cronqvist, Olsson
Referee: Taylor (England)

6.6.70 Uruguay (0) 0, Italy (0) 0 PUEBLA
Uruguay: Mazurkiewicz, Ancheta, Matosas, Ubinas, Montero Castillo, Mujica, Cubilla, Esparrago, Maneiro, Bareno (Zubia), Cortes
Italy: Albertosi, Burgnich, Facchetti, Cera, Rosato, Bertini, Riva, Domenghini (Furino), Mazzola, De Sisti, Boninsenga
Referee: Glockner (East Germany)

7.6.70 Sweden (0) 1, Israel (0) 1 TOLUCA
Sweden: Larsson S G, Selander, Axelsson, Olsson, Grip, Svensson, Bo Larsson, Nordahl, Kindvall, Persson (Palsson), Turesson (1)
Israel: Vissoker, Bar, Schwager, Rosen, Rosenthal, Primo, Spiegel, Vollach (Schuruk), Spiegler (1), Faygenbaum, Shum
Referee: Tarekegn (Ethiopia)

10.6.70 Sweden (0) 1, Uruguay (0) 0 PUEBLA
Sweden: Larsson S G, Selander, Axelsson, Nordqvist, Grip, Svensson, Bo Larsson, Eriksson, Kindvall (Turesson), Persson, Nicklasson (Grahn (1))
Uruguay: Mazurkiewicz, Ancheta, Matosas, Ubinas, Montero Castillo, Mujica, Esparrago (Fontes), Maneiro, Zubia, Cortes, Losada
Referee: Landauer (USA)

11.6.70 Italy (0) 0, Israel (0) 0 TOLUCA
Italy: Albertosi, Burgnich, Facchetti, Cera, Rosato, Bertini, Riva, Domenghini (Rivera), Mazzola, De Sisti, Boninsegna
Israel: Vissoker, Bar, Bello, Primo, Rosen, Rosenthal, Shum, Spiegel, Faygenbaum (Rom), Spiegler, Schwager
Referee: De Moraes (Brazil)

	P	W	D	L	F	A	Pts
Italy	3	1	2	0	1	0	4
Uruguay	3	1	1	1	2	1	3
Sweden	3	1	1	1	2	2	3
Israel	3	0	2	1	1	3	2

GROUP 3

2.6.70 England (0) 1, Rumania (0) 0 GUADALAJARA
England: Banks, Newton (Wright), Cooper, Mullery, Labone, Moore, Lee (Osgood), Ball, Hurst (1), Charlton R, Peters
Rumania: Adamache, Satmareanu, Lupescu, Dinu, Mocanu, Dumitru, Tataru (Neagu), Nunweiler, Dembrovschi, Dumitrache, Lucescu
Referee: Loraux (Belgium)

3.6.70 Brazil (1) 4, Czechoslovakia (1) 1 GUADALAJARA
Brazil: Felix, Carlos Alberto, Brito, Piazza, Everaldo, Clodoaldo, Gerson (Paulo Cesar), Rivelino, Jairzinho (2), Tostao, Pele (1)
Czechoslovakia: Viktor, Dobias, Migas, Horvath, Hagara, Kuna, Hrdlicka (Kvasnak), Vesely F (Vesely B), Petras (1), Adamec, Jokl
Referee: Barreto (Uruguay)

6.6.70 Rumania (0) 2, Czechoslovakia (1) 1 GUADALAJARA
Rumania: Adamache, Satmareanu, Dinu, Lupescu, Mocanu, Dumitru (Ghergeli), Nunweiler, Dembrovschi, Neagu (1), Dumitrache (1 pen), Lucescu (Tataru)
Czechoslovakia: Vencel, Dobias, Migas, Horvath, Zlocha, Kuna, Kvasnak, Vesely B, Jurkanin (Adamec), Petras (1), Jokl (Vesely F)
Referee: De Leo (Mexico)

7.6.70 Brazil (1) 1, England (0) 0 GUADALAJARA
Brazil: Felix, Carlos Alberto, Brito, Piazza, Everaldo, Clodoaldo, Paulo Cesar, Rivelino, Jairzinho (1), Tostao (Roberto), Pele
England: Banks, Wright, Cooper, Mullery, Labone, Moore, Lee (Bell), Ball, Charlton R (Astle), Hurst, Peters
Referee: Klein (Israel)

10.6.70 Brazil (2) 3, Rumania (1) 2 GUADALAJARA
Brazil: Felix, Carlos Alberto, Brito, Fontana, Everaldo (Marco Antonio), Clodoaldo (Edu), Piazza, Paulo Cesar, Jairzinho (1), Tostao, Pele (2)
Rumania: Adamache (Raducanu), Satmareanu, Lupescu, Dinu, Mocanu, Dumitru, Nunweiler, Dembrovschi (1), Lucescu, Neagu, Dumitrache (1) (Tataru)
Referee: Marshall (Austria)

11.6.70 England (0) 1, Czechoslovakia (0) 0 GUADALAJARA
England: Banks, Newton, Cooper, Mullery, Charlton J, Moore, Bell, Clarke (1 pen), Astle (Osgood), Charlton R (Ball), Peters
Czechoslovakia: Viktor, Dobias, Hrivnak, Migas, Hagara, Pollak, Kuna, Vesely F, Petras, Adamec, Capkovic (Jokl)
Referee: Machin (France)

	P	W	D	L	F	A	Pts
Brazil	3	3	0	0	8	3	6
England	3	2	0	1	2	1	4
Rumania	3	1	0	2	4	5	2
Czechoslovakia	3	0	0	3	2	7	0

GROUP 4

2.6.70 Peru (0) 3, Bulgaria (1) 2 LEON
Peru: Rubinos, Campos (Gonzalez J), De la Torre, Chumpitaz (1), Fuentes, Mifflin, Challe, Baylon (Sotil), Leon, Cubillas (1), Gallardo (1)
Bulgaria: Simeonov, Chalamanov, Dimitrov, Davidov, Aladjov, Penev, Bonev (1) (Asparoukhov), Yakimov, Popov (Marachliev), Jekov, Dermendjiev (1)
Referee: Sbardella (Italy)

3.6.70 West Germany (0) 2, Morocco (1) 1 LEON
West Germany: Maier, Vogts, Schulz, Fichtel, Hottges (Lohr), Haller (Grabowski), Beckenbauer, Overath, Seeler (1), Muller (1), Held
Morocco: Allal, Abdallah, Boujemaa, Khannoussi, Slimani, Maaroufi, Bamous (Faras), El Filali, Said, Ghazouani (Khyati), Houmane (1)
Referee: Van Ravens (Netherlands)

6.6.70 Peru (0) 3, Morocco (0) 0 LEON
Peru: Rubinos, Gonzales P, De la Torre, Chumpitaz, Fuentes, Mifflin, Challe (1), Sotil, Leon, Cubillas (2), Gallardo (Ramirez)
Morocco: Allal, Abdallah, Boujemaa (Fadili), Khannoussi, Slimani, Maaroufi, Bamous, El Filali, Said (Alaoui), Ghazouani, Houmane
Referee: Bakhramov (USSR)

7.6.70 West Germany (2) 5, Bulgaria (1) 2 LEON
West Germany: Maier, Vogts, Fichtel, Schnellinger, Hottges, Seeler (1), Beckenbauer (Weber), Overath, Libuda (1), Muller (3, 1 pen) Lohr (Grabowski)
Bulgaria: Simeonov, Gaidarski, Jetchev, Nikodimov (1), Gaganelov (Chalamanov), Penev, Bonev, Kolev (1), Marachliev, Asparoukhov, Dermendiev (Mitkov)
Referee: De Mendibil (Spain)

10.6.70 West Germany (3) 3, Peru (1) 1 LEON
West Germany: Maier, Vogts, Fichtel, Schnellinger, Hottges (Patzke), Seeler, Beckenbauer, Overath, Libuda (Grabowski), Muller (3), Lohr
Peru: Rubinos, Gonzales P, De la Torre, Chumpitaz, Fuentes, Mifflin, Challe (Cruzado), Sotil, Leon (Ramirez), Cubillas (1), Gallardo
Referee: Aguilar (Mexico)

11.6.70 Bulgaria (1) 1, Morocco (0) 1 LEON
Bulgaria: Yordanov, Chalamanov, Penev (Dimitrov), Jetchev (1), Gaidarski, Kolev, Nikodimov, Yakimov (Bonev), Popov, Asparoukhov, Mitkov
Morocco: Hazzaz, Fadili, Slimani, Khannoussi, Boujemaa, Maaroufi, Bamous (Choukri), El Filali, Said, Alaoui (Faras), Ghazouani (1)
Referee: Saldanha (Portugal)

	P	W	D	L	F	A	Pts
West Germany	3	3	0	0	10	4	6
Peru	3	2	0	1	7	5	4
Bulgaria	3	0	1	2	5	9	1
Morocco	3	0	1	2	2	6	1

QUARTER FINALS

14.6.70 Uruguay (0) 1, USSR (0) 0 (aet, 0 - 0 at 90 mins) MEXICO CITY
Uruguay: Mazurkiewicz, Ancheta, Matosas, Ubinas, Montero Castillo, Mujica, Cubilla, Maneiro, Morales (Gomez), Fontes (Esparrago (1)), Cortes
USSR: Kavazashvili, Dzodzuashvili, Afonin, Shesternev, Khurtsilava (Logofet), Kaplichny, Asatiani (Kiselev), Muntian, Byshovets, Evryushikhin, Khmelnitzki
Referee: Van Ravens (Netherlands)

14.6.70 Italy (1) 4, Mexico (1) 1 TOLUCA
Italy: Albertosi, Burgnich, Cera, Rosato, Bertini, Riva (2), Domenghini (Gori), Mazzola (Rivera (1)), De Sisti, Boninsegna
Mexico: Calderon, Vantolra, Guzman, Pena, Perez, Pulido, Gonzalez (1) (Borja), Munguia (Diaz), Padilla, Valdivia, Fragoso
Referee: Scheurer (Switzerland)

14.6.70 Brazil (2) 4, Peru (1) 2 GUADALAJARA
Brazil: Felix, Carlos Alberto, Brito, Piazza, Marco Antonio, Clodoaldo, Gerson (Paulo Cesar), Rivelino (1), Jairzinho (1) (Roberto), Tostao (2), Pele
Peru: Rubinos, Campos, Fernandez, Chumpitaz, Fuentes, Challe, Mifflin, Baylon (Sotil), Leon (Reyes), Cubillas (1), Gallardo (1)
Referee: Loraux (Belgium)

14.6.70 West Germany (0) 3, England (2) 2 (aet, 2 - 2 at 90 mins) LEON
West Germany: Maier, Vogts, Fichtel, Schnellinger, Hottges (Schulz), Seeler (1), Beckenbauer (1), Overath, Libuda (Grabowski), Muller (1), Lohr
England: Bonetti, Newton, Cooper, Mullery (1), Labone, Moore, Lee, Ball, Hurst, Charlton R (Bell), Peters (1) (Hunter)
Referee: Coerezza (Argentina)

SEMI FINALS

17.6.70 Italy (1) 4, West Germany (0) 3 (aet, 1 - 1 at 90 mins) MEXICO CITY
Italy: Albertosi, Burgnich (1), Facchetti, Cera, Rosato (Poletti), Bertini, Riva (1), Domenghini, Mazzora (Rivera (1)), De Sisti, Boninsegna (1)
West Germany: Maier, Vogts, Schnellinger (1), Schulz, Patzke (Held), Beckenbauer, Overath, Grabowski, Seeler, Muller (2), Lohr (Libuda)
Referee: Yamasaki (Peru)

17.6.70 Brazil (1) 3, Uruguay (1) 1 GUADALAJARA
Brazil: Felix, Carlos Alberto, Brito, Piazza, Everaldo, Clodoaldo (1), Gerson, Rivelino (1), Jairzinho (1), Tostao, Pele
Uruguay: Mazurkiewicz, Ubinas, Ancheta, Matosas, Mujica, Montero Castillo, Maneiro (Esparrago), Cortes, Cubilla (1), Fontes, Morales
Referee: De Mendibil (Spain)

Match for third place

20.6.70 West Germany (1) 1, Uruguay (0) 0 MEXICO CITY
West Germany: Wolter, Patzke, Weber, Schnellinger (Lorenz), Fichtel, Vogts, Overath (1), Libuda (Lohr), Seeler, Muller, Held
Uruguay: Mazurkiewicz, Ubinas, Ancheta, Matosas, Mujica, Montero Castillo, Maneiro (Sandoval), Cortes, Cubilla, Fontes (Esparrago), Morales
Referee: Sbardella (Italy)

FINAL

21.6.70 Brazil (1) 4, Italy (1) 1 MEXICO CITY
Brazil: Felix, Carlos Alberto (1), Brito, Piazza, Everaldo, Clodoaldo, Gerson (1), Rivelino, Jairzinho (1), Tostao, Pele (1)
Italy: Albertosi, Burgnich, Facchetti, Cera, Rosato, Bertini (Juliano), Riva, Domenghini, Mazzola, De Sisti, Boninsegna (1) (Rivera)
Referee: Glockner (East Germany)

WEST GERMANY

1974

FIFA's technical study of the tournament in West Germany revealed that the two teams which consistently produced the highest ratio of penetrating attacks were the finalists, West Germany and Holland. But attacks are one factor, scoring goals another. Of the three goals registered in the final, two came from the penalty spot and the Dutch concept of 'total football' was let down by poor finishing.

Even in the single goal defeat by East Germany, the West Germans had 23 attempts at scoring, 15 of them from inside the penalty area. Holland's highlight, in what proved to be a goalless draw, was when they mounted 61 penetrating attacks against Sweden and had 36 shots, again 15 of them from inside the area.

Goalscoring actually reached a new low. This was never better illustrated than when a lack of goals cost unbeaten Scotland a place in the second round and saw Italy eliminated on goal difference. In Group 1, six games produced nine goals, five of them conceded by Australia. Group 2 did have 16, but all but two were at the expense of Zaire! Holland did not concede a goal to an opponent until the final apart from an own goal, while Haiti also let in 14 in three games.

Instead of a quarter-final knock-out round, the eight qualifiers from the four groups were split into two further sections of four, causing some jockeying for positions. For example the last game in Group 1, which pitted the two halves of Germany against each other, saw the West Germans unconcerned over the outcome and preferring to avoid Holland in the second stage. Jurgen Sparwasser's 77th-minute goal settled it for the East.

Sweden and West Germany provided a thriller in the rain when they met in the second round. Swedish keeper Ronnie Hellstrom keeps out a shot from Gerd Muller (dark shirt). (ALLSPORT)

Billy Bremner (4, dark shirt) holds his head after missing from close range against Brazil, to the despair of team-mate David Hay and the relief of Brazil's Rivelino (10). (ALLSPORT)

(Far right) Holland faced their toughest opposition on the way to the final in Group 3, when Sweden held them 0-0 in Dortmund. Dutch goalkeeper Jongbloed (8) dives to thwart an attempt on goal. (ALLSPORT)

Certainly the system did not encourage goalscoring but Yugoslavia succeeded in scoring nine against Zaire, who had a player sent off, one of five dismissed in the finals, though there were 84 cautioned.

For practically the entire tournament it rained. In this there was a good omen for West Germany, who had prevailed in similar circumstances 20 years earlier. But they had their problems off the field, with scarcely secret differences between manager Helmut Schoen and captain Franz Beckenbauer over team selection. Schoen persisted with wingers and discovered a fine powerhouse in Rainer Bonhof during the competition.

Brazil were rugged without a vestige of the flair of former days. Even so they finished fourth. Jairzinho led the attack virtually on his own. Zagalo could have had Pele had he asked him to play, but seemed not to relish the prospect of the 'Black Pearl' gaining the accolade of a Brazilian victory.

Poland, who had deprived England of a place in the finals, had their strongest squad of all time. Their last match for a place in the final was against West Germany in Frankfurt. The kick-off was delayed half an hour while groundsmen attempted to remove gallons of rainwater from the pitch. Polish goalkeeper Jan Tomaszewski saved a penalty from Uli Hoeness, his second such stop in the finals, but it was Gerd Muller who scooped up the only goal in the second half. Grzegorz Lato, top scorer in the tournament with seven goals, had missed two first-half chances in a game which rose above the conditions.

Chile, who had qualified when the USSR refused to play a return game in Santiago for political reasons, were held to a goalless draw in a Group 1 game by Australia. The Aussies had a player shown two yellow cards but he was allowed to continue, until a linesman drew the referee's attention to the situation and he was sent off.

(Left) Joe Jordan (9, white shirt) celebrates a late equaliser for Scotland against Yugoslavia in Frankfurt, but it was not enough to prevent the Scots' elimination from the tournament. (ALLSPORT)

Torrential rain in Frankfurt (below) almost caused West Germany's game with Poland to be postponed. Uli Hoeness (white shirt) loses out to the grounded Jerzy Gorgon of Poland. (PRESSENS BILD)

When Yugoslavia were awarded a free-kick against Zaire, one of the Zaire defenders rushed out of the defensive wall and booted the ball into touch! He received a swift red card for his indiscretion. Scotland held Brazil without undue difficulty, in another of the five scoreless matches in the opening phase, and then managed a 1-1 draw with Yugoslavia. This left the Brazilians with the task of scoring at least three times against Zaire. They only just managed it, thanks to the African goalkeeper being beaten on his near post by an angled drive from substitute Valdomiro.

But in the second stage, the Brazilians were well beaten by Holland, whose goals from Johan Neeskens and Johan Cruyff, who had covered more ground than almost any player in the tournament, emphasised their mobility and strength. It was enough to put the Dutch into the final against the hosts West Germany.

There had never been a penalty awarded in a previous final. Inside half an hour there were two. Holland kicked off and were awarded the first within a minute of play, without a German touching the ball. Cruyff was brought down inside the area and Neeskens hit the spot kick straight at goal while goalkeeper Sepp Maier was diving to his right.

Jack Taylor the English referee had shown immense courage in this award, but there were critics of his next decision when Wim Jansen was adjudged to have clipped the legs of Bernd Holzenbein in the 26th minute. But up stepped Paul Breitner to level the scores. Two minutes from the break, Bonhof raided on the right and pulled the ball back. It fell slightly behind Muller, who checked, turned and scored.

It was a crushing blow for the Dutch who had dominated much of the play. In fact Cruyff was so incensed that he argued with Taylor as the players went off for half-time. Holland huffed and puffed in the second half but the Germans held firm to win the cup, the new FIFA World Cup.

Qualifying Tournament

99 entries

Europe (33): Albania, Austria, Belgium, Bulgaria, Cyprus, Czechoslovakia, Denmark, England, Finland, France, East Germany, West Germany, Greece, Holland, Hungary, Iceland, Republic of Ireland, Northern Ireland, Italy, Luxembourg, Malta, Norway, Poland, Portugal, Rumania, Scotland, Spain, Sweden, Switzerland, Turkey, USSR, Wales, Yugoslavia

Africa (23): Algeria, Cameroon, Congo, Dahomey, Egypt, Ethiopia, Gabon, Ghana, Guinea, Ivory Coast, Kenya, Lesotho, Madagascar, Mauritius, Morocco, Nigeria, Senegal, Sierra Leone, Sudan, Tanzania, Tunisia, Zaire, Zambia

Concacaf (14): Antigua, Canada, Costa Rica, Guatemala, Haiti, Honduras, Jamaica, Mexico, Netherlands Antilles, Puerto Rico, El Salvador, Surinam, Trinidad/Tobago, USA

South America (10): Argentina, Bolivia, Brazil, Chile, Colombia, Ecuador, Paraguay, Peru, Uruguay, Venezuela

Asia (17): Hong Kong, India, Indonesia, Iran, Iraq, Israel, Japan, North Korea, South Korea, Kuwait, Malaysia, Philippines, Sri Lanka, Syria, Thailand, United Arab Emirates, South Vietnam

Oceania (2): Australia, New Zealand

Seven countries withdrew before the qualifying tournament began: Gabon, India, Jamaica, Madagascar, Philippines, Sri Lanka, Venezuela.

The final qualifying tie between the winners of Europe Group 9 and South America Group 3 was not completed. The USSR and Chile had drawn 0 - 0 in Moscow but the Soviets refused to play the return in the National Stadium in Santiago because it had been used to house prisoners when the military overthrew the elected government. In the African Zone, Nigeria's home game with Ghana was abandoned following crowd disturbances with Ghana leading 3 - 2. Ghana were declared winners 2 - 0. Zaire had already qualified for the finals when Morocco refused to play their home game as a protest against the refereeing of the match in Zaire. In Europe's Group 3, Iceland played 'home' games in Belgium and Holland.

Final places in West Germany were to be distributed as follows: Europe (8 + West Germany)*, South America (3 + Brazil)*, Concacaf (1), Africa (1), Asia/Oceania (1).

*Play-off between USSR and Chile gave South America a further final place.

Europe

Group 1 (Austria, Sweden, Hungary, Malta)

Malta v Hungary 0 - 2; Austria v Malta 4 - 0; Hungary v Malta 3 - 0; Sweden v Hungary 0 - 0; Austria v Sweden 2 - 0; Sweden v Malta 7 - 0; Austria v Hungary 2 - 2; Malta v Austria 0 - 2; Hungary v Austria 2 - 2; Sweden v Austria 3 - 2; Hungary v Sweden 3 - 3; Malta v Sweden 1 - 2

	P	W	D	L	F	A	Pts
Sweden	6	3	2	1	15	8	8
Austria	6	3	2	1	14	7	8
Hungary	6	2	4	0	12	7	8
Malta	6	0	0	6	1	20	0

Play-off: Austria v Sweden (in Gelsenkirchen) 1 - 2

Sweden qualified

Group 2 (Italy, Turkey, Switzerland, Luxembourg)

Luxembourg v Italy 0 - 4; Switzerland v Italy 0 - 0; Luxembourg v Turkey 2 - 0; Turkey v Luxembourg 3 - 0; Italy v Turkey 0 - 0; Turkey v Italy 0 - 1; Italy v Luxembourg 5 - 0; Luxembourg v Switzerland 0 - 1; Switzerland v Turkey 0 - 0; Switzerland v Luxembourg 1 - 0; Italy v Switzerland 2 - 0; Turkey v Switzerland 2 - 0

	P	W	D	L	F	A	Pts
Italy	6	4	2	0	12	0	10
Turkey	6	2	2	2	5	3	6
Switzerland	6	2	2	2	2	4	6
Luxembourg	6	1	0	5	2	14	2

Italy qualified

Group 3 (Holland, Belgium, Norway, Iceland)

Belgium v Iceland 4 - 0; Iceland v Belgium 0 - 4; Norway v Iceland 4 - 1; Norway v Belgium 0 - 2; Holland v Norway 9 - 0; Belgium v Holland 0 - 0; Iceland v Norway 0 - 4; Iceland v Holland 0 - 5; Holland v Iceland 8 - 1; Norway v Holland 1 - 2; Belgium v Norway 2 - 0; Holland v Belgium 0 - 0

	P	W	D	L	F	A	Pts
Holland	6	4	2	0	24	2	10
Belgium	6	4	2	0	12	0	10
Norway	6	2	0	4	9	16	4
Iceland	6	0	0	6	2	29	0

Holland qualified

Group 4 (East Germany, Rumania, Finland, Albania)

Finland v Albania 1 - 0; Finland v Rumania 1 - 1; East Germany v Finland 5 - 0; Rumania v Albania 2 - 0; East Germany v Albania 2 - 0; Albania v Rumania 1 - 4; Rumania v East Germany 1 - 0; Finland v East Germany 1 - 5; East Germany v Rumania 2 - 0; Albania v Finland 1 - 0; Rumania v Finland 9 - 0; Albania v East Germany 1 - 4

	P	W	D	L	F	A	Pts
East Germany	6	5	0	1	18	3	10
Rumania	6	4	1	1	17	4	9
Finland	6	1	1	4	3	21	3
Albania	6	1	0	5	3	13	2

East Germany qualified

Group 5 (Poland, England, Wales)
Wales v England 0 - 1; England v Wales 1 - 1; Wales v Poland 2 - 0; Poland v England 2 - 0; Poland v Wales 3 - 0; England v Poland 1 - 1

	P	W	D	L	F	A	Pts
Poland	4	2	1	1	6	3	5
England	4	1	2	1	3	4	4
Wales	4	1	1	2	3	5	3

Poland qualified

Group 6 (Bulgaria, Portugal, Northern Ireland, Cyprus)
Portugal v Cyprus 4 - 0; Cyprus v Portugal 0 - 1; Bulgaria v Northern Ireland 3 - 0; Cyprus v Bulgaria 0 - 4; Cyprus v Northern Ireland 1 - 0; Northern Ireland v Portugal 1 - 1; Bulgaria v Portugal 2 - 1; Northern Ireland v Cyprus 3 - 0 (at Fulham); Northern Ireland v Bulgaria 0 - 0; Portugal v Bulgaria 2 - 2; Portugal v Northern Ireland 1 - 1; Bulgaria v Cyprus 2 - 0

	P	W	D	L	F	A	Pts
Bulgaria	6	4	2	0	13	3	10
Portugal	6	2	3	1	10	6	7
Northern Ireland	6	1	3	2	5	6	5
Cyprus	6	1	0	5	1	14	2

Bulgaria qualified

Group 7 (Spain, Yugoslavia, Greece)
Spain v Yugoslavia 2 - 2; Yugoslavia v Greece 1 - 0; Greece v Spain 2 - 3; Spain v Greece 3 - 1; Yugoslavia v Spain 0 - 0; Greece v Yugoslavia 2 - 4

	P	W	D	L	F	A	Pts
Spain	4	2	2	0	8	5	6
Yugoslavia	4	2	2	0	7	4	6
Greece	4	0	0	4	5	11	0

Play-off: Spain v Yugoslavia (in Frankfurt) 0 - 1
Yugoslavia qualified

Group 8 (Scotland, Czechoslovakia, Denmark)
Denmark v Scotland 1 - 4; Scotland v Denmark 2 - 0; Denmark v Czechoslovakia 1 - 1; Czechoslovakia v Denmark 6 - 0; Scotland v Czechoslovakia 2 - 1; Czechoslovakia v Scotland 1 - 0

	P	W	D	L	F	A	Pts
Scotland	4	3	0	1	8	3	6
Czechoslovakia	4	2	1	1	9	3	5
Denmark	4	0	1	3	2	13	1

Scotland qualified

Group 9 (USSR, Rep of Ireland, France)
France v USSR 1 - 0; Rep of Ireland v USSR 1 - 2; Rep of Ireland v France 2 - 1; USSR v Rep of Ireland 1 - 0; France v Rep of Ireland 1 - 1; USSR v France 2 - 0

	P	W	D	L	F	A	Pts
USSR	4	3	0	1	5	2	6
Rep of Ireland	4	1	1	2	4	5	3
France	4	1	1	2	3	5	3

Play-off with South American Group 3 winners
USSR v Chile 0 - 0
USSR disqualified by FIFA for refusing to play return leg in Santiago.
Chile qualified

South America
Group 1 (Uruguay, Colombia, Ecuador)
Colombia v Ecuador 1 - 1; Colombia v Uruguay 0 - 0; Ecuador v Colombia 1 - 1; Ecuador v Uruguay 1 - 2; Uruguay v Colombia 0 - 1; Uruguay v Ecuador 4 - 0

	P	W	D	L	F	A	Pts
Uruguay	4	2	1	1	6	2	5
Colombia	4	1	3	0	3	2	5
Ecuador	4	0	2	2	3	8	2

Uruguay qualified

Group 2 (Argentina, Paraguay, Bolivia)
Bolivia v Paraguay 1 - 2; Argentina v Bolivia 4 - 0; Paraguay v Argentina 1 - 1; Bolivia v Argentina 0 - 1; Paraguay v Bolivia 4 - 0; Argentina v Paraguay 3 - 1

	P	W	D	L	F	A	Pts
Argentina	4	3	1	0	9	2	7
Paraguay	4	2	1	1	8	5	5
Bolivia	4	0	0	4	1	11	0

Argentina qualified

Group 3 (Chile, Peru, Venezuela)
Venezuela withdrew
Peru v Chile 2 - 0; Chile v Peru 2 - 0
Play-off (in Montevideo): Chile v Peru 2 - 1

Concacaf
Preliminary Round
Group 1
Canada v USA 3 - 2; Canada v Mexico 0 - 1; USA v Canada 2 - 2; Mexico v USA 3 - 1; Mexico v Canada 2 - 1; USA v Mexico 1 - 2

	P	W	D	L	F	A	Pts
Mexico	4	4	0	0	8	3	8
Canada	4	1	1	2	6	7	3
USA	4	0	1	3	6	10	1

Group 2
Guatemala v El Salvador 1 - 0, 1 - 0

Group 3
Honduras v Costa Rica 2 - 1, 3 - 3

Group 4
Netherlands Antilles v Jamaica (withdrew)

Group 5
Haiti v Puerto Rico 7 - 0, 5 - 0

Group 6
Surinam v Trinidad 1 - 2; Trinidad v Surinam 1 - 1; Surinam v Antigua 3 - 1 Antigua v Surinam 0 - 6; Trinidad v Antigua 11 - 1; Antigua v Trinidad 1 - 2

	P	W	D	L	F	A	Pts
T'dad/Tobago	4	3	1	0	16	4	7
Surinam	4	2	1	1	11	4	5
Antigua	4	0	0	4	3	22	0

Final Round (in Haiti)
Honduras v Trinidad 2 - 1; Mexico v Guatemala 0 - 0; Haiti v Netherlands Antilles 3 - 0; Mexico v Honduras 1 - 1; Haiti v Trinidad 2 - 1; Guatemala v Netherlands Antilles 2 - 2; Haiti v Honduras 1 - 0; Mexico v Netherlands Antilles 8 - 0; Trinidad v Guatemala 1 - 0; Netherlands Antilles v Honduras 2 - 2; Haiti v Guatemala 2 - 1; Trinidad v Mexico 4 - 0; Honduras v Guatemala 1 - 1; Trinidad v Netherlands Antilles 4 - 0; Mexico v Haiti 1 - 0

	P	W	D	L	F	A	Pts
Haiti	5	4	0	1	8	3	8
T'dad/Tobago	5	3	0	2	11	4	6
Mexico	5	2	2	1	10	5	6
Honduras	5	1	3	1	6	6	5
Guatemala	5	0	3	2	4	6	3
N'lands/Antilles	5	0	2	3	4	19	2

Haiti qualified

Africa
1st Round
Morocco v Senegal 0 - 0, 2 - 1; Algeria v Guinea 1 - 0, 1 - 5; Egypt v Tunisia 2 - 1, 0 - 2; Sierra Leone v Ivory Coast 0 - 1, 0 - 2; Kenya v Sudan 2 - 0, 0 - 1; Mauritius v Madagascar (withdrew); Ethiopia v Tanzania 0 - 0, 1 - 1; Play-off: Ethiopia v Tanzania 3 - 0; Lesotho v Zambia 0 - 0, 1 - 6; Nigeria v Congo 2 - 1, 1 - 1; Dahomey v Ghana 0 - 5, 1 - 5; Togo v Zaire 0 - 0, 0 - 4; Cameroon v Gabon (withdrew)

2nd Round
Kenya v Mauritius 3 - 1, 2 - 2; Guinea v Morocco 1 - 1, 0 - 2; Tunisia v Ivory Coast 1 - 1, 1 - 1; Ethiopia v Zambia 0 - 0, 2 - 4: Nigeria v Ghana 2 - 3 (abandoned), 0 - 0 (Nigeria disqualified from competition by FIFA Disciplinary Committee); Cameroon v Zaire 0 - 1, 1 - 0; Play-off: Zaire v Cameroon 2 - 0

3rd Round
Ivory Coast v Morocco 1 - 1, 1 - 4; Zambia v Kenya 2 - 0, 2 - 2; Ghana v Zaire 1 - 0, 1 - 4

Final Round
Zambia v Morocco 4 - 0; Zambia v Zaire 0 - 2; Zaire v Zambia 2 - 1;
Morocco v Zambia 2 - 0; Zaire v Morocco 3 - 0;
Morocco (withdrew) v Zaire (awarded game 2 - 0)

	P	W	D	L	F	A	Pts
Zaire	4	4	0	0	9	1	8
Zambia	4	1	0	3	5	6	2
Morocco	4	1	0	3	2	9	2

Zaire qualified

Asia/ Oceana
Preliminary Round (to determine Group composition)
South Vietnam v Thailand 1 - 0; Israel v Japan 2 - 1; Hong Kong v Malaysia
1 - 0; South Korea bye

Group A (in Seoul)
Sub-Group 1
Hong Kong v South Vietnam 1 - 0; Hong Kong v Japan 1 - 0;
Japan v South Vietnam 4 - 0

	P	W	D	L	F	A	Pts
Hong Kong	2	2	0	0	2	0	4
Japan	2	1	0	1	4	1	2
South Vietnam	2	0	0	2	0	5	0

Sub-Group 2
Israel v Malaysia 3 - 0; Israel v Thailand 6 - 0; Israel v South Korea 0 - 0;
South Korea v Thailand 4 - 0; South Korea v Malaysia 0 - 0;
Malaysia v Thailand 2 - 0

	P	W	D	L	F	A	Pts
Israel	3	2	1	0	9	0	5
South Korea	3	1	2	0	4	0	4
Malaysia	3	1	1	1	2	3	3
Thailand	3	0	0	3	0	12	0

Semi-finals
South Korea v Hong Kong 3 - 1; Israel v Japan 1 - 0

Final
South Korea v Israel 1 - 0

Group B
Sub-Group 1 (in Australia)
New Zealand v Australia 1 - 1; Indonesia v New Zealand 1 - 1; Australia
v Iraq 3 - 1; Iraq v New Zealand 2 - 0; Australia v Indonesia 2 - 1; Iraq
v Indonesia 1 - 1: Australia v New Zealand 3 - 3; Indonesia v New Zealand
1 - 0; Australia v Iraq 0 - 0; Iraq v Indonesia 3 - 2; Iraq v New Zealand
4 - 0; Australia v Indonesia 6 - 0

	P	W	D	L	F	A	Pts
Australia	6	3	3	0	15	6	9
Iraq	6	3	2	1	11	6	8
Indonesia	6	1	2	3	6	13	4
New Zealand	6	0	3	3	5	12	3

Sub-Group 2 (in Tehran)
North Korea v Iran 0 - 0; Syria v Kuwait 2 - 1; Iran v Kuwait 2 - 1; North
Korea v Syria 1 - 1; Iran v Syria 1 - 0; Kuwait v North Korea 0 - 0; North
Korea v Iran 1 - 2; Syria v Kuwait 2 - 0; Iran v Kuwait 2 - 0; North Korea v
Syria 3 - 0; Syria v Iran 1 - 0; Kuwait v North Korea 2 - 0

	P	W	D	L	F	A	Pts
Iran	6	4	1	1	7	3	9
Syria	6	3	1	2	6	7	7
North Korea	6	1	3	2	5	5	5
Kuwait	6	1	1	4	4	8	3

Final Round
Australia v Iran 3 - 0, 0 - 2; Australia v South Korea 0 - 0, 2 - 2
Play-off (in Hong Kong): Australia v South Korea 1 - 0
Australia qualified

Final Tournament WEST GERMANY
First round
GROUP 1
14.6.74 West Germany (1) 1, Chile (0) 0 WEST BERLIN
West Germany: Maier, Vogts, Schwarzenbeck, Beckenbauer, Breitner (1),
Hoeness, Cullmann, Overath (Holzenbein), Grabowski, Muller, Heynckes
Chile: Vallejos, Garcia, Figueroa, Quintano, Arias, Valdes (Veliz), Rodriguez
(Lara), Reinoso, Caszely, Ahumada, Paez
Referee: Babacan (Turkey)

14.6.74 East Germany (0) 2, Australia (0) 0 HAMBURG
East Germany: Croy, Kische, Bransch, Weise, Watzlich, Sparwasser,
Irmscher, Pommerenke, Lowe (Hoffmann), Streich (1), Vogel
Australia: Reilly, Utjesenovic, Schafer, Wilson, Curran (o. g.), Richards,
Mackay, Rooney, Warren, Alston, Buljevic
Referee: N'Diaye (Senegal)

18.6.74 West Germany (2) 3, Australia (0) 0 HAMBURG
West Germany: Maier, Vogts, Schwarzenbeck, Beckenbauer, Breitner,
Hoeness, Cullmann (1) (Wimmer), Overath (1), Grabowski, Muller (1),
Heynckes (Holzenbein)
Australia: Reilly, Utjesenovic, Schafer, Wilson, Curran, Richards, Rooney,
Mackay, Campbell (Abonyi), Alston, Buljevic (Ollerton)
Referee: Kamel (Egypt)

18.6.74 Chile (0) 1, East Germany (0) 1 WEST BERLIN
Chile: Vallejos, Garcia, Figueroa, Quintano, Arias, Valdes (Yavar), Reinoso,
Paez, Socias (Farias), Ahumada (1), Veliz
East Germany: Croy, Kische, Bransch, Weise, Watzlich, Seguin (Kreische),
Irmscher, Sparwasser, Hoffmann (1), Streich, Vogel (Ducke)
Referee: Angonese (Italy)

22.6.74 Australia (0) 0, Chile (0) 0 WEST BERLIN
Australia: Reilly, Utjesenovic, Wilson, Schafer, Curran (Williams), Richards,
Rooney, Mackay, Abonyi, Alston (Ollerton), Buljevic
Chile: Vallejos, Garcia, Quintano, Figueroa, Arias, Paez, Caszely, Reinoso,
Valdes (Farias), Ahumada, Veliz (Yavar)
Referee: Namdar (Iran)

22.6.74 East Germany (0) 1, West Germany (0) 0 HAMBURG
East Germany: Croy, Kische, Weise, Bransch, Watzlich, Lauck, Irmscher
(Hamann), Kreische, Kurbjuweit, Sparwasser (1), Hoffmann
West Germany: Maier, Vogts, Schwarzenbeck (Hottges), Beckenbauer,
Breitner, Hoeness, Cullmann, Overath (Netzer), Grabowski, Muller, Flohe
Referee: Barreto (Uruguay)

	P	W	D	L	F	A	Pts
East Germany	3	2	1	0	4	1	5
West Germany	3	2	0	1	4	1	4
Chile	3	0	2	1	1	2	2
Australia	3	0	1	2	0	5	1

GROUP 2
13.6.74 Yugoslavia (0) 0, Brazil (0) 0 FRANKFURT
Yugoslavia: Maric, Buljan, Katalinski, Bogicevic, Hadziabdic, Muzinic, Oblak,
Acimovic, Petkovic, Surjak, Dzajic
Brazil: Leao, Nelinho, Mario Marinho, Pereira, Francesco Marinho, Piazza,
Rivelino, Paulo Cesar L, Valdomiro, Jairzinho, Leivinha
Referee: Scheurer (Switzerland)

14.6.74 Scotland (2) 2, Zaire (0) 0 DORTMUND
Scotland: Harvey, Jardine, McGrain, Bremner, Holton, Blackley, Dalglish
(Hutchison), Hay, Lorimer (1), Jordan (1), Law
Zaire: Kazadi, Mwepu, Mukombo, Buhanga, Lobilo, Kilasu, Myanga
(Kembo), Mana, Ndaye, Kidumu (Kibonge), Kakoko
Referee: Schulenberg (West Germany)

18.6.74 Yugoslavia (6) 9, Zaire (0) 0 GELSENKIRCHEN
Yugoslavia: Maric, Buljan, Katalinski (1), Bogicevic (1), Hadziabdic,
Acimovic, Oblak (1), Surjak (1), Petkovic (1), Bajevic (3), Dzajic (1)
Zaire: Kazadi (Tubilandu), Mwepu, Mukombo, Buhanga, Lobilo, Kilasu,
Ndaye, Mana, Kembo, Kidumu, Kakoko (Myanga)
Referee: Delgado (Colombia)

18.6.74 Scotland (0) 0, Brazil (0) 0 FRANKFURT
Scotland: Harvey, Jardine, McGrain, Buchan, Holton, Bremner, Dalglish,
Hay, Jordan, Lorimer, Morgan
Brazil: Leao, Nelinho, Pereira, Mario Marinho, Francesco Marinho, Piazza,
Rivelino, Paulo Cesar L, Jairzinho, Mirandinha, Leivinha (Paulo Cesar C)
Referee: Van Gemert (Netherlands)

22.6.74 Brazil (1) 3, Zaire (0) 0 GELSENKIRCHEN
Brazil: Leao, Nelinho, Pereira, Mario Marinho, Francesco Marinho, Piazza (Mirandhina), Rivelino (1), Paulo Cesar C, Jairzinho (1), Leivinha (Valdomiro (1)), Edu
Zaire: Kazadi, Mwepu, Mukombo, Buhanga, Lobilo, Kobonge, Tshinabu (Kembo), Mana, Ntumba, Kidumu (Kilasu), Myanga
Referee: Rainea (Rumania)

22.6.74 Yugoslavia (0) 1, Scotland (0) 1 FRANKFURT
Yugoslavia: Maric, Buljan, Katalinski, Bogicevic, Hadziabdic, Acimovic, Oblak, Surjak, Petkovic, Bajevic (Karasi (1)), Dzajic
Scotland: Harvey, Jardine, McGrain, Buchan, Holton, Bremner, Dalglish (Hutchison), Hay, Jordan (1), Lorimer, Morgan
Referee: Archundia (Mexico)

	P	W	D	L	F	A	Pts
Yugoslavia	3	1	2	0	10	1	4
Brazil	3	1	2	0	3	0	4
Scotland	3	1	2	0	3	1	4
Zaire	3	0	0	3	0	14	0

GROUP 3
15.6.74 Holland (1) 2, Uruguay (0) 0 HANOVER
Holland: Jongbloed, Suurbier, Rijsbergen, Haan, Krol, Jansen, Neeskens, Van Hanegem, Rep (2), Cruyff, Rensenbrink
Uruguay: Mazurkiewicz, Forlan, Masnik, Juaregui, Pavoni, Esparrago, Montero Castillo, Rocha, Cubilla (Milar), Morena, Mantegazza
Referee: Palotai (Hungary)

15.6.74 Sweden (0) 0, Bulgaria (0) 0 DUSSELDORF
Sweden: Hellstrom, Olsson, Karlsson, Bo Larsson, Andersson, Grahn, Kindvall (Magnusson), Tapper, Torstensson, Sandberg, Edstrom
Bulgaria: Goranov, Vassilev Z, Ivkov, Penev, Velitschkov, Kolev, Bonev, Nikodimov, Voinov (Michailov), Panov (Vassilev M), Denev
Referee: Nunez (Peru)

19.6.74 Holland (0) 0, Sweden (0) 0 DORTMUND
Holland: Jongbloed, Suurbier, Rijsbergen, Haan, Krol, Jansen, Neeskens, Van Hanegem (De Jong), Rep, Cruyff, Keizer
Sweden: Hellstrom, Olsson (Grip), Andersson, Karlsson, Nordqvist, Tapper (Persson), Grahn, Bo Larsson, Ejderstdt, Edstrom, Sandberg
Referee: Winsemann (Canada)

19.6.74 Bulgaria (1) 1, Uruguay (0) 1 HANOVER
Bulgaria: Goranov, Vassilev Z, Ivkov, Penev, Velitschkov, Kolev, Bonev (1), Nikodimov (Michailov), Voinov, Panov, Denev
Uruguay: Mazurkiewicz, Forlan, Garisto (Masnik), Jauregui, Pavoni (1), Esparrago, Mantegazza (Cardaccio), Rocha, Milar, Morena, Corbo
Referee: Taylor (England)

23.6.74 Holland (2) 4, Bulgaria (0) 1 DORTMUND
Holland: Jongbloed, Suurbier, Rijsbergen, Haan, Krol (o. g.), Jansen, Neeskens (2) (De Jong (1)), Van Hanegem (Israel), Rep (1), Cruyff, Rensenbrink
Bulgaria: Staikov, Vassilev Z, Ivkov, Penev, Velitschkov, Kolev, Bonev, Stoyanov (Michailov), Voinov, Panov (Borisov), Denev
Referee: Boskovic (Australia)

23.6.74 Sweden (0) 3, Uruguay (0) 0 DUSSELDORF
Sweden: Hellstrom, Andersson, Nordqvist, Karlsson, Grip, Grahn, Kindvall (Torstensson), Bo Larsson, Magnusson (Ahlstrom), Edstrom (2), Sandberg (1)
Uruguay: Mazurkiewicz, Forlan, Garisto (Masnik), Jauregui, Pavoni, Esparrago, Mantegazza, Rocha, Milar, Morena, Corbo (Cubilla)
Referee: Linemayr (Australia)

	P	W	D	L	F	A	Pts
Holland	3	2	1	0	6	1	5
Sweden	3	1	2	0	3	0	4
Bulgaria	3	0	2	1	2	5	2
Uruguay	3	0	1	2	1	6	1

GROUP 4
15.6.74 Italy (0) 3, Haiti (0) 1 MUNICH
Italy: Zoff, Spinosi, Morini, Burgnich, Facchetti, Mazzola, Capello, Rivera (1), Benetti (1), Chinaglia (Anastasi (1)), Riva
Haiti: Francillon, Bayonne, Nazaire, Jean-Joseph, Auguste, Francois, Vorbe, Desir, Antoine, Saint-Vil G (Barthelmy), Sanon (1)
Referee: Llobregat (Venezuela)

15.6.74 Poland (2) 3, Argentina (0) 2 STUTTGART
Poland: Tomaszewski, Szymanowski, Zmuda, Gorgon, Musial, Kasperczyk, Maszczyk, Deyna, Lato (2), Szarmach (1) (Domarski), Gadocha (Cmikiewicz)
Argentina: Carnevali, Wolff, Perfumo, Heredia (1), Sa, Bargas (Telch), Brindisi (Houseman), Babington (1), Balbuena, Ayala, Kempes
Referee: Thomas (Wales)

19.6.74 Poland (5) 7, Haiti (0) 0 MUNICH
Poland: Tomaszewski, Szymanowski, Zmuda, Gorgon (1), Musial (Gut), Kasperczyk, Maszczyk (Cmikiewicz), Deyna (1), Lato (2), Szarmach (3), Gadocha
Haiti: Francillon, Bayonne, Nazaire, Vorbe, Auguste, Francois, Desir, Andre (Barthelmy), Sanon, Antoine, Saint-Vil R (Racine)
Referee: Suppiah (Singapore)

19.6.74 Argentina (1) 1, Italy (1) 1 STUTTGART
Argentina: Carnevali, Wolff (Glaria), Perfumo (o. g.), Heredia, Telch, Sa, Houseman (1), Babington, Ayala, Kempes, Yazalde (Chazarreta)
Italy: Zoff, Spinosi, Morini (Wilson), Burgnich, Facchetti, Mazzola, Capello, Rivera (Causio), Benetti, Riva, Anastasi
Referee: Kasakov (USSR)

23.6.74 Argentina (2) 4, Haiti (0) 1 MUNICH
Argentina: Carnevali, Wolff, Perfumo, Heredia, Sa, Telch, Houseman (1) (Brinidisi), Babington, Ayala (1), Kempes (Balbuena), Yazalde (2)
Haiti: Francillon, Ducoste, Bayonne, Nazaire (Leandre M), Louis, Vorbe, Desir, Saint-Vil G (Leandre F), Antoine, Racine, Sanon (1)
Referee: Sanchez-Ibanez (Spain)

23.6.74 Poland (2) 2, Italy (0) 1 STUTTGART
Poland: Tomaszewski, Szymanowski, Zmuda, Gorgon, Musial, Kasperczyk, Maszczyk, Deyna (1), Lato, Szarmach (1) (Cmikiewicz), Gadocha
Italy: Zoff, Spinosi, Morini, Burgnich (Wilson), Facchetti, Mazzola, Benetti, Capello (1), Causio, Chinaglia (Boninsegna), Anastasi
Referee: Weyland (West Germany)

	P	W	D	L	F	A	Pts
Poland	3	3	0	0	12	3	6
Argentina	3	1	1	1	7	5	3
Italy	3	1	1	1	5	4	3
Haiti	3	0	0	3	2	14	0

Second round
GROUP A
26.6.74 Brazil (0) 1, East Germany (0) 0 HANOVER
Brazil: Leao, Pereira, Ze Maria, Mario Marinho, Francesco Marinho, Rivelino (1), Paulo Cesar C, Paulo Cesar L, Valdomiro, Jairzinho, Dirceu
East Germany: Croy, Kische, Bransch, Weise, Watzlich, Lauck (Lowe), Hamann (Irmscher), Kurbjuweit, Streich, Sparwasser, Hoffmann
Referee: Thomas (Wales)

26.6.74 Holland (2) 4, Argentina (0) 0 GELSENKIRCHEN
Holland: Jongbloed, Suurbier (Israel), Rijsbergen, Haan, Krol (1), Jansen, Neeskens, Van Hanegem, Rep (1), Cruyff (2), Rensenbrink
Argentina: Carnevali, Wolff (Glaria), Perfumo, Heredia, Sa, Telch, Balbuena, Squeo, Yazalde, Ayala, Houseman (Kempes)
Referee: Davidson (Scotland)

30.6.74 Holland (1) 2, East Germany (0) 0 GELSENKIRCHEN
Holland: Jongbloed, Suurbier, Rijsbergen, Haan, Krol, Jansen, Neeskens (1), Van Hanegem, Rep, Cruyff, Rensenbrink (1)
East Germany: Croy, Kische, Weise, Bransch, Kurbjuweit, Lauck (Kreische), Schnuphase, Sparwasser, Pommerenke, Lowe (Ducke), Hoffmann
Referee: Scheurer (Switzerland)

30.6.74 Brazil (1) 2, Argentina (1) 1 HANOVER
Brazil: Leao, Pereira, Ze Maria, Mario Marinho, Francesco Marinho, Rivelino (1), Paulo Cesar C, Paulo Cesar L, Valdomiro, Jairzinho (1), Dirceu
Argentina: Carnevali, Glaria, Bargas, Heredia, Sa (Carrascosa), Brindisi (1), Squeo, Babington, Balbuena, Ayala, Kempes (Houseman)
Referee: Loraux (Belgium)

3.7.74 Holland (0) 2, Brazil (0) 0 DORTMUND
Holland: Jongbloed, Suurbier, Rijsbergen, Haan, Krol, Jansen, Neeskens (1) (Israel), Van Hanegem, Rep, Cruyff (1), Rensenbrink (De Jong)
Brazil: Leao, Pereira, Ze Maria, Mario Marinho, Francesco Marinho, Rivelino, Paulo Cesar C, Paulo Cesar L (Mirandhina), Valdomiro, Jairzinho, Dirceu
Referee: Tschenscher (West Germany)

3.7.84 East Germany (1) 1, Argentina (1) 1 GELSENKIRCHEN
East Germany: Croy, Kische, Weise, Bransch, Kurbjuweit, Sparwasser, Schnuphase, Pommerenke, Lowe (Vogel), Streich (1) (Ducke), Hoffmann
Argentina: Fillol, Wolff, Heredia, Bargas, Carrascosa, Telch, Brindisi, Babington, Houseman (1), Ayala, Kempes
Referee: Taylor (England)

	P	W	D	L	F	A	Pts
Holland	3	3	0	0	8	0	6
Brazil	3	2	0	1	3	3	4
East Germany	3	0	1	2	1	4	1
Argentina	3	0	1	2	2	7	1

GROUP B
26.6.74 West Germany (1) 2, Yugoslavia (0) 0 DUSSELDORF
West Germany: Maier, Vogts, Schwarzenbeck, Beckenbauer, Breitner (1), Wimmer (Hoeness), Overath, Bonhof, Holzenbein (Flohe), Muller (1), Herzog
Yugoslavia: Maric, Buljan, Katalinski, Muzinic, Hadziabdic, Oblak (Jerkovic), Acimovic, Surjak, Popivoda, Karasi, Dzajic (Petkovic)
Referee: Marques (Brazil)

26.6.74 Poland (1) 1, Sweden (0) 0 STUTTGART
Poland: Tomaszewski, Gut, Gorgon, Szymanowski, Zmuda, Kasperczyk, Deyna, Maszczyk, Lato (1), Szarmach (Kmiecik), Gadocha
Sweden: Hellstrom, Andersson (Augustsson), Grip, Karlsson, Nordqvist, Bo Larsson, Torstensson, Tapper (Ahlstrom), Edstrom, Grahn, Sandberg
Referee: Barreto (Uruguay)

30.6.74 West Germany (0) 4, Sweden (1) 2 DUSSELDORF
West Germany: Maier, Vogts, Schwarzenbeck, Beckenbauer, Breitner, Hoeness (1 pen), Bonhof (1), Overath (1), Holzenbein (Flohe), Muller, Herzog (Grabowski (1))
Sweden: Hellstrom, Olsson, Karlsson, Nordqvist, Augustsson, Tapper, Bo Larsson (Ejderstedt), Grahn, Torstensson, Edstrom (1), Sandberg (1)
Referee: Kasakov (USSR)

30.6.74 Poland (1) 2, Yugoslavia (1) 1 FRANKFURT
Poland: Tomaszewski, Szymanowski, Zmuda, Gorgon, Musial, Kasperczyk, Maszczyk, Deyna (1 pen) (Domarski), Lato (1), Szarmach (Cmikiewicz), Gadocha
Yugoslavia: Maric, Buljan, Katalinski, Bogicevic, Hadziabdic, Karasi (1), Oblak (Jerkovic), Acimovic, Petkovic (Petrovic), Bajevic, Surjak
Referee: Glockner (East Germany)

3.7.74 Sweden (1) 2, Yugoslavia (1) 1 DUSSELDORF
Sweden: Hellstrom, Olsson, Karlsson, Nordqvist, Augustsson, Tapper, Grahn, Persson, Torstensson (1), Edstrom (1), Sandberg
Yugoslavia: Maric, Buljan, Katalinski, Hadziabdic, Pavlovic (Peruzovic), Bogicevic, Acimovic, Jerkovic, Petrovic (Karasi), Surjak (1), Dzajic
Referee: Pestarino (Argentina)

3. 7. 74 West Germany (0) 1, Poland (0) 0 FRANKFURT
West Germany: Maier, Vogts, Schwarzenbeck, Beckenbauer, Breitner, Hoeness, Bonhof, Overath, Grabowski, Muller (1), Holzenbein
Poland: Tomaszewski, Szymanowski, Gorgon, Zmuda, Musial, Kasperczyk (Cmikiewicz), Deyna, Maszczyk (Kmiecik), Lato, Domarski, Gadocha
Referee: Linemayr (Austria)

	P	W	D	L	F	A	Pts
West Germany	3	3	0	0	7	2	6
Poland	3	2	0	1	3	2	4
Sweden	3	1	0	2	4	6	2
Yugoslavia	3	0	0	3	2	6	0

Match for third place
6.7.74 Poland (0) 1, Brazil (0) 0 MUNICH
Poland: Tomaszewski, Szymanowski, Zmuda, Gordon, Musial, Kasperczyk (Cmikiewicz), Maszczyk, Deyna, Lato (1), Szarmach (Kapka), Gadocha
Brazil: Leao, Ze Maria, Alfredo, Mario Marinho, Francesco Marinho, Rivelino, Paulo Cesar C, Ademir (Mirandhina), Valdomiro, Jairzinho, Dirceu
Referee: Angonese (Italy)

FINAL
7.7.74 West Germany (2) 2, Holland (1) 1 MUNICH
West Germany: Maier, Vogts, Schwarzenbeck, Beckenbauer, Breitner (1 pen), Hoeness, Bonhof, Overath, Grabowski, Muller (1), Holzenbein
Holland: Jongbloed, Suurbier, Rijsbergen (De Jong), Haan, Krol, Jansen, Neeskens (1 pen), Van Hanegem, Rep, Cruyff, Rensenbrink (Van der Kerkhof)
Referee: Taylor (England)

Argentina on the way to beating
Holland in the 1978 final on a
littered pitch in Buenos Aires.

(ALLSPORT)

ARGENTINA

1978

Argentina became the third host nation to win the competition in the last four tournaments, in a tense but flowing final in which the Dutch, though forcing extra time, again had to be content with runners-up medals. There was controversy before the match over the manner of Argentina's qualification for the final. They knew just how many goals were required against Peru to overtake Brazil on goal difference.

Gamesmanship also extended to the pre-match arrangements. Argentina kept the Dutch players waiting five minutes before they left their dressing-room. Then they complained about the plaster on the arm of Rene Van de Kerkhof; tactics designed to unsettle their opponents.

Although 102 goals were scored in the tournament, the average was only slightly better than the all-time low of 1974, with the gap widening between improved but uncompromising defences and impoverished attacks. Only two goals came from free-kicks and just one following a corner, though several memorable longer-range efforts succeeded from open play. There were three own goals, three players sent off and 58 cautioned.

Of the 14 penalty kicks awarded, only two failed, including another suspect incident involving Argentina, against Poland. Kazimierz Deyna, in his 100th international, was about to take his shot when the referee repositioned the ball, possibly disturbing his concentration. Scotland, the other spot-kick failures against Peru, had unwisely celebrated before the finals and clearly underestimated the South Americans. Two long-range efforts, one from a free-kick, by Teofilo Cubillas helped Peru to beat them 3-1.

The Scots were then held 1-1 by Iran but requiring a three-goal margin to deprive Holland of a place in the second stage, they gave their best performance by far,

Clive Thomas, the Welsh referee controversially blew for time seconds before Zico scored for Brazil against Sweden in Mar del Plata. The Brazilians were furious when he refused to allow the goal. (ASP)

A jubilant Mario Kempes (below) after opening the scoring in the final. (ALLSPORT)

But Brazil, unbeaten in the three games, finished behind Austria to join Peru and Holland who had emerged from the other group. The Dutch, while still using the all-out attack and reinforced defence methods of their 'total football' era, badly missed Cruyff and lacked accuracy in front of goal.

In Group A of the second stage, West Germany and Italy played out a dull, negative scoreless draw before the Dutch produced their most successful win, 5-1 over Austria. A Paolo Rossi goal after 14 minutes gave Italy the points at the expense of the Austrians before West Germany and Holland replayed their 1974 final but shared four goals this time.

Erny Brandts scored for both sides in Holland's 2-1 win over Italy and Austria deprived the Germans of a chance of a medal by beating them 3-2, giving Italy the third-place tie behind Holland, who became finalists for the second series in a row.

In Group B, Argentina were well into their stride with Mario Kempes causing defences many anxious moments with his strong, long-striding runs and faultless finishing. He struck twice in the 16th and 71st minute in the opening match with Poland. Brazil also looked much better against Peru and deserved their three-goal victory and had the edge over Argentina in an absorbing if tension-ridden 0-0 draw with the hosts.

Though Poland kept their faint hopes alive by beating Peru 1-0, Brazil beat the Poles who had drawn level at 1-1 on half-time, scoring twice after the break in a 3-1 success. Four hours later the Argentines kicked-off against Peru knowing they needed a win of four goals to reach the final. They hit six against a totally demoralised Peruvian side, while rumours spread outside Argentina about the reasons for the collapse.

For Brazil it was a galling experience; unbeaten in six games and forced to play only in the game for third place, which they won, beating Italy 2-1 after being a goal down at half-time.

Argentina had strength, resolution and were quick in all departments. They also had outstanding individuals like their defence organiser Daniel Passarella, midfield genius Ossie Ardiles, who was at the hub of almost every attack, and Kempes, a rakish striker who deservedly won the player of the tournament award.

Against Holland they made the most of almost every opening, while the Dutch, well below their best, squandered the half-chances which came their way. Kempes' persistence gave them a 1-0 lead after 38 minutes and it seemed enough until substitute Dirk Nanninga equalised for Holland with eight minutes left. But in extra time Kempes' powers of penetration led to him scoring again after 105 minutes and making the opening for Daniel Bertoni to make it 3-1 eleven minutes later. Argentina, with racing inflation and military dictatorship, had something to celebrate.

winning 3-2. But there was more disgrace for Scotland as Willie Johnston was sent home after being found guilty of taking an illegal drug.

Argentina had started nervously themselves but finished second in their group to Italy, who had beaten them by a single goal in Buenos Aires. In Group 2 the traditional opener for the competition involving the holders resulted in a goalless draw between West Germany and Poland, who both went on to the second round, again based on two sections as in 1974.

In Group 3, Sweden and Brazil were drawing 1-1 when the South Americans were awarded a corner. Referee Clive Thomas allowed the kick to be taken although it was timed electronically at three seconds over the normal 90 minutes. Zico headed in at nine seconds on the clock but the goal was ruled out as Thomas insisted he had ended the match when the corner was taken.

Neither Italy nor West Germany managed a goal in this Group A match in Buenos Aires, but Antonio Cabrini appears to have cause for concern after being caught by Karl-Heinz Rummenigge (right).
(PRESSENS BILD)

Qualifying Tournament

106 entries

Europe (32): Austria, Belgium, Bulgaria, Cyprus, Czechoslovakia, Denmark, England, Finland, France, East Germany, West Germany, Greece, Holland, Hungary, Iceland, Republic of Ireland, Northern Ireland, Italy, Luxembourg, Malta, Norway, Poland, Portugal, Rumania, Scotland, Spain, Sweden, Switzerland, Turkey, USSR, Wales, Yugoslavia

Africa (26): Algeria, Cameroon, Central Africa, Congo, Egypt, Ethiopia, Ghana, Guinea, Ivory Coast, Kenya, Libya, Malawi, Mauritania, Morocco, Niger, Nigeria, Senegal, Sierra Leone, Sudan, Tanzania, Togo, Tunisia, Uganda, Upper Volta, Zaire, Zambia

Concacaf (17): Barbados, Canada, Costa Rica, Cuba, Dominican Republic, Guatemala, Guyana, Haiti, Honduras, Jamaica, Mexico, Netherlands Antilles, Panama, El Salvador, Surinam, Trinidad and Tobago, USA

South America (10): Argentina, Bolivia, Brazil, Chile, Colombia, Ecuador, Paraguay, Peru, Uruguay, Venezuela

Asia (18): Bahrain, Hong Kong, Indonesia, Iran, Iraq, Israel, Japan, North Korea, South Korea, Kuwait, Malaysia, Qatar, Saudi Arabia, Singapore, Sri Lanka, Syria, Thailand, United Arab Emirates

Oceania (3): Australia, New Zealand, Taiwan

Taiwan were transferred from the Asian zone into Oceania. In South America, the winners of the three groups were to play in a tournament in a neutral country. The first two teams were guaranteed final places but the third had to meet the winner of Group 9 in Europe. Sri Lanka became the first country to withdraw when its government refused to grant permission to pay the entrance fee.

Final places in Argentina were to be distributed as follows: Europe (9 + West Germany)*, South America (2 + Argentina)*, Concacaf (1), Africa (1), Asia/Oceania (1).

*Play-off between Hungary and Bolivia gave Europe a further final place

Europe

Group 1 (Poland, Portugal, Denmark, Cyprus)

Cyprus v Denmark 1 - 5; Portugal v Poland 0 - 2; Denmark v Cyprus 5 - 0; Poland v Cyprus 5 - 0; Portugal v Denmark 1 - 0; Cyprus v Portugal 1 - 2; Denmark v Poland 1 - 2; Cyprus v Poland 1 - 3; Poland v Denmark 4 - 1; Denmark v Portugal 2 - 4; Poland v Portugal 1 - 1; Portugal v Cyprus 4 - 0

	P	W	D	L	F	A	Pts
Poland	6	5	1	0	17	4	11
Portugal	6	4	1	1	12	6	9
Denmark	6	2	0	4	14	12	4
Cyprus	6	0	0	0	3	24	0

Poland qualified

Group 2 (Italy, England, Finland, Luxembourg)

Finland v England 1 - 4; Finland v Luxembourg 7 - 1; England v Finland 2 - 1; Luxembourg v Italy 1 - 4; Italy v England 2 - 0; England v Luxembourg 5 - 0; Luxembourg v Finland 0 - 1; Finland v Italy 0 - 3; Luxembourg v England 0 - 2; Italy v Finland 6 - 1; England v Italy 2 - 0; Italy v Luxembourg 3 - 0

	P	W	D	L	F	A	Pts
Italy	6	5	0	1	18	4	10
England	6	5	0	1	15	4	10
Finland	6	2	0	4	11	16	4
Luxembourg	6	0	0	6	2	22	0

Italy qualified

Group 3 (East Germany, Austria, Turkey, Malta)

Turkey v Malta 4 - 0; East Germany v Turkey 1 - 1; Malta v Austria 0 - 1; Malta v East Germany 0 - 1; Austria v Turkey 1 - 0; Austria v Malta 9 - 0; Austria v East Germany 1 - 1; East Germany v Austria 1 - 1; East Germany v Malta 9 - 0; Turkey v Austria 0 - 1; Turkey v East Germany 1 - 2; Malta v Turkey 0 - 3

	P	W	D	L	F	A	Pts
Austria	6	4	2	0	14	2	10
East Germany	6	3	3	0	15	4	9
Turkey	6	2	1	3	9	5	5
Malta	6	0	0	6	0	27	0

Austria qualified

Group 4 (Holland, Belgium, Northern Ireland, Iceland)

Iceland v Belgium 0 - 1; Iceland v Holland 0 - 1; Holland v Northern Ireland 2 - 2; Belgium v Northern Ireland 2 - 0; Belgium v Holland 0 - 2; Iceland v Northern Ireland 1 - 0; Holland v Iceland 4 - 1; Belgium v Iceland 4 - 0; Northern Ireland v Holland 0 - 1; Holland v Belgium 1 - 0; Northern Ireland v Belgium 3 - 0

	P	W	D	L	F	A	Pts
Holland	6	5	1	0	11	3	11
Belgium	6	3	0	3	7	6	6
Northern Ireland	6	2	1	3	7	6	5
Iceland	6	1	0	5	2	12	2

Holland qualified

Group 5 (Bulgaria, France, Rep of Ireland)
Bulgaria v France 2 - 2; France v Rep of Ireland 2 - 0;
Rep of Ireland v France 1 - 0; Bulgaria v Rep of Ireland 2 - 1;
Rep of Ireland v Bulgaria 0 - 0; France v Bulgaria 3 - 1

	P	W	D	L	F	A	Pts
France	4	2	1	1	7	4	5
Bulgaria	4	1	2	1	5	6	4
Rep of Ireland	4	1	1	2	2	4	3

France qualified

Group 6 (Sweden, Switzerland, Norway)
Sweden v Norway 2 - 0; Norway v Switzerland 1 - 0;
Switzerland v Sweden 1 - 2; Sweden v Switzerland 2 - 1; Norway
v Sweden 2 - 1; Switzerland v Norway 1 - 0

	P	W	D	L	F	A	Pts
Sweden	4	3	0	1	7	4	6
Norway	4	2	0	2	3	4	4
Switzerland	4	1	0	3	3	5	2

Sweden qualified

Group 7 (Scotland, Czechoslovakia, Wales)
Czechoslovakia v Scotland 2 - 0; Scotland v Wales 1 - 0; Wales
v Czechoslovakia 3 - 0; Scotland v Czechoslovakia 3 - 1;
Wales v Scotland 0 - 2; Czechoslovakia v Wales 1 - 0

	P	W	D	L	F	A	Pts
Scotland	4	3	0	1	6	3	6
Czechoslovakia	4	2	0	2	4	6	4
Wales	4	1	0	3	3	4	2

Scotland qualified

Group 8 (Yugoslavia, Spain, Rumania)
Spain v Yugoslavia 1 - 0; Rumania v Spain 1 - 0; Yugoslavia v Rumania 0 - 2;
Spain v Rumania 2 - 0; Rumania v Yugoslavia 4 - 6; Yugoslavia v Spain 0 - 1

	P	W	D	L	F	A	Pts
Spain	4	3	0	1	4	1	6
Rumania	4	2	0	2	7	8	4
Yugoslavia	4	1	0	3	6	8	2

Spain qualified

Group 9 (USSR, Hungary, Greece)
Greece v Hungary 1 - 1; USSR v Greece 2 - 0; Hungary v USSR 2 - 1;
Greece v USSR 1 - 0; USSR v Hungary 2 - 0; Hungary v Greece 3 - 0

	P	W	D	L	F	A	Pts
Hungary	4	2	1	1	6	4	5
USSR	4	2	0	2	5	3	4
Greece	4	1	1	2	2	6	3

Play-off against third-placed team in South American play-off group:
Hungary v Bolivia 6 - 0, 3 - 2
Hungary qualified

South America
Group 1 (Brazil, Paraguay, Colombia)
Colombia v Brazil 0 - 0; Colombia v Paraguay 0 - 1; Paraguay v Colombia
1 - 1; Brazil v Colombia 6 - 0; Paraguay v Brazil 0 - 1; Brazil v Paraguay 1 - 1

	P	W	D	L	F	A	Pts
Brazil	4	2	2	0	8	1	6
Paraguay	4	1	2	1	3	3	4
Colombia	4	0	2	2	1	8	2

Group 2 (Uruguay, Venezuela, Bolivia)
Venezuela v Uruguay 1 - 1; Bolivia v Uruguay 1 - 0; Venezuela v Bolivia
1 - 3; Bolivia v Venezuela 2 - 0; Uruguay v Venezuela 2 - 0; Uruguay
v Bolivia 2 - 2

	P	W	D	L	F	A	Pts
Bolivia	4	3	1	0	8	3	7
Uruguay	4	1	2	1	5	4	4
Venezuela	4	0	1	3	2	8	1

Group 3 (Chile, Peru, Ecuador)
Ecuador v Peru 1 - 1; Ecuador v Chile 0 - 1; Chile v Peru 1 - 1; Peru
v Ecuador 4 - 0; Chile v Ecuador 3 - 0; Peru v Chile 2 - 0

	P	W	D	L	F	A	Pts
Peru	4	2	2	0	8	2	6
Chile	4	2	1	1	5	3	5
Ecuador	4	0	1	3	1	9	1

Play-off group (in Colombia)
Brazil v Peru 1 - 0; Brazil v Bolivia 8 - 0; Peru v Bolivia 5 - 0

	P	W	D	L	F	A	Pts
Brazil	2	2	0	0	9	0	4
Peru	2	1	0	1	5	1	2
Bolivia	2	0	0	2	0	13	0

Brazil and Peru qualified

Concacaf
Group 1 (North) (Canada, USA, Mexico)
Canada v USA 1 - 1; USA v Mexico 0 - 0; Canada v Mexico 1 - 0;
Mexico v USA 3 - 0; USA v Canada 2 - 0; Mexico v Canada 0 - 0

	P	W	D	L	F	A	Pts
Mexico	4	1	2	1	3	1	4
USA	4	1	2	1	3	4	4
Canada	4	1	2	1	2	3	4

Play-off for second place (in Haiti):
Canada v USA 3 - 0

Group 2 (Central) (Guatemala, El Salvador, Honduras, Costa Rica, Panama)
Honduras withdrew
Panama v Costa Rica 3 - 2; Panama v El Salvador 1 - 1; Costa Rica v Panama
3 - 0; El Salvador v Panama 4 - 1; Panama v Guatemala 2 - 4; Guatemala
v Panama 7 - 0; El Salvador v Costa Rica 1 - 1; Costa Rica v Guatemala
0 - 0; Guatemala v El Salvador 3 - 1; Guatemala v Costa Rica 1 - 1;
El Salvador v Guatemala 2 - 0; Costa Rica v El Salvador 1 - 1

	P	W	D	L	F	A	Pts
Guatemala	6	3	2	1	15	6	8
El Salvador	6	2	3	1	10	7	7
Costa Rica	6	1	4	1	8	6	6
Panama	6	1	1	4	7	21	3

Group 3 (Caribbean) (Netherlands Antilles, Barbados, Cuba, Guyana, Haiti, Jamaica, Surinam, Trinidad and Tobago, Dominican Republic)

Extra preliminary round
Dominican Republic v Haiti 0 - 3, 0 - 3

Preliminary round
Guyana v Surinam 2 - 0, 0 - 3; Netherlands Antilles v Haiti 1 - 2, 0 - 7;
Jamaica v Cuba 1 - 3, 0 - 2; Barbados v Trinidad and Tobago 2 - 1, 0 - 1;
Play-off: Trinidad and Tobago v Barbados 3 - 1

Final preliminary round
Surinam v Trinidad and Tobago 1 - 1, 2 - 2; Play-off: Surinam v Trinidad and
Tobago 3 - 2; Cuba v Haiti 1 - 1, 1 - 1. Play-off: Cuba v Haiti 0 - 2

Final Round
Guatemala v Surinam 3 - 2; El Salvador v Canada 2 - 1; Mexico v Haiti 4 - 1;
Canada v Surinam 2 - 1; Haiti v Guatemala 2 - 1; Mexico v El Salvador 1 - 0;
Mexico v Surinam 8 - 1; Canada v Guatemala 2 - 1; Haiti v El Salvador 1 - 0;
Mexico v Guatemala 2 - 1; Canada v Haiti 1 - 1; El Salvador v Surinam 3 - 2;
Mexico v Canada 3 - 1; Haiti v Surinam 1 - 0; Guatemala v El Salvador 2 - 2

	P	W	D	L	F	A	Pts
Mexico	5	5	0	0	20	5	10
Haiti	5	3	1	1	6	6	7
Canada	5	2	1	2	7	8	5
El Salvador	5	2	1	2	8	9	5
Guatemala	5	1	1	3	8	10	3
Surinam	5	0	0	5	6	17	0

Mexico qualified

Africa
Extra Preliminary Round
Sierra Leone v Niger 5 - 1, 1 - 2; Upper Volta v Mauritania 1 - 1, 2 - 0

1st Round
Algeria v Libya 1 - 0, 0 - 0; Morocco v Tunisia 1 - 1, 1 - 1 (Tunisia won 4 - 2
on penalties); Togo v Senegal 1 - 0, 1 - 1; Ghana v Guinea 2 - 1, 1 - 2;
Play-off: Guinea v Ghana 2 - 0; Zaire v Central Africa (withdrew); Sierra
Leone v Nigeria 0 - 0, 2 - 6; Congo v Cameroon 2 - 2, 2 - 1; Upper Volta
v Ivory Coast 1 - 1, 0 - 2; Egypt v Ethiopia 3 - 0, 2 - 1; Kenya v Sudan
(withdrew); Uganda v Tanzania (withdrew); Zambia v Malawi 4 - 0, 1 - 0

2nd Round
Zaire withdrew
Tunisia v Algeria 2 - 0, 1 - 1; Togo v Guinea 0 - 2, 1 - 2; Ivory Coast v Congo
3 - 2, 3 - 1; Kenya v Egypt 0 - 0, 0 - 1; Uganda v Zambia 1 - 0, 2 - 4

3rd Round

Guinea v Tunisia 1 - 0, 1 - 3; Ivory Coast v Nigeria 2 - 2, 0 - 4; Egypt v Zambia 2 - 0, 0 - 0

Final tournament

Tunisia v Nigeria 0 - 0; Nigeria v Egypt 4 - 0; Egypt v Nigeria 3 - 1; Nigeria v Tunisia 0 - 1; Egypt v Tunisia 3 - 2; Tunisia v Egypt 4 - 1

	P	W	D	L	F	A	Pts
Tunisia	4	2	1	1	7	4	5
Egypt	4	2	0	2	7	11	4
Nigeria	4	1	1	2	5	4	3

Tunisia qualified

Asia and Oceania

Oceania Group (Australia, New Zealand, Taiwan)

(In Australia)

Australia v Taiwan 3 - 0; Taiwan v Australia 1 - 2; New Zealand v Taiwan 6 - 0; Taiwan v New Zealand 0 - 6; Australia v New Zealand 3 - 1; New Zealand v Australia 1 - 1

	P	W	D	L	F	A	Pts
Australia	4	3	1	0	9	3	7
New Zealand	4	2	1	1	14	4	5
Taiwan	4	0	0	4	1	17	0

Asia Group 1 (Hong Kong, Indonesia, Malaysia, Thailand, Singapore)

(In Singapore)

Singapore v Thailand 2 - 0; Hong Kong v Indonesia 4 - 1; Malaysia v Thailand 6 - 4; Hong Kong v Singapore 2 - 2; Indonesia v Malaysia 0 - 0; Thailand v Hong Kong 1 - 2; Singapore v Malaysia 1 - 0; Thailand v Indonesia 3 - 2; Malaysia v Hong Kong 1 - 1; Indonesia v Singapore 4 - 0

	P	W	D	L	F	A	Pts
Hong Kong	4	2	2	0	9	5	6
Singapore	4	2	1	1	5	6	5
Malaysia	4	1	2	1	7	6	4
Indonesia	4	1	1	2	7	7	3
Thailand	4	1	0	3	8	12	2

Group Final: Singapore v Hong Kong 0 - 1

Asia Group 2 (Israel, Japan, South Korea, North Korea)

North Korea withdrew

Israel v South Korea 0 - 0; Israel v Japan 2 - 0; Japan v Israel 0 - 2; South Korea v Israel 3 - 1; Japan v South Korea 0 - 0; South Korea v Japan 1 - 0

	P	W	D	L	F	A	Pts
South Korea	4	2	2	0	4	1	6
Israel	4	2	1	1	5	3	5
Japan	4	0	1	3	0	5	1

Asia Group 3 (Iran, Saudi Arabia, Iraq, Syria)

Iraq withdrew

Saudi Arabia v Syria 2 - 0; Syria v Saudi Arabia 2 - 1; Saudi Arabia v Iran 0 - 3; Syria v Iran 0 - 1; Iran v Syria (withdrew), match awarded to Iran 2 - 0; Iran v Saudi Arabia 2 - 0

	P	W	D	L	F	A	Pts
Iran	4	4	0	0	8	0	8
Saudi Arabia	4	1	0	3	3	7	2
Syria	4	1	0	3	2	6	2

Asia Group 4 (Bahrain, Kuwait, Qatar, UAE)

(In Qatar)

UAE withdrew

Bahrain v Kuwait 0 - 2; Bahrain v Qatar 0 - 2; Qatar v Kuwait 0 - 2; Bahrain v Kuwait 1 - 2; Qatar v Bahrain 0 - 3; Qatar v Kuwait 1 - 4

	P	W	D	L	F	A	Pts
Kuwait	4	4	0	0	10	2	8
Qatar	4	1	0	3	3	9	2
Bahrain	4	1	0	3	4	6	2

Final round

Hong Kong v Iran 0 - 2; Hong Kong v South Korea 0 - 1; South Korea v Iran 0 - 0; Australia v Hong Kong 3 - 0; Australia v Iran 0 - 1; Australia v South Korea 2 - 1; Hong Kong v Kuwait 1 - 3; South Korea v Kuwait 1 - 0; Australia v Kuwait 1 - 2; South Korea v Australia 0 - 0; Iran v Kuwait 1 - 0; Hong Kong v Australia 2 - 5; Kuwait v South Korea 2 - 2; Iran v South Korea 2 - 2; Kuwait v Hong Kong 4 - 0; Iran v Hong Kong 3 - 0; Kuwait v Australia 1 - 0; Iran v Australia 1 - 0; Kuwait v Iran 1 - 2; South Korea v Hong Kong 5 - 2

	P	W	D	L	F	A	Pts
Iran	8	6	2	0	12	3	14
South Korea	8	3	4	1	12	8	10
Kuwait	8	4	1	3	13	8	9
Australia	8	3	1	4	11	8	7
Hong Kong	8	0	0	8	5	26	0

Iran qualified

Final Tournament ARGENTINA
First round
GROUP 1

2.6.78 Argentina (1) 2, Hungary (1) 1 BUENOS AIRES

Argentina: Fillol, Olguin, Galvan, Passarella, Tarantini, Ardiles, Gallego, Valencia (Alonso), Houseman (Bertoni (1)), Luque (1), Kempes

Hungary: Gujdar, Torok (Martos), Kereki, Kocsis, Toth J, Nyilasi, Pinter, Zombori, Csapo, Torocsik, Nagy

Refree: Garrido (Portugal)

2.6.78 Italy (1) 2, France (1) 1 MAR DEL PLATA

Italy: Zoff, Scirea, Gentile, Bellugi, Cabrini, Benetti, Causio, Tardelli, Antognoni (Zaccarelli (1)), Rossi (1), Bettega

France: Bertrand-Demanes, Tresor, Janvion, Rio, Bossis, Guillou, Michel, Platini, Dalger, Lacombe (1) (Berdoll), Six (Rouyer)

Referee: Rainea (Rumania)

6.7.78 Argentina (1) 2, France (0) 1 BUENOS AIRES

Argentina: Fillol, Olguin, Galvan, Passarella (1 pen), Tarantini, Ardiles, Gallego, Valencia (Alonso), Houseman, Luque (1), Kempes

France: Bertrand-Demanes (Baratelli), Tresor, Battiston, Lopez, Bossis, Bathenay, Michel, Platini (1), Rocheteau, Lacombe, Six

Referee: Dubach (Switzerland)

6.6.78 Italy (2) 3, Hungary (0) 1 MAR DEL PLATA

Italy: Zoff, Scirea, Gentile, Bellugi, Cabrini (Cuccureddu), Benetti (1), Causio, Tardelli, Antognoni, Rossi (1), Bettega (1) (Graziani)

Hungary: Meszaros, Kereki, Martos, Kocsis, Toth J, Csapo, Pinter, Zombori, Pusztai, Fazekas (Halasz), Nagy (Toth A (1 pen))

Referee: Barretto (Uruguay)

10.6.78 Italy (0) 1, Argentina (0) 0 BUENOS AIRES

Italy: Zoff, Scirea, Gentile, Bellugi (Cuccureddu), Cabrini, Benetti, Causio, Tardelli, Antognoni (Zaccarelli), Rossi, Bettega (1)

Argentina: Fillol, Olguin, Galvan, Passarella, Tarantini, Gallego, Ardiles, Valencia, Bertoni, Kempes, Ortiz (Houseman)

Referee: Klein (Israel)

10.6.78 France (3) 3, Hungary (1) 1 MAR DEL PLATA

France: Dropsy, Tresor, Janvion, Lopez (1), Bracci, Petit, Bathenay, Papi, Rocheteau (1), Berdoll (1), Rouyer

Hungary: Gujdar, Kereki, Balint, Martos, Toth J, Nyilasi, Pinter, Zombori (1), Pusztai, Torocsik, Nagy (Csapo)

Referee: Coehlo (Brazil)

	P	W	D	L	F	A	Pts
Italy	3	3	0	0	6	2	6
Argentina	3	2	0	1	4	3	4
France	3	1	0	2	5	5	2
Hungary	3	0	0	3	3	8	0

GROUP 2

1.6.78 West Germany (0) 0, Poland (0) 0 BUENOS AIRES

West Germany: Maier, Kaltz, Vogts, Russmann, Zimmerman, Bonhof, Beer, Flohe, Muller H, Abramczik, Fischer

Poland: Tomaszewski, Gorgon, Maculewicz, Szymanowski, Zmuda, Masztaler (Kasperczak), Nawalka, Deyna, Lato, Lubanski (Boniek), Szarmach

Referee: Coerezza (Argentina)

2.6.78 Tunisia (0) 3, Mexico (1) 1 ROSARIO

Tunisia: Naili, Dhouieb (1), Jendoubi, Jebali, Kaabi (1), Ghommidh (1), Temine (Labidi), Agrebi, Akid, Tarak, Ben Aziza (Karoui)

Mexico: Reyes, Martinez Diaz, Vazquez Ayala (1 pen), Ramos, Tena, De la Torre, Cuellar, Mendizabal (Lugo Gomez), Isiordia, Rangel, Sanchez

Referee: Gordon (Scotland)

6.6.78 Poland (1) 1, Tunisia (0) 0 ROSARIO
Poland: Tomaszewski, Gordon, Szymanowski, Zmuda, Maculewicz, Nawalka, Deyna, Kasperczak, Lato (1), Lubanski (Boniek), Szarmach (Iwan)
Tunisia: Naili, Dhouieb, Jendoubi, Gasmi, Kaabi, Ghommidh, Temine, Agrebi, Akid, Tarak, Jebali
Referee: Martinez (Spain)

6.6.78 West Germany (4) 6, Mexico (0) 0 CORDOBA
West Germany: Maier, Kaltz, Vogts, Russmann, Dietz, Bonhof, Flohe (2), Muller H (1), Rummenigge (2), Fischer, Muller D (1)
Mexico: Reyes (Soto), Martinez Diaz, Tena, Ramos, Vazquez Ayala, Lopez Zarza (Lugo Gomez), Cuellar, De la Torre, Sanchez, Rangel, Mendizabal
Referee: Bouzo (Syria)

10.6.78 West Germany (0) 0, Tunisia (0) 0 CORDOBA
West Germany: Maier, Kaltz, Vogts, Russmann, Dietz, Bonhof, Flohe, Rummenigge, Muller H, Fischer, Muller D
Tunisia: Naili, Jebali, Dhouieb, Jendoubi, Kaabi, Ghommidh, Gasmi, Tarak, Agrebi, Temine, Akid (Ben Aziza)
Referee: Orosco (Peru)

10.6.78 Poland (1) 3, Mexico (0) 1 ROSARIO
Poland: Tomaszewski, Gorgon, Szymanowski, Zmuda, Kasperczak, Deyna (1), Masztaler, Maculewicz, Boniek (2), Lato (1), Iwan (Lubanski)
Mexico: Soto, Gomez C, Cisneros, De la Torre, Vazquez Ayala, Cuellar, Flores, Cardenas (Mendizabal), Ortega, Rangel (1), Sanchez
Referee: Namdar (Iran)

	P	W	D	L	F	A	Pts
Poland	3	2	1	0	4	1	5
West Germany	3	1	2	0	6	0	4
Tunisia	3	1	1	1	3	2	3
Mexico	3	0	0	3	2	12	0

GROUP 3
3.6.78 Austria (1) 2, Spain (1) 1 BUENOS AIRES
Austria: Koncilla, Pezzey, Sara, Breitenberger, Obermayer, Prohaska, Kreuz, Hickersberger (Weber), Jara, Schachner (1) (Pirkner), Krankl (1)
Spain: Miguel Angel, Marcelino, Pirri, Migueli, San Jose, De la Cruz, Asensi, Rexach (Quini), Cardenosa (Leal), Dani (1), Ruben Cano
Referee: Palotai (Hungary)

3.6.78 Sweden (1) 1, Brazil (1) 1 MAR DEL PLATA
Sweden: Hellstrom, Andersson R, Borg, Nordqvist, Erlandsson, Larsson L (Edstrom), Tapper, Linderoth, Bo Larsson, Sjoberg (1), Wendt
Brazil: Leao, Oscar, Toninho, Amaral, Edinho, Batista, Zico, Cerezo, Gil (Nelinho), Reinaldo (1), Rivelino
Referee: Thomas (Wales)

7.6.78 Austria (1) 1, Sweden (0) 0 BUENOS AIRES
Austria: Koncilia, Obermayer, Sara, Pezzey, Breitenberg, Prohaska, Hickersberger, Krieger (Weber), Jara, Krankl (1 pen), Kreuz
Sweden: Hellstrom, Andersson R, Borg, Nordqvist, Erlandsson, Larsson L, Tapper (Torstensson), Linderoth (Edstrom), Bo Larsson, Sjoberg, Wendt
Referee: Corver (Netherlands)

7.6.78 Brazil (0) 0, Spain (0) 0 MAR DEL PLATA
Brazil: Leao, Amaral, Nelinho (Gil), Oscar, Edinho, Cerezo, Batista, Zico (Mendonca), Dirceu, Toninho, Reinaldo
Spain: Miguel Angel, Olmo, Marcelino, Migueli (Biosca), Uria (Guzman), Leal, Asensi, Cardenosa, San Jose, Juanito, Santillana
Referee: Gonella (Italy)

11.6.78 Spain (0) 1, Sweden (0) 0 BUENOS AIRES
Spain: Miguel Angel, Olmo (Pirri), Marcelino, Biosca, San Jose, Uria, Leal, Asensi (1), Cardenosa, Juanito, Santillana
Sweden: Hellstrom, Andersson R, Borg, Nordqvist, Erlandsson, Larsson L, Bo Larsson, Nordin, Nilsson, Sjoberg (Linderoth), Edstrom (Wendt)
Referee: Biwersi (West Germany)

11.6.78 Brazil (1) 1, Austria (0) 0 MAR DEL PLATA
Brazil: Leao, Amaral, Toninho, Oscar, Rodrigues Neto, Batista, Cerezo (Chicao), Dirceu, Gil, Mendonca (Zico), Roberto (1)
Austria: Koncilia, Obermayer, Sara, Pezzey, Breitenberger, Prohaska, Hickersberger (Weber), Krieger (Happich), Jara, Krankl, Kreuz
Referee: Wurtz (France)

	P	W	D	L	F	A	Pts
Austria	3	2	0	1	3	2	4
Brazil	3	1	2	0	2	1	4
Spain	3	1	1	1	2	2	3
Sweden	3	0	1	2	1	3	1

GROUP 4
3.6.78 Holland (1) 3, Iran (0) 0 MENDOZA
Holland: Jongbloed, Suurbier, Rijsbergen, Krol, Haan, Jansen, Neeskens, Van de Kerkhof W, Rep, Rensenbrink (3, 2 pens), Van de Kerkhof R (Nanninga)
Iran: Hejazi, Nazari, Abdullahi, Kazerani, Eskandarian, Parvin, Ghassempour, Sadeghi, Nayeb-Agha, Faraki (Rowshan), Jahani
Referee: Archundia (Mexico)

3.6.78 Peru (1) 3, Scotland (1) 1 CORDOBA
Peru: Quiroga, Chumpitaz, Duarte, Manzo, Diaz, Velasquez, Cueto (1) (Rojas), Cubillas (2), Munante, La Rosa (Sotil), Oblitas
Scotland: Rough, Kennedy, Burns, Rioch (Gemmill), Forsyth, Buchan, Dalglish, Hartford, Jordan (1), Masson (Macari), Johnston
Referee: Eriksson (Switzerland)

7.6.78 Scotland (1) 1, Iran (0) 1 CORDOBA
Scotland: Rough, Jardine, Donachie, Gemmill, Burns, Buchan (Forsyth), Dalglish (Harper), Hartford, Jordan, Macari, Robertson
Iran: Hejazi, Nazari, Abdullahi, Kazerani, Eskandarian (o. g.), Parvin, Ghassempour, Sadeghi, Danaifar (1) (Nayeb-Agha), Faraki (Rowshan), Jahani
Referee: N'Diaye (Senegal)

7.6.78 Holland (0) 0, Peru (0) 0 MENDOZA
Holland: Jongbloed, Suurbier, Rijsbergen, Krol, Poortvliet, Neeskens (Nanninga), Van de Kerkhof W, Jansen, Haan, Van de Kerkhof R (Rep), Rensenbrink
Peru: Quiroga, Chumpitaz, Duarte, Manzo, Diaz, Velasquez, Cueto, Cubillas, Munante, La Rosa (Sotil), Oblitas
Referee: Prokop (East Germany)

11.6.78 Peru (3) 4, Iran (1) 1 CORDOBA
Peru: Quiroga, Chumpitaz, Duarte, Manzo (Leguia), Diaz, Velasquez (1), Cueto, Cubillas (3, 2 pens), Munante, La Rosa (Sotil), Oblitas
Iran: Hejazi, Nazari, Abdullahi, Kazerani, Allahvardi, Parvin, Ghassempour, Sadeghi, Danaifar, Faraki (Jahani), Rowshan (1) (Fariba)
Referee: Jarguz (Poland)

11.6.78 Scotland (1) 3, Holland (1) 2 MENDOZA
Scotland: Rough, Kennedy, Donachie, Rioch, Forsyth, Buchan, Dalglish (1), Hartford, Jordan, Gemmill (2, 1 pen), Souness
Holland: Jongbloed, Suurbier, Rijsbergen (Wildschut), Krol, Poortvliet, Neeskens (Boskamp), Jansen, Van de Kerkhof W, Rep (1), Van de Kerkhof R, Rensenbrink (1 pen)
Referee: Linemayr (Austria)

	P	W	D	L	F	A	Pts
Peru	3	2	1	0	7	2	5
Holland	3	1	1	1	5	3	3
Scotland	3	1	1	1	5	6	3
Iran	3	0	1	2	2	8	1

Second round
GROUP A
14.6.78 West Germany (0) 0, Italy (0) 0 BUENOS AIRES
West Germany: Maier, Kaltz, Vogts, Russmann, Dietz, Bonhof, Flohe (Beer), Zimmermann (Konopa), Holzenbein, Rummenigge, Fischer
Italy: Zoff, Scirea, Gentile, Bellugi, Cabrini, Tardelli, Benetti, Antognoni (Zaccarelli), Causio, Rossi, Bettega
Referee: Maksimovic (Yugoslavia)

14.6.78 Holland (3) 5, Austria (0) 1 CORDOBA
Holand: Schrijvers, Wildschut, Brandts (1) (Van Kraay), Krol, Poortvliet, Jansen, Haan, Van de Kerkhof W (1), Rep (2), Van de Kerhof R (Schoenaker), Rensenbrink (1)
Austria: Koncilia, Obermayer (1), Sara, Pezzey, Breitenberger, Hickersberger, Prohaska, Jara, Krieger, Kreuz, Krankl
Referee: Gordon (Scotland)

18.6.78 Italy (1) 1, Austria (0) 0 BUENOS AIRES
Italy: Zoff, Scirea, Bellugi (Cuccureddu), Gentile, Cabrini, Benetti, Zaccarelli, Tardelli, Causio, Rossi (1), Bettega (Graziani)
Austria: Koncilia, Obermayer, Sara, Pezzey, Strasser, Hickersberger, Prohaska, Kreuz, Krieger, Schachner (Pirkner), Krankl
Referee: Rion (Belgium)

18.6.78 West Germany (1) 2, Holland (1) 2 Cordoba
West Germany: Maier, Kaltz, Vogts, Russmann, Dietz, Bonhof, Holzenbein, Beer, Abramczik (1), Muller D (1), Rummenigge
Holland: Schrijvers, Wildschut (Nanninga), Brandts, Krol, Poortvliet, Jansen, Haan (1), Van de Kerkhof W, Rep, Van de Kerkhof R (1), Rensenbrink
Referee: Barreto (Uruguay)

21.6.78 Holland (0) 2, Italy (1) 1 BUENOS AIRES
Holland: Schrijvers (Jongbloed), Brandts (o. g., 1), Krol, Poortvliet, Jansen, Haan (1), Neeskens, Van de Kerkhof W, Rep (van Kraay), Van de Kerkhof R, Rensenbrink
Italy: Zoff, Scirea, Gentile, Cuccureddu, Cabrini, Tardelli, Zaccarelli, Benetti (Graziani), Causio (Sala C), Rossi, Bettega
Referee: Martinez (Spain)

21.6.78 Austria (0) 3, West Germany (1) 2 CORDOBA
Austria: Koncilia, Obermayer, Sara, Pezzey, Strasser, Hickersberger, Prohaska, Kreuz, Krieger, Schachner (Oberacher), Krankl (2)
West Germany: Maier, Kaltz, Vogts (o. g., 1), Russmann, Dietz, Bonhof, Holzenbein (1), Beer (Muller H), Abramczik, Muller D (Fischer), Rummenigge (1)
Referee: Klein (Israel)

	P	W	D	L	F	A	Pts
Holland	3	2	1	0	9	4	5
Italy	3	1	1	1	2	2	3
West Germany	3	0	2	1	4	5	2
Austria	3	1	0	2	4	8	2

GROUP B
14.6.78 Argentina (1) 2, Poland (0) 0 ROSARIO
Argentina: Fillol, Olguin, Galvan, Passarella, Tarantini, Ardiles, Gallego, Valencia (Villa), Houseman (Ortiz), Bertoni, Kempes (2)
Poland: Tomaszewski, Kasperczak, Szymanowski, Zmuda, Maculewicz, Masztaler (Mazur), Deyna, Nawalka, Boniek, Lato, Szarmach
Referee: Eriksson (Sweden)

14.6.78 Brazil (2) 3, Peru (0) 0 MENDOZA
Brazil: Leao, Amaral, Toninho, Oscar, Rodrigues Neto, Batista, Cerezo (Chicao), Dirceu (2), Gil (Zico (1 pen)), Mendonca, Roberto
Peru: Quiroga, Chumpitaz, Diaz (Navarro), Manzo, Duarte, Velasquez, Cueto, Cubillas, La Rosa, Munante, Oblitas (Rojas P)
Referee: Rainea (Rumania)

18.6.78 Argentina (0) 0, Brazil (0) 0 ROSARIO
Argentina: Fillol, Olguin, Galvan, Passarella, Tarantini, Ardiles (Villa), Gallego, Ortiz (Alonso), Kempes, Bertoni, Luque
Brazil: Leao, Amaral, Toninho, Oscar, Rodrigues Neto (Edinho), Chicao, Batista, Dirceu, Mendonca (Zico), Gil, Roberto
Referee: Palotai (Hungary)

18.6.78 Poland (0) 1, Peru (0) 0 MENDOZA
Poland: Kukla, Gorgon, Szymanowski, Zmuda, Maculewicz, Masztaler (Kasperczak), Nawalka, Deyna, Lato, Boniek (Lubanski), Szarmach (1)
Peru: Quiroga, Chumpitaz, Duarte, Manzo, Navarro, Cueto, Quezada, Cubillas, La Rosa (Sotil), Munante (Rojas P), Oblitas
Referee: Partridge (England)

21.6.78 Brazil (1) 3, Poland (1) 1 MENDOZA
Brazil: Leao, Amaral, Toninho, Oscar, Nelinho (1), Cerezo (Rivelino), Batista, Dirceu, Zico (Mendonca), Gil, Roberto (2)
Poland: Kukla, Gorgon, Szymanowski, Zmuda, Maculewicz, Kasperczak (Lubanski), Nawalka, Deyna, Boniek, Lato (1), Szarmach
Referee: Silvagno (Chile)

21.6.78 Argentina (2) 6, Peru (0) 0 ROSARIO
Argentina: Fillol, Olguin, Galvan, Passarella, Tarantini (1), Larrosa (Oviedo), Kempes (2), Bertoni (Houseman (1)), Luque (2), Ortiz
Peru: Quiroga, Chumpitaz, Duarte, Manzo, Rojas R, Cueto, Velasquez (Gorriti), Cubillas, Quezada, Munante, Oblitas
Referee: Wurtz (France)

	P	W	D	L	F	A	Pts
Argentina	3	2	1	0	8	0	5
Brazil	3	2	1	0	6	1	5
Poland	3	1	0	2	2	5	2
Peru	3	0	0	3	0	10	0

Match for third place
24.6.78 Brazil (0) 2, Italy (1) 1 BUENOS AIRES
Brazil: Leao, Amaral, Nelinho (1), Oscar, Rodrigues Neto, Batista, Cerezo (Rivelino), Dirceu (1), Gil (Reinaldo), Roberto, Mendonca
Italy: Zoff, Scirea, Gentile, Cuccureddu, Maldera, Cabrini, Antognoni (Sala C), Sala P, Causio (1), Rossi, Bettega
Referee: Klein (Israel)

FINAL
25.6.78 Argentina (1) 3, Holland (0) 1 (aet, 1 - 1 at 90 mins) BUENOS AIRES
Argentina: Fillol, Olguin, Galvan, Passarella, Tarantini, Ardiles (Larrosa), Gallego, Kempes (2), Bertoni (1), Luque, Ortiz (Houseman)
Holland: Jongbloed, Poortvliet, Krol, Brandts, Jansen (Suurbier), Neeskens, Haan, Van de Kerkhof W, Van de Kerkhof R, Rep (Nanninga (1)), Rensenbrink
Referee: Gonella (Italy)

French defender Marius Tresor (8)
scores for France in the semi-final
with West Germany. But it was the
Germans who won on penalties
after extra time. (COLORSPORT)

SPAIN
1982

Italy's deserved success was a personal triumph for manager Enzo Bearzot, whose diligent endeavours to unfetter his international players from the defensive strictures of their domestic football proved successful. They were technically sound, professional and clinical in their finishing. Yet few would have given much for their prospects in the opening group phase. Even by their own standards they were abysmally negative.

Italy failed to win a match, drawing all three of these section games — as did modest Cameroon, who retired undefeated from the contest — yet progressed to the next stage by virtue of their superior goalscoring: two goals to Cameroon's one!

England could also rightly claim to have been forced out of the tournament by the vagaries of its system. They, too, remained unbeaten. However, just how much of the euphoria which surrounded their performance was borne of Bryan Robson scoring after 27 seconds of the first game is debatable. For the Scots, in a difficult group, defensive errors proved costly when they had revealed imagination and skill in combating teams of differing quality in Brazil and the rather overrated USSR.

Northern Ireland were one of the few teams to play above themselves. They reached a peak against their dismally disappointing Spanish hosts, beating them 1-0 despite having to play for the greater part of the second half with ten men following the dismissal of Mal Donaghy. Their defence did not waver or allow itself to be drawn into rash tackles that would inevitably have led to cries for a Spanish penalty. Such fears were understandable, for two of Spain's three previous goals had come from the spot.

The minnows — Honduras, Algeria, Kuwait and New Zealand in particular — certainly enlivened arguably the most unenterprising World Cup of all time, despite the increase in goalscoring. Forwards were scarce, most teams packed the midfield. But whereas some like Brazil and France used the midfield as a springboard to attack from all angles, too many relied on the mistakes of the opposition to goad them on to the offensive.

Unfortunately the Eastern Europeans were dreadfully dull and predictable, especially Czechoslovakia and Yugoslavia. Poland operated only fitfully, despite their third-place rating. But El Salvador managed to shore up their leaky defence after conceding 10 goals to the Hungarians.

For the South Americans, Chile and Peru failed to excite. The holders Argentina were physically dealt with by Italy in the first half, then beaten fairly and squarely after the interval. Diego Maradona, the Argentine with the multi-million pound reputation, was an expensive disappointment.

Conversely, the admirable Brazilians for whom Zico, Falcao, Socrates and Junior gave memorable performances, were finally let down by a goalkeeping weakness and the absence of a recognised spearhead. Unquestionably the outstanding team both for the quality of their play and for entertainment value, Brazil found themselves a goal down to Italy on three occasions, which was once too much for them.

French midfielder Patrick Battiston is stretchered off after being knocked unconscious by West German goalkeeper Harald Schumacher during the semi-final in Seville. (COLORSPORT)

The Italian goalscoring hero was Paolo Rossi, the prodigal son, returning from a two-year suspension following a bribery scandal. He struggled to find his form in the opening games, but became transformed in the second round to finish as the tournament's leading goalscorer with six goals.

Italy's victory over Brazil was the second-most rewarding encounter. The top game was the pulsating end-to-end semi-final between West Germany and France. The French had displayed enterprise and charm with Marius Tresor, Michel Platini, Jean Tigana and Alain Giresse shining. All square after extra time at 3-3, the emotionally and physically drained players were called upon to settle matters by penalty kicks. It was the first time that this unsatisfactory system had been used to determine a match in the World Cup finals.

The Germans emerged 5-4 winners from the shoot-out. Two goals down in the match itself at one stage, they salvaged part of their reputation against the French, who were only slightly inferior to Brazil in terms of attractiveness. However, there were less savoury aspects of German play. Humiliated by one of the outsiders, Algeria, they gave a miserly display on other occasions. They succumbed to the feigning of injury, which oddly

Paolo Rossi, the prodigal son of Italian football, scores the third of his hat-trick against Brazil. Italy won 3-2 to ensure a place in the semi-finals. (POPPERFOTO)

Claudio Gentile (6) and his captain Dino Zoff (1) celebrate Italy's victory. (ALLSPORT)

enough helped them reach the 1966 final, and a blatant foul on French substitute Patrick Battiston by goalkeeper Harald Schumacher at a crucial moment in the semi-final disrupted the French rhythm yet went unpunished. The standard of refereeing was no higher than that of the overall play.

Just as disturbing was the furore caused by the apparent arrangement between the Germans and Austria which prevented Algeria from progressing into the second round, West Germany winning 1-0.

The Germans could claim that Karl-Heinz Rummenigge, easily their most gifted player, was handicapped throughout by injury. Indeed, he seemed to be either coming on or going off late to preserve his fitness. Yet the Italians were hit more seriously in the final, having to start without Giancarlo Antognoni and losing Francesco Graziani in the early stages.

Italy's eventual success came as something of an anti-climax; they were far superior to the Germans and won as easily as 3-1 suggested. Dino Zoff, at 40, crowned a masterly tournament by collecting the trophy as Italy's skipper.

Qualifying Tournament

108 entries

Europe (33): Albania, Austria, Belgium, Bulgaria, Cyprus, Czechoslovakia, Denmark, England, Finland, France, East Germany, West Germany, Greece, Holland, Hungary, Iceland, Republic of Ireland, Northern Ireland, Italy, Luxembourg, Malta, Norway, Poland, Portugal, Rumania, Scotland, Spain, Sweden, Switzerland, Turkey, USSR, Wales, Yugoslavia

South America (10): Argentina, Bolivia, Brazil, Chile, Colombia, Ecuador, Paraguay, Peru, Uruguay, Venezuela

Africa (28): Algeria, Cameroon, Central Africa, Egypt, Ethiopia, Gambia, Ghana, Guinea, Kenya, Lesotho, Liberia, Libya, Madagascar, Malawi, Morocco, Mozambique, Niger, Nigeria, Senegal, Sierra Leone, Somalia, Sudan, Tanzania, Togo, Tunisia, Uganda, Zaire, Zambia

Asia (18): Bahrain, China, Hong Kong, Indonesia, Iran, Iraq, Israel, Japan, North Korea, South Korea, Kuwait, Macao, Malaysia, Qatar, Saudi Arabia, Singapore, Syria, Thailand

Concacaf (15): Canada, Costa Rica, Cuba, Grenada, Guatemala, Guyana, Haiti, Honduras, Mexico, Netherlands Antilles, Panama, El Salvador, Surinam, Trinidad and Tobago, USA

Oceania (4): Australia, Fiji, New Zealand, Taiwan

The People's Republic of China was re-admitted to FIFA in 1979. Israel was added to the European zone after the draw for the qualifying competition had left them isolated once more. The continuing political uncertainty in El Salvador caused Costa Rica to refuse to play there, but it cost them the points.

However the expansion from 16 to 24 finalists produced a record entry of 108 from a FIFA membership of 147 nations. Increased final places had an encouraging effect on third world participation.

Final places in Spain were to be distributed as follows: Europe (13 + Spain), South America (3 + Argentina), Africa (2), Concacaf (2), Asia/Oceania (2).

Europe

Group 1 (West Germany, Austria, Bulgaria, Finland, Albania)
Finland v Bulgaria 0 - 2; Albania v Finland 2 - 0; Finland v Austria 0 - 2; Bulgaria v Albania 2 - 1; Austria v Albania 5 - 0; Bulgaria v West Germany 1 - 3; Albania v Austria 0 - 1; Albania v West Germany 0 - 2; West Germany v Austria 2 - 0; Bulgaria v Finland 4 - 0; Finland v West Germany 0 - 4; Austria v Bulgaria 2 - 0; Austria v Finland 5 - 1; Finland v Albania 2 - 1; West Germany v Finland 7 - 1; Austria v West Germany 1 - 3; Albania v Bulgaria 0 - 2; Bulgaria v Austria 0 - 0; West Germany v Albania 8 - 0; West Germany v Bulgaria 4 - 0

	P	W	D	L	F	A	Pts
West Germany	8	8	0	0	33	3	15
Austria	8	5	1	2	16	6	11
Bulgaria	8	4	1	3	11	10	9
Albania	8	1	0	7	4	22	2
Finland	8	1	0	7	4	27	2

West Germany and Austria qualified

Group 2 (Holland, France, Belgium, Rep of Ireland, Cyprus)
Cyprus v Rep of Ireland 2 - 3; Rep of Ireland v Holland 2 - 1; Cyprus v France 0 - 7; Rep of Ireland v Belgium 1 - 1; France v Rep of Ireland 2 - 0; Belgium v Holland 1 - 0; Rep of Ireland v Cyprus 6 - 0; Cyprus v Belgium 0 - 2; Belgium v Cyprus 3 - 2; Holland v Cyprus 3 - 0; Holland v France 1 - 0; Belgium v Rep of Ireland 1 - 0; France v Belgium 3 - 2; Cyprus v Holland 0 - 1; Holland v Rep of Ireland 2 - 1; Belgium v France 2 - 0; Holland v Belgium 3 - 0; Rep of Ireland v France 3 - 2; France v Holland 2 - 0; France v Cyprus 4 - 0

	P	W	D	L	F	A	Pts
Belgium	8	5	1	2	12	9	11
France	8	5	0	3	20	8	10
Rep of Ireland	8	4	2	2	17	11	10
Holland	8	4	1	3	11	7	9
Cyprus	8	0	0	8	4	29	0

Belgium and France qualified

Group 3 (Czechoslovakia, USSR, Wales, Turkey, Iceland)
Iceland v Wales 0 - 4; Iceland v USSR 1 - 2; Turkey v Iceland 1 - 3; Wales v Turkey 4 - 0; USSR v Iceland 5 - 0; Wales v Czechoslovakia 1 - 0; Czechoslovakia v Turkey 2 - 0; Turkey v Wales 0 - 1; Turkey v Czechoslovakia 0 - 3; Czechoslovakia v Iceland 6 - 1; Wales v USSR 0 - 0; Iceland v Turkey 2 - 0; Czechoslovakia v Wales 2 - 0; Iceland v Czechoslovakia 1 - 1; USSR v Turkey 4 - 0; Turkey v USSR 0 - 3; Wales v Iceland 2 - 2; USSR v Czechoslovakia 2 - 0; USSR v Wales 3 - 0; Czechoslovakia v USSR 1 - 1

	P	W	D	L	F	A	Pts
USSR	8	6	2	0	20	2	14
Czechoslovakia	8	4	2	2	15	6	10
Wales	8	4	2	2	12	7	10
Iceland	8	2	2	4	10	21	6
Turkey	8	0	0	8	1	22	0

USSR and Czechoslovakia qualified

Group 4 (England, Norway, Rumania, Switzerland, Hungary)
England v Norway 4 - 0; Norway v Rumania 1 - 1; Rumania v England 2 - 1; Switzerland v Norway 1 - 2; England v Switzerland 2 - 1; Switzerland v Hungary 2 - 2; England v Rumania 0 - 0; Hungary v Rumania 1 - 0; Norway v Hungary 1 - 2; Switzerland v England 2 - 1; Rumania v Norway 1 - 0; Hungary v England 1 - 3; Norway v Switzerland 1 - 1; Norway v England 2 - 1; Rumania v Hungary 0 - 0; Rumania v Switzerland 1 - 2; Hungary v Switzerland 3 - 0; Hungary v Norway 4 - 1; Switzerland v Rumania 0 - 0; England v Hungary 1 - 0

	P	W	D	L	F	A	Pts
Hungary	8	4	2	2	13	8	10
England	8	4	1	3	13	8	9
Rumania	8	2	4	2	5	5	8
Switzerland	8	2	3	3	9	12	7
Norway	8	2	2	4	8	15	6

Hungary and England qualified

Group 5 (Italy, Yugoslavia, Greece, Denmark, Luxembourg)
Luxembourg v Yugoslavia 0 - 5; Yugoslavia v Denmark 2 - 1; Luxembourg v Italy 0 - 2; Denmark v Greece 0 - 1; Italy v Denmark 2 - 0; Greece v Italy 0 - 2; Greece v Luxembourg 2 - 0; Luxembourg v Greece 0 - 2; Yugoslavia v Greece 5 - 1; Luxembourg v Denmark 1 - 2; Denmark v Italy 3 - 1; Denmark v Yugoslavia 1 - 2; Greece v Denmark 2 - 3; Yugoslavia v Italy 1 - 1; Italy v Greece 1 - 1; Yugoslavia v Luxembourg 5 - 0; Greece v Yugoslavia 1 - 2; Italy v Luxembourg 1 - 0

	P	W	D	L	F	A	Pts
Yugoslavia	8	6	1	1	22	7	13
Italy	8	5	2	1	12	5	12
Denmark	8	4	0	4	14	11	8
Greece	8	3	1	4	10	13	7
Luxembourg	8	0	0	8	1	23	0

Yugoslavia and Italy qualified

Group 6 (Scotland, Sweden, Portugal, Northern Ireland, Israel)
Israel v Northern Ireland 0 - 0; Sweden v Israel 1 - 1; Sweden v Scotland 0 - 1; Scotland v Sweden 3 - 0; Scotland v Portugal 0 - 0; Portugal v Northern Ireland 1 - 0; Portugal v Israel 3 - 0; Israel v Scotland 0 - 1; Scotland v Northern Ireland 1 - 1; Scotland v Israel 3 - 1; Northern Ireland v Portugal 1 - 0; Sweden v Northern Ireland 1 - 0; Sweden v Portugal 3 - 0; Portugal v Sweden 1 - 2; Northern Ireland v Scotland 0 - 0; Israel v Portugal 4 - 1; Northern Ireland v Israel 1 - 0; Portugal v Scotland 2 - 1

	P	W	D	L	F	A	Pts
Scotland	8	4	3	1	9	4	11
Northern Ireland	8	3	3	2	6	3	9
Sweden	8	3	2	3	7	8	8
Portugal	8	3	1	4	8	11	7
Israel	8	1	3	4	6	10	5

Scotland and Northern Ireland qualified

Group 7 (Poland, East Germany, Malta)
Malta v Poland 0 - 2; Malta v East Germany 1 - 2; Poland v East Germany 1 - 0; East Germany v Poland 2 - 3; East Germany v Malta 5 - 1; Poland v Malta 6 - 0

	P	W	D	L	F	A	Pts
Poland	4	4	0	0	12	2	8
East Germany	4	2	0	2	9	6	4
Malta	4	0	0	4	2	15	0

Poland qualified

South America

Group 1 (Bolivia, Brazil, Venezuela)
Venezuela v Brazil 0 - 1; Bolivia v Venezuela 3 - 0; Bolivia v Brazil 1 - 2;
Venezuela v Bolivia 1 - 0; Brazil v Bolivia 3 - 1; Brazil v Venezuela 5 - 0

	P	W	D	L	F	A	Pts
Brazil	4	4	0	0	11	2	8
Bolivia	4	1	0	3	5	6	2
Venezuela	4	1	0	3	1	9	2

Brazil qualified

Group 2 (Colombia, Peru, Uruguay)
Colombia v Peru 1 - 1; Uruguay v Colombia 3 - 2; Peru v Colombia 2 - 0;
Uruguay v Peru 1 - 2; Peru v Uruguay 0 - 0; Colombia v Uruguay 1 - 1

	P	W	D	L	F	A	Pts
Peru	4	2	2	0	5	2	6
Uruguay	4	1	2	1	5	5	4
Colombia	4	0	2	2	4	7	2

Peru qualified

Group 3 (Chile, Ecuador, Paraguay)
Ecuador v Paraguay 1 - 0; Ecuador v Chile 0 - 0; Paraguay v Ecuador 3 - 1;
Paraguay v Chile 0 - 1; Chile v Ecuador 2 - 0; Chile v Paraguay 3 - 0

	P	W	D	L	F	A	Pts
Chile	4	3	1	0	6	0	7
Ecuador	4	1	1	2	2	5	3
Paraguay	4	1	0	3	3	6	2

Chile qualified

Africa

1st Round (Zimbabwe, Sudan, Liberia, Togo byes)
Libya v Gambia 2 - 1, 0 - 0; Ethiopia v Zambia 0 - 0, 0 - 4; Sierra Leone
v Algeria 2 - 2, 1 - 3; Senegal v Morocco 0 - 1, 0 - 0; Guinea v Lesotho
3 - 1, 1 - 1; Tunisia v Nigeria 2 - 0, 0 - 2 (Nigeria won 4 - 3 on penalties);
Cameroon v Malawi 3 - 0, 1 - 1; Kenya v Tanzania 3 - 1, 0 - 5; Zaire
v Mozambique 5 - 2, 2 - 1; Niger v Somalia 0 - 0, 1 - 1; Egypt v Ghana
(withdrew); Madagascar v Uganda (withdrew)

2nd Round
Cameroon v Zimbabwe 2 - 0, 0 - 1; Sudan v Algeria 1 - 1, 0 - 2;
Madagascar v Zaire 1 - 1, 2 - 3; Morocco v Zambia 2 - 0, 0 - 2 (Morocco
won 5 - 4 on penalties); Nigeria v Tanzania 1 - 1, 2 - 0; Liberia v Guinea
0 - 0, 0 - 1; Niger v Togo 0 - 1, 2 - 1; Egypt v Libya (withdrew)

3rd Round
Guinea v Nigeria 1 - 1, 0 - 1; Zaire v Cameroon 1 - 0, 1 - 6; Morocco
v Egypt 1 - 0, 0 - 0; Algeria v Niger 4 - 0, 0 - 1

4th Round
Nigeria v Algeria 0 - 2, 1 - 2; Morocco v Cameroon 0 - 2, 1 - 2
Algeria and Cameroon qualified

Asia/Oceania

Group 1 (Australia, Fiji, Indonesia, New Zealand, Taiwan)
New Zealand v Australia 3 - 3; Fiji v New Zealand 0 - 4; Taiwan v New
Zealand 0 - 0; Indonesia v New Zealand 0 - 2; Australia v New Zealand
0 - 2; Australia v Indonesia 2 - 0; New Zealand v Indonesia 5 - 0; New
Zealand v Taiwan 2 - 0; Fiji v Indonesia 0 - 0; Fiji v Taiwan 2 - 1; Australia
v Taiwan 3 - 2; Indonesia v Taiwan 1 - 0; Taiwan v Indonesia 2 - 0; Fiji
v Australia 1 - 4; Taiwan v Fiji 0 - 0; Indonesia v Fiji 3 - 3; Australia v Fiji
10 - 0; New Zealand v Fiji 13 - 0; Indonesia v Australia 1 - 0; Taiwan
v Australia 0 - 0

	P	W	D	L	F	A	Pts
New Zealand	8	6	2	0	31	3	14
Australia	3	4	2	2	22	9	10
Indonesia	8	2	2	4	5	14	6
Taiwan	8	1	3	4	5	8	5
Fiji	8	1	3	4	6	35	5

Group 2 (Saudi Arabia, Bahrain, Iraq, Qatar, Syria)
(In Saudi Arabia)
Qatar v Iraq 0 - 1; Syria v Bahrain 0 - 1; Iraq v Saudi Arabia 0 - 1; Qatar
v Bahrain 3 - 0; Syria v Saudi Arabia 0 - 2; Iraq v Bahrain 2 - 0; Qatar v Syria
2 - 1; Bahrain v Saudi Arabia 0 - 1; Iraq v Syria 2 - 1; Qatar v Saudi Arabia
0 - 1

	P	W	D	L	F	A	Pts
Saudi Arabia	4	4	0	0	5	0	8
Iraq	4	3	0	1	5	2	6
Qatar	4	2	0	2	5	3	4
Bahrain	4	1	0	3	1	6	2
Syria	4	0	0	4	2	7	0

Group 3 (South Korea, Iran (withdrew), Kuwait, Malaysia, Thailand)
(In Kuwait)
Malaysia v South Korea 1 - 2; Kuwait v Thailand 6 - 0; South Korea
v Thailand 5 - 1; Kuwait v Malaysia 4 - 0; Malaysia v Thailand 2 - 2; Kuwait
v South Korea 2 - 0

	P	W	D	L	F	A	Pts
Kuwait	3	3	0	0	12	0	6
South Korea	3	2	0	1	7	4	4
Malaysia	3	0	1	2	3	8	1
Thailand	3	0	1	2	3	13	1

Group 4 (China, North Korea, Hong Kong, Japan, Macao, Singapore)
(In Hong Kong)

Preliminary Round
Hong Kong v China 0 - 1; North Korea v Macao 3 - 0;
Singapore v Japan 0 - 1

Sub-Group 4A
China v Macao 3 - 0; China v Japan 1 - 0; Japan v Macao 3 - 0

Sub-Group 4B
Hong Kong v Singapore 1 - 1; Singapore v North Korea 0 - 1; Hong Kong
v North Korea 2 - 2

Semi-finals
North Korea v Japan 1 - 0; China v Hong Kong 0 - 0 (China won 5 - 4 on
penalties)

Final
China v North Korea 4 - 2

Final round
China v New Zealand 0 - 0; New Zealand v China 1 - 0; New Zealand
v Kuwait 1 - 2; China v Kuwait 3 - 0; Saudi Arabia v Kuwait 0 - 1; Saudi
Arabia v China 2 - 4; China v Saudi Arabia 2 - 0; New Zealand v Saudi
Arabia 2 - 2; Kuwait v China 1 - 0; Kuwait v Saudi Arabia 2 - 0; Kuwait
v New Zealand 2 - 2; Saudi Arabia v New Zealand 0 - 5

	P	W	D	L	F	A	Pts
Kuwait	6	4	1	1	8	6	9
New Zealand	6	2	3	1	11	6	7
China	6	3	1	2	9	4	7
Saudi Arabia	6	0	1	5	4	16	1

Play-off: New Zealand v China 2 - 1 (in Singapore)
Kuwait and New Zealand qualified

Concacaf

Group 1 (Caribbean)
Preliminary Round
Guyana v Grenada 5 - 2, 3 - 2

Sub-Group 1A (Cuba, Surinam, Guyana)
Cuba v Surinam 3 - 0; Surinam v Cuba 0 - 0; Guyana v Surinam 0 - 1;
Surinam v Guyana 4 - 0; Cuba v Guyana 1 - 0; Guyana v Cuba 0 - 3

	P	W	D	L	F	A	Pts
Cuba	4	3	1	0	7	0	7
Surinam	4	2	1	1	5	3	5
Guyana	4	0	0	4	0	9	0

Sub-Group 1B (Haiti, Trinidad and Tobago, Netherlands Antilles)
Haiti v Trinidad and Tobago 2 - 0; Trinidad and Tobago v Haiti 1 - 0; Haiti
v Netherlands Antilles 1 - 0; Trinidad and Tobago v Netherlands Antilles
0 - 0; Netherlands Antilles v Trinidad and Tobago 0 - 0; Netherlands
Antilles v Haiti 1 - 1

	P	W	D	L	F	A	Pts
Haiti	4	2	1	1	4	2	5
T'dad & Tobago	4	1	2	1	1	2	4
N'lands Antilles	4	0	3	1	1	2	3

Group 2 (North) (Mexico, Canada, USA)

Canada v Mexico 1 - 1; USA v Canada 0 - 0; Canada v USA 2 - 1; Mexico v USA 5 - 1; Mexico v Canada 1 - 1; USA v Mexico 2 - 1

	P	W	D	L	F	A	Pts
Canada	4	1	3	0	4	3	5
Mexico	4	1	2	1	8	5	4
USA	4	1	1	2	4	8	3

Group 3 (Central) (Costa Rica, El Salvador, Guatemala, Honduras, Panama)

Panama v Guatemala 0 - 2; Panama v Honduras 0 - 2; Panama v Costa Rica 1 - 1; Panama v El Salvador 1 - 3; Costa Rica v Honduras 2 - 3; El Salvador v Panama 4 - 1; Guatemala v Costa Rica 0 - 0; Honduras v Guatemala 0 - 0; El Salvador v Costa Rica (awarded 2 - 0 to El Salvador when Costa Rica refused to play there for security reasons); Costa Rica v Panama 2 - 0; Guatemala v El Salvador 0 - 0; Guatemala v Panama 5 - 0; Honduras v Costa Rica 1 - 1; El Salvador v Honduras 2 - 1; Costa Rica v Guatemala 0 - 3; Honduras v El Salvador 2 - 0; Guatemala v Honduras 0 - 1; Costa Rica v El Salvador 0 - 0; Honduras v Panama 5 - 0; El Salvador v Guatemala 1 - 0

	P	W	D	L	F	A	Pts
Honduras	8	5	2	1	15	5	12
El Salvador	8	5	2	1	12	5	12
Guatemala	8	3	3	2	10	2	9
Costa Rica	8	1	4	3	6	10	6
Panama	8	0	1	7	3	24	1

Final round

(In Honduras)

Mexico v Cuba 4 - 0; Canada v El Salvador 1 - 0; Honduras v Haiti 4 - 0; Haiti v Canada 1 - 1; Mexico v El Salvador 0 - 1; Honduras v Cuba 2 - 0; El Salvador v Cuba 0 - 0; Mexico v Haiti 1 - 1; Honduras v Canada 2 - 1; Haiti v Cuba 0 - 2; Mexico v Canada 1 - 1; Honduras v El Salvador 0 - 0; Haiti v El Salvador 0 - 1; Cuba v Canada 2 - 2; Honduras v Mexico 0 - 0

	P	W	D	L	F	A	Pts
Honduras	5	3	2	0	8	1	8
El Salvador	5	2	2	1	2	1	6
Mexico	5	1	3	1	6	3	5
Canada	5	1	3	1	6	6	5
Cuba	5	1	2	2	4	8	4
Haiti	5	0	2	3	2	9	2

Honduras and El Salvador Qualified

Final Tournament SPAIN
GROUP 1

14.6.82 Italy (0) 0, Poland (0) 0 VIGO
Italy: Zoff, Gentile, Scirea, Collovati, Cabrini, Marini, Antognoni, Tardelli, Conti, Rossi, Graziani
Poland: Mlynarczyk, Jalocha, Majewski, Zmuda, Janas, Buncol, Lato, Boniek, Matysik, Iwan (Kusto), Smolarek
Referee: Vautrot (France)

15.6.82 Peru (0) 0, Cameroon (0) 0 LA CORUNA
Peru: Quiroga, Duarte, Salguero, Diaz, Olaechea, Uribe, Cueto, Velasquez, Leguia (La Rosa), Cubillas (Barbadillo), Oblitas
Cameroon: N'Kono, M'Bom, Aoudou, Onana, Kaham, Abega, M'Bida, Kunde, Milla (Tokoto), N'Djeya, N'Guea (Bakohen)
Referee: Wohrer (Austria)

18.6.82 Italy (1) 1, Peru (0) 1 VIGO
Italy: Zoff, Cabrini, Collovati, Gentile, Scirea, Antognoni, Marini, Tardelli, Conti (1), Graziani, Rossi (Causio)
Peru: Quiroga, Duarte, Diaz (1), Salguero, Olaechea, Cueto, Velasquez (La Rosa), Cubillas, Uribe, Oblitas, Barbadillo (Leguia)
Referee: Eschweiler (West Germany)

19.6.82 Poland (0) 0, Cameroon (0) 0 LA CORUNA
Poland: Mlynarczyk, Majewski, Janas, Zmuda, Jalocha, Lato, Buncol, Boniek, Iwan (Szarmach), Palasz (Kusto), Smolarek
Cameroon: N'Kono, Kaham, Onana, N'Djeya, M'Bom, Aoudou, Abega, Kunde, M'Bida, Milla, N'Guea (Tokoto)
Referee: Ponnet (Belgium)

22.6.82 Poland (0) 5, Peru (0) 1 LA CORUNA
Poland: Mlynarczyk, Majewski, Janas, Zmuda, Jalocha (Dziuba), Buncol (1), Matysik, Kupcewiez, Lato (1), Boniek (1), Smolarek (1) (Ciolek [1])
Peru: Quiroga, Duarte, Diaz, Salguero, Olaechea, Cubillas (Uribe), Velasquez, Cueto, Leguia, La Rosa (1), Oblitas (Barbadillo)
Referee: Rubio (Mexico)

23.6.82 Italy (0) 1, Cameroon (0) 1 VIGO
Italy: Zoff, Gentile, Collovati, Scirea, Cabrini, Oriali, Tardelli, Antognoni, Conti, Rossi, Graziani (1)
Cameroon: N'Kono, Kaham, N'Djeya, Onana, M'Bom, Aoudou, Kunde, M'Bida (1), Abega, Milla, Tokoto
Referee: Dotschev (Bulgaria)

	P	W	D	L	F	A	Pts
Poland	3	1	2	0	5	1	4
Italy	3	0	3	0	2	2	3
Cameroon	3	0	3	0	1	1	3
Peru	3	0	2	1	2	6	2

GROUP 2

16.6.82 Algeria (0) 2, West Germany (0) 1 GIJON
Algeria: Cerbah, Guendouz, Kourichi, Merzekane, Mansouri, Belloumi (1), Dhaleb, Fergani, Madjer (1) (Larbes), Zidane (Bensaoula), Assad
West Germany: Schumacher, Kaltz, Stielike, Forster K H, Briegel, Breitner, Magath (Fischer), Dremmler, Rummenigge (1), Hrubesch, Littbarski
Referee: Labo (Peru)

17.6.82 Austria (1) 1, Chile (0) 0 OVIEDO
Austria; Koncilia, Krauss, Obermayer, Pezzey, Degeorgi (Baumeister), Hattenberger, Hintermaier, Weber (Jurtin), Prohaska, Krankl, Schachner (1)
Chile: Osben, Garrido, Figueroa, Valenzuela, Bigorra, Bonvallet, Dubo, Neira (Manuel Rojas), Moscoaso (Gamboa), Yanez, Caszely
Referee: Cardellino (Uruguay)

20.6.82 West Germany (1) 4, Chile (0) 1 GIJON
West Germany: Schumacher, Kaltz, Stielike, Forster K H, Briegel, Dremmler, Breitner (Matthaus), Magath, Littbarski (Reinders [1]), Hrubesch, Rummenigge (3)
Chile: Osben, Garrido, Figueroa, Valenzuela, Bigorra, Dubo, Bonvallet, Soto (Letelier), Moscoso (1), Yanez, Gamboa (Neira)
Referee: Galler (Switzerland)

21.6.82 Algeria (0) 0, Austria (0) 2 OVIEDO
Algeria: Cerbah, Guendouz, Kourichi, Marzekane, Mansouri, Belloumi (Bensaoula), Dhaleb (Tiemcani), Fergani, Madjer, Zidane, Assad
Austria: Koncilia, Krauss, Obermayer, Degeorgi, Pezzey, Hattenberger, Hintermaier, Baumeister (Welzl), Prohaska (Weber), Krankl (1), Schachner (1)
Referee: Boscovic (Austria)

24.6.82 Algeria (3) 3, Chile (0) 2 OVIEDO
Algeria: Cerbah, Kourichi, Marzekane, Guendouz, Larbes, Mansouri (Dhaleb), Fergani, Assad (2), Bensaoula (1), Bourebbou (Yahi), Madjer
Chile: Osben, Galindo, Valenzuela, Figueroa, Bigorra, Bonvallet (Soto), Dubo, Neira (1 pen), Yanez, Caszely (Letelier [1]), Moscoso
Referee: Mendez (Guatemala)

25.6.82 West Germany (1) 1, Austria (0) 0 GIJON
West Germany: Schumacher, Kaltz, Stielike, Forster K H, Briegel, Dremmler, Breitner, Magath, Littbarski, Hrubesch (1) (Fischer), Rummenigge (Matthaus)
Austria: Koncilia, Krauss, Pezzey, Obermayer, Degeorgi, Hattenberger, Prohaska, Hintermaier, Weber, Schachner, Krankl
Referee: Valentine (Scotland)

	P	W	D	L	F	A	Pts
West Germany	3	2	0	1	6	3	4
Austria	3	2	0	1	3	1	4
Algeria	3	2	0	1	5	5	4
Chile	3	0	0	3	3	8	0

GROUP 3

13.6.82 Argentina (0) 0, Belgium (0) 1 BARCELONA
Argentina: Fillol, Olguin, Galvan, Passarella, Tarantini, Ardiles, Gallego, Maradona, Bertoni, Diaz (Valdano), Kempes
Belgium: Pfaff, Gerets, Millechamps L, de Schrijver, Baecke, Coeck, Vercauteren, Vandersmissen, Czerniatynski, Van den Bergh (1), Ceulemans
Referee: Christov (Czechoslovakia)

15.6.82 Hungary (3) 10, El Salvador (0) 1 ELCHE
Hungary: Meszaros, Martos, Balint, Toth (1), Garaba, Muller (Szentes [1]), Nyilasi (2), Sallai, Fazekas (2),Torocsik (Kiss [3]), Poloskei (1)
El Salvador: Mora, Castillo, Jovel, Rodriguez, Recinos, Rugamas (Zapata [1]), Ventura, Huezo, Hernandez F, Gonzalez, Rivas
Referee: Al-Doy (Bahrain)

18.6.82 Argentina (2) 4, Hungary (0) 1 ALICANTE
Argentina: Fillol, Olguin, Galvan, Passarella, Tarantini (Barbas), Ardiles (1), Gallego, Maradona (2), Bertoni (1), Valdano (Calderon), Kempes
Hungary: Meszaros, Martos (Fazekas),Balint, Toth, Varga, Garaba, Nyilasi, Sallai, Rab, Kiss (Szentes), Poloskei (1)
Referee: Lacarne (Algeria)

19.6.82 Belgium (1) 1, El Salvador (0) 0 ELCHE
Belgium: Pfaff, Gerets, Meeuws, Baecke, Millecamps L, Vandersmissen (Van der Elst), Coeck (1), Vercauteren, Ceulemans (Van Moer), Van den Bergh, Czerniatynski
El Salvador: Mora, Osorto (Diaz), Jovel, Rodriguez, Recinos, Fagoaga, Ventura, Huezo, Zapata, Gonzalez, Rivas
Referee: Moffat (Northern Ireland)

22.6.82 Belgium (0) 1, Hungary (1) 1 ELCHE
Belgium: Pfaff, Gerets (Plessers), Millecamps L, Meeuws, Baecke, Coeck, Vercauteren, Vandersmissen (Van Moer), Czerniatynski (1), Van den Bergh, Ceulemans
Hungary: Meszaros, Martos, Kerekes (Sallai), Garaba, Varga (1), Nyilasi, Muller, Fazekas, Torocsik, Kiss (Csongradi), Poloskei
Referee: White (England)

23.6.82 Argentina (1) 2, El Salvador (0) 0 ALICANTE
Argentina: Fillol, Olguin, Galvan, Passarella (1 pen), Tarantini, Ardiles, Gallego, Kempes, Bertoni (1) (Diaz), Maradona, Calderon (Santamaria)
El Salvador: Mora, Osorto (Arevalo), Jovel, Rodriguez, Rugamas, Fagoaga, Ventura (Alfaro), Huezo, Zapata, Gonzalez, Rivas
Referee: Barrancos (Bolivia)

	P	W	D	L	F	A	Pts
Belgium	3	2	1	0	3	1	5
Argentina	3	2	0	1	6	2	4
Hungary	3	1	1	1	12	6	3
El Salvador	3	0	0	3	1	13	0

GROUP 4

16.6.82 England (1) 3, France (1) 1 BILBAO
England: Shilton, Mills, Sansom (Neal), Thompson, Butcher, Robson (2), Coppell, Wilkins, Mariner (1), Francis, Rix
France: Ettori, Battiston, Bossis, Tresor, Lopez, Larios (Tigana), Girard, Giresse, Rocheteau (Six), Platini, Soler (1)
Referee: Garrido (Portugal)

17.6.82 Czechoslovakia (1) 1, Kuwait (0) 1 VALLADOLID
Czechoslovakia: Hruska, Barmos, Jurkemik, Fiala, Kukucka, Panenka (1 pen), Berger, Kriz (Bicovsky), Janecka (Petrzela), Nehoda, Vizek
Kuwait: Al Tarabulsi, Naeem Saed, Mayoof, Mahboub, Waleed Jasem, Al Buloushi, Saeed Al Houti, Karam (Fathi Kameel), Al Dakheel (1), Jasem Yacoub, Al Anbari
Referee: Dwomoha (Ghana)

20.6.82 England (0) 2, Czechoslovakia (0) 0 BILBAO
England: Shilton, Mills, Thompson, Butcher, Sansom, Coppell, Robson (Hoddle), Wilkins, Francis (1), Mariner, Rix
Czechoslovakia: Seman (Stromsik), Barmos, Fiala, Radimec, Vojacek, Jurkemik, Chaloupka, Vizek, Berger, Janecka (Masny), Nehodaf
Referee: Corver (Holland)

21.6.82 France (2) 4, Kuwait (0) 1 VALLADOLID
France: Ettori, Amoros, Tresor, Janvion, Bossis (1), Giresse, Platini (1) (Girard), Genghini (1), Soler, Lacombe, Six (1)
Kuwait: Al Tarabulsi, Naeem Saed, Mayoof, Mahboub, Waleed Jasem (Al Shemmari), Al Buloushi (1), Saed Al Houti, Karam (Fathi Kameel), Al Dakheel, Jasem Yacoub, Al Ambari
Referee: Stupar (USSR)

24.6.82 France (0) 1, Czechoslovakia (0) 1 VALLADOLID
France: Ettori, Amoros, Tresor, Janvion, Bossis, Giresse, Platini, Genghini, Soler (Girard), Lacombe (Couriol), Six (1)
Czechoslovakia: Stromsik, Barmos, Fiala, Stambacher, Vojacek, Jurkemik, Kriz (Masny), Bicovsky, Vizek, Janecka (Panenka [1 pen]), Nehoda
Referee: Casarin (Italy)

25.6.82 England (1) 1, Kuwait (0) 0 BILBAO
England: Shilton, Neal, Thompson, Foster, Mills, Coppell, Hoddle, Wilkins, Rix, Mariner, Francis (1)
Kuwait: Al Tarabulsi, Naeem Saed, Mahboub, Mayoof, Waleed Jasem (Al Shemmari), Saed Al Houti, Al Buloushi, Al Suwayed, Fathi Kameel, Al Dakheel, Al Anbari
Referee: Aristizabal (Colombia)

	P	W	D	L	F	A	Pts
England	3	3	0	0	6	1	6
France	3	1	1	1	6	5	3
Czechoslovakia	3	0	2	1	2	4	2
Kuwait	3	0	1	2	2	6	1

GROUP 5

16.6.82 Spain (0) 1, Honduras (1) 1 VALENCIA
Spain: Arconada, Gordillo, Camacho, Alonso, Alesanco, Tendillo (Saura), Joaquin (Sanchez), Satrustegui, Zamora, Lopez Ufarte (1 pen)
Honduras: Arzu, Gutierrez, Costly, Villegas, Bulnes, Zelaya (1), Gilberto, Maradiaga, Norales (Caballero), Betancourt, Figueroa
Referee: Ithurralde (Argentina)

17.6.82 Northern Ireland (0) 0, Yugoslavia (0) 0 ZARAGOZA
Northern Ireland: Jennings, Nicholl J, Nicholl C, McClelland, Donaghy, McIlroy, O'Neill M, McCreery, Armstrong, Hamilton, Whiteside
Yugoslavia: Pantelic, Gudelj, Zajec, Stojkovic, Petrovic, Sljivo, Zlatko Vujovic, Susic, Jovanovic, Hrstic, Surjak
Referee: Fredriksson (Sweden)

20.6.82 Spain (1) 2, Yugoslavia (1) 1 VALENCIA
Spain: Arconada, Camacho, Tendillo, Alesanco, Gordillo, Alonso, Sanchez (Saura [1]), Zamora, Juanito (1 pen), Satrustegui (Quini), Lopez Ufarte
Yugoslavia: Pantelic, Krmpotic, Zajec, Stojkovic, Jovanovic (Halilhodzic), Gudelj (1), Petrovic, Sljivo, Zlatko Vujovic (Sestic), Surjak, Susic
Referee: Lund-Sorensen (Denmark)

21.6.82 Honduras (0) 1, Northern Ireland (1) 1 ZARAGOZA
Honduras: Arzu, Gutierrez, Villegas, Cruz J L, Costly, Maradiaga, Gilberto, Zelaya, Norales (Laing [1]), Betancourt, Figueroa
Northern Ireland: Jennings, Nicholl J, Nicholl C, McClelland, Donaghy, O'Neill M (Healy), McCreery, McIlroy, Whiteside (Brotherston), Armstrong (1), Hamilton
Referee: Chan Tam Sun (Hong Kong)

24.6.82 Honduras (0) 0, Yugoslavia (0) 1 ZARAGOZA
Honduras: Arzu, Droumond, Villegas, Costly, Bulnes, Zelaya, Gilberto, Maradiaga, Cruz J (Laing), Betancourt, Figueroa
Yugoslavia: Pantelic, Krmpotic, Stojkovic, Zajec, Jovanovic (Halilhodzic), Sljivo, Gudelj, Surjak, Zlatko Vujovic (Sestic), Susic, Petrovic (1 pen)
Referee: Castro (Chile)

25.6.82 Northern Ireland (0) 1, Spain (0) 0 VALENCIA
Northern Ireland: Jennings, Nicholl J, Nicholl C, McClelland, Donaghy, O'Neill M, McCreery, McIlroy (Cassidy), Armstrong (1), Hamilton, Whiteside (Nelson)
Spain: Arconada, Camacho, Tendillo, Alesanco, Gordillo, Sanchez, Alonso, Saura, Juanito, Satrustegui (Quini), Lopez Ufarte (Gallego)
Referee: Ortiz (Paraguay)

	P	W	D	L	F	A	Pts
Northern Ireland	3	1	2	0	2	1	4
Spain	3	1	1	1	3	3	3
Yugoslavia	3	1	1	1	2	2	3
Honduras	3	0	2	1	2	3	2

GROUP 6

14.6.82 Brazil (0) 2, USSR (1) 1 SEVILLE
Brazil: Valdir Peres, Leandro, Oscar, Luizinho, Junior, Socrates (1), Serginho, Zico, Eder (1), Falcao, Dirceu (Paulo Isidoro)
USSR: Dasayev, Sulakvelidze, Chivadze, Baltacha, Demyanenko, Shengelia (Andreyev), Bessonov, Gavrilov (Susloparov), Blokhin, Bal (1), Daraselia
Referee: Lamo Castillo (Spain)

15.6.82 Scotland (3) 5, New Zealand (0) 2 MALAGA
Scotland: Rough, McGrain, Gray F, Hansen, Evans, Souness, Strachan (Narey), Dalglish (1), Wark (2), Brazil (Archibald [1]), Robertson (1)
New Zealand: Van Hattum, Elrick, Hill, Malcolmson (Cole), Almond (Herbert), Sumner (1), Mackay, Cresswell, Boath, Rufer W, Wooddin (1)
Referee: El Ghoul (Libya)

18.6.82 Brazil (1) 4, Scotland (1) 1 SEVILLE
Brazil: Valdir Peres, Leandro, Oscar (1), Luizinho, Junior, Cerezo, Falcao (1), Socrates, Serginho (Paulo Isidoro), Zico (1), Eder (1)
Scotland: Rough, Narey (1), Gray F, Souness, Hansen, Miller, Strachan (Dalglish), Hartford (McLeish), Archibald, Wark, Robertson
Referee: Siles (Costa Rica)

19.6.82 USSR (1) 3, New Zealand (0) 0 MALAGA
USSR: Dasayev, Sulakvelidze, Chivadze, Baltacha, Demyanenko (1), Shengelia, Bessonov, Bal, Daraselia (Oganesian), Gavrilov (1) (Rodionov), Blokhin (1)
New Zealand: Van Hattum, Dods, Herbert, Elrick, Boath, Cole, Sumner, Mackay, Cresswell, Rufer W, Wooddin
Referee: El Ghoul (Libya)

22.6.82 Scotland (1) 2, USSR (0) 2 MALAGA
Scotland: Rough, Narey, Gray F, Souness (1), Hansen, Miller, Strachan (McGrain), Archibald, Jordan (1) (Brazil), Wark, Robertson
USSR: Dasayev, Sulakvelidze, Chivadze (1), Baltacha, Demyanenko, Borovsky, Shengelia (1) (Andreyev), Bessonov, Gavrilov, Bal, Blokhin
Referee: Rainea (Rumania)

23.6.82 Brazil (2) 4, New Zealand (0) 0 SEVILLE
Brazil: Valdir Peres, Leandro, Oscar (Edinho), Luizinho, Junior, Cerezo, Socrates, Zico (2), Falcao (1), Serginho (1) (Paulo Isidoro), Eder
New Zealand: Van Hattum, Dods, Herbert, Elrick, Boath, Sumner, Mackay, Cresswell (Turner B), Almond, Rufer W (Cole), Wooddin
Referee: Matovinovic (Yugoslavia)

	P	W	D	L	F	A	Pts
Brazil	3	3	0	0	10	2	6
USSR	3	1	1	1	6	4	3
Scotland	3	1	1	1	8	8	3
New Zealand	3	0	0	3	2	12	0

Second round
GROUP A

28.6.82 Poland (2) 3, Belgium (0) 0 BARCELONA
Poland: Mlynarczyk, Dziuba, Zmuda, Janas, Majewski, Kupcewicz (Ciolek), Buncol, Matysik, Lato, Boniek (3), Smolarek
Belgium: Custers, Renquin, Millecamps L, Meeuws, Plessers (Baecke), Van Moer (Van der Elst), Coeck, Vercauteren, Czerniatynski, Van den Bergh, Ceulemans
Referee: Siles (Costa Rica)

1.7.82 Belgium (0) 0, USSR (0) 1 BARCELONA
Belgium: Munaron, Renquin, Millecamps L, Meeuws, de Schrijver (Millecamps M), Verheyen, Coeck, Vercauteren, Vandersmissen (Czerniatynski), Van den Bergh, Ceulemans
USSR: Dasayev, Borovsky, Chivadze, Baltacha, Demyanenko, Bal (Daraselia), Oganesian (1), Bessonov, Shengelia (Rodionov), Gavrilov, Blokhin
Referee: Vautrot (France)

4.7.82 Poland (0) 0, USSR (0) 0 BARCELONA
Poland: Mlynarczyk, Dziuba, Zmuda, Janas, Majewski, Kupcewicz (Ciolek), Buncol, Matysik, Lato, Boniek, Smolarek
USSR: Dasayev, Sulakvelidze, Chivadze, Baltacha, Demyanenko, Borovsky, Oganesian, Bessonov, Shengelia (Andreyev), Gavrilov (Daraselia), Blokhin
Referee: Valentine (Scotland)

	P	W	D	L	F	A	Pts
Poland	2	1	1	0	3	0	3
USSR	2	1	1	0	1	0	3
Belgium	2	0	0	2	0	4	0

GROUP B

29.6.82 West Germany (0) 0, England (0) 0 MADRID
West Germany: Schumacher, Kaltz, Forster K H, Stielike, Forster B, Muller (Fischer), Breitner, Dremmler, Briegel, Rummenigge, Reinders (Littbarski)
England: Shilton, Mills, Thompson, Butcher, Sansom, Coppell, Wilkins, Robson, Rix, Francis (Woodcock), Mariner
Referee: Coelho (Brazil)

2.7.82 Spain (0) 1, West Germany (0) 2 MADRID
Spain: Arconada, Camacho, Gordillo, Alonso, Tendillo, Alesanco, Juanito (Lopez Ufarte), Zamora (1), Urquiaga, Santillana, Quini (Sanchez)
West Germany: Schumacher, Kaltz, Forster K H, Stielike, Forster B, Breitner, Briegel, Dremmler, Littbarski (1), Fischer (1), Rummenigge (Reinders)
Referee: Casarin (Italy)

5.7.82 England (0) 0, Spain (0) 0 MADRID
England: Shilton, Mills, Thompson, Butcher, Sansom, Wilkins, Robson, Rix (Brooking), Francis, Mariner, Woodcock (Keegan)
Spain: Arconada, Camacho, Gordillo, Alonso, Tendillo (Macedo), Alesanco, Satrustegui, Zamora, Urquiaga, Saura (Uralde), Santillana
Referee: Ponnet (Belgium)

	P	W	D	L	F	A	Pts
West Germany	2	1	1	0	2	1	3
England	2	0	2	0	0	0	2
Spain	2	0	1	1	1	2	1

GROUP C

29.6.82 Italy (0) 2, Argentina (0) 1 BARCELONA
Italy: Zoff, Gentile, Collovati, Scirea, Cabrini (1), Oriali (Marini), Tardelli (1), Antognoni, Conti, Rossi (Altobelli), Graziani
Argentina: Fillol, Olguin, Passarella (1), Galvan, Tarantini, Ardiles, Gallego, Maradona, Bertoni, Diaz (Calderon), Kempes (Valencia)
Referee: Rainea (Rumania)

2.7.82 Brazil (1) 3, Argentina (0) 1 BARCELONA
Brazil: Valdir Peres, Leandro (Edevaldo), Oscar, Luizinho, Junior (1), Cerezo, Falcao, Socrates, Serginho (1), Zico (1) (Batista), Eder
Argentina: Fillol, Olguin, Barbas, Passarella, Tarantini, Ardiles, Galvan, Maradona, Bertoni (Santamaria), Calderon, Kempes (Diaz [1])
Referee: Rubio (Mexico)

5.7.82 Italy (2) 3, Brazil (1) 2 BARCELONA
Italy: Zoff, Collovati (Bergomi), Gentile, Scirea, Cabrini, Oriali, Antognoni, Tardelli (Marini), Conti, Graziani, Rossi (3)
Brazil: Valdir Peres, Leandro, Oscar, Luizinho, Junior, Cerezo, Falcao (1), Socrates (1), Zico, Serginho (Paulo Isidoro), Eder
Referee: Klein (Israel)

	P	W	D	L	F	A	Pts
Italy	2	2	0	0	5	3	4
Brazil	2	1	0	1	5	4	2
Argentina	2	0	0	2	2	5	0

GROUP D

28.6.82 France (1) 1, Austria (0) 0 MADRID
France: Ettori, Battiston, Janvion, Tresor, Bossis, Giresse, Genghini (1) (Girard), Tigana, Soler, Lacombe (Rocheteau), Six
Austria: Koncilia, Krauss, Obermayer, Pezzey, Degeorgi (Baumeister), Hattenberger, Hintermaier, Jara (Welzl), Schachner, Prohaska, Krankl
Referee: Palotai (Hungary)

1.7.82 Northern Ireland (1) 2, Austria (0) 2 MADRID
Northern Ireland: Platt, Nicholl J, Nicholl C, McClelland, Nelson, McCreery, O'Neill M, McIlroy, Armstrong, Hamilton (2), Whiteside (Brotherston)
Austria: Koncilia, Krauss, Obermayer, Pezzey (1), Schachner, Prohaska, Pichler, Hagmayr (Welzl), Baumeister, Pregesbauer (Hintermaier [1]), Jurtin
Referee: Prokop (East Germany)

4.7.82 Northern Ireland (0) 1, France (1) 4 MADRID
Northern Ireland: Jennings, Nicholl J, Nicholl C, McClelland, Donaghy, McIlroy, McCreery (O'Neill J), O'Neill M, Armstrong (1), Hamilton, Whiteside
France: Ettori, Amoros, Janvion, Tresor, Bossis, Giresse (2), Genghini, Tigana, Platini, Soler (Six), Rocheteau (2) (Couriol)
Referee: Jarguz (Poland)

	P	W	D	L	F	A	Pts
France	2	2	0	0	5	1	4
Austria	2	0	1	1	2	3	1
Northern Ireland	2	0	1	1	3	6	1

SEMI FINALS
8.7.82 Poland (0) 0, Italy (1) 2 BARCELONA
Poland: Mlynarczyk, Dziuba, Zmuda, Janas, Majewski, Kupcewicz, Buncol, Matysik, Lato, Ciolek (Palasz), Smolarek (Kusto)
Italy: Zoff, Bergomi, Collovati, Scirea, Cabrini, Oriali, Antognoni (Marini), Tardelli, Conti, Rossi (2), Graziani (Altobelli)
Referee: Cardellino (Uruguay)

8.7.82 West Germany (1) 3, France (1) 3 (aet, 1 -1 at 90 mins, West Germany won 5 - 4 on penalties) SEVILLE
West Germany: Schumacher, Kaltz, Forster K H, Stielike, Forster B, Briegel (Rummenigge [1]), Dremmler, Breitner, Littbarski (1), Fischer (1), Magath (Hrubesch)
France: Ettori, Amoros, Janvion, Tresor (1), Bossis, Genghini (Battiston) (Lopez), Platini (1 pen), Giresse (1), Rocheteau, Six, Tigana
Referee: Corver (Holland)

Match for third place
10.7.82 France (1) 2, Poland (2) 3 ALICANTE
France: Castaneda, Amoros, Mahut, Tresor, Janvion (Lopez), Tigana (Six), Girard (1), Larios, Couriol (1), Soler, Bellone
Poland: Mlynarczyk, Dziuba, Janas, Zmuda, Majewski (1), Matysik (Wojcicki), Kupcewicz (1), Buncol, Lato, Szarmach (1), Boniek
Referee: Garrido (Portugal)

FINAL
11.7.82 West Germany (0) 1, Italy (0) 3 MADRID
West Germany: Schumacher, Kaltz, Forster K H, Stielike, Forster B, Breitner (1), Dremmler (Hrubesch), Littbarski, Briegel, Fischer, Rummenigge (Muller)
Italy: Zoff, Bergomi, Cabrini, Collovati, Scirea, Gentile, Oriali, Tardelli (1), Conti, Graziani (Altobelli [1]) (Causio), Rossi (1)
Referee: Arnaldo Coelho (Brazil)

MEXICO
1986

To the English mind, the lasting memory of Mexico was of Diego Maradona. Alas, it was not as the genuinely outstanding individual of the tournament, but simply because he propelled the ball with his hand for Argentina's opening goal against England in the quarter-finals. Years afterwards, the infamy of this action was still being ridiculed in two separate advertisements on commercial television.

Commercial considerations had dominated the competition itself. To satisfy TV scheduling, matches were played in the hottest part of the day, with no time added on for stoppages. In one venue, Monterrey, in appalling conditions of heat and humidity, only nine goals were scored in the six group games played there.

Despite these restraints, the generally low goalscoring and the unsatisfactory matter of deciding games on penalty kicks, it was widely regarded as the best World Cup since the finals were previously held in Mexico 16 years earlier. Though France, Brazil, Denmark and the USSR produced floods of attacking fluency, they were eventually left flawed. Ultimately it was the Maradona-inspired aristry of Argentina which grappled with the doggedly determined West Germans.

Arguably the finest match was the quarter-final between France and Brazil; the best of the old and new worlds, but both linked with that inimitable Latin style of skill interwoven with improvisation. It was a travesty that it had to be decided on penalties.

Denmark took maximum points from their matches in Group E, including this 2 - 0 victory over West Germany. Danish striker Preben Elkjaer tussles for possession with Karl-Heinz Forster (white shirt). (ALLSPORT)

(Above) Luis Brown (extreme right) heads Argentina into the lead in the 1986 World Cup final. Brown gallantly played out the final stages of the game despite suffering a dislocated shoulder.
(ALLSPORT)

Gary Lineker (10), about to complete a memorable hat-trick for England against Poland in Monterrey. A 3-0 win saw England through to the second round.
(ALLSPORT)

French skipper Platini in action against Canada. Having played some of the best football of the tournament, France again went out at the semi-final stage. (ALLSPORT)

It had needed two weeks and 36 matches to eliminate just eight of the 24 finalists. England began disastrously, their 4-3-3 formation fortunately giving way, when injury and suspension hit Bryan Robson and Ray Wilkins respectively, to a 4-4-2 system which shot Gary Lineker to prominence with a hat-trick against Poland. Lineker snapped up two more goals against the ponderous Paraguayans and one against Argentina; these six goals made him the competition's leading marksman.

There was no doubting Argentina's superiority in the match against England. But that short-arm jab from Maradona let manager Bobby Robson off the hook by handing him the perfect excuse in defeat. Ironically, Maradona's second goal was arguably one of the finest ever seen in any match. Collecting the ball ten yards inside his own half on the right, he jinked his way past two opponents and accelerated before turning inside a third and rounding a fourth. His *coup de grace* was to dummy goalkeeper Peter Shilton before slipping the ball nonchalantly into the net. After that, Robson threw caution to the wind employing two wingers, but it was too little, too late.

France made light of the blistering heat and stamina-sapping altitude in Mexico City to dispose of the holders Italy with a display of flair and finesse which was reminiscent of their peak two years previously when they became European champions.

Though the USSR had given an early indication of the threat they posed, demoralising the Hungarians in a 6-0 win, their fast, attacking ideas foundered against the counter-punching Belgians. This 4-3 defeat echoed Italy's similar victory over the Germans in 1970.

Brazil, with question marks over their ageing stars like Socrates, Falcao and Junior plus the injured Zico, had a fortunate escape against Spain in their opening group game. Neither Australian referee Christopher Bambridge nor American linesman David Socha were positioned to notice that a drive by Michel which beat Carlos, the Brazilian goalkeeper, clearly bounced down off the crossbar over the line. Moreover there was a suspicion of offside when Socrates headed the only goal of the game.

The talented but indisciplined Uruguayans had had players sent off against Denmark and Scotland. Under the threat of expulsion from the competition they were subdued against Argentina, but restricted them to a 1-0 scoreline. As for the driving dynamics of the Danes, these faltered on defensive errors against the Spaniards who made them pay severely in a 5-1 success, while Brazil, who had been successfully rotating their veterans, lost out to France.

Meanwhile the Germans, underestimated as ever, had stumbled along to the final in characteristically unspectacular style. They were beaten 2-0 in the last group game by Denmark, almost held by Morocco and survived the penalty kick lottery against Mexico.

However their midfield held Michel Platini in a vice-like grip and the defence stifled everything else that the French could create in one semi-final, while a Maradona double accounted for Belgium in the other.

In the final, Argentina led 2-0 with 17 minutes remaining, only for the Germans to level the score with two goals in eight minutes. And for once it was Maradona in the role of goal maker who brought Argentina their second World Cup in eight years. He released a perfect pass to Jorge Burruchaga who ran half the length of the pitch before drawing Harald Schumacher and clinching victory in a spectacular climax to a memorable final. After 13 tournaments, FIFA had a competition more truly representative of its world-wide membership, if rather fewer great teams and referees. But without this sufficient guarantee of places its member nations would certainly fragment.

Qualifying Tournament

Record 119 entries*

Italy as champions and Mexico as hosts already qualified

Africa (29 entries): Algeria, Angola, Benin, Cameroon, Egypt, Ethiopia, Gambia, Ghana, Guinea, Ivory Coast, Kenya, Lesotho, Liberia, Libya, Madagascar, Malawi, Mauritius, Morocco, Niger, Nigeria, Senegal, Sierra Leone, Sudan, Tanzania, Togo, Tunisia, Uganda, Zambia, Zimbabwe

Asia (26): Bahrain, Bangladesh, Brunei, China, Hong Kong, India, Indonesia, Iran, Iraq, Israel, Japan, North Korea, South Korea, Kuwait, Macao, Malaysia, Nepal, Oman, Qatar, Saudi Arabia, Singapore, Syria, Thailand, UAE, North Yemen, South Yemen

Concacaf (18): Antigua, Barbados, Canada, Costa Rica, Grenada, Guatemala, Guyana, Haiti, Honduras, Jamaica, Mexico, Netherlands Antilles, Panama, Puerto Rico, El Salvador, Surinam, Trinidad and Tobago, USA

Europe (33): Albania, Austria, Belgium, Bulgaria, Cyprus, Czechoslovakia, Denmark, England, Finland, France, East Germany, West Germany, Greece, Holland, Hungary, Iceland, Northern Ireland, Rep of Ireland, Italy, Luxembourg, Malta, Norway, Poland, Portugal, Rumania, Scotland, Spain, Sweden, Switzerland, Turkey, USSR, Wales, Yugoslavia

Oceania (3): Australia, Taipei, New Zealand

South America (10): Argentina, Bolivia, Brazil, Chile, Colombia, Ecuador, Paraguay, Peru, Uruguay, Venezuela

Final places in Mexico were to be distributed as follows: Africa (2), Asia (2), Concacaf (1 + Mexico), Europe (13 + Italy)**, Oceania (0)**, South America (4).

*Subsequent additional entries for Lebanon in Asia and Israel added to Oceania, took the total to 121.

**Oceania's representative would be required to play the 13th placed team in Europe for a final place.

Europe

Group 1 (Poland, Belgium, Greece, Albania)

Belgium v Albania 3 - 1; Poland v Greece 3 - 1; Poland v Albania 2 - 2; Greece v Belgium 0 - 0; Albania v Belgium 2 - 0; Greece v Albania 2 - 0; Belgium v Greece 2 - 0; Belgium v Poland 2 - 0; Greece v Poland 1 - 4; Albania v Poland 0 - 1; Poland v Belgium 0 - 0; Albania v Greece 1 - 1

	P	W	D	L	F	A	Pts
Poland	6	3	2	1	10	6	8
Belgium	6	3	2	1	7	3	8
Greece	6	1	2	3	5	10	4
Albania	6	1	2	3	6	9	4

Poland qualified

Group 2 (West Germany, Czechoslovakia, Sweden, Portugal, Malta)

Sweden v Malta 4 - 0; Sweden v Portugal 0 - 1; Portugal v Czechoslovakia 2 - 1; West Germany v Sweden 2 - 0; Czechoslovakia v Malta 4 - 0; Portugal v Sweden 1 - 3; Malta v West Germany 2 - 3; Malta v Portugal 1 - 3; Portugal v West Germany 1 - 2; West Germany v Malta 6 - 0; Malta v Czechoslovakia 0 - 0; Czechoslovakia v West Germany 1 - 5; Sweden v Czechoslovakia 2 - 0; Sweden v West Germany 2 - 2; Czechoslovakia v Portugal 1 - 0; Portugal v Malta 3 - 2; Czechoslovakia v Sweden 2 - 1; West Germany v Portugal 0 - 1; West Germany v Czechoslovakia 2 - 2; Malta v Sweden 1 - 2

	P	W	D	L	F	A	Pts
West Germany	8	5	2	1	22	9	12
Portugal	8	5	0	3	12	10	10
Sweden	8	4	1	3	14	9	9
Czechoslovakia	8	3	2	3	11	12	8
Malta	8	0	1	7	6	25	1

West Germany and Portugal qualified

Group 3 (England, Northern Ireland, Rumania, Turkey, Finland)

Finland v Northern Ireland 1 - 0; Northern Ireland v Rumania 3 - 2; England v Finland 5 - 0; Turkey v Finland 1 - 2; Northern Ireland v Finland 2 - 1; Turkey v England 0 - 8; Northern Ireland v England 0 - 1; Rumania v Turkey 3 - 0; Northern Ireland v Turkey 2 - 0; Rumania v England 0 - 0; Finland v England 1 - 1; Finland v Rumania 1 - 1; Rumania v Finland 2 - 0; Turkey v Northern Ireland 0 - 0; England v Rumania 1 - 1; Finland v Turkey 1 - 0; Rumania v Northern Ireland 0 - 1; England v Turkey 5 - 0; England v Northern Ireland 0 - 0; Turkey v Rumania 1 - 3

	P	W	D	L	F	A	Pts
England	8	4	4	0	21	2	12
Northern Ireland	8	4	2	2	8	5	10
Rumania	8	3	3	2	12	7	9
Finland	8	3	2	3	7	12	8
Turkey	8	0	1	7	2	24	1

England and Northern Ireland qualified

Group 4 (France, Yugoslavia, East Germany, Bulgaria, Luxembourg)

Yugoslavia v Bulgaria 0 - 0; Luxembourg v France 0 - 4; East Germany v Yugoslavia 2 - 3; Luxembourg v East Germany 0 - 5; France v Bulgaria 1 - 0; Bulgaria v Luxembourg 4 - 0; France v East Germany 2 - 0; Yugoslavia v Luxembourg 3 - 0; Yugoslavia v France 0 - 0; Bulgaria v East Germany 1 - 0; Luxembourg v Yugoslavia 0 - 1; Bulgaria v France 2 - 0; East Germany v Luxembourg 3 - 1; Bulgaria v Yugoslavia 2 - 1; East Germany v France 2 - 0; Luxembourg v Bulgaria 1 - 3; Yugoslavia v East Germany 1 - 2; France v Luxembourg 6 - 0; France v Yugoslavia 2 - 0; East Germany v Bulgaria 2 - 1

	P	W	D	L	F	A	Pts
France	8	5	1	2	15	4	11
Bulgaria	8	5	1	2	13	5	11
East Germany	8	5	0	3	16	9	10
Yugoslavia	8	3	2	3	7	8	8
Luxembourg	8	0	0	8	2	27	0

France and Bulgaria qualified

Group 5 (Austria, Hungary, Holland, Cyprus)

Cyprus v Austria 1 - 2; Hungary v Austria 3 - 1; Holland v Hungary 1 - 2; Austria v Holland 1 - 0; Cyprus v Hungary 1 - 2; Cyprus v Holland 0 - 1; Holland v Cyprus 7 - 1; Hungary v Cyprus 2 - 0; Austria v Hungary 0 - 3; Holland v Austria 1 - 1; Austria v Cyprus 4 - 0; Hungary v Holland 0 - 1

	P	W	D	L	F	A	Pts
Hungary	6	5	0	1	12	4	10
Holland	6	3	1	2	11	5	7
Austria	6	3	1	2	9	8	7
Cyprus	6	0	0	6	3	18	0

Hungary qualified

Play-off between the runners-up of Groups 1 and 5
Belgium v Holland 1 - 0, 1 - 2
Belgium qualified

Group 6 (USSR, Denmark, Rep of Ireland, Switzerland, Norway)

Rep of Ireland v USSR 1 - 0; Norway v Switzerland 0 - 1; Denmark v Norway 1 - 0; Norway v USSR 1 - 1; Switzerland v Denmark 1 - 0; Norway v Rep of Ireland 1 - 0; Denmark v Rep of Ireland 3 - 0; Switzerland v USSR 2 - 2; Rep of Ireland v Norway 0 - 0; USSR v Switzerland 4 - 0; Rep of Ireland v Switzerland 3 - 0; Denmark v USSR 4 - 2; Switzerland v Rep of Ireland 0 - 0; USSR v Denmark 1 - 0; Denmark v Switzerland 0 - 0; Norway v Denmark 1 - 5; USSR v Rep of Ireland 2 - 0; USSR v Norway 1 - 0; Switzerland v Norway 1 - 1; Rep of Ireland v Denmark 1 - 4

	P	W	D	L	F	A	Pts
Denmark	8	5	1	2	17	6	11
USSR	8	4	2	2	13	8	10
Switzerland	8	2	4	2	5	10	8
Rep of Ireland	8	2	2	4	5	10	6
Norway	8	1	3	4	4	10	5

Denmark and USSR qualified.

Group 7 (Spain, Scotland, Wales, Iceland)

Iceland v Wales 1 - 0; Spain v Wales 3 - 0; Scotland v Iceland 3 - 0; Scotland v Spain 3 - 1; Wales v Iceland 2 - 1; Spain v Scotland 1 - 0; Scotland v Wales 0 - 1; Wales v Spain 3 - 0; Iceland v Scotland 0 - 1; Iceland v Spain 1 - 2; Wales v Scotland 1 - 1; Spain v Iceland 2 - 1

	P	W	D	L	F	A	Pts
Spain	6	4	0	2	9	8	8
Scotland	6	3	1	2	8	4	7
Wales	6	3	1	2	7	6	7
Iceland	6	1	0	5	4	10	2

Spain qualified

Runner-up played winner of Oceania group
Scotland v Australia 2 - 0, 0 - 0
Scotland qualified

Oceania
1st Round

Israel v Taipei 6 - 0; Taipei v Israel 0 - 5; New Zealand v Australia 0 - 0; New Zealand v Taipei 5 - 1; Israel v Taipei 1 - 2; Taipei v New Zealand 0 - 5; Australia v Israel 1 - 1; Australia v Tapei 7 - 0; New Zealand v Israel 3 - 1; Taipei v Australia 0 - 8; Australia v New Zealand 2 - 0; Israel v New Zealand 3 - 0

	P	W	D	L	F	A	Pts
Australia	6	4	2	0	20	2	10
Israel	6	3	1	2	17	6	7
New Zealand	6	3	1	2	13	7	7
Taipei	6	0	0	6	1	36	0

Australia qualified for play-off: see above

South America
Group 1 (Argentina, Peru, Colombia, Venezuela)

Colombia v Peru 0 - 1; Venezuela v Argentina 2 - 3; Colombia v Argentina 1 - 3; Venezuela v Peru 0 - 1; Peru v Colombia 0 - 0; Argentina v Venezuela 3 - 0; Peru v Venezuela 4 - 1; Argentina v Colombia 1 - 0; Venezuela v Colombia 2 - 2; Peru v Argentina 1 - 0; Colombia v Venezuela 2 - 0; Argentina v Peru 2 - 2

	P	W	D	L	F	A	Pts
Argentina	6	4	1	1	12	6	9
Peru	6	3	2	1	8	4	8
Colombia	6	2	2	2	6	6	6
Venezuela	6	0	1	5	5	15	1

Argentina qualified

Group 2 (Chile, Ecuador, Uruguay)

Ecuador v Chile 1 - 1; Uruguay v Ecuador 2 - 1; Chile v Ecuador 6 - 2; Chile v Uruguay 2 - 0; Ecuador v Uruguay 0 - 2; Uruguay v Chile 2 - 1

	P	W	D	L	F	A	Pts
Uruguay	4	3	0	1	6	4	6
Chile	4	2	1	1	10	5	5
Ecuador	4	0	1	3	4	11	1

Uruguay qualified

Group 3 (Brazil, Paraguay, Bolivia)

Bolivia v Paraguay 1 - 1; Bolivia v Brazil 0 - 2; Paraguay v Bolivia 3 - 0; Paraguay v Brazil 0 - 2; Brazil v Paraguay 1 - 1; Brazil - Bolivia 1 - 1

	P	W	D	L	F	A	Pts
Brazil	4	2	2	0	6	2	6
Paraguay	4	1	2	1	5	4	4
Bolivia	4	0	2	2	2	7	2

Brazil qualified

Play-off between the runners-up of Groups 1 and 2
Chile v Peru 4 - 2, 1 - 0

Play-off between the runners-up of Group 3 and third-placed team in Group 1
Paraguay v Colombia 3 - 0, 1 - 2

Final qualifier from above matches
Paraguay v Chile 3 - 0, 2 - 2
Paraguay qualified

Africa
1st Round

Egypt v Zimbabwe 1 - 0, 1 - 1; Kenya v Ethiopia 2 - 1, 3 - 3; Mauritius v Malawi 0 - 1, 0 - 4; Zambia v Uganda 3 - 0, 0 - 1; Madagascar v Lesotho (withdrew); Tanzania v Sudan 1 - 1, 0 - 0; Sierra Leone v Morocco 0 - 1, 0 - 4; Libya v Niger (withdrew); Benin v Tunisia 0 - 2, 0 - 4; Ivory Coast v Gambia 4 - 0, 2 - 3; Nigeria v Liberia 3 - 0, 1 - 0; Angola v Senegal 1 - 0, 0 - 1 (Angola won 4 - 3 on penalties); Guinea v Togo (withdrew)

2nd Round

Zambia v Cameroon 4 - 1, 1 - 1; Morocco v Malawi 2 - 0, 0 - 0; Angola v Algeria 0 - 0, 2 - 3; Kenya v Nigeria 0 - 3, 1 - 3; Egypt v Madagascar 1 - 0, 0 - 1 (Egypt won 4 - 2 on penalties); Guinea v Tunisia 1 - 0, 0 - 2; Sudan v Libya 0 - 0, 0 - 4; Ivory Coast v Ghana 0 - 0, 0 - 2

3rd Round

Algeria v Zambia 2 - 0, 1 - 0; Ghana v Libya 0 - 0, 0 - 2; Nigeria v Tunisia 1 - 0, 0 - 2; Egypt v Morocco 0 - 0, 0 - 2

4th Round

Tunisia v Algeria 1 - 4, 0 - 3; Morocco v Libya 3 - 0, 0 - 1
Algeria and Morocco qualified

Concacaf
1st Round
Group 1 (El Salvador, Puerto Rico, Canada, Jamaica (expelled), Netherlands Antilles, USA)
El Salvador v Puerto Rico 5 - 0, 3 - 0; Netherlands Antilles v USA 0 - 0, 0 - 4; Canada (walked over)

Group 2 (Barbados (withdrew), Costa Rica (walked over), Panama, Honduras, Guatemala (walked over))
Panama v Honduras 0 - 3, 0 - 1

Group 3 (Trinidad and Tobago, Grenada (withdrew), Antigua, Haiti, Surinam, Guyana)
Antigua v Haiti 0 - 4, 2 - 1; Surinam v Guyana 1 - 0, 1 - 1; Trinidad and Tobago (walked over)

2nd Round
Group 1 (El Salvador, Honduras, Surinam)
Surinam v El Salvador 0 - 3; El Salvador v Surinam 3 - 0; Surinam v Honduras 1 - 1; Honduras v Surinam 2 - 1; El Salvador v Honduras 1 - 2; Honduras v El Salvador 0 - 0

	P	W	D	L	F	A	Pts
Honduras	4	2	2	0	5	3	6
El Salvador	4	2	1	1	7	2	5
Surinam	4	0	1	3	2	9	1

Group 2 (Canada, Haiti, Guatemala)
Canada v Haiti 2 - 0; Canada v Guatemala 2 - 1; Haiti v Guatemala 0 - 1; Guatemala v Canada 1 - 1; Haiti v Canada 0 - 2; Guatemala v Haiti 4 - 0

	P	W	D	L	F	A	Pts
Canada	4	3	1	0	7	2	7
Guatemala	4	2	1	1	7	3	5
Haiti	4	0	0	4	0	9	0

Group 3 (USA, Costa Rica, Trinidad and Tobago)
Trinidad and Tobago v Costa Rica 0 - 3; Costa Rica v Trinidad and Tobago 1 - 1; Trinidad and Tobago v USA 1 - 2; USA v Trinidad and Tobago 1 - 0; Costa Rica v USA 1 - 1; USA v Costa Rica 0 - 1

	P	W	D	L	F	A	Pts
Costa Rica	4	2	2	0	6	2	6
USA	4	2	1	1	4	3	5
T'dad & Tobago	4	0	1	3	2	7	1

3rd Round

Costa Rica v Honduras 2 - 2; Canada v Costa Rica 1 - 1; Honduras v Canada 0 - 1; Costa Rica v Canada 0 - 0; Honduras v Costa Rica 3 - 1; Canada v Honduras 2 - 1

	P	W	D	L	F	A	Pts
Canada	4	2	2	0	4	2	6
Honduras	4	1	1	2	6	6	3
Costa Rica	4	0	3	1	4	6	3

Canada qualified

Asia

1st Round

Group 1

Sub-Group 1A (Saudi Arabia, UAE, Oman (withdrew))

Saudi Arabia v UAE 0 - 0, 0 - 1

Sub - Group 1B (Iraq, Lebanon, Qatar, Jordan)

Jordan v Qatar 1 - 0; Iraq v Lebanon 6 - 0; Lebanon v Iraq 0 - 6; Qatar v Lebanon 7 - 0 (Lebanon subsequently withdrew, record expunged); Jordan v Iraq 2 - 3; Qatar v Iraq 3 - 0; Qatar v Jordan 2 - 0; Iraq v Jordan 2 - 0; Iraq v Qatar 2 - 1

	P	W	D	L	F	A	Pts
Iraq	4	3	0	1	7	6	6
Qatar	4	2	0	2	6	3	4
Jordan	4	1	0	3	3	7	2

Group 2

Sub-Group 2A (Kuwait, North Yemen, Syria)

Syria v Kuwait I - 0; North Yemen v Syria 0 - 1; Kuwait v North Yemen 5 - 0; Kuwait v Syria 0 - 0; Syria v North Yemen 3 - 0; North Yemen v Kuwait 1 - 3

	P	W	D	L	F	A	Pts
Syria	4	3	1	0	5	0	7
Kuwait	4	2	1	1	8	2	5
North Yemen	4	0	0	4	1	12	0

Sub-Group 2B (Bahrain, South Yemen, Iran excluded)

South Yemen v Bahrain 1 - 4; Bahrain v South Yemen 3 - 3

Group 3

Sub-Group 3A (Malaysia, Nepal, South Korea)

Nepal v South Korea 0 - 2; Malaysia v South Korea 1 - 0; Nepal v Malaysia 0 - 1; Malaysia v Nepal 5 - 0; South Korea v Nepal 4 - 0; South Korea v Malaysia 2 - 0

	P	W	D	L	F	A	Pts
South Korea	4	3	0	1	8	1	6
Malaysia	4	2	1	1	6	2	5
Nepal	4	0	1	3	0	11	1

Sub-Group 3B (Thailand, India, Bangladesh, Indonesia)

Indonesia v Thailand 1 - 0; Indonesia v Bangladesh 2 - 0; Indonesia v India 2 - 1; Thailand v Bangladesh 3 - 0; Thailand v India 0 - 0; Thailand v Indonesia 0 - 1; Bangladesh v India 1 - 2; Bangladesh v Indonesia 2 - 1; Bangladesh v Thailand 1 - 0; India v Indonesia 1 - 1; India v Thailand 1 - 1; India v Bangladesh 2 - 1

	P	W	D	L	F	A	Pts
Indonesia	6	4	1	1	8	4	9
India	6	2	3	1	7	6	7
Thailand	6	1	2	3	4	4	4
Bangladesh	6	2	0	4	5	10	4

Group 4

Sub-Group 4A (China, Hong Kong, Macao, Brunei)

Macao v Brunei 2 - 0; Hong Kong v China 0 - 0; Macao v China 0 - 4; Hong Kong v Brunei 8 - 0; China v Brunei 8 - 0; Brunei v China 0 - 4; Brunei v Hong Kong 1 - 5; Brunei v Macao 1 - 2; Macao v Hong Kong 0 - 2; Hong Kong v Macao 2 - 0; China v Macao 6 - 0; China v Hong Kong 1 - 2

	P	W	D	L	F	A	Pts
Hong Kong	6	5	1	0	19	2	11
China	6	4	1	1	23	2	9
Macao	6	2	0	4	4	15	4
Brunei	6	0	0	6	2	29	0

Sub-Group 4B (Japan, North Korea, Singapore)

Singapore v North Korea 1 - 1; Singapore v Japan 1 - 3; Japan v North Korea 1 - 0; North Korea v Japan 0 - 0; Japan v Singapore 5 - 0; North Korea v Singapore 2 - 0

	P	W	D	L	F	A	Pts
Japan	4	3	1	0	9	1	7
North Korea	4	1	2	1	3	2	4
Singapore	4	0	1	3	2	11	1

2nd Round

UAE v Iraq 2 - 3, 2 - 1; Bahrain v Syria 1 - 1, 0 - 1; South Korea v Indonesia 2 - 0, 4 - 1; Japan v Hong Kong 3 - 0, 2 - 1

3rd Round

Syria v Iraq 0 - 0; Iraq v Syria 3 - 1
Japan v South Korea 1 - 2; South Korea v Japan 1 - 0
Iraq and South Korea qualified

Final Tournament MEXICO
First round
GROUP A

31.5.86 Bulgaria (0) 1, Italy (1) 1 MEXICO CITY
Bulgaria: Mikhailov, Arabov, Zdravkov, Dimitrov, Markov A, Sirakov (1), Iskrenov (Kostadinov), Sadkov, Mladenov, Gospodinov (Jeliaskov), Getov
Italy: Galli, Bergomi, Cabrini, De Napoli, Vierchowod, Scirea, Conti (Vialli), Di Gennaro, Galderisi, Bagni, Altobelli (1)
Referee: Fredriksson (Sweden)

2.6.86 Argentina (2) 3, South Korea (0) 1 MEXICO CITY
Argentina: Pumpido, Clausen, Brown, Ruggeri (1), Garre, Giusti, Batista (Olarticoechea), Burruchaga, Pasculli (Tapia), Maradona, Valdano (2)
South Korea: Oh Yun-Kyo, Park Kyung-Hoon, Jung Yong-Hwan, Cho Min-Kook, Kim Yong-See (Byun Byung-Joo), Huh Jung-Moo, Kim Pyung- Suk (Cho Kwang-Rae), Park Chang-Sun (1), Choi Soon-Ho, Kim Joo- Sung, Cha Bum-Kun
Referee: Sanchez Arminio (Spain)

5.6.86 Italy (1) 1, Argentina (1) 1 PUEBLA
Italy: Galli, Bergomi, Cabrini, De Napoli (Baresi), Vierchowod, Scirea, Conti (Vialli), De Gennaro, Galderisi, Bagni, Altobelli (1 pen)
Argentina: Pumpido, Cuciuffo, Brown, Ruggeri, Garre, Giusti, Batista (Olarticoechea), Burruchaga, Borghi (Enrique), Maradona (1), Valdano
Referee: Keizer (Holland)

2.6.86 South Korea (0) 1, Bulgaria (1) 1 MEXICO CITY
South Korea: Oh Yun-Kyo, Park Kyung-Hoon, Jung Yong-Hwan, Cho Young-Jeung, Cho Kwang-Rae (Choe Min-Kook), Huh Jung-Moo, Park Chang-Sun, No Soo-Jin (Kim Jong-Boo [1]), Byun Byung-Joo, Kim Joo-Sung, Cha Bum-Kun
Bulgaria: Mikhailov, Arabov, Zdravkov, Dimitrov, Petrov, Sirakov, Iskrenov, Sadkov, Mladenov, Gospodinov (Jeliaskov), Getov (1) (Kostadinov)
Referee: Al-Shanar (Saudi Arabia)

10.6.86 Argentina (1) 2, Bulgaria (0) 0 MEXICO CITY
Argentina: Pumpido, Cuciuffo, Brown, Ruggeri, Garre, Giusti, Batista (Enrique), Burruchaga (1), Borghi (Olarticoechea), Maradona, Valdano (1)
Bulgaria: Mikhailov, Sirakov, Markov A., Dimitrov, Jordanov, Markov P, Petrov, Jeliaskov, Mladenov (Velitchkov), Sadkov, Getov
Referee: Ulloa (Costa Rica)

10.6.86 South Korea (0) 2, Italy (1) 3 PUEBLA
South Korea: On Yun-Kyo, Park Kyung-Hoon, Jung Yong-Hwan, Cho Young-Jeung, Cho Kwang-Rae (o. g.), Huh Jung-Moo, Park Chang-Sun, Byun Byung-Joo (Kim Jong-Boo), Choi Soon-Ho (1), Kim Joo-Sung (Chung Jong-Soo), Cha Bum-Kun
Italy: Galli, Collovati, Cabrini, De Napoli, Vierchowod, Scirea, Conti, Di Gennaro, Galderisi (Vialli), Bagni (Baresi), Altobelli (2)
Referee: Socha (USA)

	P	W	D	L	F	A	Pts
Argentina	3	2	1	0	6	2	5
Italy	3	1	2	0	5	4	4
Bulgaria	3	0	2	1	2	4	2
South Korea	3	0	1	2	4	7	1

GROUP B

3.6.86 Belgium (1) 1, Mexico (2) 2 MEXICO CITY
Belgium: Pfaff, Gerets, Van der Elst F, Broos, De Wolf, Scifo, Vandereycken, Vercauteren, Desmet (Claesen), Vandenbergh (1) (Demol), Ceulemans
Mexico: Larios, Trejo, Quirarte, Felix Cruz, Servin, Munoz, Aguirre, Negrete, Boy (Espana), Sanchez (1), Flores (Javier Cruz)
Referee: Esposito (Argentina)

4.6.86 Paraguay (1) 1, Iraq (0) 0 TOLUCA
Paraguay: Fernandez, Torales, Zabula, Schettina, Delgado, Nunez, Ferreira, Romero (1), Cabanas, Canete, Mendoza (Guasch)
Iraq: Hammoudi, Allawi, Shaker N, Shaker B, Hussein, Mohammed (Hameed), Radi, Saeed, Gorgis (Quassen), Hashem, Uraibi
Referee: Picon (Mauritius)

7.6.86 Mexico (1) 1, Paraguay (0) 1 MEXICO CITY
Mexico: Larios, Trejo, Quirarte, Felix Cruz, Servin, Munoz, Aguirre, Negrete, Boy (Espana), Sanchez, Flores (1) (Javier Cruz)
Paraguay: Fernandez, Torales (Hicks), Zabala, Schettina, Delgado, Nunez, Ferreira, Romero (1), Cabanas, Canete, Mendoza (Guasch)
Referee: Courtney (England)

8.6.86 Iraq (0) 1, Belgium (2) 2 TOLUCA
Iraq: Hammoudi, Allawi, Shaker N, Shaker B, Hussein, Mohammed, Radi (1), Saddam (Hameed), Gorgis, Hashem, Uraibi
Belgium: Pfaff, Gerets, Van der Elst F, Demol (Grun), De Wolf, Scifo (1) (Clysters), Vandereycken, Vercauteren, Desmet, Claesen (1 pen), Ceulemans
Referee: Diaz (Colombia)

11.6.86 Paraguay (0) 2, Belgium (1) 2 TOLUCA
Paraguay: Fernandez, Torales, Zabala, Delgado, Guasch, Nunez, Ferreira, Romero, Cabanas (2), Canete, Mendoza (Hicks)
Belgium: Pfaff, Grun (Van der Elst L), Broos, Renquin, Vervoort, Scifo, Demol, Ceulemans, Vercauteren (1), Veyt (1), Claesen
Referee: Dochev (Bulgaria)

11.6.86 Iraq (0) 0, Mexico (0) 1 MEXICO CITY
Iraq: Jasim, Majeed, Allawi, Nadhum, Hussein, Ghanem, Hashem, Radi, Abid (Shaker N), Minshed, Kassim (Hameed)
Mexico: Larios, Amador (Dominguez), Quirarte (1), Felix Cruz, Servin, De los Cobos (Javier Cruz), Aguirre, Negrete, Boy, Espana, Flores
Referee: Petrovic (Yugoslavia)

	P	W	D	L	F	A	Pts
Mexico	3	2	1	0	4	2	5
Paraguay	3	1	2	0	4	3	4
Belgium	3	1	1	1	5	5	3
Iraq	3	0	0	3	1	4	0

GROUP C

1.6.86 Canada (0) 0, France (0) 1 LEON
Canada: Dolan, Lenarduzzi, Wilson, Bridge, Samuel, Ragan, Valentine, Norman, James (Segota), Sweeney (Lowery), Vrablic
France: Bats, Amoros, Tusseau, Battiston, Bossis, Fernandez, Giresse, Tigana, Papin (1), Platini, Rocheteau (Stopyra)
Referee: Silva Arce (Chile)

2.6.86 USSR (3) 6, Hungary (0) 0 IRAPUATO
USSR: Dasayev, Larionov, Bessonov, Kuznetsov, Demyanenko, Yaremchuk (2), Yakovenko (1) (Yevtushenko), Rats, Belanov (1 pen) (Rodionov [1]), Zavarov, Aleinikov (1)
Hungary: Disztl P, Sallai, Roth (Bursca), Garaba, Kardos, Kiprich, Nagy, Detari, Peter (Dajka), Esterhazy, Bognar
Referee: Agnolin (Italy)

5.6.86 France (0) 1, USSR (0) 1 LEON
France: Bats, Amoros, Ayache, Battiston, Bossis, Fernandez (1), Giresse (Vercruysse), Tigana, Papin (Bellone), Platini, Stopyra
USSR: Dasayev, Larionov, Bessonov, Kuznetsov, Demyanenko, Yaremchuk, Yakovenko, Rats (1), Belanov, Zavarov (Blokhin), Aleinikov
Referee: Arrpi Filho (Brazil)

6.6.86 Hungary (1) 2, Canada (0) 0 IRAPUATO
Hungary: Szendrei, Sallai, Varga, Garaba, Kardos, Kiprich, Nagy (Dajka), Detari (1), Burcsa (Roth), Esterhazy (1), Bognar
Canada: Lettieri, Lenarduzzi, Wilson (Sweeney), Bridge, Samuel, Ragan, Valentine, Norman, James (Segota), Gray, Vrablic
Referee: Al-Sharis (Syria)

9.6.86 Hungary (0) 0, France (1) 3 LEON
Hungary: Disztl P, Sallai, Roth, Varga, Kardos, Garaba, Hannich (Nagy), Detari, Dajka, Esterhazy, Kovacs (Bognar)
France: Bats, Ayache, Amoros, Battiston, Bossis, Fernandez, Giresse, Tigana (1), Papin (Rocheteau [1]), Platini, Stopyra (1) (Ferreri)
Referee: Silva (Portugal)

9.6.86 USSR (0) 2, Canada (0) 0 IRAPUATO
USSR: Chanov, Morozov, Bubnov, Kuznetsov, Bal, Litovchenko, Yevtushenko, Aleinikov, Rodionov, Protasov (Belanov), Blokhin (1) (Zavarov [1])
Canada: Lettieri, Lenarduzzi, Wilson, Bridge, Samuel, Ragan, Valentine, Norman, James (Segota), Gray (Pakos), Mitchell
Referee: Traore (Mali)

	P	W	D	L	F	A	Pts
USSR	3	2	1	0	9	1	5
France	3	2	1	0	5	1	5
Hungary	3	1	0	2	2	9	2
Canada	3	0	0	3	0	5	0

GROUP D

1.6.86 Spain (0) 0, Brazil (0) 1 GUADALAJARA
Spain: Zubizarreta, Tomas, Camacho, Maceda, Giocoechea, Julio Alberto, Michel, Victor, Butragueno, Francisco (Senor), Julio Salinas
Brazil: Carlos, Branco, Edson, Edhino, Julio Cesar, Junior (Falcao), Alemao, Casagrande (Muller), Careca, Socrates (1), Elzo
Referee: Bambridge (Australia)

3.6.86 Algeria (0) 1, Northern Ireland (1) 1 GUADALAJARA
Algeria: Larbi, Medjadi, Mansouri, Kourichi, Guendouz, Kaci Said, Assad, Benmabrouk, Zidane (1) (Belloumi), Maroc, Madjer (Harkouk)
Northern Ireland: Jennings, Nicholl, Donaghy, O'Neill, McDonald, Worthington, Penney (Stewart), McIlroy, McCreery, Hamilton, Whiteside (1) (Clarke)
Referee: Butenko (USSR)

7.6.86 Northern Ireland (0) 1, Spain (2) 2 GUADALAJARA
Northern Ireland: Jennings, Nicholl, Donaghy, O'Neill, McDonald, Worthington (Hamilton), Penney (Stewart), McIlroy, McCreery, Clarke (1), Whiteside
Spain: Zubizarreta, Tomas, Camacho, Gallego, Giocoechea, Gordillo (Caldere), Michel, Victor, Butragueno (1), Francisco, Julio Salinas (1) (Senor)
Referee: Brummener (Austria)

6.6.86 Brazil (0) 1, Algeria (0) 0 GUADALAJARA
Brazil: Carlos, Edson (Falcao), Branco, Edinho, Julio Cesar, Junior, Alemao, Casagrande (Muller), Careca (1), Socrates, Elzo
Algeria: Drid, Medjadi, Mamsouri, Megharia, Guendouz, Kaci Said, Assad (Bensaoula), Benmabrouk, Menad, Belloumi (Zidane), Madjer
Referee: Molina (Guatemala)

12.6.85 Algeria (0) 0, Spain (1) 3 MONTERREY
Algeria: Drid (Larbi), Megharia, Mansouri, Kourichi, Guendouz, Kaci Said, Madjer, Maroc, Harkouk, Belloumi, Zidane (Menad)
Spain: Zubizarreta, Tomas, Camacho, Gallego, Goicoechea, Caldere (2), Michel (Senor), Victor, Butragueno (Eloy [1]), Francisco, Julio Salinas
Referee: Takada (Japan)

12.6.86 Northern Ireland (0) 0, Brazil (2) 3 GUADALAJARA
Northern Ireland: Jennings, Nicholl, Donaghy, O'Neill, McDonald, McCreery, McIlroy, Stewart, Clarke, Whiteside (Hamilton), Campbell (Armstrong)
Brazil: Carlos, Josimar (1), Julio Cesar, Edinho, Branco, Elzo, Alemao, Junior, Socrates (Zico), Muller (Casagrande), Careca (2)
Referee: Kirschen (East Germany)

	P	W	D	L	F	A	Pts
Brazil	3	3	0	0	5	0	6
Spain	3	2	0	1	5	2	4
Northern Ireland	3	0	1	2	2	6	1
Algeria	3	0	1	2	1	5	1

GROUP E

4.6.86 Uruguay (1) 1, West Germany (0) 1 QUERETARO
Uruguay: Alvez, Gutierrez, Acevedo, Diogo, Bossio, Batista, Alzamendi (1) (Ramos), Barrios (Saralegui), Da Silva, Francescoli, Santin
West Germany: Schumacher, Briegel, Berthold, Forster, Augenthaler, Eder, Matthaus (Rummenigge), Magath, Brehme (Littbarski), Voller, Allofs (1)
Referee: Christov (Czechoslovakia)

4.6.86 Scotland (0) 0, Denmark (0) 1 NEZA
Scotland: Leighton, Gough, Malpas, Souness, McLeish, Miller, Strachan (Bannon), Aitken, Nicol, Nicholas, Sturrock (McAvennie)
Denmark: Rasmussen, Busk, Olsen M, Nielsen, Lerby, Olsen J (Molby), Berggreen, Elkjaer (1), Laudrup, Bertelsen, Arnesen (Sivebaek)
Referee: Nemeth (Hungary)

8.6.86 Denmark (2) 6, Uruguay (1) 1 NEZA
Denmark: Rasmussen, Busk, Olsen M, Nielsen, Lerby (1), Andersen, Berggreen, Elkjaer (3), Laudrup (1) (Olsen J [1]), Bertelsen (Molby), Arnesen
Uruguay: Alvez, Gutierrez, Acevedo, Diogo, Bossio, Batista, Alzamendi (Ramos), Saralegui, Da Silva, Francescoli (1), Santin (Salazar)
Referee: Marquez (Mexico)

8.6.89 West Germany (1) 2, Scotland (1) 1 QUERETARO
West Germany: Schumacher, Briegel (Jakobs), Berthold, Forster, Augenthaler, Eder, Matthaus, Magath, Littbarski (Rummenigge), Voller (1), Allofs
Scotland: Leighton, Gough, Malpas, Souness, Narey, Miller, Strachan (1), Aitken, Nicol (McAvennie), Archibald, Bannon (Cooper)
Referee: Igna (Romania)

13.6.86 Scotland (0) 0, Uruguay (0) 0 NEZA
Scotland: Leighton, Gough, Albiston, Aitken, Narey, Miller, Strachan, McStay, Sharp, Nicol (Cooper), Sturrock (Nicholas)
Uruguay: Alvez, Diogo, Acevedo, Gutierrez, Pereyra, Batista, Ramos (Saralegui), Barrios, Cabrera, Francescoli (Alzamendi), Santin
Referee: Quiniou (France)

13.6.86 Denmark (1) 2, West Germany (0) 0 QUERETARO
Denmark: Hogh, Sivebaek, Busk, Olsen M, Andersen, Arnesen, Lerby, Molby, Laudrup, Olsen J (1 pen) (Simonsen), Elkjaer (Eriksen [1])
West Germany: Schumacher, Berthold, Jakobs, Forster (Rummenigge), Herget, Eder, Brehme, Matthaus, Voller, Rolff (Littbarski), Allofs
Referee: Ponnet (Belgium)

	P	W	D	L	F	A	Pts
Denmark	3	3	0	0	9	1	6
West Germany	3	1	1	1	3	4	3
Uruguay	3	0	2	1	2	7	2
Scotland	3	0	1	2	1	3	1

GROUP F

2.6.86 Morocco (0) 0, Poland (0) 0 MONTERREY
Morocco: Zaki, Labd, Lemriss, El-Biyaz, Bouyahiaoui, Mustapha El-Haddaoui (Souleimani), Dolmy, Bouderbala, Krimau, Timoumi (Khairi), Merry
Poland: Milynarczyk, Ostrowski, Wojcicki, Majewski, Matysik, Kubicki, Komornicki (Przybys), Buncol, Smolarek, Dziekanowski (Urban), Boniek
Referee: Martinez Bazan (Uruguay)

3.6.86 Portugal (0) 1, England (0) 0 MONTERREY
Portugal: Bento, Alvaro, Frederico, Oliveira, Inacio, Diamantino (Jose Antonio), Andre, Carlos Manuel (1), Pacheco, Sousa, Gomes (Futre)
England: Shilton, Stevens, Sansom, Hoddle, Fenwick, Butcher, Robson (Hodge), Wilkins, Hateley, Lineker, Waddle (Beardsley)
Referee: Roth (West Germany)

6.6.86 England (0) 0, Morocco (0) 0 MONTERREY
England: Shilton, Stevens, Sansom, Hoddle, Fenwick, Butcher, Robson (Hodge), Wilkins, Hateley (Stevens G A), Lineker, Waddle
Morocco: Zaki, Labd, Lemriss (Heina), El-Biyaz, Bouyahiaoui, Khairi, Dolmy, Bouderbala, Krimau, Timoumi, Merry (Souleimani)
Referee: Gonzalez (Paraguay)

7.6.86 Poland (0) 1, Portugal (0) 0 MONTERREY
Poland: Mlynarczyk, Ostrowski, Wojcicki, Majewski, Matysik, Urban, Komornicki (Karas), Pawlak, Smolarek (1) (Zgutczynski), Dziekanowski, Boniek
Portugal: Damas, Alvaro, Frederico, Oliveira, Inacio, Diamantino, Andre (Magalhaes), Carlos Manuel, Pacheco, Sousa, Gomes (Futre)
Referee: Ali ben Nasser (Tunisia)

11.6.86 England (3) 3, Poland (0) 0 MONTERREY
England: Shilton, Stevens, Sansom, Hoddle, Fenwick, Butcher, Steven, Reid, Lineker (3) (Dixon), Beardsley (Waddle), Hodge
Poland: Milynarczyk, Ostrowski, Wojcicki, Matysik (Buncol), Urban, Majewski, Smolarek, Komonicki (Karas), Pawlak, Dziekanowski, Boniek
Referee: Daina (Switzerland)

11.6.86 Portugal (0) 1, Morocco (2) 3 GUADALAJARA
Portugal: Damas, Alvaro (Aguas), Frederico, Oliveira, Inacio, Magalhaes, Carlos Manuel, Pacheco, Sousa (Diamantino [1]), Gomes, Futre
Morocco: Zaki, Labd, Lemriss, El-Biyaz, Bouyahiaoui, Dolmy, Mustapha El-Haddaoui (Souleimani), Bouderbala, Krimau (1), Timouni, Khairi (2)
Referee: Snoddy (Northern Ireland)

	P	W	D	L	F	A	Pts
Morocco	3	1	2	0	3	1	4
England	3	1	1	1	3	1	3
Poland	3	1	1	1	1	3	3
Portugal	3	1	0	2	2	4	2

Second round

15.6.86 Mexico (1) 2, Bulgaria (0) 0 MEXICO CITY
Mexico: Larios, Amador, Quirarte, Felix Cruz, Servin (1), Espana, Aguirre, Munoz, Boy (De los Cobos), Sanchez, Negrete (1)
Bulgaria: Mikhailov, Arabov, Zdravkov, Dimitrov, Petrov, Jordanov, Sadkov, Kostadinov, Getov (Sirakov), Gospodinov, Paschev (Iskrenov)
Referee: Arppi Filho (Brazil)

15.6.86 USSR (1) 3, Belgium (0) 4 (aet, 2 - 2 at 90 mins) LEON
USSR: Dasayev, Bessonov, Bal, Kuznetsov, Demyanenko, Yaremchuk, Yakovenko (Yevtushenko), Aleinikov, Rats, Belanov (3, 1 pen), Zavarov (Rodionov)
Belgium: Pfaff, Gerets, Grun (Clijsters), Vervoort, Demol (1), Renquin, Scifo (1), Vercauteren, Claesen (1), Veyt, Ceulemans (1)
Referee: Frederiksson (Sweden)

16.6.86 Brazil (1) 4, Poland (0) 0 GUADALAJARA
Brazil: Carlos, Josimar (1), Branco, Edinho (1), Julio Cesar, Alemao, Muller (Silas), Socrates (1 pen) (Zico), Careca (1 pen), Junior, Elzo
Poland: Mlynarczyk, Ostrowski, Majewski, Wojcicki, Przybs (Furtok), Urban (Zmuda), Karas, Tarasiewicz, Dziekanowski, Boniek, Smolarek
Referee: Roth (West Germany)

16.6.86 Argentina (1) 1, Uruguay (0) 0 PUEBLA
Argentina: Pumpido, Cuciuffo, Brown, Garre, Giusti, Ruggeri, Batista (Olarticoechea), Burruchaga, Pasculli (1), Maradona, Valdano
Uruguay: Alvez, Rivero, Bossio, Gutierrez, Acevedo (Paz), Pereyra, Ramos, Cabrera (Da Silva), Francescoli, Barrios, Santin
Referee: Agnolin (Italy)

17.6.86 France (1) 2, Italy (0) 0 MEXICO CITY
France: Bats, Ayache, Amoros, Battiston, Bossis, Fernandez (Tusseau), Giresse, Tigana, Rocheteau, Platini (1) (Ferreri), Stopyra (1)
Italy: Galli, Bergomi, Cabrini, De Napoli, Vierchowod, Scirea, Conti, Bagni, Galderisi (Vialli), Baresi (Di Gennaro), Altobelli
Referee: Esposito (Argentina)

17.6.86 Morocco (0) 0, West Germany (0) 1 MONTERREY
Morocco: Zaki, Labd, Lemriss, Bouyahiaoui, Dolmy, Mustapha El-Haddaoui, Bouderbala, Krimau, Timoumi, Hcina, Khairi
West Germany: Schumacher, Berthold, Briegel, Jakobs, Forster, Eder, Matthaus (1), Rummenigge, Voller (Littbarski), Magath, Allofs
Referee: Petrovic (Yugoslavia)

18.6.86 England (1) 3, Paraguay (0) 0 MEXICO CITY
England: Shilton, Stevens, Sansom, Hoddle, Martin, Butcher, Steven, Reid (Stevens G A), Lineker (2), Beardsley (1) (Hateley), Hodge
Paraguay: Fernandez, Torales (Guasch), Zabala, Schettina, Delgado, Nunez, Ferreira, Romero, Cabanas, Canets, Mendoza
Referee: Al-Sharif (Syria)

18.6.86 Denmark (1) 1, Spain (1) 5 QUERETARO
Denmark: Hogh, Andersen (Eriksen), Olsen M, Busk, Nielsen, Lerby, Olsen J (1 pen) (Molby), Bertelsen, Laudrup, Berggreen, Elkjaer
Spain: Zubizarreta, Tomas, Camacho, Gallego, Giocoechea (1 pen), Julio Alberto,Victor, Michel (Francisco), Butragueno (4, 1 pen), Caldere, Julio Salinas (Eloy)
Referee: Keizer (Holland)

QUARTER FINALS
21.6.86 Brazil (1) 1, France (1) 1 (aet, 1 - 1 at 90 mins, France won 4 - 3 on penalties)   GUADALAJARA
Brazil: Carlos, Josimar, Branco, Edinho, Julio Cesar, Elzo, Muller (Zico), Alemao, Careca (1), Socrates, Junior (Silas)
France: Bats, Amoros, Tusseau, Battiston, Bossis, Fernandez, Giresse (Ferreri), Tigana, Rocheteau (Bellone), Platini (1), Stopyra
Referee: Igna (Romania)

21.6.86 West Germany (0) 0, Mexico (0) 0 (aet, West Germany won 4 - 1 on penalties)   MONTERREY
West Germany: Schumacher, Berthold, Briegel, Jakobs, Forster, Eder (Littbarski), Matthaus, Brehme, Rummenigge (Hoeness), Magath, Allofs
Mexico: Larios, Amador (Javier Cruz), Felix Cruz, Quirarte, Servin, Munoz, Aguirre, Espana, Boy (De los Cobos), Negrete, Sanchez
Referee: Diaz (Colombia)

22.6.86 Argentina (0) 2, England (0) 1 MEXICO CITY
Argentina: Pumpido, Ruggeri, Cuciuffo, Olarticoechea, Brown, Giusti, Batista, Burruchaga (Tapia), Enrique, Maradona (2), Valdano
England: Shilton, Stevens, Sansom, Hoddle, Butcher, Fenwick, Steven (Barnes), Reid (Waddle), Lineker (1), Beardsley, Hodge
Referee: Ali ben Nasser (Tunisia)

22.6.86 Spain (0) 1, Belgium (1) 1 (aet, 1 - 1 at 90 mins, Belgium won 5 - 4 on penalties)   PUEBLA
Spain: Zubizarreta, Chendo, Camacho, Gallego, Tomas (Senor [1]), Michel, Victor, Caldere, Butragueno, Julio Alberto, Julio Salinas (Eloy)
Belgium: Pfaff, Gerets, Renquin, Demol, Vervoort, Grun, Scifo, Veyt (Broos), Claesen, Ceulemans (1), Vercauteren (Van der Elst L)
Referee: Kirschen (East Germany)

SEMI FINALS
25.6.86 Argentina (0) 2, Belgium (0) 0 MEXICO CITY
Argentina: Pumpido, Cuciuffo, Ruggeri, Brown, Olarticoechea, Giusti, Batista, Burruchaga (Bochini), Enrique, Maradona (2), Valdano
Belgium: Pfaff, Gerets, Renquin (Desmet), Demol, Vervoort, Veyt, Grun, Scifo, Claesen, Ceulemans, Vercauteren
Referee: Marquez (Mexico)

25.6.86 France (0) 0, West Germany (1) 2 GUADALAJARA
France: Bats, Amoros, Ayache, Battiston, Bossis, Fernandez, Giresse (Vercruysse), Tigana, Bellone (Xuereb), Platini, Stopyra
West Germany: Schumacher, Brehme (1), Briegel, Jakobs, Forster, Eder, Matthaus, Rolff, Rummenigge (Voller [1]), Magath, Allofs
Referee: Agnolin (Italy)

Match for third place
28.6.86 Belgium (1) 2, France (2) 4 PUEBLA
Belgium: Pfaff, Gerets, Vervoort, Demol, Renquin (Van der Elst F), Grun, Scifo (Van der Elst L), Mommens, Claesen (1), Ceulemans (1), Veyt
France: Rust, Bibard, Amoros (1 pen), Le Roux (Bossis), Battiston, Vercruysse, Genghini (1), Tigana (Tusseau), Papin (1), Ferreri (1), Bellone
Referee: Courtney (England)

FINAL
29.6.86 Argentina (1) 3, West Germany (0) 2 MEXICO CITY
Argentina: Pumpido, Cuciuffo, Olarticoechea, Ruggeri, Brown (1), Giusti, Burruchaga (1) (Trobbiani), Batista, Valdano (1), Maradona, Enrique
West Germany: Schumacher, Berthold, Briegel, Jakobs, Forster, Eder, Brehme, Matthaus, Allofs (Voller [1]), Magath (Hoeness), Rummenigge (1)
Referee: Arppi Filho (Brazil)

ITALY

1990

In a reversal of the result of the final in Mexico four years earlier, West Germany gained revenge over Argentina in a totally unsatisfactory match which was an affront to the game and an appalling advertisement for the world championship. It epitomised much of what had been an undistinguished tournament.

Argentina finished the game with nine men and the Germans won with a disputed penalty five minutes from time. Pedro Monzon became the first player to be sent off in a World Cup final and was later followed by team-mate Gustavo Dezotti. West Germany equalled Brazil's and Italy's record of three World Cup wins and Franz Beckenbauer, who had captained their 1974 side, became the first manager to win the trophy having led the team to victory as a player in a previous tournament.

With four players suspended, Argentina concentrated on defence in the final. They had reached this stage in fortuitous circumstances while piling up a disgraceful total of red and yellow cards. They rarely showed any ambition to attack the opposition's goal, often resorting to attacking the opposing player. At the end of the tournament they had amassed 22 yellow and three red cards in an overall tally of 164 bookings and 16 dismissals, a record total as match officials threw cautions to the wind. FIFA's insistence on clamping down on infringements of the law put incredible pressure on the referees, who were struggling to understand the offside law in many instances and were falling foul of the idea that they had to decide whether a tackle was legitimate or not by the antics of the victim. Again a wide interpretation of the laws meant a wholly unsatisfactory outcome.

In the first half of the final the physically formidable Germans attacked relentlessly without sufficient guile. Rudi Voller missed three reasonable scoring opportunities while Argentina's only reply came from a poorly directed free kick from Diego Maradona, who had gone through the entire tournament with a bored and bemused countenance. He had made one telling contribution in the second round when he contrived a defence-splitting pass which sealed Brazil's fate, but apart from being the most fouled player, he contributed little and was surrounded by a set of quite ordinary colleagues.

At the start of the second half, Monzon replaced Oscar Ruggeri in the Argentine defence but played only 20 minutes before he brought down Jurgen Klinsmann and was shown the red card. Worse followed, as Voller was tripped by Robert Sensini and the impressive Andreas Brehme converted low to the right of the Argentine goalkeeper Goycochea with five minutes remaining. Two minutes from the final whistle Dezotti wrestled Kohler for the ball and was sent off. Maradona joined Sensini among the yellow cards for protesting amidst a group of furious Argentines.

The game for third place was this time one of the more enjoyable of the entire month-long extravaganza. Instead of adopting the approach of beaten semi-finalists with little heart for the fray, both Italy and England put on a creditable performance. The Italians won 2-1 in a closely fought affair which confirmed England as worthy winners of the fair play award. They had only five players booked throughout the tournament and committed just 106 fouls. At the end of the game Peter Shilton announced his retirement from international football after collecting 125 caps. He had been unable to bow out in style; he was at fault with Italy's first goal, dallying in front of goal and allowing himself to be dispossessed. He had also been caught off his line in the semi-final with West Germany when a free-kick took a high deflection off the wall.

The hosts Italy were always going to struggle for goals.

England celebrate as a goal by David Platt (kneeling) in the last minute of extra time wins the second round match against Belgium.

The unmistakeable expression of Salvatore 'Toto' Schillaci, top scorer in the 1990 finals.

Although they had discovered a marksman in the Sicilian, Salvatore Schillaci, a chunky, ebullient little man, they could not provide him with the support up front which he obviously needed. He finished top scorer in the competition with six goals. Yet for all the Italians technical accomplishments on the ball, they lacked the necessary drive in the last third of the field. Individually there was much to admire in Giannini, Donadoni, Baresi and even the £7.7 million Roberto Baggio, who had some inspired moments. But the penalty shoot-out with Argentina was to provide a cruel exit. Schillaci was the player caught most offside during Italia '90.

So ironically, the tournament which began with Argentina being humiliated in losing to the Cameroon, who finished the match with nine men, ended with the South Americans themselves losing two men and the match to a theatrical West Germany, for whom Lothar Matthaus proved a midfield dynamo.

There was little doubt that the 1990 finals revealed a levelling of standards. Of the lesser nations only South Korea and the United Arab Emirates failed to make an impression. The Cameroon, unbeaten in their only previous appearance in the World Cup finals eight years earlier, were a revelation. With better discipline they might have reached the final itself. Their combined play and individual flair was a joy to behold and they went some way towards assuming the mantle of Brazil.

Egypt excelled in defence with Hany Ramzi outstanding at the heart of their rearguard and the USA recovered from a naive display in their opening game when they were thrashed 5-1 by the Czechs to improve noticeably in their remaining group matches though they still lost 1-0 to Italy and 2-1 to Austria. Indeed against the Italians they might well have scored on the counter attack on at least two occasions. Costa Rica, given little chance by the critics or themselves, began by beating Scotland 1-0 and at times mirrored the best passing movements of

Brazil. But they had a vulnerability in defence which was exposed in the second round when the aerial threat posed by Czechoslovakia resulted in Tomas Skuhravy scoring a rare headed hat-trick in a 4-1 win.

Arguably the two most disappointing teams were Sweden and Austria. The Austrians had clearly played their best football in the warm up games before the finals and well though the Swedes played at times in their group, they had nothing to show for their endeavours. Again the Soviet Union were exasperating. After a lethargic opening in which they were well beaten 2-0 by a lively Rumanian team, they were unlucky to lose by the same margin to Argentina, having a player sent off rather harshly it seemed, and being denied a penalty when Diego Maradona showed he had added a further dimension to his handling prowess at the other end of the field. The Argentines were clearly determined to show that it was not only their stocky captain who could use his hands to good effect. Alas, others lacked his subtle approach and Claudio Caniggia was booked for leaping up basketball fashion in midfield, the resultant yellow card costing him a place in the final.

Of the more fancied sides, Holland were arguably the most disappointing. Their big four of Marco Van Basten, Ruud Gullit, Ronald Koeman and Frank Rijkaard all had problems. Van Basten scarcely did anything right and appeared uninterested for long periods. Gullit was a shadow of his former buccaneering self but having had a year out with injury he at least had an excuse. Koeman did not have the same reason for a low-key performance and Rijkaard disgraced himself in the second round game with West Germany when he was sent off for spitting twice at the West German Rudi Voller, whom he apparently goaded into also being dismissed with him.

Brazil might have progressed further than the second round had they played with the conviction in attack that the previous wearers of the yellow shirts had done. They were beaten by a late goal against Argentina after controlling almost the entire game. Uruguay, having cleaned up their act from four years earlier, were a curious mixture; their defensive organisation was almost faultless but they were let down by players like Enzo Francescoli and Ruben Sosa who had been expected to shine during the finals. Sosa missed a penalty against Spain after Villaroya handled under the crossbar, the misdemeanour passing unpunished by the referee, who had previously booked the Spaniard for another handling offence.

The Scots were dreadful against Costa Rica despite missing chances close in, but lifted themselves against the Swedes and were denied a place in the second round when they conceded a late scrambled goal to the Brazilians. As for the Republic of Ireland, they reached the second round by giving every ounce of energy they possessed and came through the first of the penalty shoot-out lotteries against Rumania. They were narrowly beaten by Italy in the quarter-final. Yet their opening fixture with England might well have been a poor First Division game in the Football League and received widespread criticism.

However England did better against the uninspired, dispirited Dutch who obviously had trouble in the camp; the players had apparently wanted Johan Cruyff to take over as coach after they had succeeded in having Thijs Libregts removed, and were unhappy with Leo Beenhakker's appointment. This game ended goalless and for periods against the Egyptians, England were nonplussed. They were outplayed for long periods against Belgium, who twice hit a post, before David Platt snatched a memorable late winner in extra time; and they had to dig deep into their determination to come back against the Cameroon to win 3-2 with two penalties from Gary Lineker, after trailing 2-1.

Ironically England's good fortune evaporated after their most convincing performance in the semi-final with West Germany. This was also decided on penalties; the quartet of German efforts were despatched with teutonic efficiency leaving Stuart Pearce and Chris Waddle to fail in their attempts. But England had had many plusses. Des Walker and Mark Wright excelled in defence as did Lineker in attack. Paul Gascoigne was accuracy itself with dead ball kicks, many of which he himself earned through his tireless running with the ball.

The tournament failed to reveal many new outstanding individuals. Indeed one of the most effective to emerge was 38-year-old Roger Milla of the Cameroon, brought out of semi-retirement on the island of Reunion, which said little for others ten years his junior. Yugoslavia's Dragan Stojkovic was often influential in a team which threatened to do better but never quite achieved it, while several teams suffered from having one outstanding player through whom almost everything had to flow. Belgium, who had a purple patch in one of the better contests with Uruguay, had above-average players but invariably looked to the scurrying expertise of Enzo Scifo. Michel was in a similar position for Spain, who proved to be as inconsistent as ever, and Gheorghe Hagi often ventured individual sorties for Rumania which came to nothing, when the team as a unit had been more effective in the first game against the Soviet Union without him. To a lesser extent Colombia relied on Carlos Valderrama, but he was overshadowed by the eccentricities of goalkeeper Rene Higuita, who was finally caught out attempting some sleight of foot outside his penalty area against the Cameroon in extra time. The incident just about summed up the entire tournament, which despite ultimately producing worthy champions in West Germany, will be remembered most for its errors and omissions.

Andreas Brehme (3) scores from the penalty spot to win the World Cup for West Germany.

Qualifying Tournament
112 entries*
Argentina as champions and Italy as hosts already qualified
AFRICA (24): Algeria, Angola, Burkina Faso, Cameroon, Egypt, Gabon, Ghana, Guinea, Ivory Coast, Kenya, Lesotho, Liberia, Libya, Malawi, Morocco, Nigeria, Rwanda, Sudan, Togo, Tunisia, Uganda, Zaire, Zambia, Zimbabwe
CONCACAF(15): Antigua, Canada, Costa Rica, Cuba, Guatemala, Guyana, Honduras, Jamaica, Mexico, Netherlands Antilles, Panama, Puerto Rico, El Salvador, Trinidad and Tobago, USA
EUROPE(33): Albania, Austria, Belgium, Bulgaria, Cyprus, Czechoslovakia, Denmark, England, Finland, France, East Germany, West Germany, Greece, Holland, Hungary, Iceland, Northern Ireland, Rep of Ireland, Italy, Luxembourg, Malta, Norway, Poland, Portugal, Rumania, Scotland, Spain, Sweden, Switzerland, Turkey, USSR, Wales, Yugoslavia
OCEANIA (4 + 1): Australia, Fiji, New Zealand, Taipei + Israel
SOUTH AMERICA(10): Argentina, Bolivia, Brazil, Chile, Colombia, Ecuador, Paraguay, Peru, Uruguay, Venezuela
ASIA (25): Bahrain, Bangladesh, China, Hong Kong, India, Indonesia, Iran, Iraq, Japan, Jordan, North Korea, South Korea, Kuwait, Malaysia, Nepal, Oman, Pakistan, Qatar, Saudi Arabia, Singapore, Syria, Thailand, UAE, North Yemen, South Yemen

*India subsequently withdrew.

Final places in Italy were to be distributed as follows: Africa (2), Asia (2), Concacaf (2), Europe (13 + Italy), Oceania (0)**, South America (3;+ Argentina)**

**Oceania's representative would be required to play the winner of Group 2 in South America for a final place.

Europe
Group 1 (Denmark, Bulgaria, Rumania, Greece)
Greece v Denmark 1 - 1; Bulgaria v Rumania 1 - 3; Rumania v Greece 3 - 0; Denmark v Bulgaria 1 - 1; Greece v Rumania 0 - 0; Bulgaria v Denmark 0 - 2; Rumania v Bulgaria 1 - 0; Denmark v Greece 7 - 1; Bulgaria v Greece 4 - 0; Denmark v Rumania 3 - 0; Greece v Rumania 1 - 0; Rumania v Denmark 3 - 1

	P	W	D	L	F	A	Pts
Rumania	6	4	1	1	10	5	9
Denmark	6	3	2	1	15	6	8
Greece	6	1	2	3	3	15	4
Bulgaria	6	1	1	4	6	8	3

Rumania qualified

Group 2 (England, Poland, Sweden, Albania)
England v Sweden 0 - 0; Poland v Albania 1 - 0; Albania v Sweden 1 - 2; Albania v England 0 - 2; England v Albania 5 - 0; Sweden v Poland 2 - 1; England v Poland 3 - 0; Sweden v England 0 - 0; Sweden v Albania 3 - 1; Poland v England 0 - 0; Poland v Sweden 0 - 2; Albania v Poland 1 - 2

	P	W	D	L	F	A	Pts
Sweden	6	4	2	0	9	3	10
England	6	3	3	0	10	0	9
Poland	6	2	1	3	4	8	5
Albania	6	0	0	6	3	15	0

Sweden and England qualified

Group 3 (USSR, East Germany, Austria, Iceland, Turkey)
Iceland v USSR 1 - 1; Turkey v Iceland 1 -1; USSR v Austria 2 - 0; East Germany v Iceland 2 - 0; Austria v Turkey 3 - 2; Turkey v East Germany 3 - 1; East Germany v Turkey 0 - 2; USSR v East Germany 3 - 0; Turkey v USSR 0 - 1; East Germany v Austria 1 - 1; USSR v Iceland 1 - 1; Iceland v Austria 0 - 0; Austria v Iceland 2 - 1; Austria v USSR 0 - 0; Iceland v East Germany 0 - 3; Iceland v Turkey 2 - 1; East Germany v USSR 2 - 1; Turkey v Austria 3 -0; USSR v Turkey 2 - 0; Austria v East Germany 3 - 0

	P	W	D	L	F	A	Pts
USSR	8	4	3	1	11	4	11
Austria	8	3	3	2	9	9	9
Turkey	8	3	1	4	12	10	7
East Germany	8	3	1	4	9	13	7
Iceland	8	1	4	3	6	11	6

USSR and Austria qualified

Group 4 (West Germany, Holland, Wales, Finland)
Finland v West Germany 0 - 4; Holland v Wales 1 - 0; Wales v Finland
2 - 2; West Germany v Holland 0 - 0; Holland v West Germany 1 - 1; Wales
v West Germany 0 - 0; Finland v Holland 0 - 1; Finland v Wales
1 - 0; West Germany v Finland 6 - 1; Wales v Holland 1 - 2; West Germany
v Wales 2 - 1; Holland v Finland 3 - 0

	P	W	D	L	F	A	Pts
Holland	6	4	2	0	8	2	10
West Germany	6	3	3	0	13	3	9
Finland	6	1	1	4	16	3
Wales	6	0	2	4	4	8	2

Holland and West Germany qualified

Group 5 (France, Scotland, Yugoslavia, Norway, Cyprus)
Norway v Scotland 1 - 2; France v Norway 1 - 0; Scotland v Yugoslavia
1 - 1; Cyprus v France 1 - 1; Cyprus v Norway 0 - 3; Yugoslavia v France
3 - 2; Yugoslavia v Cyprus 4 - 0; Cyprus v Scotland 2 - 3; Scotland
v France 2 - 0; Scotland v Cyprus 2 - 1; France v Yugoslavia 0 - 0; Norway
v Cyprus 3 - 1; Norway v Yugoslavia 1 - 2; Norway v France 1 - 1;
Yugoslavia v Scotland 3 - 1; Yugoslavia v Norway 1-0; France v Scotland 3 -
0; Cyprus v Yugoslavia 1 - 2; Scotland v Norway 1 - 1; France v Cyprus 2-0

	P	W	D	L	F	A	Pts
Yugoslavia	8	6	2	0	16	6	14
Scotland	8	4	2	2	12	12	10
France	8	3	3	2	10	7	9
Norway	8	2	2	4	10	9	6
Cyprus	8	0	1	7	6	20	1

Yugoslavia and Scotland qualified

Group 6 (Spain, Hungary, Northern Ireland, Rep of Ireland, Malta)
Northern Ireland v Malta 3 - 0; Northern Ireland v Rep of Ireland 0 - 0;
Hungary v Northern Ireland 1 - 0; Spain v Rep of Ireland 2 - 0; Malta
v Hungary 2 - 2; Spain v Northern Ireland 4 - 0; Malta v Spain 0 - 2;
Northern Ireland v Spain 0 - 2; Hungary v Rep of Ireland 0 - 0; Spain
v Malta 4 - 0; Hungary v Malta 1 -1 ; Malta v Northern Ireland 0 - 2; Rep of
Ireland v Spain 1 - 0; Rep of Ireland v Malta 2 - 0; Rep of Ireland
v Hungary 2 - 0; Northern Ireland v Hungary 1 - 2; Hungary v Spain 2 - 2;
Rep of Ireland v Northern Ireland 3 - 0; Spain v Hungary 4 - 0; Malta
v Rep of Ireland 0 - 2

	P	W	D	L	F	A	Pts
Spain	8	6	1	1	20	3	13
Rep of Ireland	8	5	2	1	10	2	12
Hungary	8	2	4	2	8	12	8
Northern Ireland	8	2	1	5	6	12	5
Malta	8	0	2	6	3	18	2

Spain and Rep of Ireland qualified

Group 7 (Belgium, Portugal, Czechoslovakia, Switzerland, Luxembourg)
Luxembourg v Switzerland 1 - 4; Luxembourg v Czechoslovakia 0 - 2;
Belgium v Switzerland 1 - 0; Czechoslovakia v Belgium 0 - 0; Portugal
v Luxembourg 1 - 0; Portugal v Belgium 1 - 1; Portugal v Switzerland 3 - 1;
Belgium v Czechoslovakia 2 - 1; Czechoslovakia v Luxembourg 4 - 0;
Luxembourg v Belgium 0 - 5; Switzerland v Czechoslovakia 0 - 1; Belgium
v Portugal 3 - 0; Switzerland v Portugal 1 - 2; Czechoslovakia v Portugal
2 - 1; Luxembourg v Portugal 0 - 3; Switzerland v Belgium 2 - 2;
Czechoslovakia v Switzerland 3 - 0; Belgium v Luxembourg 1 - 1; Portugal
v Czechoslovakia 0 - 0; Switzerland v Luxembourg 2 - 1

	P	W	D	L	F	A	Pts
Belgium	8	4	4	0	15	5	12
Czechoslovakia	8	5	2	1	13	3	12
Portugal	8	4	2	2	11	8	10
Switzerland	8	2	1	5	10	14	5
Luxembourg	8	0	1	7	3	22	1

Belgium and Czechoslovakia qualified

Africa
1st Round
Group 1
Angola v Sudan 0 - 0, 2 - 1; Zimbabwe v Lesotho (withdrew); Zambia
v Rwanda (withdrew); Uganda v Malawi 1 - 0, 1 - 3

Group 2
Libya v Burkina Faso 3 - 0, 0 - 2; Ghana v Liberia 0 - 0, 0 - 2; Tunisia
v Guinea 5 - 0, 0 - 3; Gabon v Togo (withdrew)

2nd Round
Group A (Algeria, Ivory Coast, Zimbabwe, Libya)
Algeria v Zimbabwe 3 - 0; Ivory Coast v Libya 1 - 0; Libya v Algeria (Libya
refused to play claiming state of war against the USA; match awarded
2 - 0 to Algeria); Zimbabwe v Ivory Coast 0 - 0;(Libya withdrew at this
point and their record was expunged); Ivory Coast v Algeria 0 - 0;
Zimbabwe v Algeria 1 - 2; Ivory Coast v Zimbabwe 5 - 0; Algeria v Ivory
Coast 1 - 0

	P	W	D	L	F	A	Pts
Algeria	4	3	1	0	6	1	7
Ivory Coast	4	1	2	1	5	1	4
Zimbabwe	4	0	1	3	1	10	1

Group B (Egypt, Kenya, Malawi, Liberia)
Egypt v Liberia 2 - 0; Kenya v Malawi 1 - 1; Malawi v Egypt 1 - 1;Liberia
v Kenya 0 - 0; Kenya v Egypt 0 - 0; Liberia v Malawi 1 - 0; Malawi v Kenya
1 - 0; Liberia v Egypt 1 - 0; Egypt v Malawi 1 - 0; Kenya v Liberia 1 - 0;
Egypt v Kenya 2 - 0; Malawi v Liberia 0 - 0

	P	W	D	L	F	A	Pts
Egypt	6	3	2	1	6	2	8
Liberia	6	2	2	2	2	3	6
Malawi	6	1	3	2	3	4	5
Kenya	6	1	3	2	2	4	5

Group C (Cameroon, Nigeria, Gabon, Angola)
Nigeria v Gabon 2 - 1; Cameroon v Angola 1 - 1; Gabon v Cameroon
1 - 3; Angola v Nigeria 2 - 2; Nigeria v Cameroon 2 - 0; Angola v Gabon
2 - 0; Angola v Cameroon 1 - 2; Gabon v Nigeria 2 - 1; Nigeria v Angola
1 - 0; Cameroon v Gabon 2 - 1; Cameroon v Nigeria 1 - 0; Gabon v Angola
1 - 0

	P	W	D	L	F	A	Pts
Cameroon	6	4	1	1	9	6	9
Nigeria	6	3	1	2	7	5	7
Angola	6	1	2	3	6	7	4
Gabon	6	2	0	4	5	9	4

Group D (Morocco, Zaire, Tunisia, Zambia)
Morocco v Zambia 1 - 0; Zaire v Tunisia 3 - 1; Tunisia v Morocco 2 - 1;
Zambia v Zaire 4 - 2; Zaire v Morocco 0 - 0; Zambia v Tunisia 1 - 0; Zambia
v Morocco 2 - 1; Tunisia v Zaire 1 - 0; Morocco v Tunisia 0 - 0; Zaire
v Zambia 1 - 0; Tunisia v Zambia 1 - 0; Morocco v Zaire 1 - 1

	P	W	D	L	F	A	Pts
Tunisia	6	3	1	2	5	5	7
Zambia	6	3	0	3	7	6	6
Zaire	6	2	2	2	7	7	6
Morocco	6	1	3	2	4	5	5

3rd Round
Algeria v Egypt 0 - 0,0 - 1; Cameroon v Tunisia 2 - 0, 1 - 0
Egypt and Cameroon qualified

Asia
1st Round
Group 1 (Iraq, Qatar, Jordan, Oman)
Qatar v Jordan 1 - 0; Oman v Iraq 1 - 1; Oman v Qatar 0 - 0; Jordan v Iraq
0 - 1; Jordan v Oman 2 - 0; Qatar v Iraq 1 - 0; Jordan v Qatar 1 - 1; Iraq
v Oman 3 - 1: Qatar v Oman 3 - 0; Iraq v Jordan 4 - 0; Oman v Jordan
0 - 2; Iraq v Qatar 2 - 2

	P	W	D	L	F	A	Pts
Qatar	6	3	3	0	8	5	9
Iraq	6	3	2	1	11	5	8
Jordan	6	2	1	3	5	7	5
Oman	6	0	2	4	2	11	2

Group 2 (Saudi Arabia, Syria, North Yemen, Bahrain (withdrew))
North Yemen v Syria 0 - 1; Saudi Arabia v Syria 5 - 4; North Yemen v Saudi
Arabia 0 - 1; Syria v North Yemen 2 - 0; Syria v Saudi Arabia 0 - 0; Saudi
Arabia v North Yemen 1 - 0

	P	W	D	L	F	A	Pts
Saudi Arabia	4	3	1	0	7	4	7
Syria	4	2	1	1	7	5	5
North Yemen	4	0	0	4	0	5	0

Group 3 (Kuwait, UAE, Pakistan, South Yemen (withdrew))
Pakistan v Kuwait 0 - 1; Kuwait v UAE 3 - 2; UAE v Pakistan 5 - 0; Kuwait
v Pakistan 2 - 0; UAE v Kuwait 1 - 0; Pakistan v UAE 1 - 4

	P	W	D	L	F	A	Pts
UAE	4	3	0	1	12	4	6
Kuwait	4	3	0	1	6	3	6
Pakistan	4	0	0	4	1	12	0

Group 4 (South Korea, Singapore, Malaysia, Nepal, India (withdrew))
All matches played in Singapore
Malaysia v Nepal 2 - 0; Singapore v South Korea 0 - 3; Malaysia v
Singapore 1 - 0; Nepal v South Korea 0 - 9; Singapore v Nepal 3 - 0; South
Korea v Malaysia 3 - 0 (all matches played in South Korea); Singapore
v Malaysia 2 - 2; South Korea v Nepal 4 - 0; Malaysia v South Korea 0 - 3;
Nepal v Singapore 0 - 7; Singapore v South Korea 0 - 3; Malaysia v Nepal
3 - 0

	P	W	D	L	F	A	Pts
South Korea	6	6	0	0	25	0	2
Malaysia	6	3	1	2	8	8	7
Singapore	6	2	1	3	12	9	5
Nepal	6	0	0	6	0	28	0

Group 5 (China, Iran, Thailand, Bangladesh)
Thailand v Bangladesh 1 - 0; China v Bangladesh 2 - 0; Thailand v Iran 0 - 3;
Bangladesh v Iran 1 - 2; Thailand v China 0 - 3; Bangladesh v China 0 - 2;
Bangladesh v Thailand 3 - 1; Iran v Bangladesh 3 - 0; Iran v Thailand 3 - 0;
China v Iran 2 - 0; Iran v China 3 - 2; China v Thailand 2 - 0

	P	W	D	L	F	A	Pts
China	6	5	0	1	13	3	10
Iran	6	5	0	1	12	5	10
Bangladesh	6	1	0	5	4	9	2
Thailand	6	1	0	5	2	14	2

Group 6 (North Korea, Japan, Indonesia, Hong Kong)
Indonesia v North Korea 0 - 0; Hong Kong v Japan 0 - 0; Hong Kong v
North Korea 1 - 2; Indonesia v Japan 0 - 0; Hong Kong v Indonesia 1 - 1;
Japan v North Korea 2 - 1; Japan v Indonesia 5 - 0; Japan v Hong Kong 0 -
0; Indonesia v Hong Kong 3 - 2; North Korea v Japan 2 - 0; North Korea
v Hong Kong 4 - 1; North Korea v Indonesia 2 - 1

	P	W	D	L	F	A	Pts
North Korea	6	4	1	1	11	5	9
Japan	6	2	3	1	7	3	7
Indonesia	6	1	3	2	5	10	5
Hong Kong	6	0	3	3	5	10	3

2nd Round (in Singapore)
UAE v North Korea 0 - 0; China v Saudi Arabia 2 - 1; South Korea v Qatar
0 - 0; Qatar v Saudi Arabia 1 - 1; South Korea v North Korea 1 - 0; China
v UAE 1 - 2; China v South Korea 0 - 1; North Korea v Qatar 2 - 0; Saudi
Arabia v UAE 0 - 0; UAE v Qatar 1 - 1; North Korea v China 0 - 1; Saudi
Arabia v South Korea 0 - 2; UAE v South Korea 1 - 1; Saudi Arabia v North
Korea 2 - 0; Qatar v China 2 - 1

	P	W	D	L	F	A	Pts
South Korea	5	3	2	0	5	1	8
UAE	5	1	4	0	4	3	6
Qatar	5	1	3	1	4	5	5
China	5	2	0	3	5	6	4
Saudi Arabia	5	1	2	2	4	5	4
North Korea	5	1	1	3	2	4	3

South Korea and UAE qualified

Concacaf
1st Round
Guyana v Trinidad and Tobago 0 - 4, 0 - 1; Cuba v Guatemala 0 - 1, 1 - 1;
Jamaica v Puerto Rico 1 - 0, 2 - 1; Antigua v Netherlands Antilles 0 - 1,
1 - 0 (Netherlands Antilles won 3 - 1 on penalties); Costa Rica v Panama
1 - 1, 2 - 0

2nd Round
Netherlands Antilles v El Salvador 0 - 1, 0 - 5; Jamaica v USA 0 - 0, 1 - 5;
Trinidad and Tobago v Honduras 0 - 0, 1 - 1; Costa Rica v Mexico
(disqualified); Guatemala v Canada 1 0, 2 - 3

3rd Round
Guatemala v Costa Rica 1 - 0; Costa Rica v Guatemala 2 - 1; Costa Rica
v USA 1 - 0; USA v Costa Rica 1 - 0; USA v Trinidad and Tobago 1 - 1;
Trinidad and Tobago v Costa Rica 1 - 1; Costa Rica v Trinidad and Tobago
1 - 0; USA v Guatemala 2 - 1; El Salvador v Costa Rica 2 - 4 (match
abandoned after 84 mins; score allowed to stand), Costa Rica
v El Salvador 1 - 0; Trinidad and Tobago v El Salvador 2 - 0; El Salvador
v Trinidad and Tobago 1 - 0; Guatemala v Trinidad and Tobago 0 - 1;
Trinidad and Tobago v Guatemala 2 - 1; El Salvador v USA (in Honduras)
0 - 1; Guatemala v USA 0 - 0; USA v El Salvador 0 - 1; Trinidad and Tobago
v USA 0 - 1; Guatemala v El Salvador and El Salvador v Guatemala not
played due to deterioration of the political situation in El Salvador, FIFA
annulled the fixtures

	P	W	D	L	F	A	Pts
Costa Rica	8	5	1	2	10	6	11
USA	8	4	3	1	6	3	11
T'dad/Tobago	8	3	3	2	7	5	9
Guatemala	6	1	1	4	4	7	3
El Salvador	6	0	2	4	2	8	2

Costa Rica and USA qualified

South America
Group 1 (Uruguay, Peru, Bolivia)
Bolivia v Peru 2 - 1; Peru v Uruguay 0 - 2; Bolivia v Uruguay 2 - 1;
Peru v Bolivia 1 - 2; Uruguay v Bolivia 2 - 0; Uruguay v Peru 2 - 0

	P	W	D	L	F	A	Pts
Uruguay	4	3	0	1	7	2	6
Bolivia	4	3	0	1	6	5	6
Peru	4	0	0	4	2	8	0

Uruguay qualified

Group 2 (Paraguay, Colombia, Ecuador)
Colombia v Ecuador 2 - 0; Paraguay v Colombia 2 - 1; Ecuador v Colombia
0 - 0; Paraguay v Ecuador 2 - 1; Colombia v Paraguay 2 - 1; Ecuador
v Paraguay 3 - 1

	P	W	D	L	F	A	Pts
Colombia	4	2	1	1	5	3	5
Paraguay	4	2	0	2	6	7	4
Ecuador	4	1	1	2	4	5	3

Colombia qualified for play-off with Oceania winner

Group 3 (Brazil, Chile, Venezuela)
Venezuela v Brazil 0 - 4; Venezuela v Chile 1 - 3; Chile v Brazil 1 - 1; Brazil v
Venezuela 6 - 0; Chile v Venezuela 5 - 0; Brazil v Chile 1 - 0 (abandoned
59th minute; match awarded 2 - 0 to Brazil)

	P	W	D	L	F	A	Pts
Brazil	4	3	1	0	13	1	7
Chile	4	2	1	1	9	4	5
Venezuela	4	0	0	4	1	18	0

Brazil qualified

Oceania
1st round
Group 1
Taipei v New Zealand 0 - 4, 1-4

Group 2
Fiji v Australia 1 - 0, 1 - 5

2nd round
Israel v New Zealand 1 - 0; Australia v New Zealand 4 - 1; Israel
v Australia 1 - 1; New Zealand v Australia 2 - 0; New Zealand v Israel 2 - 2;
Australia v Israel 1 - 1

	P	W	D	L	F	A	Pts
Israel	4	1	3	0	5	4	5
Australia	4	1	2	1	6	5	4
New Zealand	4	1	1	2	5	7	3

Play-off: Colombia v Israel 1 - 0, 0 - 0
Colombia qualified

Final Tournament ITALY
First Round
GROUP A

9.6.90 Italy (0) 1, Austria (0) 0 ROME
Italy: Zenga, Maldini, Ferri, Baresi, Bergomi, De Napoli, Ancelotti (De Agostini), Donadoni, Giannini, Carnevale (Schillaci (1)), Vialli
Austria: Lindenberger, Russ, Streiter, Pecl, Aigner, Artner (Zsak), Herzog, Schottel, Linzmaier (Hortnagl), Ogris, Polster
Referee: Wright (Brazil)

10.6.90 Czechoslovakia (2) 5, USA (0) 1 FLORENCE
Czechoslovakia: Stejskal, Hasek (1), Kocian, Kadlec, Straka, Moravcik (Weiss), Chovanec, Kubik, Bilek (1 pen), Knoflicek (Luhovy (1)), Skuhravy (2)
USA: Meola, Armstrong, Stollmeyer (Balboa), Windischmann, Trittschuh, Caligiuri (1), Ramos, Harkes, Wynalda, Vermes, Murray (Sullivan)
Referee: Rothlisberger (Switzerland)

14.6.90 Italy (1) 1, USA (0) 0 ROME
Italy: Zenga, Bergomi, Ferri, Baresi, Maldini, De Napoli, Berti, Giannini (1), Donadoni, Carnevale (Schillaci), Vialli
USA: Meola, Armstrong, Windischmann, Doyle, Banks (Stollmeyer), Ramos, Balboa, Caligiuri, Harkes, Vermes, Murray (Sullivan)
Referee: Codesal (Mexico)

15.6.90 Austria (0) 0, Czechoslovakia (0) 1 FLORENCE
Austria: Lindenberger, Russ (Ogris), Aigner, Pecl, Pfeffer, Hortnagl, Zsak, Schottel (Streiter), Herzog, Rodax, Polster
Czechoslovakia: Stejskal, Hasek, Kadlec, Kocian, Nemecek, Moravcik, Chovanec (Bielik), Kubik, Bilek (1 pen), Skuhravy, Knoflicek (Weiss)
Referee: Smith (Scotland)

19.6.90 Italy (1) 2, Czechoslovakia (0) 0 ROME
Italy: Zenga, Bergomi, Ferri, Baresi, Maldini, Donadoni (De Agostini), De Napoli (Vierchowod), Giannini, Berti, Baggio (1), Schillaci (1)
Czechoslovakia: Stejskal, Hasek, Kadlec, Kinier, Nemecek (Bielik), Moravcik, Chovanec, Weiss (Griga), Bilek, Skuhravy, Knoflicek
Referee: Quiniou (France)

19.6.90 Austria (0) 2, USA (0) 1 FLORENCE
Austria: Lindenberger, Streiter, Aigner, Pecl, Pfeffer, Artner, Zsak, Herzog, Rodax (1) (Glatzmeyer), Polster (Reisinger), Ogris (1)
USA: Meola, Doyle, Windischmann, Banks (Wynalda), Armstrong, Caligiuri (Bliss), Harkes, Ramos, Balboa, Murray (1), Vermes
Referee: Sharif Jamal (Egypt)

	P	W	D	L	F	A	Pts
Italy	3	3	0	0	4	0	6
Czechoslovakia	3	2	0	1	6	3	4
Austria	3	1	0	2	2	3	2
United States	3	0	0	3	2	8	0

GROUP B

8.6.90 Argentina (0) 0, Cameroon (0) 1 MILAN
Argentina: Pumpido, Ruggeri (Caniggia), Fabbri, Simon, Lorenzo, Batista, Sensini (Calderon), Balbo, Basualdo, Burruchaga, Maradona
Cameroon: Nkono, Tataw, Ebwelle, Massing, Ndip, Kunde, Mbouh, Kana-Biyik, Mfede (Libih), Makanaky (Milla), Omam-Biyik (1)
Referee: Vautrot (France)

9.6.90 USSR (0) 0, Rumania (1) 2 BARI
USSR: Dasayev, Kuznetsov, Khidiatulin, Gorlukovich, Rats, Aleinikov, Bessonov, Litovchenko (Yaremchuk), Zavarov, Protasov, Dobrovolski (Borodyuk)
Rumania: Lung, Rednic, Andone, Popescu, Klein, Rotariu, Timofte, Sabau, Lupescu, Lacatus (2, 1 pen) (Dumitrescu), Raducioiu (Balint)
Referee: Cardellino (Uruguay)

13.6.90 Argentina (1) 2, USSR (0) 0 NAPLES
Argentina: Pumpido (Goycochea), Monzon (Lorenzo), Serrizuela, Simon, Olarticoechea, Batista, Basualdo, Burruchaga (1), Troglio (1), Maradona, Caniggia
USSR: Uvarov, Bessonov, Kuznetsov, Khidiatulin, Gorlukovich, Zygmantovich, Aleinikov, Shalimov, Zavarov (Liuti), Dobrovolski, Protasov (Litovchenko)
Referee: Fredriksson (Sweden)

14.6.90 Cameroon (0) 2, Rumania (0) 1 BARI
Cameroon: Nkono, Tataw, Onana, Ndip, Ebwelle, Kunde (Pagal), Mbouh, Mfede, Maboang (Milla (2)), Makanaky, Omam-Biyik
Rumania: Lung, Rednic, Andone, Popescu, Klein, Rotariu, Sabau, Timofte, Hagi (Dumitrescu), Raducioiu (Balint (1)), Lacatus
Referee: Valente (Portugal)

18.6.90 Argentina (0) 1, Rumania (0) 1 NAPLES
Argentina: Goycochea, Simon, Serrizuela, Monzon (1), Troglio (Giusti), Batista, Burruchaga (Dezotti), Basualdo, Olarticoechea, Maradona, Caniggia
Rumania: Lung, Rednic, Andone, Popescu, Klein, Rotariu, Sabau (Mateut), Lupescu, Hagi, Lacatus, Balint (1) (Lupu)
Referee: Valente (Portugal)

18.6.90 USSR (2) 4, Cameroon (0) 0 BARI
USSR: Uvarov, Khidiatulin, Kuznetsov, Demianenko, Gorlukovich, Aleinikov, Litovchenko (Yaremchuk), Zygmantovich (1), Shalimov (Zavarov (1)), Protasov (1), Dobrovolski (1)
Cameroon: Nkono, Onana, Ebwelle, Kunde (Milla), Tataw, Ndip, Kana-Biyik, Mbouh, Mfede, Makanaky (Pagal), Omam-Biyik
Referee: Wright (Brazil)

	P	W	D	L	F	A	Pts
Cameroon	3	2	0	1	3	5	4
Rumania	3	1	1	1	4	3	3
Argentina	3	1	1	1	3	2	3
USSR	3	1	0	2	4	4	2

GROUP C

10.6.90 Brazil (1) 2, Sweden (0) 1 TURIN
Brazil: Taffarel, Mauro Galvao, Mozer, Ricardo Gomes, Jorginho, Branco, Dunga, Alemao, Valdo (Silas), Muller, Careca (2)
Sweden: Ravelli, Nilsson R, Larsson P, Ljung (Stromberg), Limpar, Thern, Schwarz, Ingesson, Nilsson J, Brolin (1), Magnusson (Pettersson)
Referee: Lanese (Italy)

11.6.90 Costa Rica (0) 1, Scotland (0) 0 GENOA
Costa Rica: Conejo, Chavarria, Flores, Marchena, Montero, Chavez, Gonzalez, Gomez, Ramirez, Jara (Medford), Cayasso (1)
Scotland: Leighton, Gough (McKimmie), McPherson, McLeish, Malpas, McStay, Aitken, McCall, Bett (McCoist), Johnston, McInally
Referee: Loustau (Argentina)

16.6.90 Brazil (1) 1, Costa Rica (0) 0 TURIN
Brazil: Taffarel, Mauro Galvao, Jorginho, Mozer, Ricardo Gomes, Branco, Dunga, Alemao, Valdo (Silas), Careca (Bebeto), Muller (1)
Costa Rica: Conejo, Flores, Chavarria, Marchena, Gonzalez, Montero, Chavez, Gomez, Ramirez, Jara (Myers), Cayasso (Guimaraes)
Referee: Jouini (Tunisia)

16.6.90 Scotland (1) 2, Sweden (0) 1 GENOA
Scotland: Leighton, McPherson, Levein, McLeish, Malpas, Aitken, MacLeod, McCall (1), Fleck (McCoist), Durie (McStay), Johnston (1 pen)
Sweden: Ravelli, Nilsson R, Larsson P (Stromberg (1)), Hysen, Schwarz, Ingesson, Thern, Limpar, Nilsson J, Brolin, Pettersson (Ekstrom)
Referee: Maciel (Paraguay)

20.6.90 Brazil (0) 1, Scotland (0) 0 TURIN
Brazil: Taffarel, Jorginho, Mauro Galvao, Ricardo Rocha, Ricardo Gomes, Branco, Alemao, Dunga, Valdo, Careca, Romario (Muller (1))
Scotland: Leighton, McKimmie, McPherson, Aitken, McLeish, Malpas, McCall, McStay, MacLeod (Gillespie), Johnston, McCoist (Fleck)
Referee: Kohl (Austria)

20.6.90 Costa Rica (0) 2, Sweden (1) 1 GENOA
Costa Rica: Conejo, Marchena, Flores (1), Gonzalez, Montero, Chavarria, Gomez (Medford (1)), Chaves, Cayasso, Ramirez, Jara
Sweden: Ravelli, Nilsson R, Larsson P, Hysen, Schwarz, Pettersson, Stromberg (Engqvist), Ingesson, Nilsson J, Ekstrom (1), Brolin (Gren)
Referee: Petrovic (Yugoslavia)

	P	W	D	L	F	A	Pts
Brazil	3	3	0	0	4	1	6
Costa Rica	3	2	0	1	3	2	4
Scotland	3	1	0	2	2	3	2
Sweden	3	0	0	3	3	6	0

GROUP D

9.6.90 Colombia (0) 2, UAE (0) 0 BOLOGNA
Colombia: Higuita, Escobar, Gildardo Gomez, Herrera, Perea, Gabriel Gomez, Valderrama (1), Redin (1), Alvarez, Rincon, Iguaran (Estrada)
UAE: Faraj, Mubarak K G, Abdulrahman I, Abdulrahman E (Sultan), Mohamed Y, Juma'a, Abdullah Moh, Abbas, Mubarak N, Mubarak K (Bilal), Talyani
Referee: Courtney (England)

10.6.90 Yugoslavia (0) 1, West Germany (2) 4 MILAN
Yugoslavia: Ivkovic, Vulic, Hadzibegic, Jozic (1), Spasic, Katanec, Baljic, Susic (Brnovic), Savicevic (Prosinecki), Stojkovic, Vujovic
West Germany: Illgner, Reuter, Berthold, Augenthaler, Brehme, Buchwald, Matthaus (2), Bein (Moller), Hassler (Littbarski), Klinsmann (1), Voller (1)
Referee: Mikkelsen (Denmark)

14.6.90 Yugoslavia (0) 1, Colombia (0) 0 BOLOGNA
Yugoslavia: Ivkovic, Stanojkovic, Spasic, Hadzibegic, Jozic (1), Brnovic, Susic, Katanec (Jarni), Stojkovic, Sabanadzovic, Vujovic (Pancev)
Colombia: Higuita, Herrera, Perea, Gildardo Gomez, Escobar, Gabriel Gomez, Alvarez, Valderrama, Redin (Estrada), Rincon (Hernandez), Iguaran
Referee: Agnolin (Italy)

15.6.90 West Germany (2) 5, UAE (0) 1 MILAN
West Germany: Illgner, Reuter, Buchwald, Augenthaler, Brehme, Berthold (Littbarski), Matthaus, Hassler, Bein (1), Klinsmann (1) (Riedle), Voller (2)
UAE: Faraj, Abdulrahman E, Mubarak K G, Mohamed Y, Abdulrahman I, (Al Haddad), Addullah Moh, Juma'a, Mubarak N, Mubarak K (1) (Hussain), Abbas, Talyani
Referee: Spirin (USSR)

19.6.90 West Germany (0) 1, Colombia (0) 1 MILAN
West Germany: Illgner, Reuter, Buchwald, Augenthaler, Pflugler, Berthold, Matthaus, Hassler (Thon), Bein (Littbarski (1)), Klinsmann, Voller
Colombia: Higuita, Herrera, Escobar, Perea, Gildardo Gomez, Gabriel Gomez, Alvarez, Estrada, Fajardo, Valderrama, Rincon (1)
Referee: Snoddy (N. Ireland)

19.6.90 Yugoslavia (2) 4, UAE (1) 1 BOLOGNA
Yugoslavia: Ivkovic, Stanojkovic, Spasic, Hadzibegic, Jozic, Brnovic, Susic (1), Stojkovic, Sabanadzovic (Prosinecki (1)), Pancev (2), Vujovic (Vulic)
UAE: Faraj, Mubarak K G, Abdulrahman I, Abdulrahman E, Al Haddad, Juma'a (1), (Mubarak F K), Abdullah Moh, Abbas, Mubarak N (Sultan), Mubarak I, Talyani
Referee: Takada (Japan)

	P	W	D	L	F	A	Pts
West Germany	3	2	1	0	10	3	5
Yugoslavia	3	2	0	1	6	5	4
Colombia	3	1	1	1	3	2	1
UAE	3	0	0	3	2	11	0

GROUP E

12.6.90 Belgium (0) 2, South Korea (0) 0 VERONA
Belgium: Preud'homme, Gerets, Clijsters, Demol, Dewolf (1), Emmers, Van der Elst, Scifo, Versavel, De Gryse (1), Van der Linden (Ceulemans)
South Korea: Choi In-Young, Choi Kang-Hee, Chung Yong-Hwan, Hong Myung-Bo, Park Kyung-Joon, Gu Sang-Bum, Lee Young-Jin (Cho Min-Kook), Noh Soo-Jin (Lee Tae-Hoo), Choi Soon-Ho, Hwang Seon-Hong, Kim Joo-Sung
Referee: Mauro (USA)

13.6.90 Spain (0) 0, Uruguay (0) 0 UDINE
Spain: Zubizarreta, Chendo, Sanchis, Andrinua, Jimenez, Martin Vazquez, Roberto, Villaroya (Gorriz), Michel, Manolo (Paz), Butragueno
Uruguay: Alvez, Herrera, Gutierrez, De Leon, Dominguez, Ruben Pereira (Correa), Perdomo, Paz, Alzamendi (Aguilera), Francescoli, Sosa
Referee: Kohl (Austria)

17.6.90 Spain (1) 3, South Korea (1) 1 UDINE
Spain: Zubizarreta, Chendo, Andrinua, Sanchis, Gorriz, Michel (3), Villaroya, Roberto (Bakero), Martin Vazquez, Butragueno (Fernando), Julio Salinas
South Korea: Choi In-Young, Park Kyung-Joon (Chung Jong-Soo), Choi Kang-Hee, Hong Myung-Bo, Yoon Deuk-Yeo, Hwang Kwan-Bo (1), Chung Hae-Won (Noh Soo-Jin), Kim Joo-Sung, Gu Sang-Bum, Byun Byung-Joo, Choi Soon-Ho
Referee: Guerrero (Ecuador)

17.6.90 Belgium (2) 3, Uruguay (0) 1 VERONA
Belgium: Preud'homme, Gerets, Grun, Clijsters (1) (Emmers), Demol, Dewolf, Versavel (Vervoort), Van der Elst, Scifo (1), De Gryse, Ceulemans (1)
Uruguay: Alvez, Herrera, Gutierrez, De Leon, Dominguez, Ostolaza (Bengoechea (1)), Perdomo, Paz, Alzamendi (Aguilera), Francescoli, Sosa
Referee: Kirschen (East Germany)

21.6.90 Spain (2) 2, Belgium (1) 1 VERONA
Spain: Zubizarreta, Chendo, Sanchis, Andrinua, Villaroya, Gorriz, Michel (1 pen), Roberto, Martin Vazquez, Butragueno (Alcorta), Julio Salinas (Pardeza)
Belgium: Preud'homme, Staelens (Van der Linden), Albert, Demol, Dewolf, Van der Elst, Emmers (Plovie), Vervoort (1), Scifo, De Gryse, Ceulemans
Referee: Loustau (Argentina)

21.6.90 Uruguay (0) 1, South Korea (0) 0 UDINE
Uruguay: Alvez, Gutierrez, De Leon, Herrera, Dominguez, Perdomo, Ostolaza (Aguilera), Francescoli, Paz, Martinez, Sosa (1) (Fonseca (1))
South Korea: Choi In-Young, Park Kyung-Joon, Choi Kang-Hee, Chung Jong-Soo, Hong Myung-Bo, Yoon Deuk-Yeo, Hwang Kwan-Bo (Chung Hae-Won), Lee Heung-Sil, Kim Joo-Sung (Hwang Seon-Hong), Byun Byung-Joo, Choi Soon-Ho
Referee: Lanese (Italy)

	P	W	D	L	F	A	Pts
Spain	3	2	1	0	5	2	5
Belgium	3	2	0	1	6	3	4
Uruguay	3	1	1	1	2	3	3
South Korea	3	0	0	3	1	6	0

GROUP F

11.6.90 England (1) 1, Rep of Ireland (0) 1 CAGLIARI
England: Shilton, Stevens, Walker, Butcher, Pearce, Robson, Beardsley (McMahon), Gascoigne, Waddle, Barnes, Lineker (1) (Bull)
Rep of Ireland: Bonner, Morris, McCarthy, Moran, Staunton, McGrath, Houghton, Sheedy (1), Aldridge (McLoughlin), Townsend, Cascarino
Referee: Schmidhuber (West Germany)

12.6.90 Egypt (0) 1, Holland (0) 1 PALERMO
Egypt: Shoubeir, Hassan I, Yaken, Ramzi H, Yassine, Youssef, Ramzi A (Abdel Rahmane), Hassan H, Abdelhamid (Tolba), Abdelghani (1 pen), Abdou
Holland: Van Breukelen, Van Aerle, Rutjes, Koeman R, Van Tiggelen, Vanenburg (Kieft (1)), Wouters, Rijkaard, Koeman E (Witschge), Van Basten, Gullit
Referee: Aladren (Spain)

16.9.90 England (0) 0, Holland (0) 0 CAGLIARI
England: Shilton, Parker, Walker, Wright, Butcher, Pearce, Robson (Platt), Waddle (Bull), Gascoigne, Barnes, Lineker
Holland: Van Breukelen, Van Aerle, Rijkaard, Koeman R, Van Tiggelen, Wouters, Gullit, Witschge, Van't Schip (Kieft), Gillhaus, Van Basten
Referee: Petrovic (Yugoslavia)

17.6.90 Egypt (0) 0, Rep of Ireland (0) 0 PALERMO
Egypt: Shoubeir, Hassan I, Yaken, Ramzi H, Yassine, Abdelghani, Orabi, Tolba (Abou Seid), Youssef, Abdou (Abdelhamid), Hassan H
Rep of Ireland: Bonner, Morris, McCarthy, Moran, Staunton, McGrath, Houghton, Townsend, Sheedy (McLoughlin), Aldridge (McLoughlin), Cascarino (Quinn)
Referee: Van Langehove (Belgium)

21.6.90 England (0) 1, Egypt (0) 0 CAGLIARI
England: Shilton, Parker, Wright (1), Walker, Pearce, Waddle (Platt), McMahon, Gascoigne, Barnes, Lineker, Bull (Beardsley)
Egypt: Shoubeir, Hassan I, Yaken, Ramzi H, Yassine, Youssef, Abdelghani, Abdou (Soliman), Ramzi A, Abdelhamid (Abdel Rahmane), Hassan H
Referee: Rothlisberger (Switzerland)

21.6.90 Rep of Ireland (0) 1, Holland (1) 1 PALERMO
Rep of Ireland: Bonner, Morris, McCarthy, Moran, Staunton, McGrath, Houghton, Townsend, Sheedy (Whelan), Aldridge (Cascarino), Quinn (1)
Holland: Van Breukelen, Van Aerle, Rijkaard, Koeman R, Van Tiggelen, Wouters, Witschge (Fraser), Van Basten, Gullit (1), Gillhaus, Kieft (Van Loen)
Referee: Vautrot (France)

	P	W	D	L	F	A	Pts
England	3	1	2	0	2	1	4
Rep of Ireland	3	0	3	0	2	2	3
Holland	3	0	3	0	2	2	3
Egypt	3	0	2	1	1	2	2

Second round

23.6.90 Cameroon (0) 2, Colombia (0) 1 (aet, 0-0 at 90 mins) NAPLES
Cameroon: Nkono, Tataw, Ndip, Onana, Ebwelle, Kana-Biyik, Mbouh, Maboang, Mfede (Milla (2)), Omam-Biyik, Makanaky (Djonkep)
Colombia: Higuita, Herrera, Perea, Escobar, Gildardo Gomez, Alvarez, Gabriel Gomez (Redin (1)), Rincon, Fajardo (Iguaran), Valderrama, Estrada
Referee: Lanese (Italy)

23.6.90 Czechoslovakia (1) 4, Costa Rica (0) 1 BARI
Czechoslovakia: Stejskal, Hasek, Kadlec, Kocian, Straka, Moravcik, Chovanec, Kubik (1), Bilek, Skuhravy (3), Knoflicek
Costa Rica: Barrantes, Chavarria (Guimaraes), Marchena, Flores, Montero, Chavez, Ramirez, Gonzalez (1), Obando (Medford), Cayasso, Jara
Referee: Kirschen (East Germany)

24.6.90 Argentina (0) 1, Brazil (0) 0 TURIN
Argentina: Goycochea, Basualdo, Monzon, Simon, Ruggeri, Olarticoechea, Giusti, Burruchaga, Maradona, Troglio (Calderon), Caniggia (1)
Brazil: Taffarel, Jorginho, Ricardo Rocha, Ricardo Gomes, Mauro Galvao (Renato), Branco, Alemao (Silas), Dunga, Valdo, Careca, Muller
Referee: Quiniou (France)

24.6.90 West Germany (0) 2, Holland (0) 1 MILAN
West Germany: Illgner, Reuter, Kohler, Augenthaler, Brehme (1), Buchwald, Berthold, Matthaus, Littbarski, Voller, Klinsmann (1) (Riedle)
Holland: Van Breukelen, Van Aerle (Kieft), Koeman R (1 pen), Van Tiggelen, Wouters, Rijkaard, Witschge (Gillhaus), Winter, Gullit, Van Basten, Van't Schip
Referee: Loustau (Argentina)

25.6.90 Rep of Ireland (0) 0, Rumania (0) 0
(aet, Rep of Ireland won 5-4 on penalties) GENOA
Rep of Ireland: Bonner, Morris, McCarthy, Moran, Staunton (O'Leary), McGrath, Townsend, Houghton, Sheedy, Aldridge (Cascarino), Quinn
Rumania: Lung, Rednic, Andone, Popescu, Klein, Rotariu, Lupescu, Sabau (Timofte), Hagi, Raducioiu (Lupu), Balint
Referee: Wright (Brazil)

25.6 90 Italy (0) 2, Uruguay (0) 0 ROME
Italy: Zenga, Bergomi, Ferri, Baresi, Maldini, De Agostini, De Napoli, Berti (Serena (1)) Giannini, Schillaci (1), Baggio (Vierchowod)
Uruguay: Alvez, Saldana, Gutierrez, De Leon, Dominguez, Ostolaza (Alzamendi), Perdomo, Francescoli, Ruben Pereira, Aguilera (Sosa), Fonseca
Referee: Courtney (England)

26.6.90 Spain (0) 1, Yugoslavia (0) 2 (aet, 1-1 at 90 mins) VERONA
Spain: Zubizarreta, Chendo, Gorriz, Andrinua (Jimenez), Sanchis, Villaroya, Martin Vazquez, Roberto, Michel, Butragueno (Rafa Paz), Julio Salinas (1)
Yugoslavia: Ivkovic, Sabanadzovic, Spasic, Brnovic, Katanec (Vulic), Hadzibegic, Jozic, Susic, Stojkovic (2), Pancev (Savicevic), Vujovic
Referee: Schmidhuber (West Germany)

26.6.90 England (0) 1, Belgium (0) 0 (aet) BOLOGNA
England: Shilton, Parker, Butcher, Wright, Walker, Pearce, Waddle, Gascoigne, McMahon (Platt (1)), Barnes (Bull), Lineker
Belgium: Preud'homme, Gerets, Grun, Demol, Clijsters, Dewolf, Van der Elst, Scifo, Versavel (Vervoort), Ceulemans, De Gryse (Claesen)
Referee: Middelsen (Denmark)

QUARTER FINALS

30.6.90 Argentina (0) 0, Yugoslavia (0) 0
(aet, Argentina won 3-2 on penalties) FLORENCE
Argentina: Goycochea, Simon, Ruggeri, Serrizuela, Basualdo, Olarticoechea (Troglio), Giusti, Burruchaga, Calderon (Dezotti), Caniggia, Maradona
Yugoslavia: Ivkovic, Hadzibegic, Spasic, Brnovic, Vulic, Sabanadzovic, Jozic, Susic (Savicevic), Prosinecki, Stojkovic, Vujovic
Referee: Rothlisberger (West Germany)

30.6.90 Rep of Ireland (0) 0, Italy (1) 1 ROME
Rep of Ireland: Bonner, Morris, McCarthy, Moran, Staunton, McGrath, Houghton, Townsend, Sheedy, Quinn (Cascarino), Aldridge (Sheridan)
Italy: Zenga, Bergomi, Ferri, Baresi, Maldini, De Agostini, De Napoli, Giannini (Ancelotti), Baggio (Serena), Schillaci (1)
Referee: Valente (Portugal)

1.7.90 Czechoslovakia (0) 0, West Germany (1) 1 MILAN
Czechoslovakia: Stejskal, Hasek, Straka, Kocian, Kadlec, Moravcik, Chovanec, Bilek (Nemecek), Kubik (Griga), Skuhravy, Knoflicek
West Germany: Illgner, Berthold, Kohler, Augenthaler, Brehme, Buchwald, Matthaus (1 pen), Bein (Moller), Littbarski, Riedle, Klinsmann
Referee: Kohl (Austria)

1.7.90 Cameroon (0) 2, England (1) 3 (aet, 2-2 at 90 mins) NAPLES
Cameroon: Nkono, Tataw, Kunde (1 pen), Ebwelle, Maboang (Milla), Libih, Pagal, Makanaky, Mfede (Ekeke (1)), Omam-Biyik
England: Shilton, Parker, Butcher (Steven), Wright, Walker, Pearce, Waddle, Platt (1), Gascoigne, Barnes (Beardsley), Lineker (2 pens)
Referee: Codesal (Mexico)

SEMI FINALS

3.7.90 Argentina (0) 1, Italy (1) 1
(aet, 1-1 at 90 mins, Argentina won 4-3 on penalties) NAPLES
Argentina: Goycochea, Simon, Ruggeri, Serrizuela, Giusti, Calderon (Troglio), Burruchaga, Basualdo (Batista), Olarticoechea, Caniggia (1), Maradona
Italy: Zenga, Bergomi, Baresi, Ferri, De Napoli, De Agostini, Donadoni, Maldini, Giannini (Baggio), Schillaci (1), Vialli (Serena)
Referee: Vautrot (France)

4.7.90 West Germany (0) 1, England (0) 1
(aet, 1-1 at 90 mins, West Germany won 4-3 on penalties) TURIN
West Germany: Illgner, Berthold, Augenthaler, Buchwald, Kohler, Hassler (Reuter), Matthaus, Thon, Brehme (1), Klinsmann, Voller (Riedle)
England: Shilton, Parker, Butcher (Steven), Wright, Walker, Pearce, Platt, Gascoigne, Waddle, Beardsley, Lineker (1)
Referee: Wright (Brazil)

Match for third place

7.7.9 Italy (0) 2, England (0) 1 BARI
Italy: Zenga, Bergomi, Baresi, Ferrara, Maldini, Vierchowod, De Agostini (Berti), Ancelotti, Giannini (Ferri), Baggio (1), Schillaci (1 pen)
England: Shilton, Stevens, Wright (Waddle), Parker, Walker, Dorigo, Steven, Platt (1), McMahon (Webb), Beardsley, Lineker
Referee: Quiniou (France)

FINAL

8.7.90 West Germany (0) 1, Argentina (0) 0 ROME
West Germany: Illgner, Berthold (Reuter), Kohler, Augenthaler, Buchwald, Brehme (1 pen), Littbarski, Hassler, Matthaus, Voller, Klinsmann
Argentina: Goycochea, Lorenzo, Serrizuela, Sensini, Ruggeri (Monzon), Simon, Basualdo, Burruchaga (Calderon), Maradona, Troglio, Dezotti
Referee: Codesal (Mexico)

USA
1994

The draw for the qualifying tournament was made in New York in December 1991 and three months later the first match was played. The 21 months of football that decided who would be going to America for the 1994 finals are recorded in diary form:

March 1992

21 First of 582 scheduled qualifying matches for the 1994 finals sees Puerto Rico beat the Dominican Republic 2-1 in Santo Domingo, watched by a crowd of 8000. Mark Lugris (Puerto Rico) scores the first goal after 23 minutes. First bookings: Arcadio Santana (Dominican Republic), Ramiro Agustin Brja and Franko Pronesa (both Puerto Rico). First protest: Dominican Republic against Puerto Rico, alleging entire squad ineligible for possessing US passports.

22 First red card: Trevor Joseph (St Lucia) v St Vincent and the Grenadines. St Lucia won 1-0.

23 Nine venues announced for the finals: Chicago, Dallas, East Rutherford (New Jersey), Boston (Foxboro), Los Angeles (Pasadena), Orlando, Pontiac (Detroit), San Francisco (Palo Alto) and Washington. The selection of the Pontiac venue brings indoor football to the World Cup for the first time.

April 1992

16 FIFA turn down the Dominican Republic's protest.

17 Belgium manager Paul Van Himst picks uncapped Gunther Hofmans (Ekeren) in the squad to play Cyprus.

19 After drawing 1-1 in the Netherlands Antilles, the Antigua team demands a walkover, protesting that the 80 minute delay to the kick-off was due to the hosts failing to provide transport from their hotel.

22 Hofmans appears as substitute in the last 15 minutes in Belgium's 1-0 win.

28 Lithuania celebrates its World Cup comeback with a 2-2 draw in Northern Ireland. It was their first tie in the competition since the 1938 series.

May 1992

6 Gavrila Balint scores a hat-trick in Rumania's 7-0 win over the Faroes. His father gave him the middle name of Pele . . . The Ukraine wants the CIS disbanded and all new ex-Soviet states to play-off for the World Cup place . . . Dallas chosen as broadcasting centre for the finals.

7 Las Vegas named as venue for the Finals draw in December 1993.

13 Sao Tome e Principe withdraw from the competition.

June 1992

11 Alketas Panagoulias returns as national manager of Greece in succession to Antonis Georghiadis.

12 Javier Clemente is to leave Espanol Barcelona to succeed Vicente Miera as national manager of Spain with a two-year contract worth £500,000 plus £150,000 if they qualify. But he wants Miera to stay for the Olympic finals.

29 Pasadena is chosen as the venue for the 1994 Final itself. The tournament will open in Chicago . . . FIFA agree in principle to South Africa returning to the fold and they could replace either Burkina Faso or Sierra Leone, who have withdrawn, in the World Cup.

July 1992

1 FIFA approve Russia replacing the CIS in the present competition . . . Switzerland bid for the 1998 World Cup.

2 Michel Platini quits as France's manager as his country is given the 1998 World Cup by 12-7 over Morocco. The

105

Swiss bid is ruled out because of the use of temporary stands, now outlawed by FIFA.

3 FIFA Congress does not agree a two-thirds majority to an African proposal aimed at increasing third world representation on the executive committee . . . With South Africa's return and other new members admitted, FIFA now has 178 countries under its control.

9 Gerard Houllier is appointed as France's manager.

August 1992

9 FIFA General Secretary Sepp Blatter says yellow card tallies may be discounted after the first round group matches in the finals.

10 FIFA invite South Africa to replace Sao Tome e Principe in the tournament. Benin and Namibia replace Malawi and Burkina Faso respectively.

11 English-born Swiss manager Roy Hodgson axes Kubilay Turkyilmaz, his Swiss-born striker of Turkish descent, from the squad.

17 Andreas Brehme, scorer of the winning penalty in the 1990 World Cup Final, retires from the German national team.

26 Latvia hold European Champions Denmark to a goalless draw.

27 Uruguay ban all transfers to foreign clubs until after the qualifying rounds, but Miljan Miljanic, veteran Yugoslav coach of international repute, rejects an offer to manage the national team.

29 Libya pulls out of the World Cup.

September 1992

1 FIFA postpone decision on Yugoslavia's future under UN sanctions.

3 Zimbabwe offer new bonuses for qualifying success.

7 FIFA again postpone a decision on Yugoslavia after plea from Prime Minister Milan Panic.

9 Norway take ten goals off San Marino with Oldham Athletic's Gunnar Halle scoring a hat-trick.

18 FIFA agree to the principle of selected referees from other continents controlling matches in other zones. Thus Pierluigi Pairetto (Italy) will handle Tunisia v Benin and Brizio Carter (Mexico) the England v Norway tie.

23 Latvia and Lithuania hold Spain and Denmark respectively to goalless draws.

24 Financial problems force Uganda, Mauritania and Sudan to withdraw.

27 Death of Hermann Neuberger, FIFA Vice-President and Chairman of the World Cup Organising Committee at 72.

October 1992

1 Franco Baresi, AC Milan captain, announces his decision to retire from the national team in Italy.

5 Ruud Gullit withdraws from the Dutch national team for 'personal reasons'.

10 South Africa lose 4-0 in Nigeria.

11 Morocco are leading Ethiopia 5-0 when the match is abandoned after 55 minutes. Ethiopia with no substitutes have five injured players.

14 England surprisingly held 1-1 by Norway . . . Italy give away two goals in the first 21 minutes but hit back with two in the last seven to draw 2-2 with Switzerland . . . Holland also 2-0 down to Poland force a similar draw.

20 Six members of Ethiopia's squad go missing during a stopover in Rome, awaiting their plane to Morocco . . . Germany will play at Chicago in the 1994 finals.

22 'Striker' is voted mascot of the 1994 finals. Twenty-five thousand Americans voted and the announcement was made at Mann's Chinese Theatre in Hollywood.

25 The Tanzania v Madagascar match goes ahead 24 hours late after the visitors were given extra time recovering from a bus crash two weeks earlier when two players were slightly injured. The match ends in a 0-0 draw.

27 Cesar Menotti quits as national team manager of Mexico after internal FA politics threaten President Francisco Ibarra, who hired him.

28 Menotti withdraws his resignation as Ibarra returns from a business trip to regain control . . . Blatter hints that sudden death might replace penalty shoot-outs and three points for a win used in the first round in an effort to make the game more attractive.

November 1992

2 Baresi ends his international exile after 32 days. 'I wanted a break, but I didn't realise I would miss the national team so much. Playing for your country is the greatest honour for any player.'

4 Local newspapers allege Menotti is having tax problems as the Ibarra controversy continues.

16 Arrigo Sacchi dispels all doubts about his feelings towards Baresi's return by welcoming him back to the national camp . . . Much injured Ian Durrant returns to Scotland's squad after four years absence.

17 Joao Havelange proclaims the 'back pass' rule to be a success . . . Japan and South Africa bid for the 2002 and 2006 World Cups respectively . . . Platini says he would have stayed as France's manager but for disinterest in his plans by clubs.

19 Roberto Baggio's rib injury will keep him out until 1993: "I've never been kicked so much in my life." Italy drew 0-0 with Scotland.

23 The US announces an ambitious schedule of matches for 1993 with Denmark, Rumania, Russia (twice), Germany (twice), England, Brazil as opponents and participation in the Concacaf and South American Championships.

29 Costa Rica surprisingly beat Mexico 2-0.

30 Hristo Stoichkov (Barcelona) is dropped by Bulgaria after quitting training camp to play in a Spanish League game.

December 1992

2 Milan Panic again asks for more World Cup leniency for Yugoslavia.

3 FIFA agree to Beirut being declared safe enough to host matches in Group D of the Asian Zone.

4 FIFA ends ban on Fernando Astengo the Chile captain involved in the World Cup game in Brazil during 1989 which led to the country being thrown out of the 1994 competition and finally reject Yugoslavia's plea.

6 In Mexico's 11-0 thrashing of St Vincent, there are three hat-tricks: Hermosilio (four goals), Uribe and Bernal.

8 Gullit ends his premature retirement from the Dutch team.

12 Czech Federation holds last meeting agreeing for a combined national team to continue until after the 1994 World Cup.

13 Tommy Lindholm, coach to TPS Turku, is appointed national team manager, succeeding Jukka Vakkila.

14 Italy choose nine AC Milan players for the match with Malta.

15 Marco Van Basten quits training early on eve of the tie v Turkey complaining of a right ankle injury . . . Menotti quits as Mexico's manager after ousting of Ibarra and criticism of him not selecting national hero Hugo Sanchez in the team.

16 Among the 20 players selected for US training camp in California there are no foreign-based candidates.

18 Van Basten is European Footballer of the Year, but is to undergo surgery on his ankle.

19 Baresi is sent off for a professional foul, listed officially as serious ungentlemanly conduct, in Italy's 2-1 win over Malta.

20 Zimbabwe beat Egypt 2-1 in something of an African upset.

27 Miguel Mejia Baran, former assistant to Bora Milutinovic in 1986, is appointed Mexico's manager.

30 FIFA confirm Libya's withdrawal from the competition.

January 1993

3 Valeri Lobanovski, ex-USSR national coach, is dismissed from his position in charge of the UAE.

6 Liberia becomes the 11th African country to pull out of the tournament.

7 Manager Roger Milla confirms that the Cameroon will play Zaire despite cash problems which led them being thrown out of a Yaounde hotel . . . Kevin Moran (Republic of Ireland) is cleared by FIFA to play v Northern Ireland following case of mistaken identity. Polish referee Ryszard Wojcik had booked Niall Quinn during the match with Denmark, but wrongly reported Moran after it . . . The US appoint ex-NBC Sports director Michael Weisman to organise preparatory TV programmes in 1994.

8 Herbert Prohaska is appointed Austria's national team manager . . . Antoni Piechniczek takes over the UAE. He is a former Poland manager.

17 Fawzi Roussi scores three goals as Tunisia win 5-0 in Benin.

18 Angola and Egypt draw 0-0 in Luanda after a postponement from the previous Sunday when the referee's travel problems delayed his arrival.

21 Carlos Queiros, Portugal's manager omits Paulo Futre because of the stress the player has had since walking out on Atletico Madrid.

26 Rotterdam city officials ask the Dutch FA to switch the match with Turkey to an afternoon kick-off to avoid crowd trouble . . . Tanzania withdraw.

27 Blatter says that the kick-in could replace the throw-in after the 1994 finals . . . Pele predicts the 1994 finals will be a success as will the US team in it.

February 1993

8 Pele backs the kick-in.

10 Blatter says that preliminary rounds will be needed in Europe for the next World Cup, to streamline the competition and prevent meaningless matches from cluttering the fixture list.

14 Azeglio Vicini, former Italian manager, criticises Sacchi for using too many players and not concentrating on a settled squad of 18.

17 England captain David Platt scores four goals in a 6-0 win over San Marino, but misses a late penalty which would have equalled Malcolm Macdonald's record.

24 Death of former England captain Bobby Moore at 51 . . . US ticket sales boom for first round games in Chicago, New York and Washington.

26 Mexico recall Sanchez.

28 After Egypt's 2-1 win over Zimbabwe, the visitors protest that their players and coaches had been struck by missiles from the crowd in Cairo's Nasser Stadium.

March 1993

1 Oman will compete in the World Cup after all. The FA's decision to withdraw is overturned by the Sports Ministry.

8 Greece fined £9000 by FIFA for fireworks and other missiles in the match with Luxembourg . . . Bruce Grobbelaar (Liverpool) is referred for a brain scan after headaches following Zimbabwe's match with Egypt . . . San Marino take their first competitive point after a 0-0 draw with Turkey.

11 Bolivia's hopes are threatened when FA officials cancel the championship until September because of a players strike in support of freedom of contract . . . World Cup failure costs Tunisian manager Mrad Mahjoub his job. Youssef Zouaoui of Club Africain takes over.

12 FIFA order replay of Egypt v Zimbabwe on neutral territory.

15 The date of the above match is postponed because of Egypt's religious holiday.

16 US officials deny problems in Boston where no executive committee has been established.

17 FIFA set April 15 in Lyon as the date and venue for Egypt v Zimbabwe.

19 Sacchi calls up uncapped Alessandro Melli (Parma) and G Sergio Porrini (Atalanta) v Malta . . . Johan Cruyff's two year extension to his Barcelona contract allows him to manage Holland if they reach the finals.

20 Asian Confederation officials say the winner of the Oceania Group can be admitted to their Zone in future if FIFA grant Asia an extra place in the finals.

22 Belgium recall Brazilian born, Sicily domiciled Luis Oliveira (Cagliari) against Wales . . . Spain include nine Barcelona players in the squad v Denmark.

25 Defender Marcelo Balboa ends four months of negotiation by agreeing his contract to play for the USSF.

30 Australian team manager Eddie Thomson and his assistant Les Scheinflug are given new contracts until 1998.

31 Oliveira plays in the second half for Belgium v Wales, but they are well beaten 2-0.

April 1993

2 FIFA order inquiry into crowd incidents at Turkey v England.

8 Grobbelaar defies Liverpool and flies off to join Zimbabwe's training camp . . . Hungarian manager Emerich Jenei quits after 1-0 defeat by Greece.

9 Mark Raven, England supporter blinded in one eye by a missile from Turkish fans in Izmir, demands stern FIFA action against the Turkish FA . . . Ferenc Puskas is appointed caretaker-manager of Hungary . . . Pele predicts 'best organised World Cup ever' as he launches a competition for MasterCard which will honour the top player in each of the 24 qualifying countries.

10 Kazu Miura scores four times as Japan beat Bangladesh 8-0.

12 Faustino Asprilla, Parma's Colombian international, damages his achilles tendon falling on broken glass at his mother's home in Tulua.

13 Milan Macala quits as manager replaced by Vaclav Jezek, who will now be the last Czechoslovakian team manager . . . Hodgson's contract extends to 1996.

18 Piyapong pue-on scores three goals in a 4-1 win over Bangladesh.

19 Only one Real Madrid player in Spain's squad v Northern Ireland: Fernando Hierro . . . US Footballer of the Year Balboa out for six months when X-rays reveal ligament and cartilage damage in right knee.

20 FIFA announce six months suspension on stadia in Cairo and Izmir for recent crowd disturbances . . . Havelange praises preparations in Boston.

21 Jose Estanislao Malinowski quits as manager of Honduras after 3-1 defeat by Canada.

22 FIFA warn Zimbabwe could be suspended from World Cup if Sports Ministry dismisses the local FA general council over corruption allegations.

28 Zambia's squad of 18 players and staff die in an air crash after taking off from Gabon on refuelling stop on way to Senegal. Kalusha Bwalya (PSV Eindhoven) and Charles Musonda (Anderlecht) are not in the party . . . Ally McCoist (Rangers) breaks his leg during Scotland's 5-0 defeat in Portugal . . . Luis Cubilla, Uruguayan manager, writes to Italian-based Uruguayans Sosa, Fonseca, Herrera, Francescoli and Aguilera to end their boycott in protest of Cubilla's criticism of their attitude in the 1990 World Cup finals . . . Zimbabwe manager Reinhard Fabisch quits at cash crisis following dismissal of key officials in the FA.

May 1993

1 Switzerland's 1-0 win over Italy is their first over their neighbours since the 1954 World Cup. Dino Baggio is sent off for the first time in his career by Aron Schmidhuber, who had cautioned him a month earlier in a UEFA Cup tie . . . Schmidhuber voted top referee by FIFA . . . First defeat for Italian team in 15 matches under Sacchi.

2 Honduras lose 4-1 in Tegucigalpa to Mexico. Three players are sent off and riot police wrestle with irate fans.

3 Another hat-trick for Piyapong pue-on against Sri Lanka and one for Ali Al-Hadiyak in Kuwait's 10-1 victory over Macao.

5 Zambia holds trials for a new national team . . . Asman Adnan has hat-trick in Malaysia's 9-0 win over luckless Macao.

7 Amid heavy security, Lebanon and India drew 2-2 in Beirut . . . FIFA order Wankdorf stadium in Berne too dangerous for international matches. It was the scene of the 1954 final.

9 Mexico qualify for the finals, beating Canada 2-1 in Toronto.

10 Hans Ooft has contract as Japan's manager extended by a year after pleasing results in the competition.

12 Malta record their first World Cup victory: 1-0 in Estonia.

14 Hat-tricks for Saeed Owairan and Hamza Idris as Macao are beaten again, this time 8-0 by Saudi Arabia.

20 Cubilla reports agreement with Sosa, Francescoli and Aguilera, though Sosa opts out of the Copa America.

22 Cai Sheng scores a hat-trick as China beat Pakistan 5-0 in Jordan.

23 Greece qualifies for the finals for the first time after drawing 1-1 with Russia in Moscow.

24 Wynton Rufer tells the New Zealand FA he will not play in the match with Australia as he wants to help Werder Bremen in their German Bundesliga championship bid.

25 Denmark may blood uncapped Martin Johansen (FC Copenhagen) against Albania.

June 1993

1 Bosnian born defender Izudin Dervic is to make his international debut for Iceland v Russia. England are well beaten 2-0 in Norway . . .

2 Johansen goes on in the 64th minute but the scoring is all over at 4-0 for the Danes ... Despite a 1-1 draw, Russia qualify ... Peter Dubovsky has a hat-trick for Czechoslovakia in the 5-2 win over Rumania ... Tomas Brolin is another treble-shooter in the 5-0 success against Israel ... Germany make a bid for the 2006 World Cup ... FIFA decide that the 1994 finalists should decide in December whether to move to three points for a win in next year's first round.

7 Cornel Dinu axed as Rumanian national manager after 5-2 defeat by Czechoslovakia.

9 Specialist surgeon Marc Martens operates again on Van Basten's ankle, then warns the player may be finished.

11 Rune Bratseth, Norway captain, undergoes knee surgery which will keep him out of action for around three months.

14 Brazil's manager Carlos Alberto Parreira attacks plans to play World Cup finals in high daytime temperatures and humidity.

16 Van Basten has plaster and stitches removed and his surgeon expresses satisfaction with the operation.

17 Malta's national coach Pippo Psaila claims Portuguese sources approached his players to help Portugal produce a high score in their match.

19 Portugal only manage four goals against the Maltese.

22 Psaila quits, blaming differences with the FA over his role.

23 Anghel Iordanescu is the new manager of Rumania on a two-year contract ... Ali Modir Rousta scores four goals as Iran beat Taiwan 6-0 in the second match of a double-header in which Oman and Syria draw 0-0 before a crowd of 80,000 ... The Chorzow ground is suspended by FIFA because of crowd trouble at the Poland v England match. The Polish FA is fined £8000 ... Honduras are fined £12,000 and threatened with suspension from the 1998 World Cup after crowd trouble in matches with Canada and Mexico.

29 Ian Porterfield, ex-Chelsea manager, is appointed adviser to the Zambian national team; his position funded by the British Foreign Office and British companies.

30 Brazil have 14 foreign-based players in their full-strength squad.

July 1993

4 A rebuilt Zambia beat Morocco 2-1.

6 Pietro Ghedin, an Italian, is the new Malta coach.

9 Abel Balbo is recalled to the Argentine squad.

10 Milutin Soskic, ex-Yugoslav goalkeeper with Partizan Belgrade is appointed US goalkeeping coach.

17 Several fans are injured, one seriously, after rioting breaks out when Senegal lose 3-1 at home to Morocco.

18 Ramallo scores three goals as Bolivia win 7-1 in Venezuela.

25 Brazil lose a qualifying match for the first time, 2-0 v Bolivia in high-altitude La Paz; their hosts even allowing themselves the luxury of a missed penalty.

26 The Brazilian squad returns home to a barrage of criticism. Assistant coach Mario Zagalo has to be restrained by officials after a taxi driver shouts insults at Parreira.

27 Mark Bosnich (Aston Villa) decides to remain in England rather than keep goal for Australia v Canada.

29 Australian FA apply to FIFA for the temporary suspension of Bosnich ... Brazil axe six players from the team beaten in Bolivia ... FIFA shut the Dakar stadium in Senegal and they will have to play Zambia in Abidjan, Ivory Coast.

30 FIFA suspend Bosnich for two matches; the player may take legal action.

August 1993

1 Brazil beat Venezuela 5-1 ... Asprilla misses a penalty in Colombia's goalless draw with Paraguay ... England's Paul Gascoigne is alleged in the newspapers to be suffering from bulimia, the eating disorder, but intends suing over the story.

2 FIFA announce that the Bolivian defender Miguel Rimba and Brazilian reserve goalkeeper Zetti are temporarily suspended for failing dope tests. Traces of cocaine are reported to have been found, though both players deny taking anything stronger than coca tea ... Heavily-criticised Careca withdraws from the Brazil squad.

5 Frenchman Philippe Troussier is dismissed by Ivory Coast as manager, one match away from a possible place in the finals ... Uruguayan players are banned from drinking Bolivia's traditional coca leaf tea.

6 Bayern Munich force defender Jorginho to commute to and from Brazil's World Cup matches ... FIFA clear Rimba and Zetti of dope suspicion.

8 Eduardo Hurtado scores three times as Ecuador beat Venezuela 5-0.

11 Australia's World Cup squad end a 24-hour pay revolt by agreeing a 300 percent rise in bonuses.

15 Australia beat Canada on penalty kicks.

16 Asprilla walks out on the Colombian squad with no apparent explanation. He is to be banned for life from the national team ... FIFA fine Bolivia and Brazil £12,000 each for carelessness over the dope incident.

17 Asprilla, Colombia's prodigal son, is welcomed back after apologising ... Cubilla quits the Uruguayan post and is replaced by a former assistant Ildo Maneiro.

18 Johnson Bwalya, Swiss based Zambian player, voices recent concern that the recent air crash might have been caused by sabotage.

22 Brazil are back on track after beating Ecuador 2-0.

24 Furious Bolivians are unhappy with FIFA, said to be preparing to ban qualifying matches at high altitude.

25 Michael Laudrup returns to the Danish team in the 4-0 win over Lithuania ... A group of Dutch MPs protest that famine aid money sent to Zambia by the government was allowed to be switched into supporting the Zambian national team's World Cup effort.

29 Brazil hit Bolivia for six without reply.

September 1993

1 Uruguay manager Maneiro sends an SOS to Italy for Paulo Montero (Atalanta), the Uruguayan defender because of injury to Carlos Zoca.

3 Romario, who stormed out of Brazil's training camp last December after being axed from the team to play Germany, is in line to be recalled.

5 Asprilla scores twice as Colombia beat Argentina 5-0 in Buenos Aires. Having ended Argentina's unbeaten 31 match run earlier in Barranquilla, they now inflict the host nation's worst defeat on their own soil since 1910. Argentina must now play-off with Australia to qualify for the USA.

6 Twenty people die in celebrations after Colombia's historic victory in Buenos Aires.

12 Uruguay cling to hopes of qualifying with a controversial 2-1 win over Bolivia. Enzo Francescoli converts a disputed third-minute penalty. Later Juan Manuel Pena (Bolivia) and Carlos Aguilera (Uruguay) are sent off.

13 Bolivia protests about the refereeing of Colombian Armando Perez Hoyos. Andy Roxburgh resigns as Scotland's coach. FIFA instructs both host teams in next Sunday's South American qualifiers to kick-off at the same time.

15 Poland recall Andrzej Rudy and their captain Roman Szewczyk for the match in Norway. The Poles have not lost to the Norwegians for 47 years. Zambia fail in plea to have Gabonese officials replaced for the match in Morocco.

19 Brazil end Uruguayan aspirations as Romario scores twice in a 2-0 win and maintain their record of appearing in every World Cup finals. They are joined by Bolivia after a 1-1 draw in Guayaquil against Ecuador.

21 Greek manager Alketas Panagoulias is standing for parliament.

22 The Dutch take seven goals off San Marino, who finish with ten men when Marco Mazza is sent off in the 70th minute. John Bosman scores a hat-trick. Dick Advocaat has used 35 different players in a year. Julio Salinas scores three and makes the other two Spanish goals as Albania are beaten 5-1. Goalkeeper Andoni Zubizarreta equals Jose Camacho's record of 81 caps for Spain. Norway win a stormy affair with Poland 1-0, described by their manager Egil Olsen as 'more like war than soccer'. Erik Thorstvedt his goalkeeper and Polish defender Szewczyk are sent off.

23 Argentina will include Maradona against Australia, providing he is fit enough after manager Basile and the player make their peace.

24 Spain deny that an agent travelling with the party to Albania was involved in a bribery attempt.

26 Zimbabwe beat Guinea with a third minute goal from Agent Sawu, recently on trial at Liverpool. Two goals from Rashidi Yekini (Vitoria Setubal, Portugal) puts Nigeria within a point of qualifying after beating the Ivory Coast 4-1. Zambia, unbeaten since the air disaster, beat Senegal 4-0 and are similarly poised.

October 1993

2 Five lion cubs born in La Paz zoo are given the names of Bolivian players.

4 Spain select ten six-foot tall players for the Republic of Ireland match.

5 No place for Ruud Gullit in the Dutch team. Three Rumanians including Gheorghe Hagi are doubtful for the match with Wales.

8 A 1-1 draw in Algeria puts Nigeria through to their first World Cup finals.

10 Morocco edge out Zambia to book their passage and Cameroon will accompany them following a 3-1 win over Zimbabwe, whose coach Reinhard Fabisch is ordered from the bench for throwing coins at a linesman's feet.

11 Zambia complain to FIFA about the Gabonese officials at the Morocco game following their 1-0 defeat. Belgium are unhappy about an English referee Philip Don being appointed for Wales' match with Cyprus, who are to detail Glasgow born Costas Costa an ex-Celtic and Newcastle trialist to mark Ryan Giggs.

12 Argentina recall Maradona for the Aussie clincher. Graham Taylor selects only three of the players who drew 2-2 with Holland in April, but is unhappily snappy with reporters at the press conference.

13 German referee Karl Josef Assenmacher disallows a good Dutch goal by Frank Rijkaard then fails to send off Ronald Koeman for a professional foul on David Platt. Koeman subsequently scores from a free-kick as the Dutch beat England 2-0. The Republic of Ireland lose in Dublin for the first time in eight years as Spain win 3-1. Wales beat Cyprus 2-0, the visitors finishing with nine men; one of the dismissals involving Costa. France concede a goal to Israel's Reuben Atar in the last minute and lose 3-2. Sweden come from behind to beat Finland 3-2 and reach the finals. Norway complete a Scandinavian double by beating Poland 3-0. Improving Bulgaria defeat Austria 4-1 and Rumania have an important 2-1 win over Belgium.

19 Assenmacher is sacked by FIFA for his next international fixture: Belgium v RCS. Franz Beckenbauer says that Kevin Keegan should be the next England manager. Eric Cantona says he will not play at the Parc des Princes again after the crowd's verbal treatment of Jean Pierre Papin. Iraq sack coach Adman Derjal. Iraq FA President Udai, son of Saddam Hussein appoints Aman Baba Dawood in his place. FIFA reject Zambia's complaint.

22 Iraq beat Gulf rivals Iran 2-1, one player from each side is sent off and five booked. After Saudi Arabia score an injury-time equaliser against South Korea some 5,000 Saudis invade the pitch and a few South Koreans throw bottles.

24 Saudi Arabia miss a penalty in the 1-1 draw with Iraq and the fans let off fireworks.

25 Kazu Miura scores as Japan inflict a first defeat of the tournament on South Korea. Saudi Arabia axes its Brazilian coach of ten months, Jose Candido.

27 Worries over the worsening security situation in Belfast cast doubts over the clash of the Irish, but FIFA intend leaving the decision to the Northern Ireland FA.

28 The Saudis qualify after beating Iran 4-3, but South Korea leave the field in tears despite beating arch-rivals North Korea 3-0, thinking the Japanese have beaten Iraq 2-1, thus preventing them from qualifying. But later they learn Jaffar Omran Salman had equalised for the Iraqis with ten seconds remaining. South Korea qualify.

31 Maradona crosses the ball for Abel Balbo to put Argentina ahead in Australia who deserve their 1-1 draw.

November 1993

2 The Northern Ireland FA insist the game will go ahead at Belfast's Windsor Park.

7 FIFA intend to instruct referees to crack down on players feigning injury in the finals. They will be booked. The USA want to start a professional league after the World Cup.

10 Portugal score only three against Estonia and must beat Italy to qualify themselves. Wales are on £50,000 a man bonus against Rumania. A 2-0 win for Wales will be enough. San Marino have one professional in their squad and he plays for a Fourth Division team in Italy. England must win by seven goals and hope Poland beat Holland.

16 After an offer from a British tabloid newspaper of £10,000 a man for Poland to beat Holland, a Dutch advertising company offers San Marino £37,000 to beat England.

17 San Marino score after eight seconds following a suicidal back-pass attempt by Stuart Pearce. England recover to score seven, but Holland make it after winning 3-1 in Poland. Defensive errors and a missed penalty by Paul Bodin contribute to Rumania beating Wales 2-1, the first Rumanian goal is scored by Hagi. At the end of the game a distress rocket fired into the crowd kills an elderly spectator. Belgium, though held scoreless by the RCS, hold on to qualify despite having Phillipe Albert sent off after an hour. The Republic of Ireland become the only representatives from the British Isles after a 1-1 draw in Northern Ireland, but are grateful to Spain's ten men beating Denmark 1-0. The goal was highly controversial: Danish goalkeeper Peter Schmeichel was obstructed. Spain had had their own goalkeeper Zubizarreta sent off for a professional foul inside ten minutes. Shock for France: beaten 2-1 by Bulgaria, who deprive them of a trip to the USA. Emil Kostadinov (Porto, Portugal) scores his second goal in-off-the-bar in the dying seconds. Dino Baggio rescues a nervous Italy seven minutes from time in the 1-0 win over Portugal and Switzerland join them in the finals after beating Estonia 4-0. But the Italians' goal was suspiciously near to offside and shortly afterwards Fernando Couto was sent off for Portugal. The 24th and final place in the USA is taken by Argentina who profit from a deflected own goal to beat Australia 1-0.

Qualifying Tournament

136 entries*
Germany as champions and the USA as hosts already qualified

ASIA (27): Bahrain, Bangladesh, China, Chinese Taipei (Taiwan), Hong Kong, India, Indonesia, Iran, Iraq, Japan, Jordan, North Korea, South Korea, Kuwait, Lebanon, Macao, Malaysia, Oman, Pakistan, Qatar, Saudi Arabia, Singapore, Sri Lanka, Syria, Thailand, United Arab Emirates, Yemen.

AFRICA (34): Algeria, Angola, Botswana, Burkina Faso, Burundi, Cameroon, Congo, Ivory Coast, Egypt, Ethiopia, Gabon, Gambia, Ghana, Guinea, Kenya, Liberia, Libya, Madagascar, Malawi, Mali, Morocco, Niger, Nigeria, Sao Tome and Principe, Senegal, Sierra Leone, Sudan, Tanzania, Togo, Tunisia, Uganda, Zaire, Zambia, Zimbabwe.

CONCACAF (23): Antigua, Barbados, Canada, Costa Rica, Cuba, Dominican Republic, El Salvador, Guatemala, Guyana, Haiti, Honduras, Jamaica, Mexico, Netherlands Antilles, Nicaragua, Panama, Puerto Rico, St Lucia, St Vincent and the Grenadines, Surinam, Trinidad and Tobago, USA.

SOUTH AMERICA (9): Argentina, Bolivia, Brazil, Colombia, Ecuador, Paraguay, Peru, Uruguay, Venezuela.

EUROPE/ISRAEL (35 + 1): Albania, Austria, Belgium, Bulgaria, Cyprus, Czechoslovakia, Denmark, England, Faroes, Finland, France, Germany, Greece, Holland, Hungary, Iceland, Northern Ireland, Republic of Ireland, Israel, Italy, Liechtenstein, Luxembourg, Malta, Norway, Poland, Portugal, Rumania, San Marino, Scotland, Spain, Sweden, Switzerland, Turkey, USSR, Wales, Yugoslavia.

OCEANIA (7): Australia, Fiji, New Zealand, Solomon Islands, Tahiti, Vanuatu, Western Samoa.

*The list of entries as at 15 September 1991 also listed the following late entries: Vietnam, Mauritania, Mozambique, Swaziland, but those named as excused were: Mauritius, Aruba, Grenada, Papua New Guinea. In addition Chile were suspended.

Final places in the USA were to be distributed as follows: Asia (2), Africa (3), Concacaf (1 + USA)**, South America (3)**, Europe (12 + Germany), Oceania (0)**

**The Concacaf runner-up competed against the winner of the Oceania eliminations, the winner of which played the fourth team from South America.

Western Samoa, Cuba, Sierra Leone and Burkina Faso later withdrew. Yugoslavia were suspended as the result of United Nations sanctions. South Africa replaced Sao Tome, Benin instead of Malawi and Namibia for Burkina Faso as late replacements.

Europe/Israel

Group 1 (Italy, Scotland, Portugal, Switzerland, Malta)

Estonia v Switzerland 0 - 6; Switzerland v Scotland 3 - 1; Italy v Switzerland 2 - 2; Scotland v Portugal 0 - 0; Malta v Estonia 0 - 0; Scotland v Italy 0 - 0; Switzerland v Malta 3 - 0; Malta v Italy 1 - 2; Malta v Portugal 0 - 1; Scotland v Malta 3 - 0; Portugal v Italy 1 - 3; Italy v Malta 6 - 1; Switzerland v Portugal 1 - 1; Italy v Estonia 2 - 0; Malta v Switzerland 0 - 2; Portugal v Scotland 5 - 0; Switzerland v Italy 1 - 0; Estonia v Malta 0 - 1; Estonia v Scotland 0 - 3; Scotland v Estonia 3 - 1; Portugal v Malta 4 - 0; Estonia v Portugal 0 - 2; Scotland v Switzerland 1 - 1; Estonia v Italy 0 - 3; Italy v Scotland 3 - 1; Portugal v Switzerland 1 - 0; Portugal v Estonia 3 - 0; Italy v Portugal 1 - 0; Malta v Scotland 0 - 2; Switzerland v Estonia 4 - 0

	P	W	D	L	F	A	Pts
Italy	10	7	2	1	22	7	16
Switzerland	10	6	3	1	23	6	15
Portugal	10	6	2	2	18	5	14
Scotland	10	4	3	3	14	13	11
Malta	10	1	1	8	3	23	3
Estonia	10	0	1	9	1	27	1

Italy and Switzerland qualified

Group 2 (England, Holland, Poland, Norway, Turkey, San Marino)

Norway v San Marino 10 - 0; Norway v Holland 2 - 1; Poland v Turkey 1 - 0; San Marino v Norway 0 - 2; England v Norway 1 - 1; Holland v Poland 2 - 2; Turkey v San Marino 4 - 1; England v Turkey 4 - 0; Turkey v Holland 1 - 3; England v San Marino 6 - 0; Holland v Turkey 3 - 1; San Marino v Turkey 0 - 0; Holland v San Marino 6 - 0; Turkey v England 0 - 2; England v Holland 2 - 2; Norway v Turkey 3 - 1; Poland v San Marino 1 - 0; San Marino v Poland 0 - 3; Poland v England 1 - 1; Norway v England 2 - 0; England v Poland 3 - 0; Norway v Poland 1 - 0; San Marino v Holland 0 - 7; Holland v England 2 - 0; Poland v Norway 0 - 3; Turkey v Poland 2 - 1; Turkey v Norway 2 - 1; San Marino v England 1 - 7; Poland v Holland 1 - 3

	P	W	D	L	F	A	Pts
Norway	10	7	2	1	25	5	16
Holland	10	6	3	1	29	9	15
England	10	5	3	2	26	9	13
Poland	10	3	2	5	10	15	8
Turkey	10	3	1	6	11	19	7
San Marino	10	0	1	9	2	46	1

Norway and Holland qualified

Group 3 (Spain, Republic of Ireland, Denmark, Northern Ireland, Albania, Lithuania, Latvia)

Spain v Albania 3 - 0; Northern Ireland v Lithuania 2 - 2; Republic of Ireland v Albania 2 - 0; Albania v Lithuania 1 - 0; Latvia v Lithuania 1 - 2; Latvia v Denmark 0 - 0; Northern Ireland v Albania 3 - 0; Republic of Ireland v Latvia 4 - 0; Lithuania v Denmark 0 - 0; Latvia v Spain 0 - 0; Denmark v Republic of Ireland 0 - 0; Northern Ireland v Spain 0 - 0; Lithuania v Latvia 1 - 1; Albania v Latvia 1 - 1; Northern Ireland v Denmark 0 - 1; Spain v Republic of Ireland 0 - 0; Spain v Latvia 5 - 0; Albania v Northern Ireland 1 - 2; Spain v Lithuania 5 - 0; Denmark v Spain 1 - 0; Republic of Ireland v Northern Ireland 3 - 0; Denmark v Latvia 2 - 0; Lithuania v Albania 3 - 1; Republic of Ireland v Denmark 1 - 1; Spain v Northern Ireland 3 - 1; Latvia v Albania 0 - 1; Lithuania v Northern Ireland 0 - 1; Albania v Republic of Ireland 1 - 2; Denmark v Albania 4 - 0; Lithuania v Spain 0 - 2; Latvia v Northern Ireland 1 - 2; Latvia v Republic of Ireland 0 - 2; Lithuania v Republic of Ireland 0 - 1; Denmark v Lithuania 4 - 0; Albania v Denmark 0 - 1; Northern Ireland v Latvia 2 - 0; Republic of Ireland v Lithuania 2 - 0; Albania v Spain 1 - 5; Denmark v Northern Ireland 1 - 0; Republic of Ireland v Spain 1 - 3; Northern Ireland v Republic of Ireland 1 - 1; Spain v Denmark 1 - 0

	P	W	D	L	F	A	Pts
Spain	12	8	3	1	27	4	19
Rep of Ireland	12	7	4	1	19	6	18
Denmark	12	7	4	1	15	2	18
Northern Ireland	12	5	3	4	14	13	13
Lithuania	12	2	3	7	8	21	7
Latvia	12	0	5	7	4	21	5
Albania	12	1	2	9	6	26	4

Spain and Republic of Ireland qualified

Group 4 (Belgium, RCS, Rumania, Wales, Cyprus, Faroe Islands)

Belgium v Cyprus 1 - 0; Rumania v Faroe Islands 7 - 0; Rumania v Wales 5 - 1; Faroe Islands v Belgium 0 - 3; Faroe Islands v Cyprus 0 - 2; RCS v Belgium 1 - 2; Wales v Faroe Islands 6 - 0; RCS v Faroe Islands 4 - 0; Belgium v Rumania 1 - 0; Cyprus v Wales 0 - 1; Rumania v RCS 1 - 1; Belgium v Wales 2 - 0; Cyprus v Rumania 1 - 4; Cyprus v Belgium 0 - 3; Cyprus v RCS 1 - 1; Wales v Belgium 2 - 0; Rumania v Cyprus 2 - 1; Cyprus v Faroe Islands 3 - 1; RCS v Wales 1 - 1; Belgium v Faroe Islands 3 - 0; RCS v Rumania 5 - 2; Faroe Islands v Wales 0 - 3; Faroe Islands v RCS 0 - 3; Wales v RCS 2 - 2; Faroe Islands v Rumania 0 - 4; Rumania v Belgium 2 - 1; Wales v Cyprus 2 - 0; RCS v Cyprus 3 - 0; Belgium v RCS 0 - 0; Wales v Rumania 1 - 2

	P	W	D	L	F	A	Pts
Rumania	10	7	1	2	29	12	15
Belgium	10	7	1	2	16	5	15
RCS	10	4	5	1	21	9	13
Wales	10	5	2	3	19	12	12
Cyprus	10	2	1	7	8	18	5
Faroe Islands	10	0	0	10	1	38	0

Rumania and Belgium qualified

Group 5 (Russia, Hungary, Greece, Iceland, Luxembourg)

Greece v Iceland 1 - 0; Hungary v Iceland 1 - 2; Luxembourg v Hungary 0 - 3; Iceland v Greece 0 - 1; Russia v Iceland 1 - 0; Russia v Luxembourg 2 - 0; Greece v Hungary 0 - 0; Greece v Luxembourg 2 - 0; Hungary v Greece 0 - 1; Luxembourg v Russia 0 - 4; Russia v Hungary 3 - 0; Luxembourg v Iceland 1 - 1; Russia v Greece 1 - 1; Iceland v Russia 1 - 1; Iceland v Hungary 2 - 0; Hungary v Russia 1 - 3; Iceland v Luxembourg 1 - 0; Luxembourg v Greece 1 - 3; Hungary v Luxembourg 1 - 0; Greece v Russia 1 - 0

	P	W	D	L	F	A	Pts
Greece	8	6	2	0	10	2	14
Russia	8	5	2	1	15	4	12
Iceland	8	3	2	3	7	6	8
Hungary	8	2	1	5	6	11	5
Luxembourg	8	0	1	7	2	17	1

Greece and Russia qualified

Group 6 (France, Austria, Sweden, Bulgaria, Finland, Israel)

Finland v Bulgaria 0 - 3; Bulgaria v France 2 - 0; Finland v Sweden 0 - 1; Sweden v Bulgaria 2 - 0; France v Austria 2 - 0; Austria v Israel 5 - 2; Israel v Sweden 1 - 3; France v Finland 2 - 1; Israel v Bulgaria 0 - 2; Israel v France 0 - 4; Austria v France 0 - 1; Austria v Bulgaria 3 - 1; Bulgaria v Finland 2 - 0; France v Sweden 2 - 1; Bulgaria v Israel 2 - 2; Finland v Austria 3 - 1; Sweden v Austria 1 - 0; Sweden v Israel 5 - 0; Finland v Israel 0 - 0; Sweden v France 1 - 1; Austria v Finland 3 - 0; Bulgaria v Sweden 1 - 1; Finland v France 0 - 2; Bulgaria v Austria 4 - 1; France v Israel 2 - 3; Sweden v Finland 3 - 2; Israel v Austria 1 - 1; Israel v Finland 1 - 3; Austria v Sweden 1 - 1; France v Bulgaria 1 - 2

	P	W	D	L	F	A	Pts
Sweden	10	6	3	1	19	8	15
Bulgaria	10	6	2	2	19	10	14
France	10	6	1	3	17	10	13
Austria	10	3	2	5	15	16	8
Finland	10	2	1	7	9	18	5
Israel	10	1	3	6	10	27	5

Sweden and Bulgaria qualified

Africa

1st Round

Group A (Algeria, Ghana, Burundi, Uganda (withdrew))

Algeria v Burundi 3 - 1; Burundi v Ghana 1 - 0; Ghana v Algeria 2 - 0; Burundi v Algeria 0 - 0; Ghana v Burundi 1 - 0; Algeria v Ghana 2 - 1

	P	W	D	L	F	A	Pts
Algeria	4	2	1	1	5	4	5
Ghana	4	2	0	2	4	3	4
Burundi	4	1	1	2	2	4	3

Group B (Cameroon, Zaire, Swaziland, Liberia (withdrew))

Cameroon v Swaziland 5 - 0; Swaziland v Zaire 1 - 0; Zaire v Cameroon 1 - 2; Swaziland v Cameroon 0 - 0; Zaire v Swaziland not played because of political unrest; Cameroon v Zaire 0 - 0

	P	W	D	L	F	A	Pts
Cameroon	4	2	2	0	7	1	6
Swaziland	3	1	1	1	1	5	3
Zaire	3	0	1	2	1	3	1

Group C (Egypt, Zimbabwe, Angola, Togo)

Zimbabwe v Togo 1 - 0; Egypt v Angola 1 - 0; Togo v Egypt 1 - 4; Zimbabwe v Egypt 2 - 1; Angola v Zimbabwe 1 - 1; Togo v Zimbabwe 1 - 2; Angola v Egypt 0 - 0; Egypt v Togo 3 - 0; Zimbabwe v Angola 2 - 1; Angola v Togo not played because of political unrest; Egypt v Zimbabwe 0 - 0 (after 2 - 1 win declared null and void after crowd trouble); Togo v Angola 0 - 1

	P	W	D	L	F	A	Pts
Zimbabwe	6	4	2	0	8	4	10
Egypt	6	3	2	1	9	3	8
Angola	5	1	2	2	3	4	4
Togo	5	0	0	5	2	11	0

Group D (Nigeria, Congo, South Africa, Libya (withdrew))

Nigeria v South Africa 4 - 0; South Africa v Congo 1 - 0; Congo v Nigeria 0 - 1; South Africa v Nigeria 0 - 0; Congo v South Africa 0 - 1; Nigeria v Congo 2 - 0

	P	W	D	L	F	A	Pts
Nigeria	4	3	1	0	7	0	7
South Africa	4	2	1	1	2	4	5
Congo	4	0	0	4	0	5	0

Group E (Ivory Coast, Niger, Botswana, Sudan (withdrew))

Ivory Coast v Botswana 6 - 0; Niger v Ivory Coast 0 - 0; Botswana v Niger 0 - 1; Botswana v Ivory Coast 0 - 0; Ivory Coast v Niger 1 - 0; Niger v Botswana 2 - 1

	P	W	D	L	F	A	Pts
Ivory Coast	4	2	2	0	7	0	6
Niger	4	2	1	1	3	2	5
Botswana	4	0	1	3	1	9	1

Group F (Morocco, Tunisia, Benin, Ethiopia)
Morocco v Ethiopia 5 - 0; Tunisia v Benin 5 - 1; Benin v Morocco 0 - 1; Ethiopia v Tunisia 0 - 0; Ethiopia v Benin 3 - 1; Tunisia v Morocco 1 - 1; Benin v Tunisia 1 - 5; Ethiopia v Morocco 0 - 1; Morocco v Benin 5 - 0; Tunisia v Ethiopia 3 - 0; Benin v Ethiopia 1 - 0; Morocco v Tunisia 0 - 0.

	P	W	D	L	F	A	Pts
Morocco	6	4	2	0	13	1	10
Tunisia	6	3	3	0	14	2	9
Ethiopia	6	1	1	4	3	11	3
Benin	6	1	0	5	3	19	2

Group G (Senegal, Gabon, Mozambique, Mauritania (withdrew))
Gabon v Mozambique 3 - 1; Mozambique v Senegal 0 - 1; Gabon v Senegal 3 - 2; Mozambique v Gabon 1 - 1; Senegal v Mozambique 6 - 1; Senegal v Gabon 1 - 0.

	P	W	D	L	F	A	Pts
Senegal	4	3	0	1	10	4	6
Gabon	4	2	1	1	7	5	5
Mozambique	4	0	1	3	3	11	1

Group H (Zambia, Madagascar, Namibia, Tanzania (withdrew))
Madagascar v Namibia 3 - 0; Zambia v Tanzania 2 - 0; Tanzania v Madagascar 0 - 0; Namibia v Zambia 0 - 4; Tanzania v Namibia 2 - 0; Madagascar v Zambia 2 - 0; Tanzania v Zambia 1 - 3; Namibia v Madagascar 0 - 1; Zambia v Namibia 4 - 0; Zambia v Madagascar 3 - 1.

	P	W	D	L	F	A	Pts
Zambia	4	3	0	1	11	3	6
Madagascar	4	3	0	1	7	3	6
Namibia	4	0	0	4	0	12	0

Group I (Kenya, Guinea, Mali and Gambia withdrew)
Guinea v Kenya 4 - 0; Kenya v Guinea 2 - 0.

	P	W	D	L	F	A	Pts
Guinea	2	1	0	1	4	2	2
Kenya	2	1	0	1	2	4	2

2nd Round
Group A (Algeria, Nigeria, Ivory Coast)
Algeria v Ivory Coast 1 - 1; Ivory Coast v Nigeria 2 - 1; Nigeria v Algeria 4 - 1; Ivory Coast v Algeria 1 - 0; Nigeria v Ivory Coast 4 - 1; Algeria v Nigeria 1 - 1.

	P	W	D	L	F	A	Pts
Nigeria	4	2	1	1	10	5	5
Ivory Coast	4	2	1	1	5	6	5
Algeria	4	0	2	2	3	7	2

Nigeria qualified

Group B (Morocco, Zambia, Senegal)
Morocco v Senegal 1 - 0; Zambia v Morocco 2 - 1; Senegal v Morocco 1 - 3; Senegal v Zambia 0 - 0; Zambia v Senegal 4 - 0; Morocco v Zambia 1 - 0.

	P	W	D	L	F	A	Pts
Morocco	4	3	0	1	6	3	6
Zambia	4	2	1	1	6	2	5
Senegal	4	0	1	3	1	8	1

Morocco qualified

Group C (Cameroon, Zimbabwe, Guinea)
Cameroon v Guinea 3 - 1; Guinea v Zimbabwe 3 - 0; Zimbabwe v Cameroon 1 - 0; Guinea v Cameroon 0 - 1; Zimbabwe v Guinea 1 - 0; Cameroon v Zimbabwe 3 - 1.

	P	W	D	L	F	A	Pts
Cameroon	4	3	0	1	7	3	6
Zimbabwe	4	2	0	2	3	6	4
Guinea	4	1	0	3	4	5	2

Cameroon qualified

Asia
1st Round
Group A (China, Iraq, Jordan, Yemen, Pakistan)
1st series in Jordan
Jordan v Yemen 1 - 1; Pakistan v China 0 - 5; Jordan v Iraq 1 - 1; Yemen v Pakistan 5 - 1; Jordan v China 0 - 3; Yemen v Iraq 1 - 6; Pakistan v Iraq 0 - 8; Yemen v China 1 - 0; Iraq v China 1 - 0; Jordan v Pakistan 3 - 1.
2nd series in China
China v Pakistan 3 - 0; Yemen v Jordan 1 - 1; Iraq v Jordan 4 - 0; Pakistan v Yemen 0 - 3; China v Jordan 4 - 1; Iraq v Yemen 3 - 0; China v Yemen 1 - 0; Iraq v Pakistan 4 - 0; China v Iraq 2 - 1; Pakistan v Jordan 0 - 5.

	P	W	D	L	F	A	Pts
Iraq	8	6	1	1	28	4	13
China	8	6	0	2	18	4	12
Yemen	8	3	2	3	12	13	8
Jordan	8	2	3	3	12	15	7
Pakistan	8	0	0	8	2	36	0

Group B (Iran, Syria, Oman, Taiwan, Myanmar (withdrew))
1st series in Iran
Taiwan v Syria 0 - 2; Iran v Oman 0 - 0; Iran v Taiwan 5 - 0; Oman v Syria 0 - 0; Iran v Syria 1 - 1; Oman v Taiwan 2 - 1.
2nd series in Syria
Oman v Iran 0 - 1; Syria v Taiwan 8 - 1; Taiwan v Iran 0 - 6; Syria v Oman 2 - 1; Taiwan v Oman 1 - 7; Syria v Iran 1 - 1.

	P	W	D	L	F	A	Pts
Iran	6	3	3	0	15	2	9
Syria	6	3	3	0	14	4	9
Oman	6	2	2	2	10	5	6
Taiwan	6	0	0	6	3	31	0

Group C (North Korea, Qatar, Singapore, Vietnam, Indonesia)
1st series in Qatar
North Korea v Vietnam 3 - 0; Qatar v Indonesia 3 - 1; North Korea v Singapore 2 - 1; Qatar v Vietnam 4 - 0; North Korea v Indonesia 4 - 0; Vietnam v Singapore 2 - 0; Qatar v Singapore 4 - 1; Vietnam v Indonesia 1 - 0; Indonesia v Singapore 0 - 2; Qatar v North Korea 1 - 2.
2nd series in Singapore
Indonesia v Qatar 1 - 4; Vietnam v North Korea 0 - 1; Singapore v North Korea 1 - 3; Vietnam v Qatar 0 - 4; Indonesia v North Korea 1 - 2; Singapore v Vietnam 1 - 0; Indonesia v Vietnam 2 - 1; Singapore v Qatar 1 - 0; North Korea v Qatar 2 - 2; Singapore v Indonesia 2 - 1.

	P	W	D	L	F	A	Pts
North Korea	8	7	1	0	19	6	15
Qatar	8	5	1	2	22	8	11
Singapore	8	5	0	3	12	12	10
Indonesia	8	1	0	7	6	19	2
Vietnam	8	1	0	7	4	18	2

Group D (South Korea, Bahrain, Hong Kong, Lebanon, India)
1st series in Lebanon
Hong Kong v Bahrain 2 - 1; Lebanon v India 2 - 1; Bahrain v South Korea 0 - 0; Lebanon v Hong Kong 2 - 2; India v Hong Kong 1 - 2; Lebanon v South Korea 0 - 1; India v South Korea 0 - 3; Lebanon v Bahrain 0 - 0; Bahrain v India 2 - 1; Hong Kong v South Korea 0 - 3.
2nd series in South Korea
Bahrain v Lebanon 0 - 0; South Korea v Hong Kong 4 - 1; India v Bahrain 0 - 3; South Korea v Lebanon 2 - 0; Hong Kong v Lebanon 1 - 2; South Korea v India 7 - 0; Bahrain v Hong Kong 3 - 0; India v Lebanon 1 - 2; Hong Kong v India 1 - 3; South Korea v Bahrain 3 - 0.

	P	W	D	L	F	A	Pts
South Korea	8	7	1	0	23	1	15
Bahrain	8	3	3	2	9	6	9
Lebanon	8	2	4	2	8	9	8
Hong Kong	8	2	1	5	9	19	5
India	8	1	1	6	8	22	3

Group E (Saudi Arabia, Kuwait, Malaysia, Macao)
1st series in Malaysia
Macao v Saudi Arabia 0 - 6; Malaysia v Kuwait 1 - 1; Macao v Kuwait 1 - 10; Malaysia v Saudi Arabia 1 - 1; Kuwait v Saudi Arabia 0 - 0; Malaysia v Macao 9 - 0.
2nd series in Saudi Arabia
Kuwait v Malaysia 2 - 0; Saudi Arabia v Macao 8 - 0; Kuwait v Macao 8 - 0; Saudi Arabia v Malaysia 3 - 0; Macao v Malaysia 0 - 5; Saudi Arabia v Kuwait 2 - 0.

	P	W	D	L	F	A	Pts
Saudi Arabia	6	4	2	0	20	1	10
Kuwait	6	3	2	1	21	4	8
Malaysia	6	2	2	2	16	7	6
Macao	6	0	0	6	1	46	0

Group F (United Arab Emirates, Japan, Thailand, Sri Lanka, Bangladesh)
1st series in Japan

Japan v Thailand 1 - 0; Sri Lanka v UAE 0 - 4; Japan v Bangladesh 8 - 0; Thailand v Sri Lanka 1 - 0; Sri Lanka v Bangladesh 0 - 1; UAE v Thailand 1 - 0; Japan v Sri Lanka 5 - 0; UAE v Bangladesh 1 - 0; Japan v UAE 2 - 0; Thailand v Bangladesh 4 - 1

2nd series in United Arab Emirates

Thailand v Japan 0 - 1; UAE v Sri Lanka 3 - 0; Bangladesh v Japan 1 - 4; Thailand v UAE 1 - 2; Bangladesh v UAE 0 - 7; Sri Lanka v Thailand 0 - 3; Bangladesh v Thailand 1 - 4; Sri Lanka v Japan 0 - 6; Bangladesh v Sri Lanka 3 - 0; UAE v Japan 1 - 1

	P	W	D	L	F	A	Pts
Japan	8	7	1	0	28	2	15
UAE	8	6	1	1	19	4	13
Thailand	8	4	0	4	13	7	8
Bangladesh	8	2	0	6	7	28	4
Sri Lanka	8	0	0	8	0	26	0

2nd round
Tournament in Qatar

North Korea v Iraq 3 - 2; Saudi Arabia v Japan 0 - 0; Iran v South Korea 0 - 3; North Korea v Saudi Arabia 1 - 2; Japan v Iran 1 - 2; Iraq v South Korea 2 - 2; North Korea v Japan 0 - 3; Iran v Iraq 1 - 2; South Korea v Saudi Arabia 1 - 1; Iraq v Saudi Arabia 1 - 1; Japan v South Korea 1 - 0; Iran v North Korea 2 - 1; South Korea v North Korea 3 - 0; Saudi Arabia v Iran 4 - 3; Iraq v Japan 2 - 2

	P	W	D	L	F	A	Pts
Saudi Arabia	5	2	3	0	8	6	7
South Korea	5	2	2	1	9	4	6
Japan	5	2	2	1	7	4	6
Iraq	5	1	3	1	9	9	5
Iran	5	2	0	3	8	11	4
North Korea	5	1	0	4	5	12	2

Saudi Arabia and South Korea qualified

Concacaf
(Antigua, Barbados, Bermuda, Canada, Costa Rica, Cuba, Dominican Republic, El Salvador, Guatemala, Guyana, Haiti, Honduras, Jamaica, Mexico, Netherlands Antilles, Nicaragua, Panama, Puerto Rico, St Lucia, St Vincent, Surinam, Trinidad & Tobago)

Pre-Preliminary Round
Dominican Republic v Puerto Rico 1 - 2; Puerto Rico v Dominican Republic 1 - 1; St Lucia v St Vincent 1 - 0; St Vincent v St Lucia 3 - 1

Preliminary Round
Bermuda v Haiti 1 - 0; Haiti v Bermuda 2 - 1; Jamaica v Puerto Rico 2 - 1; Puerto Rico v Jamaica 0 - 1; St Vincent w.o Cuba withdrew; Netherlands Antilles v Antigua 1 - 1; Antigua v Netherlands Antilles 3 - 0; Guyana v Surinam 1 - 2; Surinam v Guyana 1 - 1; Barbados v Trinidad & Tobago 1 - 2; Trinidad & Tobago v Barbados 3 - 0

1st Round
Central Region
Guatemala v Honduras 0 - 0; Honduras v Guatemala 2 - 0; Panama v Costa Rica 1 - 0; Costa Rica v Panama 5 - 1; Nicaragua v El Salvador 0 - 5; El Salvador v Nicaragua 5 - 1

Caribbean Region
Surinam v St Vincent 0 - 0; St Vincent v Surinam 2 - 1; Antigua v Bermuda 0 - 3; Bermuda v Antigua 2 - 1; Trinidad & Tobago v Jamaica 1 - 2; Jamaica v Trinidad & Tobago 1 - 1

2nd Round
Group A
Costa Rica v Honduras 2 - 3; St Vincent v Mexico 0 - 4; Mexico v Honduras 2 - 0; St Vincent v Costa Rica 0 - 1; Mexico v Costa Rica 4 - 0; St Vincent v Honduras 0 - 4; Honduras v St Vincent 4 - 0; Costa Rica v Mexico 2 - 0; Honduras v Costa Rica 2 - 1; Mexico v St Vincent 11 - 0; Costa Rica v St Vincent 5 - 0; Honduras v Mexico 1 - 1

	P	W	D	L	F	A	Pts
Mexico	6	4	1	1	22	3	9
Honduras	6	4	1	1	14	6	9
Costa Rica	6	3	0	3	11	9	6
St Vincent	6	0	0	6	0	29	0

Group B
Bermuda v El Salvador 1 - 0; Jamaica v Canada 1 - 1; Bermuda v Jamaica 1 - 1; El Salvador v Canada 1 - 1; Canada v Jamaica 1 - 0; El Salvador v Canada 4 - 1; Canada v El Salvador 2 - 3; Jamaica v Bermuda 3 - 2; Canada v Bermuda 4 - 2; Jamaica v El Salvador 0 - 2; Bermuda v Canada 0 - 0; El Salvador v Jamaica 2 - 1

	P	W	D	L	F	A	Pts
El Salvador	6	4	1	1	12	6	9
Canada	6	2	3	1	9	7	7
Jamaica	6	1	2	3	6	9	4
Bermuda	6	1	2	3	7	12	4

3rd Round
Honduras v Canada 2 - 2; El Salvador v Mexico 2 - 1; Canada v El Salvador 2 - 0; Mexico v Honduras 3 - 0; Canada v Honduras 3 - 1; Mexico v El Salvador 3 - 1; Honduras v El Salvador 2 - 0; Mexico v Canada 4 - 0; Honduras v Mexico 1 - 4; El Salvador v Canada 1 - 2; Canada v Mexico 1 - 2; El Salvador v Honduras 2 - 1

	P	W	D	L	F	A	Pts
Mexico	6	5	0	1	17	5	10
Canada	6	3	1	2	10	10	7
El Salvador	6	2	0	4	6	11	4
Honduras	6	1	1	4	7	14	3

Mexico qualified

Oceania
Group 1 (Australia, Tahiti, Solomon Islands)
Solomon Islands v Tahiti 1 - 1; Solomon Islands v Australia 1 - 2; Tahiti v Australia 0 - 3; Australia v Tahiti 2 - 0; Australia v Solomon Islands 6 - 1; Tahiti v Solomon Islands 4 - 2

	P	W	D	L	F	A	Pts
Australia	4	4	0	0	13	2	8
Tahiti	4	1	1	2	5	8	3
Solomon Islands	4	0	1	3	5	13	1

Group 2 (New Zealand, Fiji, Vanuatu)
New Zealand v Fiji 3 - 0; Vanuatu v New Zealand 1 - 4; New Zealand v Vanuatu 8 - 0; Fiji v Vanuatu 3 - 0; Fiji v New Zealand 0 - 0; Vanuatu v Fiji 0 - 3

	P	W	D	L	F	A	Pts
New Zealand	4	3	1	0	15	1	7
Fiji	4	2	1	1	6	3	5
Vanuatu	4	0	0	4	1	18	0

2nd Round
New Zealand v Australia 0 - 1; Australia v New Zealand 3 - 0

Play-off
Canada v Australia 2 - 1; Australia v Canada 2 - 1 (aet; Australia won 4 - 1 on penalties)

South America
Group A (Argentina, Colombia, Paraguay, Peru)
Colombia v Paraguay 0 - 0; Peru v Argentina 0 - 1; Paraguay v Argentina 1 - 3; Peru v Colombia 0 - 1; Colombia v Argentina 2 - 1; Paraguay v Peru 2 - 1; Argentina v Peru 2 - 1; Paraguay v Colombia 1 - 1; Argentina v Paraguay 0 - 0; Colombia v Peru 4 - 0; Argentina v Colombia 0 - 5; Peru v Paraguay 2 - 2

	P	W	D	L	F	A	Pts
Colombia	6	4	2	0	13	2	10
Argentina	6	3	1	2	7	9	7
Paraguay	6	1	4	1	6	7	6
Peru	6	0	1	5	4	12	1

Colombia qualified

Group B (Brazil, Uruguay, Ecuador, Bolivia, Venezuela)
Ecuador v Brazil 0 - 0; Venezuela v Bolivia 1 - 7; Bolivia v Brazil 2 - 0; Venezuela v Uruguay 0 - 1; Uruguay v Ecuador 0 - 1; Venezuela v Brazil 1 - 5; Bolivia v Uruguay 3 - 1; Ecuador v Venezuela 5 - 0; Bolivia v Ecuador 1 - 0; Uruguay v Brazil 1 - 1; Bolivia v Venezuela 7 - 0; Uruguay v Ecuador 2 - 0; Brazil v Bolivia 6 - 0; Uruguay v Venezuela 4 - 0; Brazil v Venezuela 4 - 0; Ecuador v Uruguay 0 - 1; Uruguay v Bolivia 2 - 1; Venezuela v Ecuador 2 - 1; Brazil v Uruguay 2 - 0; Ecuador v Bolivia 1 - 1

	P	W	D	L	F	A	Pts
Brazil	8	5	2	1	20	4	12
Bolivia	8	5	1	2	22	11	11
Uruguay	8	4	2	2	10	7	10
Ecuador	8	1	3	4	7	7	5
Venezuela	8	1	0	7	4	34	2

Brazil and Bolivia qualified

Play-off
Australia v Argentina 1 - 1; Argentina v Australia 1 - 0
Argentina qualified

GUIDE TO THE 1994 FINALS

All kick-off times BST

FIRST ROUND

Group A
USA, Rumania, Switzerland, Colombia

Sat 18 June	USA	v	Switzerland	Detroit	16.30
Sat 18 June	Colombia	v	Rumania	Los Angeles	0.30
Wed 22 June	Switzerland	v	Rumania	Detroit	21.00
Wed 22 June	USA	v	Colombia	Los Angeles	0.30
Sun 26 June	USA	v	Rumania	Los Angeles	21.00
Sun 26 June	Switzerland	v	Colombia	San Francisco	21.00

Group B
Brazil, Russia, Cameroon, Sweden

Sun 19 June	Cameroon	v	Sweden	Los Angeles	0.30
Mon 20 June	Brazil	v	Russia	San Francisco	21.00
Fri 24 June	Brazil	v	Cameroon	San Francisco	21.00
Fri 24 June	Sweden	v	Russia	Detroit	0.30
Tue 28 June	Russia	v	Cameroon	San Francisco	21.00
Tue 28 June	Brazil	v	Sweden	Detroit	21.00

Group C
Germany, Spain, Bolivia, South Korea

Fri 17 June	Germany	v	Bolivia	Chicago	20.00
Fri 17 June	Spain	v	South Korea	Dallas	0.30
Tue 21 June	Germany	v	Spain	Chicago	21.00
Thu 23 June	Bolivia	v	South Korea	Boston	21.00
Mon 27 June	Germany	v	South Korea	Dallas	21.00
Mon 27 June	Bolivia	v	Spain	Chicago	21.00

Group D
Argentina, Greece, Bulgaria, Nigeria

Tue 21 June	Argentina	v	Greece	Boston	17.30
Tue 21 June	Nigeria	v	Bulgaria	Dallas	0.30
Sat 25 June	Argentina	v	Nigeria	Boston	21.00
Sun 26 June	Bulgaria	v	Greece	Chicago	17.30
Thu 30 June	Argentina	v	Bulgaria	Dallas	0.30
Thu 30 June	Greece	v	Nigeria	Boston	0.30

Group E
Italy, Ireland, Norway, Mexico

Sat 18 June	Italy	v	Ireland	New York	21.00
Sun 19 June	Norway	v	Mexico	Washington	21.00
Thu 23 June	Italy	v	Norway	New York	21.00
Fri 24 June	Ireland	v	Mexico	Orlando	17.30
Tue 28 June	Ireland	v	Norway	New York	17.30
Tue 28 June	Italy	v	Mexico	Washington	17.30

Group F
Belgium, Holland, Morocco, Saudi Arabia

Sun 19 June	Belgium	v	Morocco	Orlando	17.30
Mon 20 June	Holland	v	Saudi Arabia	Washington	0.30
Sat 25 June	Belgium	v	Holland	Orlando	17.30
Sat 25 June	Morocco	v	Saudi Arabia	New York	0.30
Wed 29 June	Belgium	v	Saudi Arabia	Washington	17.30
Wed 29 June	Morocco	v	Holland	Orlando	17.30

SECOND ROUND

Sat 2 July	Winner Group C	v	3rd A/B/F	Chicago	18.00
Sat 2 July	2nd Group C	v	2nd Group A	Washington	21.30
Sun 3 July	2nd Group F	v	2nd Group B	Dallas	18.00
Sun 3 July	Winner group A	v	3rd C/D/E	Los Angeles	21.30
Mon 4 July	Winner Group F	v	2nd Group E	Orlando	17.00
Mon 4 July	Winner Group B	v	3rd A/C/D	San Francisco	20.30
Tue 5 July	Winner Group D	v	3rd B/E/F	Boston	18.00
Tue 5 July	Winner Group E	v	2nd Group D	New York	21.30

QUARTER FINALS

Sat 9 July	Winner (Boston)	v	Winner (Washington)	Boston	17.00
Sat 9 July	Winner (Orlando)	v	Winner (San Francisco)	Dallas	20.30
Sun 10 July	Winner (New York)	v	Winner (Chicago)	New York	17.00
Sun 10 July	Winner (Los Angeles)	v	Winner (Dallas)	San Francisco	20.30

SEMI FINALS

Wed 13 July	Winner (New York)	v	Winner (Boston)	New York	21.00
Wed 13 July	Winner (San Francisco)	v	Winner (Dallas)	Los Angeles	0.30

Sat 16 July	MATCH FOR THIRD PLACE	Los Angeles	20.30

Sun 17 July	WORLD CUP FINAL	Los Angeles	20.30

IRELAND IN THE WORLD CUP

Niall Quinn, 1990 World Cup quarter-final, Rome (ALLSPORT/RICHIARDI)

THE ROAD TO ITALY

1930-90

Ireland came of age when they reached the finals of the World Cup for the first time in 1990. But this achievement crowned not only the qualifying campaign which Jack Charlton's team had begun in Belfast in September 1988, but more than fifty years of gallant and sometimes not so gallant failure.

Since the founding of the Football Association of Ireland in 1921 and its affiliation to FIFA in 1923, Ireland had entered the World Cup qualifying competition 12 times without success and with only two near misses to speak of: in 1966 when they took Spain to a play-off in Paris and in 1982 when they defeated Holland and France in Dublin, finishing above the Dutch and ultimately losing out to the French only on goal difference. To be grouped in the first place with Belgium, France and Holland as they were on that occasion was appalling luck.

The atmosphere and the level of expectation had changed significantly, however, by the time Ireland kicked off the qualifying series for 1990. First, Ireland under new manager Jack Charlton had finally proved themselves capable of coming through a qualifying group and reaching a major finals in the recent European Championships. Second, in the finals themselves in the summer of 1988 they had performed spectacularly well.

Now, in the World Cup, while theirs was not an easy group it was one in which they had little to fear. In a pool of five from which two qualified for the finals, Spain would undoubtedly start as favourites to win it thanks in no small measure to their formidable home record in Seville. Hungary, however, were a team in decline. Their

astonishing 6-0 reverse against the Soviet Union in the 1986 World Cup finals had been followed by a dreadful European Championships. Malta were the bottom seeds and the group was completed by neighbours Northern Ireland, who were looking to achieve a third successive appearance in the World Cup finals and could not be underestimated despite a poor European Championships.

Ireland line up before the home qualifier versus Malta in 1989. From left: Moran, Bonner, Houghton, Staunton, Hughton, Cascarino, McGrath, Whelan, Sheedy, Stapleton, O'Leary (ALLSPORT/BILLY STICKLAND)

With their first three matches all away from home, Ireland avoided defeat against two of their main rivals. Starting in Belfast they fought out a 0-0 draw with Northern Ireland, then travelled to Seville to face Spain. Level at half time, the Irish went down to second-half goals from Manolo and Butragueno. Defeat in Budapest the following

1934 Qualifying
GROUP 11
25.2.1934 Ireland 4 Belgium 4 DUBLIN
Ireland: Foley, Lynch, Burke, Gaskins, O'Reilly, Kendrick, Kennedy, Byrne D, Moore (4), O'Keeffe, Kelly

8.4.1934 Holland 5 Ireland 2 AMSTERDAM
Ireland: Foley, Gaskins, Byrne P, O'Reilly, Chatton, Kendrick, Kennedy, Squires (1), Moore (1), Jordan, Meehan

1938 Qualifying
GROUP 2
10.10.1937 Norway 3 Ireland 2 OSLO
Ireland: McKenzie, Williams, Hoy, O'Reilly, Turner, Kinsella, Donnelly T, Donnelly J, Dunne (1), Jordan, Geoghegan (1)

7.11.1937 Ireland 3 Norway 3 DUBLIN
Ireland: McKenzie, O'Neill, Gorman, O'Reilly, Turner, Arrigan, O'Flanagan (1), Dunne (1), Duggan (1), Carey, Foy

1950 Qualifying
GROUP 4
2.6.1949 Sweden 3 Ireland 1 STOCKHOLM
Ireland: Godwin, Carey, Keane, Gannon, Martin, Moroney, O'Driscoll, Coad, Walsh (1), McGowan, Eglinton

8.9.1949 Ireland 3 Finland 0 DUBLIN
Ireland: Godwin, Carey, Aherne, Gannon, Martin (2), Moroney, Gavin (1), Fitzsimons, Carroll (Daly), Desmond, O'Connor

9.10.1949 Finland 1 Ireland 1 HELSINKI
Ireland: Godwin, Carey, Aherne, Coffey, Martin, Moroney, Gavin, Farrell (1), Walsh, Desmond, O'Connor

13.11.1949 Ireland 1 Sweden 3 DUBLIN
Ireland: Godwin, Carey, Aherne, Walsh W, Martin (1), Ryan, Corr, Farrell, Walsh D, Desmond, O'Connor

1954 Qualifying
GROUP 4
4.10.1953 Ireland 3 France 5 DUBLIN
Ireland: O'Neill, Dunne, Aherne, Farrell, Martin, O'Farrell (1), Fitzsimons, Moroney, Walsh (1), Ryan (1), Eglinton

28.10.1953 Ireland 4 Luxembourg 0 DUBLIN
Ireland: O'Neill, Dunne, Lawler, Gannon, Cantwell, Ryan (1), Munroe, Cummins, Gibbons, Fitzsimons (2), Eglinton (1)

25.11.1953 France 1 Ireland 0 PARIS
Ireland: O'Neill, Clinton, Lawler, Gannon, Martin, Farrell, Ringstead, Ryan, Walsh, Fitzsimons, Eglinton

7.3.1954 Luxembourg 0 Ireland 1 LUXEMBOURG
Ireland: Scannell, Clinton, Traynor, Gallagher, Martin, Saward, Gavin, Kelly, Cummins (1), Harnett

1958 Qualifying
GROUP 1
3.10.1956 Ireland 2 Denmark 1 DUBLIN
Ireland: O'Neill, Dunne S, Cantwell, Dunne T, Mackey, Nolan, Gavin (1), Whelan, Curtis (1), Fitzsimons, Haverty

8.5.1957 England 5 Ireland 1 LONDON
Ireland: Kelly, Donovan, Cantwell, Farrell, Mackey, Saward, Ringstead, Whelan, Curtis (1), Fitzsimons, Haverty

19.5.1957 Ireland 1 England 1 DUBLIN
Ireland: Godwin, Dunne, Cantwell, Nolan, Hurley, Saward, Ringstead (1), Whelan, Curtis, Fitzsimons, Haverty

2.10.1957 Denmark 0 Ireland 2 COPENHAGEN
Ireland: Godwin, Dunne, Cantwell, Saward, Hurley, O'Farrell, Ringstead, Fitzsimons, Curtis (1), Cummins (1), Haverty

1962 Qualifying
GROUP 8
3.5.1961 Scotland 4 Ireland 1 GLASGOW
Ireland: Dwyer, McNally, Cantwell, McEvoy, Hurley, Saward, Giles, Fogarty, Curtis, Cummins, Haverty (1)

7.5.1961 Ireland 0 Scotland 3 DUBLIN
Ireland: Dwyer, Kelly, Cantwell, McEvoy, Hurley, Meagan, Fagan, Giles, Fitzgerald, Cummins, Haverty

8.10.1961 Ireland 1 Czechoslovakia 3 DUBLIN
Ireland: Dwyer, Kelly, Cantwell, Nolan, Hurley, McGrath, O'Neill, Fogarty (1), Fitzgerald, Giles (1), Haverty

29.10.1961 Czechoslovakia 7 Ireland 1 PRAGUE
Ireland: Dwyer, Kelly, Cantwell, Nolan, Hurley, McGrath, O'Neill, Fogarty (1), Fitzgerald, Giles, Haverty

1966 Qualifying
GROUP 9
5.5.1965 Ireland 1 Spain 0 DUBLIN
Ireland: Dunne P, Brennan, Dunne A, McGrath, Hurley, Hennessy, O'Neill, Giles, Cantwell, McEvoy, Haverty

27.10.1965 Spain 4 Ireland 1 SEVILLE
Ireland: Dunne P, Foley, Dunne A, McGrath, Cantwell, Meagan, O'Neill, McEvoy (1), Barber, Giles, Haverty

10.11.1965 Ireland 0 Spain 1 PARIS
Ireland: Dunne P, Brennan, Dunne A, Foley, Cantwell, Meagan, O'Neill, Dunphy, McEvoy, Giles, Haverty

1970 Qualifying
GROUP 2
4.5.1969 Ireland (1) 1 Czechoslovakia (0) 2 DUBLIN
Ireland: Kelly, Brennan, Dempsey, Hurley, Mulligan, Giles, Finucane, O'Neill, Leech (Hand), Treacy, Rogers (1)

27.5.1969 Denmark (1) 2 Ireland 0 COPENHAGEN
Ireland: Kelly, Brennan, Mulligan, Rogers, Finucane, Dempsey (Dunne), Newman, Leech, Givens, Dunphy, Treacy

8.6.1969 Ireland (0) 1 Hungary (1) 2 DUBLIN
Ireland: Kelly, Brennan, Dunne, Conway, Finucane, Mulligan, Dunphy, Leech, Hurley (O'Neill), Rogers, Givens (1)

7.10.1969 Czechoslovakia (3) 3 Ireland 0 PRAGUE
Ireland: Fitzpatrick, Kinnear, Brennan, Mulligan, Carroll, Finucane, Conroy, Conway, Givens, Hale, Conmy

15.10.1969 Ireland (1) 1 Denmark (0) 1 DUBLIN
Ireland: Kelly, Kinnear, Brennan, Mulligan, Byrne, Conway, Dunphy, Rogers, Conroy, Givens (1), Treacy

5.11.1969 Hungary (1) 4 Ireland 0 BUDAPEST
Ireland: Kelly, Brennan, Dunne, Conway, Dempsey, Mulligan, Rogers, Conroy (Treacy), Givens, Dunphy, Kinnear

1974 Qualifying
GROUP 9
18.10.1972 Ireland (0) 1 Soviet Union (0) 2 DUBLIN
Ireland: Kelly, Kinnear, McConville, Hand, Carroll, Campbell, Rogers (Leech), Martin, Heighway, Treacy, Conroy (1)

15.11.1972 Ireland (1) 2 France (0) 1 DUBLIN
Ireland: Kelly, McConville, Kinnear, Mulligan, Holmes, Hand, Byrne, Treacy (1), Giles (Campbell), Conroy (1), Givens

13.5.1973 Soviet Union (0) 1 Ireland 0 MOSCOW
Ireland: Kelly, Carroll, McConville, Hand, Holmes, Mulligan, Martin, Giles, Givens, Treacy, Conroy

19.5.1973 France (0) 1 Ireland (0) 1 PARIS
Ireland: Kelly, Holmes, McConville, Mulligan, Carroll (Herrick), Byrne, Hand, Martin (1), Dennehy, Treacy, Givens

1978 Qualifying
GROUP 5
17.11.1976 France 2 Ireland 0 PARIS
Ireland: Kearns, Mulligan, Holmes, Daly, O'Leary, Martin, Brady, Stapleton (Walsh), Heighway, Giles, Givens

30.3.1977 Ireland 1 France 0 DUBLIN
Ireland: Kearns, Mulligan, Holmes, Daly, O'Leary, Martin, Brady (1), Treacy, Heighway, Giles, Givens

1.6.1977 Bulgaria 2 Ireland 0 SOFIA
Ireland: Kearns, Mulligan, Holmes, Daly (Campbell), O'Leary, Martin, Brady, Stapleton, Heighway, Giles, Givens

12.10.1977 Ireland 0 Bulgaria 0 DUBLIN
Ireland: Peyton, Mulligan, Holmes, Daly, O'Leary, Lawrenson, Brady, Stapleton, Heighway, Giles, Givens

1982 Qualifying
GROUP 2
26.3.1980 Cyprus (1) 2 Ireland (3) 3 NICOSIA
Ireland: Peyton, Grealish, Grimes, Lawrenson (1), O'Leary D, Brady, Daly, Murphy (O'Brien F), Heighway (Ryan), Stapleton, McGee (2)

10.9.1980 Ireland (0) 2 Holland (0) 1 DUBLIN
Ireland: Peyton, Langan, O'Leary D, O'Leary P, Hughton, Lawrenson (1), Daly (1), Grealish, Brady, Stapleton, Givens

15.10.1980 Ireland (1) 1 Belgium (1) 1 DUBLIN
Ireland: Peyton, Langan, Moran, Lawrenson, Hughton, Brady, Daly, Grealish (1), Stapleton, Heighway, Givens (McGee)

28.10.1980 France (1) 2 Ireland 0 PARIS
Ireland: Peyton, Langan, Lawrenson, Moran, Hughton, Martin (Ryan), Brady, Grealish, Heighway, Stapleton, Robinson

19.11.1980 Ireland (4) 6 Cyprus 0 DUBLIN
Ireland: Peyton, Langan, Hughton (1), Lawrenson, Moran, Daly (2, 1 pen), Grealish (1), Brady, Stapleton (1), Heighway, Robinson (1) [Givens]

25.3.1981 Belgium (0) 1 Ireland 0 BRUSSELS
Ireland: McDonagh, Langan, Martin, Moran, Hughton, Daly, Grealish, Brady, Robinson, Stapleton (Walsh), Heighway

9.9.198• Holland (1) 2 Ireland (1) 2 ROTTERDAM
Ireland: McDonagh, Langan, Devine, Lawrenson, O'Leary D, Brady, Martin (Whelan), Grealish, Heighway (Ryan), Stapleton (1), Robinson (1)

14.10.1981 Ireland (3) 3 France (1) 2 DUBLIN
Ireland: McDonagh, Langan, O'Leary D, Moran, Hughton, Whelan, Martin, Lawrenson, Brady, Stapleton (1) [Givens], Robinson (1)

1986 Qualifying
GROUP 6
12.9.1984 Ireland 1 Soviet Union 0 DUBLIN
Ireland: McDonagh, Devine, Hughton, Grealish, O'Leary, Lawrenson, Brady, Whelan, Robinson, Walsh (1) [O'Keefe], Galvin

17.10.1984 Norway 1 Ireland 0 OSLO
Ireland: McDonagh, Devine, Hughton, Grealish, O'Leary, Lawrenson, Brady, Whelan (O'Callaghan), Robinson (Walsh), Stapleton, Galvin

14.11.1984 Denmark 3 Ireland 0 COPENHAGEN
Ireland: McDonagh, Lawrenson, Beglin, Grealish, O'Leary, McCarthy, Brady, Stapleton, Walsh, Sheedy, Galvin (O'Callaghan)

1.5.1985 Ireland 0 Norway 0 DUBLIN
Ireland: Bonner, Langan (McGrath), Beglin, Lawrenson, O'Leary, Daly, Brady (Whelan), Stapleton, Robinson, Waddock, Galvin

2.6.1985 Ireland 3 Switzerland 0 DUBLIN
Ireland: McDonagh, Langan, Beglin, Daly (Whelan), O'Leary, McCarthy, Brady, Grealish (1) [McGrath], Robinson, Stapleton (1), Sheedy (1)

11.9.1985 Switzerland 0 Ireland 0 BERNE
Ireland: McDonagh, Hughton, Beglin, McCarthy, O'Leary, Brady, Daly (McGrath), Lawrenson, Cascarino, Stapleton, Sheedy (O'Callaghan)

16.10.1985 Soviet Union 2 Ireland 0 MOSCOW
Ireland: McDonagh, Hughton, Beglin (O'Callaghan), McCarthy, O'Leary, Brady, Waddock, Lawrenson, Cascarino, Stapleton, Grealish (Whelan)

13.11.1985 Ireland 1 Denmark 4 DUBLIN
Ireland: McDonagh, Lawrenson, Beglin, Moran, O'Leary, Brady, McGrath, Grealish (Byrne P), Cascarino, Stapleton (1), Sheedy (Robinson)

1990 Qualifying
GROUP 6
14.9.1988 Northern Ireland 0 Ireland 0 BELFAST
Ireland: Peyton, Morris, Hughton, McGrath, McCarthy, Moran, Houghton, Whelan, Aldridge, Cascarino, Sheedy

16.11.1988 Spain (0) 2 Ireland 0 SEVILLE
Ireland: Bonner, Morris, McCarthy, Staunton, O'Leary, Moran, Houghton, Sheridan (O'Brien), Aldridge (Quinn), Cascarino, Galvin

8.3.1989 Hungary 0 Ireland 0 BUDAPEST
Ireland: Bonner, Morris, Hughton, McGrath, McCarthy, Moran, Whelan, Houghton, Aldridge (Brady), Cascarino (Quinn), Sheedy

26.4.1989 Ireland (1) 1 Spain 0 DUBLIN
Ireland: Bonner, Hughton, Staunton, McCarthy, Moran, Whelan, McGrath, Houghton, Stapleton (Townsend), Cascarino, Sheedy

28.5.1989 Ireland (1) 2 Malta 0 DUBLIN
Ireland: Bonner, Hughton, Staunton, O'Leary, Moran (1), Whelan, McGrath, Houghton (1) [Townsend], Stapleton (Aldridge), Cascarino, Sheedy

4.6.1989 Ireland (1) 2 Hungary 0 DUBLIN
Ireland: Bonner, Hughton, Staunton, O'Leary, McGrath (1) [Morris], Moran, Houghton, Townsend, Aldridge (Brady), Cascarino (1), Sheedy

11.10.1989 Ireland (1) 3 Northern Ireland 0 DUBLIN
Ireland: Bonner, Morris, Staunton (O'Leary), McCarthy, Moran, Whelan (1), Townsend, Houghton(1), Aldridge, Cascarino (1), Sheedy

15.11.1989 Malta 0 Ireland (1) 2 TA'QALI
Ireland: Bonner, McGrath, Moran (Morris), Staunton, O'Leary, Houghton, Sheedy, Townsend, Whelan, Aldridge (2, 1 pen), Cascarino

spring would have made things very difficult despite Hungary having dropped a point in Valletta, but another 0-0 draw was achieved fairly comfortably.

Ireland had set themselves up well. They were undefeated in 12 matches at home and if they could continue that form now, qualification would be in their sights. Spain were first up at Lansdowne Road in front of a capacity crowd of 49,000. It was an own goal by Hierro just before half time that they had to thank for it but Ireland took the points. Then at the end of the domestic season Ireland entertained Malta and Hungary on successive Sunday afternoons in Dublin. Both games were won by two goals to nil with a goal in each half, Ray Houghton and Kevin Moran scoring against Malta, Paul McGrath and Tony Cascarino against Hungary.

A fourth win at Lansdowne Road in October against Northern Ireland would now all but seal qualification as Hungary kept themselves alive with a win in Belfast. It was a tense occasion until Ronnie Whelan put Ireland ahead just before half time. Then within three minutes of the restart Kevin Sheedy crossed for Tony Cascarino to head in. Ray Houghton wrapped the game up with a clever chip and Ireland needed only a point from their last match in Malta to qualify, and that only in the unlikely event of Hungary winning in Seville the same day. In the event the Hungarians lost heavily and two goals from John Aldridge gave Ireland victory in Valletta, in front of a huge army of travelling fans enjoying the Mediterranean sunshine.

Lucky for some: Ireland had made it to the World Cup at the 13th attempt.

ITALIA '90

1990 Finals
GROUP F

11.6.1990 England (1) 1 Ireland (0) 1 CAGLIARI
Ireland: Bonner, Morris, Moran, McCarthy, Staunton, McGrath, Houghton, Townsend, Sheedy (1), Aldridge (McLoughlin), Cascarino

17.6.1990 Egypt 0 Ireland 0 PALERMO
Ireland: Bonner, Morris, Moran, McCarthy, Staunton, McGrath, Houghton, Townsend, Sheedy, Aldridge (McLoughlin), Cascarino (Quinn)

21.6.1990 Holland (1) 1 Ireland (0) 1 PALERMO
Ireland: Bonner, Morris, Moran, McCarthy, Staunton, McGrath, Houghton, Townsend, Sheedy (Whelan), Aldridge (Cascarino), Quinn (1)

Second round
25.6.1990 Ireland 0 Rumania 0 aet GENOA
Ireland: Bonner, Morris, Moran, McCarthy, Staunton (O'Leary), McGrath, Houghton, Townsend, Sheedy, Aldridge (Cascarino), Quinn
Ireland won 5-4 on penalties: Sheedy, Houghton, Townsend, Cascarino, O'Leary

Quarter-finals
30.6.1990 Ireland 0 Italy (1) 1 ROME
Ireland: Bonner, Morris, Moran, McCarthy, Staunton, McGrath, Houghton, Townsend, Sheedy, Aldridge (Sheridan), Quinn (Cascarino)

The draw for the 1990 finals was made in Rome and in an echo of the European Championships of 1988 it again brought together Ireland, Holland and England. In reality such a draw did Ireland no favours. Holland besides being European Champions were many people's favourites to win the World Cup, and while a return clash with England was relished by some after the 1-0 win in Stuttgart two years earlier, they would undeniably be difficult opponents. Of Egypt, the resident minnow in Group F, little was known except that they had come through the tough African qualifying section and would be no pushover. That match was scheduled for the late afternoon heat of Palermo in Sicily, where the Irish were based for the first round games.

Nonetheless it was a confident group of players that Jack Charlton and Maurice Setters led first to Malta to complete their preparation for the finals, including a final warm-up game against the Maltese national side which Ireland won 3-0. Attention then began to focus on the opening match of the group, Ireland versus England in Cagliari. Some 15,000 Irish supporters headed for Sardinia for the game.

Jack Charlton regarded it as crucial to his 'game plan' for the group that Ireland must not lose this match, but they

Jack Charlton makes a point to Maurice Setters on the Irish bench during the quarter-final in Rome (ALLSPORT/BILLY STICKLAND)

did not start well. After eight minutes, the team seemed to lose its concentration when Chris Waddle apparently failed to keep the ball in play on the right-hand touchline. But no whistle came, Waddle whipped the ball across and Gary Lineker stole in ahead of Mick McCarthy, nudged the ball past Bonner and followed it into the net.

The game was a scrappy one, played against the backdrop of an incredible thunderstorm which broke over the Sant'Elia stadium just after the interval, but the Irish gradually began to get the better of the play. They survived a strong penalty claim after an hour when Kevin Moran tripped Waddle, and eventually claimed an equaliser with thirteen minutes left on the clock. A mistake by England substitute Steve McMahon on the edge of the area gave Kevin Sheedy a half chance; he struck the ball firm and true with his left foot and Ireland were level. Charlton was visibly the happier of the two managers after the game.

The following night Holland were held 1-1 by Egypt and the group was wide open. It remained so when Holland and England drew 0-0 in Cagliari and sent Ireland into their next game against Egypt knowing that a win would almost certainly put them through to the second round one way or another. But it was to prove a frustrating afternoon for the Irish. A dull game produced few scoring opportunities and Charlton was scornful of Egypt's lack of ambition. He perhaps realised that Ireland now had it all to do in the final game against Holland.

A draw would probably be sufficient but that depended on the result of the England-Egypt match being played out simultaneously in Sardinia. If the two games produced identical draws, it would bring about the bizarre scenario of lots being drawn to separate all four teams in the group. Again things could not have got off to a worse start as an out-of-sorts Ruud Gullit chose the worst possible moment to rediscover the art of goalscoring. Previously even hitting the target had seemed

Paolo Maldini of Italy joins the Irish wall of (left to right) McGrath, Houghton and Sheedy (ALLSPORT/BILLY STICKLAND)

beyond him. His goal gave Holland the lead after 10 minutes but with England 1-0 up against Egypt an equaliser would be enough. Salvation arrived with just over a quarter of an hour remaining in the then improbable form of Niall Quinn, preferred by Charlton to Tony Cascarino. Hans van Breukelen in the Dutch goal spilled a back pass following a long kick downfield from Bonner and Quinn was first to the ball.

'For God's sake Niall, don't miss it!' thought Quinn to himself, no doubt echoing the cries of Irish men and women everywhere. He didn't, Ireland had come back to level again and a place in the second round was theirs. Yet that was not quite the end of the story. Finishing in joint second place with the Dutch with an identical record, Ireland would learn who their next opponents were by means of drawing lots. The luck of the Irish sent them to Genoa to face Rumania. The Dutch went to Milan to play the eventual champions West Germany.

Rumania had been one of the surprise teams of the first round. They were an attractive footballing side and above all they had Gheorghe Hagi. At times in the first half in Genoa he threatened to win the game on his own, but Irish resilience and determination on another warm afternoon kept them in the game. Extra time was required but never looked like producing a goal. Penalty kicks would decide the outcome.

If anyone suspected the Irish of playing for the draw (it was after all their fourth draw out of four in Italy) this hardly tallied with the nature of Jack Charlton's contingency plans for the penalty shoot-out. The five penalty takers were decided upon only when Charlton strolled onto the pitch at the end of extra time and said to his exhausted players, 'Right, who fancies one?'

Kevin Sheedy fancied one and how it showed as he smashed Ireland's first penalty into the roof of the net and clenched his fist in triumph. Ray Houghton did the same and Andy Townsend also made no mistake. But all the while four Rumanian penalties were expertly dispatched past Bonner. Tony Cascarino stepped up for Ireland's fourth penalty and scuffed his kick horribly - but somehow, with the goalkeeper committed, the ball found its way into the net. It was a turning point. The fifth Rumanian penalty was superbly saved by Bonner and David O'Leary, who had appeared as substitute just after the start of extra time, now needed only to convert his kick and Ireland were in the

Packy Bonner, hero of the penalty shoot-out that decided the second round tie in Genoa (ALLSPORT/BILLY STICKLAND)

quarter-finals. O'Leary kept his cool, sidefooted firmly to the keeper's left and was submerged by the congratulations of his ecstatic team-mates.

Later that evening Ireland learned that as expected their opponents in the quarter-final would be Italy. Either way, the Irish were going to Rome where they first kept an appointment with Pope John Paul II. The Holy Father, a goalkeeper himself in his youth, seemed especially keen to greet Packy Bonner. For the 20,000 Irish fans who taken over the Luigi Ferraris stadium five days earlier, the news was less good. They were to be allocated just 2,000 places in the 73,000 capacity Stadio Olimpico for the quarter-final. High-level representations managed to secure another 10,000 tickets but this was one occasion when Jackie's Army would struggle to make themselves heard.

'All one of you has to do tonight,' insisted Jack Charlton to his players before the game, 'is score a goal . . . and we can win this thing.' He was talking about the World Cup itself. This was Ireland's moment of truth. If they could overcome Italy in Rome, no greater obstacle would stand in their way.

Though Zenga was forced to make a good save from a looping Niall Quinn header, Italy enjoyed the better of the game in the first half and Schillaci's goal was untidy but deserved. The more the game went on, however, the more rattled the Italians became by their inability to put Ireland away. There was an almost visible fear of an Irish equaliser among the *azzuri*. But it never came and for the Irish the Italian adventure was over. They flew back to Dublin to be greeted by half a million fans and to look forward to the next World Cup.

Frustration on the face of Tony Cascarino as he goes for goal during the 0-0 draw with Egypt in Palermo (ALLSPORT/ SIMON BRUTY)

JACK CHARLTON

When Jack Charlton took over as manager of the Irish national team in 1986 he was a surprise appointment, not least because he was English. It was a gamble by the FA of Ireland which has paid off handsomely both for them and for Charlton himself, a man who had always made it his business to surprise people in football with his achievements.

Born on 8 May 1935 in Ashington, Northumberland, Jack signed for Leeds United in 1952. But it was his younger brother Bobby who took the eye, playing for Manchester United in the European Cup and for England in the World Cup finals of 1958 and 1962. Things began to change, however, with the arrival of Don Revie as manager at Elland Road. He believed Jack could be good enough to play for England and so it proved. Leeds won the Second Division Championship in 1964 and the following season Charlton made his debut for England at centre-half when he was almost 30 years old. He retained his place in the side for the World Cup finals in 1966 and played in all six matches as England won the trophy.

He continued to shine as the defensive mainstay of a Leeds United side that was starting to dominate English football, receiving due recognition when he was voted Footballer of the Year in 1967. For Leeds he picked up a string of honours in amongst all their famous near misses: they were League Cup and Fairs Cup winners in 1968, League Champions in 1969, Fairs Cup winners again in 1971 and FA Cup winners in 1972. He won the last of his 35 England caps in 1970 and retired from playing in 1973 having made 772 appearances in all competitions for Leeds in which he scored 95 goals.

Charlton now turned his attention to club management, taking over at Middlesbrough and enjoying immediate success when Boro were promoted to Division One as runaway champions in 1974. After four seasons in charge at Ayresome Park, in 1977 Charlton took over as manager of Sheffield Wednesday. He led them to the semi-finals of the FA Cup in 1983 but promotion to the top flight eluded them. When Arthur Cox resigned as manager of Newcastle in 1984 having led them back to Division One, Charlton was the obvious choice to take over at St James Park, but

Ireland's manager, pictured before the game with England in 1991 at Wembley, a happy return for Jack (ALLSPORT/ SHAUN BOTTERILL)

he resigned after just one full season, the target of some fans' discontent after the sale of Chris Waddle.

Just months later, however, he began a new chapter when he made a successful application to manage the Irish national team, having previously been rejected as a candidate for the England job. On the face of it Charlton seemed to have something to prove as a result. His first game in charge was lost, at home to Wales at Lansdowne Road, but that was to become a landmark for Ireland: they would not lose again at home for six years when the Welsh were victorious at Dalymount Park. Lansdowne Road remained impregnable for another 18 months.

Charlton took over a side which in terms of achievement had not made the most of some outstanding individual players, the likes of Johnny Giles, Frank Stapleton, Mark

Lawrenson and Liam Brady. The new manager's remedy for this was soon apparent: his approach was to be uncompromising and would look uncomplicated. He felt that the natural pressing game played by club sides in the British Isles *could* work at international level if it was applied in all areas of the field, including the attacking third where traditionally international defenders were allowed to pass the ball about at will. Conversely, he was confident that if his own defenders did not try to hold onto the ball in their own half of the pitch but cleared their lines, teams would find it very difficult to score against Ireland.

For all the attention which Ireland's playing style under Charlton attracted, the fact was that he had some very good players at his disposal. Stapleton, Brady and Lawrenson were still available to him, as were Paul McGrath of Manchester United and Ronnie Whelan of Liverpool. Two Oxford United players, John Aldridge and Ray Houghton, were capped by Charlton well before they moved on to a grander club stage at Liverpool. Both qualified to play for Ireland through their Irish ancestry rather than being Ireland-born but Charlton and the FAI

were singularly unfussy about that. If a player was qualified to play for Ireland and he was good enough, then he played.

Charlton and Ireland made a decent fist of their attempt to qualify for the European Championship finals of 1988 but with all their matches completed it looked as if Bulgaria would pip them for first place in the group. Needing only a draw at home to Scotland in Sofia they lost in amazing fashion, beaten by a last minute goal from Gary Mackay which sent Ireland to the finals in Germany instead. The draw pitted Ireland against England, Holland and the Soviet Union.

After five minutes of the opening game of the group against England in Stuttgart, Ray Houghton headed Ireland into a lead which they refused to give up. It was a famous victory and possibly remains the most significant of Charlton's time in charge. A stunning goal from Ronnie Whelan against the Soviets had Ireland on the brink of qualification for the semi-finals but they conceded an equaliser and needed to draw their last match against Holland to progress. They were cruelly denied by a

IRELAND UNDER CHARLTON

1986				Spain	A	L	0-2	Chile	H	D	1-1
Wales	H	L	0-1	1989				United States	A	D	1-1
Uruguay	H	D	1-1	France	H	D	0-0	Hungary	A	W	2-1
Iraq	A	L	0-1	Hungary	A	D	0-0	Poland	A	D	3-3
Iceland	A	W	2-1	Spain	H	W	1-0	Turkey	A	W	3-1
Czechoslovakia	N	W	1-0	Malta	H	W	2-0	1992			
Belgium	A	D	2-2	Hungary	H	W	2-0	Wales	H	L	0-1
Scotland	H	D	0-0	West Germany	H	D	1-1	Switzerland	H	W	2-1
Poland	A	L	0-1	Northern Ireland	H	W	3-0	United States	H	W	4-1
1987				Malta	A	W	2-0	Albania	H	W	2-0
Scotland	A	W	1-0	1990				United States	A	L	1-3
Bulgaria	A	L	1-2	Wales	H	W	1-0	Italy	N	L	0-2
Belgium	H	D	0-0	Soviet Union	H	W	1-0	Portugal	N	W	2-0
Brazil	H	W	1-0	Finland	H	D	1-1	Latvia	H	W	4-0
Luxembourg	A	W	2-0	Turkey	A	D	0-0	Denmark	A	D	0-0
Luxembourg	H	W	2-1	Malta	A	W	3-0	Spain	A	D	0-0
Bulgaria	H	W	2-0	England	N	D	1-1	1993			
Israel	H	W	2-0	Egypt	N	D	0-0	Wales	H	W	2-1
1988				Holland	N	D	1-1	Northern Ireland	H	W	3-0
Rumania	H	W	2-0	Rumania	N	W	5-4p	Denmark	H	D	1-1
Yugoslavia	H	W	2-0	Italy	N	L	0-1	Albania	A	W	2-1
Poland	H	W	3-1	Morocco	H	W	1-0	Latvia	A	W	2-0
Norway	A	D	0-0	Turkey	H	W	5-0	Lithuania	A	W	1-0
England	N	W	1-0	England	H	D	1-1	Lithuania	H	W	2-0
Soviet Union	N	D	1-1	1991				Spain	H	L	1-3
Holland	N	L	0-1	Wales	A	W	3-0	Northern Ireland	A	D	1-1
Northern Ireland	A	D	0-0	England	A	D	1-1				
Tunisia	H	W	4-0	Poland	H	D	0-0				

Jack Charlton smiles as his captain and defensive partner Bobby Moore lifts the World Cup for England at Wembley in 1966 (ALLSPORT)

bizarre goal scored by an offside Wim Kieft with just seven minutes remaining. But Ireland had arrived on the international stage.

Fortress Lansdowne Road came to Ireland's rescue in the qualifying tournament for the 1990 World Cup finals after they failed to score in their first three matches away from home and so Charlton had followed qualification for

Bonner beats Ruud Gullit to the ball in Gelsenkirchen during the 1988 European finals (ALLSPORT/COR MOOY)

Euro '88 by leading his team to Italy for their first ever appearance in the finals of the World Cup. Ireland's preparation was relaxed and confident and Charlton made only one change to his starting line-up during the tournament, replacing Tony Cascarino with Niall Quinn after two games. There were few who could fault either his selection or his handling of the team.

His task coming out of the World Cup finals was to maintain Ireland's momentum and qualify for the 1992 finals of the European Championship. He achieved the first but ultimately the second of these aims eluded him. Ireland dropped crucial points at home and away against Poland and passed up a glorious chance to effectively eliminate England when they enjoyed much the better of the game at Wembley but had to settle for a draw. But there was still much to be happy about in the performances of Niall Quinn up front, Andy Townsend in midfield and Steve Staunton in defence. Optimism for the forthcoming World Cup qualifying campaign was high and it proved well founded.

When the final whistle blew in Belfast and then minutes later in Seville to clinch Ireland's World Cup place, Charlton's record as manager in terms of qualification for major finals, performance at major finals, and win-loss record overall, far surpassed any previous Irish manager. Furthermore he had raised the status of association football in the country to a level the FAI could only have dreamed of. It was not a bad record, all told, for an Englishman.

THE ROAD TO AMERICA

Whatever else Ireland's qualifying campaign for the 1994 World Cup turned out to be, it was clear from the outset that it would be a footballing marathon. The emergence of new nation states, in part from the political upheaval in Eastern Europe, had overloaded the European qualifying section. It meant that Ireland's group contained an unprecedented seven countries.

Realistically the two qualifying spots would be fought out between Ireland, Spain and Denmark, the unlikely winners of the 1992 European Championships. Ireland, much to Jack Charlton's irritation, had missed out on those finals and so it was that while the top nations of Europe were finalising their preparations for the tournament in Sweden, the Irish were kicking off their long series of World Cup matches at home to Albania. Despite being goalless at half time, the game was always Ireland's. Goals from John Aldridge and Paul McGrath secured the two points.

Latvia also came to Lansdowne Road and were defeated courtesy of a second-half John Aldridge hat-trick before Charlton's team moved on to perhaps the crucial matches of the campaign, away to Denmark and Spain. In Copenhagen the Danes, still on a high after their Euro victory but having already failed to win (or indeed score) in Latvia and Lithuania, were given little respect by Ireland. This was particularly evident in the positive perfomances of the central midfield partners, Andy Townsend and Roy Keane. The game finished 0-0 and one hurdle had been negotiated.

Spain in Seville would be a different proposition. Ireland had been beaten there 2-0 in a World Cup qualifier in 1988 when the game and the atmosphere in which it was played had left a sour taste. It was with some satisfaction then that the Irish left this time with another 0-0 scoreline, though it could easily have been a win with the Spaniards reduced to ten men for the final quarter of an hour and a goal from John Aldridge disallowed. Again it was the performance of Keane which caught the eye, specifically the eye of Diego Maradona who was playing club football for Sevilla and declared himself more than impressed with the young Nottingham Forest midfielder.

Ireland were now clear favourites to qualify, an impression strengthened by their demolition of neighbours Northern Ireland in March. Faced with an inexperienced side from the North, they threatened to run riot as they went in at half time 3-0 up. The second half was an anti-climax but Billy Bingham, the Northern Ireland manager, was stung by reaction to the result and the embarrassing ease with which it had been achieved. When Ireland came to Belfast for the return, he vowed, it would not be so easy for them.

Neither did Ireland cruise quite so serenely through their next encounter at Lansdowne Road against Denmark.

1994 Qualifying
GROUP 3

26.5.1992 Ireland (0) 2 Albania 0 DUBLIN
Ireland: Bonner, Irwin, Staunton, O'Leary, McGrath (1), Townsend, Keane, Houghton, Quinn, Aldridge (1) [Coyne], Sheedy (McCarthy)

9.9.1992 Ireland (1) 4 Latvia 0 DUBLIN
Ireland: Bonner, Irwin, Staunton, Kernaghan, McGrath, Townsend, Keane, Whelan, Quinn (Coyne), Aldridge (3, 1 pen), Sheedy (1) [Phelan]

14.10.1992 Denmark 0 Ireland 0 COPENHAGEN
Ireland: Bonner, Irwin, Phelan, Moran, Kernaghan, Townsend, Keane, Houghton (Kelly), Quinn, Aldridge, McGoldrick

18.11.1992 Spain 0 Ireland 0 SEVILLE
Ireland: Bonner, Irwin, Phelan, Moran, McGrath, Townsend, Keane, Houghton, Staunton, Quinn, Aldridge

31.3.1993 Ireland (3) 3 Northern Ireland 0 DUBLIN
Ireland: Bonner, Irwin, Phelan, Moran, McGrath, Townsend (1), Keane, Houghton, Staunton (1), Quinn (1) [McGoldrick], Coyne (Cascarino)

28.4.1993 Ireland (0) 1 Denmark (1) 1 DUBLIN
Ireland: Bonner, Irwin, McGoldrick, McGrath, Kernaghan, Townsend, Keane, Houghton, Staunton, Quinn (1), Aldridge (Cascarino)

26.5.1993 Albania (1) 1 Ireland (1) 2 TIRANA
Ireland: Bonner, Irwin, Phelan, Kernaghan, Moran, Townsend, Keane, Houghton, Staunton (1), Quinn, Aldridge (Cascarino [1])

9.6.1993 Latvia 0 Ireland (2) 2 RIGA
Ireland: Bonner, Irwin, Phelan, Kernaghan, McGrath (1), Townsend, Keane, Houghton, Staunton, Aldridge (1) [Sheridan], Quinn (Cascarino)

16.9.1993 Lithuania 0 Ireland (1) 1 VILNIUS
Ireland: Bonner, Irwin, Phelan, Kernaghan, McGrath, Townsend, Keane, Houghton, Staunton (1), Aldridge (Whelan), Quinn

8.9.1993 Ireland (2) 2 Lithuania 0 DUBLIN
Ireland: Bonner, Irwin, Kernaghan (1), Moran, Phelan, Townsend (Whelan), Keane, Houghton, Staunton, Aldridge (1), Quinn (Cascarino)

13.10.1993 Ireland (0) 1 Spain (3) 3 DUBLIN
Ireland: Bonner, Irwin, Phelan, Moran (Sheridan [1]), Kernaghan, McGrath, Keane, Houghton, Staunton (Cascarino), Whelan, Quinn

17.11.1993 Northern Ireland (0) 1 Ireland (0) 1 BELFAST
Ireland: Bonner, Irwin, Phelan, Kernaghan, McGrath, Houghton (McLoughlin [1]), Keane, Townsend, McGoldrick, Aldridge (Cascarino), Quinn

The team that faced Denmark in Copenhagen. From left: Townsend, Bonner, Houghton, Irwin, Kernaghan, McGoldrick, Quinn, Keane, Phelan, Moran, Aldridge (ALLSPORT/INPHO)

The Danes met fire with fire and scored first as a result of a defensive mix-up which saw Bonner stranded as the ball was lofted over him by Kim Vilfort. Though Niall Quinn's header from a corner in the second half salvaged a point, it had not been a good performance. But the business of getting results was foremost as the Irish now embarked, at the end of the domestic season, on a three-match series away in Albania, Latvia and Lithuania.

It did not get off to the best of starts when Paul McGrath failed to report for the trip to Albania, for which he later apologised to his team-mates. Without him they quickly went a goal down in Tirana but recovered to win with goals from Staunton and Cascarino, whose winner came just 13 minutes from time and three minutes after he had been introduced as substitute. With McGrath back, the team headed for the Baltic States in June and won 2-0 against Latvia in Riga, where Spain and Denmark had both failed to score. Aldridge opened the scoring with Ireland's 400th goal in international football and the second arrived just before half time from the prodigal McGrath. A week later on a difficult pitch in Vilnius a first-half goal from Staunton secured a third consecutive away victory.

A win over Lithuania in the return in Dublin the following September meant that Ireland had taken maximum points from the three Eastern European teams, but in this game they had not scored the goals expected of them, seeming to ease off at 2-0 and allowing the Lithuanians back into the game. It did not seem important. Spain were due at Lansdowne Road in October and victory for Ireland would mean qualification for the USA. But as Dublin prepared to celebrate, Ireland were upset by the absence of key players through injury, John Aldridge and Andy Townsend especially. They never looked comfortable but it was still a shock for the home crowd to see three goals

put past Bonner in the first half an hour. The game was lost but ultimately the goal pulled back by John Sheridan in the second half ranked among the most significant of the campaign.

When Denmark somewhat fortunately defeated Northern Ireland 1-0 later that evening, it was clear that a result of some sort would be needed by Ireland in Belfast and qualification would only be certain with a win. Spain and Denmark feared all-Irish collusion. Nothing could have been further from the truth.

Jack Charlton's team faced an improving Northern Ireland side and one which was determined to avenge their defeat in Dublin. If this meant stopping Ireland from qualifying for the World Cup finals then so much the better. Adding to Ireland's difficulties were the increasingly unstable political situation in the North and the fact that no tickets could be made available to supporters from the Republic. The FA of Ireland demanded that the game be moved away from Windsor Park but the Irish FA would not entertain the idea. Belfast it had to be.

On a cold night with the Spain-Denmark game being played simultaneously in Seville, Ireland's worst fears looked like being realised when Jimmy Quinn volleyed in a tremendous goal from 25 yards with less than 20 minutes remaining. But with Spain leading in Seville, an equaliser was all that was needed and it came from the left foot of substitute Alan McLoughlin who lashed the ball through a crowd of players from the edge of the area to level the scores. At the end of the match there were more tense moments as the last minutes of the game in Seville were played out. But in the end, Ireland had qualified - level on points and on goal difference with Denmark, they won through to the finals by virtue of having scored more goals than the Danes. It could hardly have been closer.

Marco Tardelli (above), scorer of Italy's second goal in the 1982 final, celebrates his country's third World Cup triumph. (ALLSPORT)

GROUP A

UNITED STATES

RUMANIA

SWITZERLAND

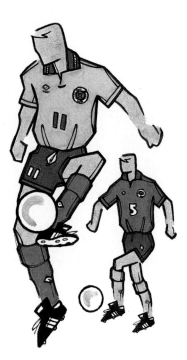

COLOMBIA

GROUP B

BRAZIL

RUSSIA

SWEDEN

CAMEROON

GROUP C

GERMANY

SPAIN

SOUTH KOREA

BOLIVIA

GROUP D

ARGENTINA

GREECE

BULGARIA

NIGERIA

GROUP E

ITALY

IRELAND

NORWAY

MEXICO

GROUP F

BELGIUM

HOLLAND

MOROCCO

SAUDI ARABIA

(Above) West German defender Dietmar Jakobs clears from Argentina's Jorge Valdano. (ALLSPORT)

THE WORLD CUP 22

The 22 players who took Ireland to America:

PACKY BONNER
The popular Celtic keeper was an ever-present in the 1994 World Cup qualifying matches, keeping a clean sheet on eight occasions. He made his debut for Ireland back in 1981 and won his 69th cap in Belfast. He kept goal in the European Championship finals of 1988 and played all five games in Italia '90, making the crucial save in the penalty shoot-out against Rumania in Genoa.

DENIS IRWIN
The 28-year-old full-back performed consistently well for Ireland throughout the 1994 qualifying campaign, playing in all 12 matches to bring his tally of caps to 24. He made his debut against Morocco in 1990 shortly after joining Manchester United with whom he won a League Championship medal in 1993. He generally plays on the left for United but is now established on the opposite flank for Ireland.

STEVE STAUNTON
Made his name as a full-back with Liverpool but more recently has been a vital member of the Irish team on the left side of midfield, from where he has contributed some important goals. His 43 appearances since his debut in 1988 include all five matches in Italia '90 and 10 qualifying matches for 1994. Now plays his club football under Ron Atkinson at Aston Villa alongside Paul McGrath, Ray Houghton and Andy Townsend.

DAVID O'LEARY
Veteran centre-half who first played for Ireland at Wembley in 1976 and has won 67 caps. Not always Jack Charlton's choice in defence, he missed out on the European Championships in 1988 but returned to enjoy a moment of glory in the World Cup when in his only appearance in the finals his penalty took Ireland through to the quarter-finals. Played in the very first World Cup qualifier for 1994 at home to Albania.

PAUL McGRATH
The rock on which the success of the Irish team has been built whether playing at centre-half or in midfield, McGrath made his international debut in 1985 and won his 63rd cap in Belfast. He survived major

injury problems and confounded more than one predicted retirement to play in nine qualifying games for 1994. Played all five World Cup games in Italy but missed the Soviet Union match in the 1988 European Championship finals.

ANDY TOWNSEND
Made his debut in 1989 and did well enough in the run-up to the World Cup finals to establish himself in

129

the side. He played all five games in Italy, converting a penalty in the shoot-out against Rumania in confident fashion. A hard-working and exciting midfielder who won his 41st cap in Belfast, he played 11 games in the 1994 qualifying campaign, missing only the defeat against Spain through injury.

ROY KEANE

Made the central midfield berth his own in the 1994 qualifying campaign in formidable partnership with Andy Townsend. Keane was given his international debut in 1991 just a week after playing in the FA Cup final for Nottingham Forest. He joined Denis Irwin at Manchester United in the summer of 1993 for a record fee and completed a full set of 1994 qualifying games in Belfast to win his 19th cap.

RAY HOUGHTON

Glasgow-born midfielder who made his debut for Ireland in 1986 while with Oxford United but confirmed his international pedigree with a move to Liverpool in 1987. He played in all three European Championship games in 1988, heading the winner against England, and in all five World Cup matches in Italy, scoring from the penalty spot against Rumania. Missed only one match in the 1994 qualifying series and now has 56 caps.

JOHN ALDRIDGE

Famously took a long time to score his first international goal but has claimed a regular place since it arrived in a friendly against Tunisia in 1988. He played all three games in the European Championship finals that year and started all five World Cup matches in Italy. His 10 appearances in the 1994 qualifying campaign brought his total of caps to 56. A goal against Lithuania

John Aldridge shows his delight as he notches a hat-trick at Lansdowne Road against Turkey in 1990 (ALLSPORT/INPHO)

in Dublin took his tally to 13 including two hat-tricks.

NIALL QUINN

Following his debut for Ireland in 1986 he appeared mainly as substitute but a highly successful move to Manchester City revitalised his club career and he made the centre-forward position in the national team his own after being preferred to Tony Cascarino against Holland in the World Cup finals. An ever-present in the 1994 qualifiers, he won his 42nd cap in Belfast before a bad injury jeopardised his chances of making the finals.

KEVIN SHEEDY

Made his debut in 1984 but started only the USSR game in the Euro '88 finals. But then with his best club form already behind him he continued to shine at international level for Ireland and played all five World Cup games in Italy, equalising against England and converting the all-important first penalty in the shoot-out in Genoa. He started the first two games of the 1994 qualifying campaign and scored on his 45th and last appearance.

TOMMY COYNE

Scored on his debut against Switzerland in 1992 while with Celtic and has won eight caps, but started just one game in the 1994 World Cup qualifiers against Northern Ireland in Dublin, filling in for his club colleague at Tranmere Rovers, John Aldridge. Also appeared as substitute in the first two matches at home to Albania and Latvia.

MICK McCARTHY

Now retired and managing Millwall, he made 57 appearances for Ireland including one as substitute in the first World Cup qualifier for 1994 against Albania. His international debut was in 1984 but he became a mainstay of the central defence under Jack Charlton in partnership mainly with Kevin Moran.

Played all three games at the European Championship finals in 1988 and was an ever-present in Italy also.

ALAN KERNAGHAN

Now a regular in central defence for Ireland, he made his debut against Latvia in Dublin in September 1992, the first of nine appearances for Ireland, all in the 1994 World Cup qualifying campaign. He made his name at Middlesbrough but was transferred for a big fee to Manchester City shortly into the 1993-94 season. Scored his first goal for Ireland against Lithuania at Lansdowne Road.

RONNIE WHELAN

Injuries and stiff competition for midfield places have restricted his appearances but Whelan started the game against Spain in Dublin to win his 47th cap. His debut came back in 1981 and the highlight of his international career was the spectacular goal he scored against the Soviet Union in the Euro '88 finals. He played all three games in Germany but made just one appearance as substitute against Holland in Italia '90.

KEVIN MORAN

The longest serving member of the 1994 World Cup qualifying pool after David O'Leary, Moran made his debut in 1980 and continues to play club and international football at the highest level at the age of 37. An ever-present in both the European Championship and World Cup finals for Ireland, he won his 68th cap against Spain in Dublin, the last of six games he started in the 1994 qualifying campaign.

DAVID KELLY

Filled in for the first-choice strikers on a number of occasions without ever threatening to make the position his own, despite a hat-trick on his debut against Israel in 1987 whilst still playing in the Third Division with Walsall. His strike rate for Ireland is impressive but all his goals have come in friendlies. His appearance in the World Cup qualifying campaign was restricted to just 20 minutes as substitute in Copenhagen.

TERRY PHELAN

Made his debut in a friendly against Hungary in 1991 and at left-back proved to be a consistent performer in nine starts during the 1994 World Cup qualifiers, after appearing first as substitute against Latvia in Dublin. The game in Belfast brought him his 18th cap. He joined Manchester City in a £2.5 million transfer from Wimbledon and now lines up alongside Alan Kernaghan and Niall Quinn at Maine Road.

JOHN SHERIDAN

Has appeared fitfully since Jack Charlton gave him his debut in 1988 and in major finals has played just once for Ireland, as substitute against Italy in the World Cup quarter-final of 1990. He scored what turned out to be more than just a consolation goal after coming on as substitute against Spain in the 3-1 defeat in Dublin but his only other appearance in the World Cup qualifiers was in Latvia.

EDDIE McGOLDRICK

A versatile player who has played variously at full-back, sweeper and wide midfield, he made his debut in 1992 and won his 9th cap when he was called into the side for the crucial game in Belfast. In all he started three games in the 1994 qualifiers with a further appearance as substitute. A move to Arsenal in the summer of 1993 and the opportunity to play against European club sides could only benefit his international career.

TONY CASCARINO

A place mainly on the substitutes' bench - his seven appearances in the 1994 qualifiers were all as sub - has not prevented Cascarino contributing some vital goals for Ireland including the winner against Albania in Tirana. Made his debut in 1985 while still with Gillingham and he made two appearances from the bench in Euro '88. He played in every match in Italy, the last three as substitute, and scored the fourth penalty in Genoa.

ALAN McLOUGHLIN

Appeared twice as substitute in the World Cup finals in Italy against England and Egypt but his slow progress at club level since leaving Swindon Town has been reflected in limited opportunities for Ireland. When he came on as substitute in Belfast it was for his 14th cap and his first competitive international appearance for two years, but his left-foot drive took Ireland to America.

Terry Phelan in World Cup action (ALLSPORT/DAVID CANNON)

11 WORLD CUP ALL-TIME GREATS

The great Pele in action for Brazil in the 1970 World Cup final against Italy.

FRANZ BECKENBAUER

WEST GERMANY

Few experts would argue against giving Franz Beckenbauer the title of the most complete footballer produced by West Germany. He had twelve years at the top in the international arena, made 103 appearances for his country and led his team to World Cup success as captain in 1974 and as manager in 1990.

As a schoolboy he played for 1906 Munchen, then at 13 he joined Bayern Munich. It was 1958 and he graduated through the club's junior ranks. Schools and youth matches provided an honours background which was to be handsomely enhanced in later years at higher level.

Born in Munich on 11 September 1945, he was 18 when he made his debut in Bayern's first team. In those days he was a left-winger, but soon found himself playing more in a midfield role. The Bayern coaches realised that his was no ordinary talent.

From his earliest games, it was evident that he had a maturity about his play far above his years. There was much more. He had speed, control and vision. Beckenbauer was also inclined to be an introvert and from this stemmed the beginnings of the accusations of a certain arrogance. The legend of 'Kaiser Franz' was born.

But a wider audience for his attributes was not yet visible. Bayern Munich were not members of the Bundesliga when it was formed in 1963-64. The top club in the city was 1860 Munich.

However, two seasons later Bayern found themselves promoted into the new German super-league, challenging their established rivals. That season 1860 Munich won the Bundesliga, but Bayern and Beckenbauer finished third.

Beckenbauer had by this time added a couple of appearances for West Germany's 'B' team but his prowess was such that in his club's initial season in the highest grade, he found himself selected to play for the full national team.

Appropriately it was in a World Cup qualifying match, against Sweden in Stockholm and the Germans won 2-1. In his fourth international he was on the losing side at Wembley in a 1-0 defeat inflicted by England. Five months later he returned, to face even greater disappointment in the World Cup Final.

Interestingly enough, these two games were the only ones in which the Germans lost during Beckenbauer's first 14 appearances. In fact there might have been a happier ending for him in that World Cup Final had it not been for the role handed to him by manager Helmut Schoen.

The Germans rightly considered Bobby Charlton to be the danger. But instead of detailing a more defensive player to shadow the Manchester United maestro, Schoen put the responsibility on Beckenbauer. Moreover, despite Charlton's comparatively quiet afternoon, the two cancelled each other out.

It was two years before Beckenbauer had the chance to restore pride lost in these defeats by England. In June 1968 in Hanover he did so with a vengeance, scoring the only goal of the match. Even more satisfaction was to come his way two years later.

On the way to the 1970 World Cup in Mexico, West Germany had a useful run of success which stretched to ten games without defeat. Morocco, Bulgaria and Peru were also accounted for in the finals themselves before a quarter-final with England.

Beckenbauer was to be switched to playing as a sweeper where his capacity for reading the game found a fresh dimension. Against England he needed all his skill to extricate West Germany from the position in which they found themselves. Two goals down and looking well beaten, the Germans discovered hidden reserves of stamina and concentration, inspired by Beckenbauer's presence.

In fact it was his low, penetrating drive which reduced the deficit to 2-1 and led to the Germans coming back to win the game 3-2. It was only Beckenbauer's second goal since his effort against England in Hanover two years before.

But if that was a high point in his career, the next was the lowest. The semi-final with Italy also went into extra

1972 to 1977 he was to become permanent skipper.

In 1972 West Germany won the European Championship impressively under Beckenbauer's command. At the end of the year he was elected European Footballer of the Year, an honour he was to receive again in 1976. For three successive years he helped Bayern to European Cup honours.

With a technique rarely matched anywhere, he appeared almost casual but always in charge of the

Helmut Schoen, the West German team manager and his captain Franz Beckenbauer. This partnership followed a similar association between Sepp Herberger and Fritz Walter and even earlier between Otto Nerz and Fritz Szepan.

time before West Germany lost 4-3. For Beckenbauer, it was a tragedy. He was seriously injured and forced to play with a dislocated shoulder, his arm being strapped across his chest. Schoen had already used both substitutes.

Yet his career developed further at club and country level. Bayern were to start their domination of domestic and European football and the national team about to reach its peak. Beckenbauer was himself appointed captain for the first time against Turkey in April 1971. From

situation. His distribution was faultless and he could take the ball past opponents with either speed or a neat swerve. More importantly he could change pace and direction at will.

In 1974 he led West Germany to a World Cup victory and continued his career outside Germany in 1977 with New York Cosmos, returning to finish his playing career at Hamburg. In 1984, he became West Germany's team manager, taking them to the runners-up spot in the 1986 World Cup, before bowing out as a winner again in 1990.

BOBBY CHARLTON

ENGLAND

Bobby Charlton was the epitome of the spirit that helped to revive Manchester United after the Munich air disaster in 1958 and the conscientious will-to-succeed that led England to its World Cup triumph eight years later. Of more practical importance, when he had the ball the crowd expected something positive to happen and were rarely disappointed.

Charlton established three records for his club and another for his country which might well stand for all time. He played in more games, scored more goals and was United's most capped player as well as being the highest goalscorer in his country's history.

But there was far more to Charlton than mere records. At his peak there was no more explosive forward anywhere in the country, combining that rare commodity for an Englishman, flair, with his powerful shooting ability.

Born into the famous footballing family of Ashington known as the Milburn club, he was the nephew of Jackie Milburn and the younger brother of Jack Charlton. He signed for Manchester United in 1953 straight from school and in doing so thwarted the aims of 17 other clubs who were chasing this schoolboy starlet.

He played with the other Matt Busby Babes in three FA Youth Cup winning teams from 1954 to 1956 inclusive and was given his first opportunity in the League side on 6 October 1956 as deputy for the injured Tommy Taylor, ironically against Charlton Athletic, scoring twice on this impressive debut. That season United won the championship and he scored ten goals in only 14 appearances.

The following season he had won a regular place in the side when the heart of the club was ripped out by the air crash in West Germany. Charlton miraculously escaped injury, being flung to safety, strapped to his seat with his shoes torn off. Despite the mental torment which must have resulted from this traumatic experience, he was quickly back in action.

Charlton assumed a responsibility which matured and enhanced him as a player and he became the focal point of the United reconstruction. Moreover he made his debut for England in the aftermath of the same tragedy, scoring in a 4-0 win over Scotland. Two more goals in the next success 2-1 against Portugal brought him his third appearance in Yugoslavia. But a 5-0 defeat cost him his place in the World Cup team in Sweden, his inside-right berth going to Bobby Robson.

In hindsight his omission proved to be a costly error. After that he was rarely absent on international duty, taking his total of appearances to 106 and a record 49 goals. Without doubt his finest moments came in the 1966 World Cup.

Yet England began the series looking anything but potential champions. They gave a lack-lustre performance against Uruguay and in subsequent matches needed the spark provided by Charlton's pace and blistering shots to ignite them. He scored two unforgettable goals against Portugal in the semi-final which set up the final accolade at West Germany's expense. Deservedly he had already been elected as Footballer of the Year and added the European crown later in the year.

In 1968 Charlton was on hand for another Wembley moment, when he scored twice in Manchester United's 4-1 win over Benfica in the European Cup final, one of his goals being a rare header.

But there had been disappointments during his career. His first FA Cup Final appearance against Aston Villa in 1957 ended in defeat as did the following year's effort against Bolton Wanderers when United's courageous post-Munich team lost 2-0. Charlton had a shot which rebounded off a post in the latter game, when Bolton were still only one goal ahead.

In the 1962 World Cup, Charlton, now settled at outside-left, was one of England's outstanding players in an ordinary squad. His acceleration and unexpected shooting from long range made him the most dangerous of opponents. His sweeping crossfield passes could also change the point of attack in impressively accurate fashion.

Subsequently he moved to inside-left and later wore the No.9 shirt as a deep-lying centre-forward, from which position he plotted the 1966 World Cup successes.

Born 11 October 1937, he was 32 at the time of the 1970 World Cup in Mexico. His last game for England was in the 3-2 defeat sustained against West Germany. Perhaps his greatest compliment has come since then, as his country has never been able to replace him with a player of similar calibre.

Charlton captained Manchester United from 1968 to 1973. He had won two League championsip medals in 1965 and 1967, an FA Cup winners medal in 1963, six Under-23 caps, an OBE in 1969 and the CBE in 1974.

In April 1973 he left Old Trafford and became player-manager of Preston North End. But like many an outstanding player before and since, his flirtation with the managerial side was not a success and he resigned over a disagreement with the board. He did have a short spell as Wigan Athletic's caretaker-manager while on that club's board but later became a director of Manchester United and organised a school for youngsters learning soccer skills.

His total number of League appearances for Manchester United came to 606 with 199 goals. In all senior club games he appeared 754 times and scored 247 goals.

The Charlton brothers Jack and Bobby (right) were stalwarts in England's World Cup triumph in 1966. (HULTON)

JOHAN CRUYFF

HOLLAND

Probably the outstanding European player in the 1970s and certainly the most gifted Dutchman of the same era, Johan Cruyff's name was synonymous with the 'total football' which brought fame to Holland during this exciting period in the country's history.

Born in a poor quarter of Amsterdam on 25 April 1947, he had close connections with Ajax. In fact his mother worked at the ground as a cleaner. He joined them when he was still at school as a ten-year-old. By the age of 17 he was making his first team debut and in that 1964-65 season scored four goals.

The following season he was a regular choice and his 16 League goals contributed to Ajax winning the championsnip. In 1966-67 they achieved the League and Cup double and Cruyff led the Dutch League goalscorers with 33 goals. A third title win in succession underlined Ajax's supremacy at home but in 1968-69 they made strenuous efforts to extend their dominance to the European Cup.

Ajax reached the final — Cruyff contributing five goals on the way — where they met AC Milan. Unfortunately they were exposed by the tactically wise Italian side, whose counter-attacking produced an emphatic 4-1 win.

Cruyff had been given the Dutch Footballer of the Year awards in 1968 and 1969. Moreover he had already been blooded into the national team, although his early experiences had been shattering to his morale. After his debut against Hungary in 1966 at the age of 19, he played his second game against Czechoslovakia. During the game he was involved in a stormy argument with the East German referee Rudi Glockner and was sent off for apparently striking the official.

Film of the event make it clear that it had been a gesture rather than a blow, but the Dutch Federation still suspended him from the national team for a year, later commuting the sentence to six months, though it was ten months before he was restored to the side against, ironically, East Germany.

Slightly built, this lanky forward had razor-sharp reactions, excellent control, speed, acceleration and the ability to change direction instantly. His problem was a demonstrative temperament which certainly cost him dearly in his younger days.

Ajax had another determined try for the European Cup in 1970-71, but made an inauspicious start in Albania where they were held to a 2-2 draw by 17 Nentori. They did better in the return leg winning 2-0 and took a 3-0 lead over Basle in the first leg of the second round. In Switzerland they won again, 2-1.

In the quarter-finals they were drawn against Celtic and Cruyff put them ahead at home with his first goal in the competition that season. Ajax went on to win 3-0 and though they lost 1-0 away, they emerged 3-1 on aggregate and faced Atletico Madrid in the semi-final. Again they were beaten by a single goal in Spain but retrieved the deficit 3-0 in Amsterdam.

The European Cup final was played at Wembley and Panathinaikos, the Greek team, found Ajax far too clever for them. The Dutch side won 2-0, without convincing sceptics that they were a team of all the talents. But their coach Rinus Michels had knocked them into shape and surprisingly decided to move on to Barcelona.

Michels was succeeded by the Rumanian Stefan Kovacs who allowed the players far more relaxation in the playing system he adapted from Michels' more disciplined strategy. The change added comprehensively to Ajax's potential and they crowned their performances with a stunning 2-0 final win over Internazionale, Cruyff scoring both goals. Ajax again retained the trophy in 1973, beating Juventus 1-0 in the final in Belgrade.

Johan Cruyff in full
flight for Holland
on the way to the
1974 final in West
Germany.

Then, following protracted negotiations, Cruyff was transferred to Barcelona where he joined his former boss Michels. The fee was £922,300 with some £400,000 going to Cruyff, who thus became one of the best-paid professional sportsmen in the world at the time.

Later that year he was voted European Footballer of the Year for the second time, having first received the award in 1971. Although his goalscoring output was not phenomenal he had taken his total of League goals to 187 by the time he moved to Spain. In 1971-72 he had been top scorer in the Dutch League with 25 goals. However the danger he posed to defenders was enough to create havoc and his final pass was invariably of pin-point accuracy, leaving colleagues with inviting openings. Overall he was to score 215 goals in Dutch League games, 47 League goals for Barcelona and 25 in the North American Soccer League.

Holland qualified for the World Cup finals in 1974 and improved as the tournament progressed in West Germany, revealing the all-out attack and defence in depth epitomised by Ajax. But they were frustrated in the final by a shrewd German team. Two years on, Holland finished third in the European Championship and Cruyff helped them to reach the 1978 World Cup finals, but decided to retire before the games in Argentina. He had scored 33 goals in 48 internationals. Subsequently he came out of retirement, playing for Los Angeles, Washington, Feyenoord, Ajax again and Levante.

As a coach, Cruyff guided his old club Barcelona to their historic European Cup triumph in 1992, having previously won the Cup Winners Cup with Barsa in 1989 and Ajax in 1987. It was then announced that Cruyff would be taking charge of the Dutch national team for the World Cup finals in 1994 but terms could not be agreed

GIACINTO FACCHETTI

ITALY

The second most honoured player in Italian history, Giacinto Facchetti appeared on 94 occasions for the national team and captained them 70 times. Although he began his career as a full-back he ended it as a sweeper.

However his early development was as slow as a footballer as it was quick as an athlete. At school he clocked 8.8 seconds for the 80 metres and 10.6 for the 80 metres hurdles. He was Italian junior champion at the time.

But as to his prowess on the field of play, he was tall, inclined to be ungainly, but quick. Unfortunately he had limited control of the ball . Originally a centre-forward he moved back to play in the defence.

Born 18 July 1942 in Treviglio, he eventually joined his local club CS Trevigliese. Helenio Herrera, often referred to as the high priest of *catenaccio* (blanket defence), was coach of Internazionale and had an idea that Facchetti 's rough edges could be smoothed out.

In 1960 he signed this tall, well-built teenager and proceeded to knock him into the kind of shape necessary to be a top-flight player. Herrera used Facchetti at left-back, despite the player 's tendency to favour his right foot. This did not prevent him from becoming an excellent overlapping defender. In fact the problem was to dissuade him from continually attacking.

In 1960-61 he made three League appearances, scoring in one of the games, and the following season added a further 15 outings. By the age of 20 he had become a regular choice. In 1962-63 Inter won the Italian championship and Facchetti was awarded his first cap for his country against Turkey in a European Nations Cup game in Istanbul. It was an inexperienced team, but the Italians managed to win 1-0 and went on to improve.

Facchetti scored four League goals for Inter that season and in the years that followed, invariably contributed a useful share of goalscoring. In 1965-66 he reached double figures, an excellent total for any defender, but astonishing by Italian standards. Facchetti added championship medals in 1965, 1966 and 1971 and European Cup success also came his way.

In 1964 he achieved a winner 's medal when Inter beat Real Madrid 3-1 in the Champions Cup final. A year later he won a second, having scored against Liverpool in the semi-final. His marksmanship was of even more value in the semi-final with CSKA Sofia in 1966-67 when he scored in two 1-1 draws against the Bulgarian Army team.

Internationally, he remained a regular choice but there was disappointment for him personally and the team in general over their miserable performance in the 1966 World Cup. But a few months later he became captain of Italy, this honour being given to the most capped player in the team.

Facchetti led the team out for the first time in Milan in a friendly with the USSR on 1 November 1966 in his 25th international. Italy won 1-0. Though settled at left-back, Inter tried to utilise his attacking gifts in a different way.

He was tried on the left-wing in a game with relegation-threatened Sampdoria. Inter won 5-0, Facchetti scored one goal and had another disallowed. But he had a nightmare game in the following match with Bologna, missing an easy chance. Finding little room in which to work, he was totally frustrated. That was the end of Facchetti as a forward, but back in his usual position of left-back he was irresistible. He could shorten or lengthen his stride and had a subtle change of pace which frequently wrong-footed opponents. He was most effective when moving into the middle of the field.

In 1968 he led Italy to victory in the European Championships, and though the 1970 World Cup left the team as beaten finalists, Facchetti and his side were

Giacinto Facchetti was an outstanding outfield player for both club and country, captaining the national side on numerous occasions.
(POPPERFOTO)

critically appraised. In October 1971 he won his 60th cap against Sweden in a European Championship game, to become Italy's most capped player. The previous holder had been Umberto Caligaris, also a left-back.

That 1971-72 season saw another milestone passed when he overtook the record total of goals scored by a full-back in Italian League football. The previous holder Sergio Cervato had contributed most of his from free-kicks and penalties, while Facchetti had scored chiefly from open play.

However he was dropped from the national team after losing the quarter-final of the European Championship to Belgium 2-1 in 1972, only to return for his 65th cap against Turkey in a World Cup game the following February. Facchetti played in the 1974 World Cup finals but was switched to sweeper in the next friendly with Yugoslavia in the following September.

He went on to play 94 times, his last appearance being against England at Wembley in 1977. Unassuming off the field, forceful on it, Facchetti held a justifiable reputation as a sportsman in 476 League games which yielded 59 goals for Internazionale. He became their most capped player and still holds the club record for League appearances.

GARY LINEKER

ENGLAND

In the 1990 World Cup finals in Italy, Gary Lineker enhanced his reputation as a top-class marksman by scoring four times, including two penalties. It took his overall goals tally in World Cup finals to 10, and Bobby Charlton's career record of 49 goals for England was in his sights.

Sadly, Lineker's international career was to end on something of a sour note. Having already decided to retire after captaining his country in the European Championship finals in 1992, he was inexplicably substituted by England manager Graham Taylor in the last match of a disappointing tournament, still one goal short of Charlton's tally. Nonetheless, Lineker's 48 goals in 80 appearances for England was a record to be proud of.

Born in Leicester on 30 November 1960 and raised locally, he became an apprentice with City and developed as a striker, despite the fact that he stood only 5ft 6in at the time. He made his debut in 1978-79 and scored once in seven outings. But it took him three seasons before he could command a regular place.

However, he was able to take his full part in Leicester returning to Division One at the end of the 1982-83 season, and in the full glare of First Division publicity the following term, he showed enough promise to find himself selected for international honours. His first taste at top level came as substitute for England against Scotland in May 1984.

But he had to wait until the following year and nine more matches before being given a further outing. This time he began in the No.10 shirt and scored one of England's goals in a 2-1 win. Yet again he was not retained. He was used as substitute in three of the next four matches, but was not chosen to start a game until West Germany provided the opposition. That was in Mexico City in June 1985.

England won 3-0 and although Lineker did not figure among the scorers, he kept his position for five more matches. In those ten games he had scored six goals, but still critics pointed to the fact that three had been achieved against Turkey and two more against the USA.

Domestically, other moves were afoot. Everton had been sufficiently impressed with him to contact Leicester where he had rejected a new contract. A tribunal set the fee at £800,000 even though City wanted £1 million.

Lineker was yet to be given a complete vote of confidence in the run-up to the World Cup finals in Mexico. Thus he went into the tournament with something to prove not only for England but to himself and his critics. Yet the hallmarks of a goalscorer above the average were already evident in his play. In his first season for Everton he had scored 30 goals.

He had shown directness and speed, allied to an ability to dart into scoring positions in the penalty area. An accuracy in finishing had also made him a marked man, but he had finished with a highly respectable total of League goals in the First Division.

In the opening two matches against Portugal and Morocco, the England attack failed miserably and there were no goals. Lineker was paired with Mark Hateley for these games. But changes were forced upon Bobby Robson for the game with Poland which included a switch of tactics from 4-3-3 to 4-4-2. This, allied to the fact that he was now partnered by Peter Beardsley, changed Lineker's fortunes in dramatic style.

He responded with a hat-trick against Poland and almost overnight became a sensation. Two more goals came from the in-form Lineker against Paraguay and one in the controversial quarter-final with Argentina. By the end of the World Cup he was being hailed as a world-class striker.

The 1986 World Cup transformed Gary Lineker from a more than useful club player into an international class striker.

Barcelona stepped in to sign him in a £2.75 million transfer and Lineker made the transition to Spanish League football in a surprisingly smooth way. Though the Catalan club finished second behind Real Madrid in the Spanish championship, Lineker's marksmanship won full acclaim from the Barcelona faithful. If there was any lingering doubt over his ability, it was dispelled when England played Spain on their own territory.

He scored four times as England won 4-2. It had been a splendid year for him. He had entered the World Cup as both the Football Writers Association and Professional Footballers Association choice as player of the year. At the end of the period he came second in the European poll, largely as a result of the impression his goalscoring had made in the Mexico World Cup.

The arrival of Johan Cruyff as coach at Barcelona in the wake of Terry Venables' departure, was the beginning of the end of Lineker's association with the Spanish club. Cruyff insisted on playing him wide on the right, and it was no surprise when, after Lineker had helped Barcelona to beat Sampdoria in the Cup Winners Cup in 1989, he joined Tottenham Hotspur for a fee of £1.25 million.

In three seasons at White Hart Lane he scored 67 League goals and collected an FA Cup winner's medal, his first domestic honour in England, before leaving for Japan to play in the inaugural season of the new J-League.

DIEGO MARADONA

ARGENTINA

Many cynics have said that Diego Maradona won the 1986 World Cup for Argentina single-handed. His contribution to the overall team effort was indeed substantial, and he might well have tipped the scales of victory towards half a dozen teams engaged in the tournament, had he changed sides accordingly.

Born in Buenos Aires on 30 October 1960 into a poor family, he revealed exceptional ability at an early age. His debut in senior circles came with Argentinos Juniors when he was still ten days short of his 16th birthday. Maradona's team lost 1-0 to Talleres Cordoba on that occasion, but it was not long before he was on the winning side more often than not.

In his first half-season with the club he scored twice in 11 matches but in the following term increased his output to 19 in 49 matches. In February of that same year, 1977, he was selected to play for the national team against Hungary in a 4-1 win. He had already become something of a boy wonder, being compared with Brazil's Pele at the same age.

He had made such progress that the Argentina team manager Luis Cesar Menotti was worried about his future. He felt the pressures on the youngster would increase, especially as the country was getting prepared to host the 1978 World Cup. At the time it seemed that Maradona would be a certainty. But Menotti left him out, hoping that he could develop towards the 1982 series at a steadier pace.

It was a brave move on the part of Menotti, and one which could have backfired on him had Argentina failed to win the World Cup; the fans would never have forgiven him for omitting Maradona in those circumstances.

However it was a shattering blow to the young player's ego when he was omitted. Yet he continued to show outstanding form for Argentinos Juniors and by 1980 had

scored 116 goals in 166 League games. Then Boca Juniors signed him and he added 28 goals for them in 40 matches.

By the time he had settled down with his new club, the 1982 World Cup finals were due to be played in Spain. Maradona had become a marked man and it was obvious that he would be given special attention during the tournament. Unfortunately for him, Maradona's temperament was not of the same maturity as his football and he was sent off against Brazil for retaliation.

After the finals, Maradona remained in Spain having been transferred to Barcelona for a then world record fee of £4,235,000. But it was not a happy time for him. He suffered a bout of hepatitis, which kept him out of action for three months, and then a severe ankle injury, the result of many blatant fouls committed on him.

In two seasons with the Catalan club he appeared in only 36 League games and scored 22 goals. But with friendlies and cup games added on he reached an overall total of 74 matches with 45 goals, though he was used in a number of games when he was not fully fit.

In the summer of 1984, he was the subject of the most costly transfer in the history of the game. The fee has been scaled up and down in the years since the move, but Napoli had to pay £6.9 million for his services at the moment they secured his signature. It was a calculated gamble and one which also brought huge receipts to the club, who sold 40,000 season tickets at £150 each within hours of the capture.

There was little respite for Maradona in Italian football. Alas, Napoli could do no better than finish eighth in his first season. Maradona's contribution was 14 goals in 30 games. But there was no denying his ability.

An attacking player of exceptional quality, as well as supreme confidence, he often attempted and many times succeeded in beating player after player with speed and alacrity. His chief fault was wanting to keep possession. Another vital part of his make-up was the accuracy of his free-kicks.

Napoli did a little better in 1985-86, winning more games to finish third. Maradona scored 11 goals but had problems with knee ligament damage, the result of a bizarre incident in a World Cup qualifying game with Venezuela in 1985. As the players were leaving the field surrounded by spectators, Maradona received a kick on the knee.

There was some doubt as to whether he would be fit enough to play in Mexico, but it was unthinkable that Argentina would even contemplate leaving him out. They included him and kept their fingers crossed. They need not have worried. In the opening game against South Korea he contributed to all three Argentine goals, then pounced on a half-chance to score in a 1-1 draw with Italy. In the later stages came his amazing double over England and two more goals at the expense of Belgium. In the final he was again the player to catch the eye.

For Maradona the 1990 tournament was a very different affair. Suffering with an injury and jeered everywhere outside Naples, he somehow managed to lead his team to another final which they lost this time to West Germany. His troubles continued when he was subsequently forced to leave Napoli and banned by FIFA after revelations about his use of drugs. He made a comeback and played for Argentina in their deciding World Cup qualifier against Australia but in truth he was a shadow of his former self.

The 1986 World Cup finals were a personal triumph for Diego Maradona. He gave a hint of what was to come in Argentina's opening match (right) against South Korea.

BOBBY MOORE

ENGLAND

Few players can have looked back on such a distinguished international career as Bobby Moore's. It lasted eleven and a half years, during which he was absent from the England team on just 12 occasions, and those due to injury or the need to give other players a chance.

Born in Barking on 12 April 1941, his early football was played with Barking and Leyton Schools then Woodford Youth Club. He joined West Ham United in June 1958 and was soon given his first League outing in the September of that year against Manchester United at Upton Park. That same season he was capped by England at youth level and played in the Hammers' FA Youth Cup final side.

He played 18 times for the England youth team and graduated to the Under-23's. He was awarded his first full cap in a pre-World Cup friendly against Peru in 1962, wearing the No. 4 shirt. In the finals in Chile, Moore was one of only two real successes in the side.

He was never absent on more than two occasions in succession and he reached his zenith when he captained England superbly in the 1966 World Cup. As one of the twin centre-backs his role was not restricted to the tight-marking of an opponent. His impeccable positioning enabled him to give the extra cover and depth required.

Moore's other outstanding capabilities were centred on his expert reading of the game, vision and constructive prowess in quickly turning defence into attack with precision and accuracy. These characteristics and his strong physique more than compensated for a slight lack of pace and suspect heading ability. Again, to offset this his tackling was well judged and measured and he was rarely caught off balance; in Moore, England truly had a world class player.

At club level, Moore helped West Ham to their 1964 FA Cup and 1965 European Cup Winners' Cup successes. He played in a record 544 League games for them before ending his career at Fulham where he added a further 124 before retiring. In all, he made 1,000 senior appearances for club and country.

Although there were much publicised differences between him and Ron Greenwood, the West Ham manager, and to a lesser extent with Sir Alf Ramsey who led England, his conduct on the field and off it was usually free of indiscretion.

However his greatest test came in Colombia before the 1970 World Cup when he was involved in the notorious affair of the 'stolen' bracelet. This was not the most suitable preliminary exercise to a tough campaign in Mexico, but Moore survived it.

He remained as calm and self-controlled in the days which followed the incident as he was cool and disciplined on the field. In Mexico he probably played better than he had four years earlier; that performance had led to the award of an OBE in January 1967.

Moore's other slip off the field was on a Friday night at Blackpool before West Ham's cup tie in January 1971. The late, late show received considerable publicity. The following day Blackpool beat West Ham 4-0. Then Moore was dropped. He missed the next two games and was required to sit on the bench for a third before making his only league appearance in a No. 12 shirt as a completion of his penance.

The following season he was called upon to deputise in goal for the injured Bobby Ferguson in a League Cup semi-final with Stoke when the goalkeeper was concussed. Moore pulled off a penalty save but was beaten by the rebound shot.

He captained England on numerous occasions. His first match leading his country was in 1963 against

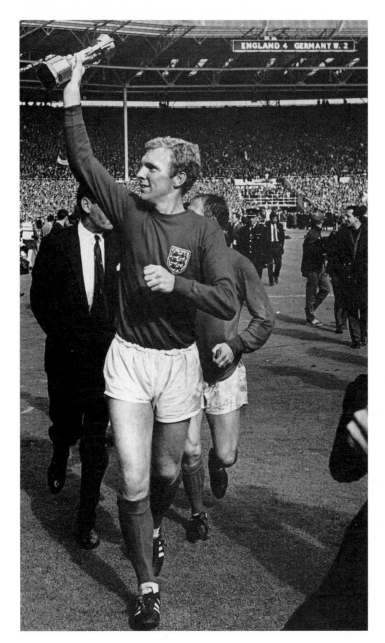

Bobby Moore trots round Wembley with the World Cup in 1966 after leading England to success.

Czechoslovakia in the absence of Jimmy Armfield. It was only his second time in the No.6 shirt he made famous. At the time he was 22.

Moore became the permanent skipper the following year, succeeding Armfield in a match with Uruguay. His last appearance was against Italy in 1973 when England had still not quite recovered from the shock of failing to qualify for the World Cup.

The following spring, Moore was transferred to Fulham for £20,000. In 1975 he made one last appearance at Wembley in the FA Cup Final. Ironically it was for Fulham against his old club West Ham. But it was to receive a runners-up medal. Then when he left Fulham he had a brief association with Seattle Sounders in the USA.

His first appointment as manager was in charge of the non-league club Oxford City. After a spell in Hong Kong,

he satisfied his ambition of taking charge of a Football League club when he accepted the managership of Southend United. After two years with them he remained on their board of directors. Subsequently he had interests in journalism and publishing outlets.

Although his final appearance at Wembley had ended in defeat, the hallowed turf at the home of English football had provided Moore with arguably his three finest moments: the 1964 FA Cup win, the 1965 European Cup Winners' success and the 1966 World Cup triumph. In 1964 he had been the recipient of the Footballer of the Year award.

Fittingly, it was at Wembley that Bobby made his last public appearance when, fighting bravely against illness, he commentated for radio on England's home fixture against San Marino. He died just a few days later aged 51.

GERD MULLER

WEST GERMANY

In West Germany he became known as 'Der Bomber', but the best description of Gerd Muller as a marksman could be summed up by the phrase 'pouncing poacher'. Few players of international class can have been so lethal inside the penalty area. Only 5ft 8in, this chunky, thick-thighed centre-forward had a low centre of gravity, fine balance and an agile sense of anticipation.

His record merely serves to underline his expertise as a goalscorer. Between 1966 and 1974 he scored 68 goals in 62 appearances for West Germany. In all competitive games he scored 628 times, and in a short extension of his career in the USA, he added 38 goals for Fort Lauderdale.

Born 11 November 1945 in the Bavarian village of Zinsen, he grew up to discover that there was no proper football pitch in his area. He had to travel seven miles by bus to have a trial with TSV Nordlingen. Muller's father died and the youngster had to leave school at 15 whereupon he became an apprentice weaver.

But Nordlingen had been impressed and signed him. Muller had made a scoring debut in what was his first game on a marked-out pitch, despite wearing borrowed boots. In fact he scored two goals. Still, he had a problem: he was overweight and earned the nickname of 'Dicker' (fatty).

Even so, in two seasons for Nordlingen he scored 46 goals. His scoring ability was duly noted by several clubs although the man who took most interest in him was Wilhelm Neudecker, President of Bayern Munich. Neudecker persuaded his coach Tchik Cajkovski, the former Yugoslavian international, to sign him. But Cajkovski regarded Muller as 'a bear among racehorses'!

Muller's debut for Bayern's reserves was a painful one; he broke his arm. In those days, Bayern was still a club in the Regional League of Southern Germany and eventually Muller made his senior bow against Freiburger and scored twice in an 11-2 win. His 35 goals that season helped Bayern win promotion to the Bundesliga.

In 1965-66 he hit 15 goals in 33 games and also deputised in goal for the injured Sepp Maier against Hamburg. By this time, Muller had had reduced his weight by more than 20 lb and his reactions sharpened. In 1966-67 he was joint top scorer in the League with 28 goals.

There were German Cup victories in 1966 and 1967 and the European Cup Winners' Cup trophy in the latter year, in which Muller scored eight goals, including four against Standard Liege in the semi-finals.

More domestic honours followed. In 1968-69 Bayern achieved their first Bundesliga title and Muller was confirmed as their ace marksman with 30 goals. Moreover he had also established himself in the national side.

His first appearance was the match after West Germany had lost the 1966 World Cup final to England at Wembley. It was on 12 October. His colleagues that day included Maier, Grabowski and Netzer. West Germany won 2 - 0 but Muller did not score. In fact he was left out until the game with Albania in the following April, when he scored four times in a 6 - 0 win.

Despite this haul, he was far from a regular choice until 1969. In the 1969-70 domestic season he scored 38 League goals as well as nine in World Cup qualifying games which helped West Germany reach the finals in Mexico. There he finished as leading scorer in the tournament with 10 goals. Recognition of his performances at club and country level followed when he was voted European Footballer of the Year.

After winning the Cup in 1971, Bayern won three Bundesliga titles in a row and each season Muller was West Germany's leading League scorer with 40, 36 and then joint top with 30 goals from 1972 to 1974.

In 1974 West Germany reached the World Cup final itself and though the team was past its peak, it achieved a notable victory. Muller's winning goal in the final against Holland was a half-chance from his only opening in the match. He retired from international football after this game, but continued to take the honours at Bayern.

That same year, Bayern had won the first of three successive European Cup Finals. He was joint top scorer for the last time in the Bundesliga with 24 goals in 1978. The following season he wanted to retire completely, but went to the North American Soccer League instead.

His tally of goals in the Bundesliga had been 365 goals in 427 games. Muller's 350th effort had arrived against Werder Bremen on 21 January 1978. He also reached his 600th competitive goal in the same season. Between 1969-70 and 1976-77 he scored 36 goals for Bayern in the European Cup. His aggregate of 14 goals in World Cup finals came from 10 in 1970, four in 1974.

In 1972 he led the West German attack in the European Championships, scoring two goals in the 3 - 0 win over the USSR in the final. It was Germany's most accomplished performance, and Muller with his uncanny positioning and accuracy was its ideal spearhead.

Gerd Muller (right, dark shirt) heads West Germany's third and final goal in the 3-0 win over Australia in the 1974 World Cup. Aussie goalkeeper Jack Reilly is well beaten. (POPPERFOTO)

PELE

BRAZIL

It says much for Pele, arguably the most accomplished footballer of all time, that two of his most audacious attempts at scoring, both of which failed to produce a goal, are remembered as fondly as the many that proved successful. Both were in the 1970 World Cup; a lob from his own half against Czechoslovakia and a brilliant dummy he sold the Uruguayan goalkeeper.

Among those unforgettably recorded was his first goal in the 1958 World Cup finals against Wales when he controlled the ball on his thigh, hooked it over his head, pivoted and drove the ball in. Then there was the occasion for Santos against Fluminense in the Maracana Stadium in Rio when from his own penalty area he dribbled past seven opponents before scoring.

Born 23 October 1940 in Tre Coracoes in the state of Minas Gerais, he came from a footballing family. His father, Joao Ramos do Nascimento, known as Dondinho, was a professional. Moreover, the nickname of Pele for someone born Edson Arantes do Nascimento has never been properly explained. To this day, the family always refer to Pele as Dico.

Pele's footballing career began when the family moved to Bauru in Sao Paulo. His first games were for a team called Ameriquinha, organised by his school friends. But it was when he joined Baquinha — little BAC, the junior team run by Bauru Athletic Club — that his fortunes changed.

Pele was 13 years old. Bauru had appointed Waldemar de Brito as coach. A member of Brazil's 1934 World Cup team, Waldemar was a friend of Pele's father. He proved of exceptional influence in Pele's formative years.

Waldemar was strict but fair and a thorough coach. He taught his young players everything he knew. But without Pele's inherent ability there would have been no outstanding talent to develop. Waldemar never attempted to curb the youngster's natural gifts, rather concentrating on his weaknesses.

He kept in close contact with Dondinho and the family, to such an extent that when Bangu tried to persuade Pele to sign for them Waldemar persuaded the family to wait, and suggested that Santos would prove a better grounding for Pele.

Thus at 15, Pele moved on, graduating from youth team to senior status. He was still 16 when he played his first game for the first team, a friendly against AIK Stockholm. Santos won with a late penalty but in Pele's next game against Corinthians of Santo Andre he scored his first goal in a 7-1 win on 7 September 1956.

While still not 17, he was chosen to play in Brazil's Roca Cup squad for the two games with Argentina. In his first on 7 July 1957 he made his debut as substitute midway through the second half and scored within 10 minutes. Brazil lost 2-1, but in the return game Pele was on from the start and scored again in a 2-0 success which clinched the trophy for Brazil.

That season with Santos he was the leading scorer in the Sao Paulo League with 36 goals. The following year he hit a record 53. But his prospects for the World Cup team looked bleak. He was almost left behind because of a knee injury.

In fact he did not play until Brazil's third game, against the USSR. He hit a post in the 2-0 win and scored the only goal of the next game with Wales. In the semi-final against France he produced a hat-trick, and two more goals followed in the final with Sweden.

The next two World Cup tournaments ended in personal despair for Pele. In 1962 he began well enough, scoring in the 2-0 success over Mexico, but was injured in the goalless draw with Czechoslovakia and took no further part in the tournament, which Brazil won. Four

Pele (10) receives the outstretched arms of Rivelino (11) and Tostao (9) having scored the opening goal of the 1970 World Cup final against Italy.
(POPPERFOTO)

years later in England, he was severely mauled by Bulgarian and Portuguese defenders and had to be assisted from the pitch in the latter encounter.

But in 1970 everything went according to plan. At 29, Pele had achieved just about everything possible in the game. His best scoring year had been 1959 when he reached 126 goals in all matches. In 1969 he reached his 1000th goal in his 909th game. Pele even completed his national service in the Army, serving in the 6th Coast Guard.

Frequently the victim of unscrupulous defenders, Pele, rarely retaliated though he was sent off early in his career when he did so. In later years he invariably humiliated his opponents with feints and footwork achieving his own kind of retribution with consummate ease.

In Mexico in 1970 he revealed his full range of artistry. His wide peripheral vision, made acute by Waldemar's insistence that players should glance around before receiving the ball, kept him vital seconds ahead in reading the game. His control was peerless and the final in particular showed his unselfishness as he memorably laid on a goal for his captain, Carlos Alberto.

His 111th and last international was against Austria in July 1971, his last game for Santos in October 1974. He retired, only to reappear for New York Cosmos and almost single-handedly popularised the game in the USA. He played his last match in New Jersey on 1 October 1977, before a crowd of 75,646. During the game he appeared for both sides — New York and Santos. It was his 1,363rd match and he scored his 1,281st goal. Later he added two more goals in special appearances. For Brazil alone he had scored 97.

Pele has remained in the public eye at home and abroad. He remains an excellent ambassador for the game, though he has been critical of Brazilian football. His popularity is such that he has considered entering politics. He continues to make public appearances on World Cup occasions and was on hand for the 1990 World Cup draw in December 1989.

MICHEL PLATINI

FRANCE

Michel Platini was the midfield inspiration of the French team which won the European Championship with an irresistible display of incisive, attacking play in the 1984 tournament. It was a memorable year for him. He became European Footballer of the Year for the second time and helped Juventus to the Italian championship in which he finished as leading goalscorer.

Platini also played in the 1978, 1982 and 1986 World Cup competitions, stamping his own authority on the fluidly attractive style for which the French became renowned.

Born in Joeuf on 21 June 1955 his early football was played with Nancy, where his father Aldo was one of the coaches. In seven seasons there he scored 98 goals in 175 League appearances. He also made his first steps in international football as a member of the French team in the 1976 Olympics in Montreal, after his full debut against Czechoslovakia in March of the same year. In this game he scored in a 2-2 draw.

In 1978 he scored the goal in the French Cup final which took the trophy to Nancy at the expense of Nice and went on to play in the World Cup finals in Argentina. The French took the lead in under a minute in the opening match with Italy, but while they promised much, results were ultimately disappointing.

But for Platini there was a move to St Etienne which was to produce a championship in 1981 in which he contributed 21 invaluable goals, and two cup final appearances on the losing side. In 107 League games he scored 58 goals for St Etienne.

In the 1982 World Cup, France's hopes were finally dashed after an exhausting 3-3 draw with West Germany and the subsequent penalty shoot-out which ended 5-4 in the Germans' favour. After the tournament, Platini moved to Italy, Juventus having paid £1.2 million for him.

Although Juventus had to be content with the runners-up position in the Italian First Division, Platini enjoyed an excellent initial season finishing as the League's leading goalscorer on 16 goals. In 1983-84 both club and player did better than that, Juventus winning the title and Platini again top scoring with 20 goals.

In 1984 France had the advantage of hosting the final tournament in the European Championship. Platini scored the only goal of the game with Denmark, three of the five against Belgium including a penalty and all three at the expense of Yugoslavia, who were beaten 3-2. He then hit the winner in the thrilling 3-2 win in extra time against Portugal, and to complete a remarkable tournament, scored the first goal in the final, which saw Spain defeated 2-0.

He had scored more goals for France than any other player in the country's history and overtook Just Fontaine's previous record of 31 goals. At 29, Platini was at his most assertive. Truly a mercurial midfield master, he initiated and completed attacks with skilled understanding and control.

His dead-ball expertise was honed by hours of practice, swerving the ball round wooden dummies. Free-kicks and penalties swelled his tally of goals. But it was his mobile contribution which made him such a dangerous opponent, able to elude the closest of markers. Platini would patiently hover for just one lapse to steal into a space and produce an opening either for a colleague or for himself.

Juventus won the 1985 European Cup, Platini converting a penalty against Liverpool in the awful aftermath of the Heysel Stadium disaster. The previous year he had won a Cup Winners' Cup medal in the 2-1 victory over Porto. In 1985-86 Juventus won another championship, Platini scoring 12 goals. The season before that he had been leading scorer with 18 goals. His last campaign for Juventus was in 1986-87.

In the 1986 World Cup in Mexico, Platini was a closely watched player. Although he equalised for France in the absorbing clash with Brazil, the match had to be decided on penalties and Platini missed from the spot. It was not the first set-back in his career, but as a player it was one of his last.

In his first season with Juventus, Platini had to settle for a runners-up medal in the European Cup, the Italian champions losing to Hamburg. But his experiences at club and international level had included nine consecutive seasons in one or other of the three European competitions. He had scored 27 goals in these three tournaments.

For Juventus in League games alone, he scored 68 goals in 147 matches. For France, whom he captained in the European Championship, Platini appeared on 72 occasions and added 41 goals to his record.

His ability to direct the ball with precision either for other players or for himself had made him unique in his era, where specialists had increasingly become uncommon and individual accomplishment rarer. At the age of 32 he decided to retire.

However he was not kept out of the spotlight for long. Having dabbled in television as a football commentator, he was asked to take over the French national team and had to wrestle with the problem faced by all outstanding players when required to manage others: transferring their own natural ability to those less gifted.

Michel Platini in aerial action for France against Hungary in the 1986 World Cup in Mexico. (ALLSPORT)

DINO ZOFF

ITALY

Like a vintage wine, Dino Zoff improved with age. He was 40 when he captained Italy to their 1982 World Cup success and although he had one or two disappointments in his career, consistency was a key factor in his longevity as an international goalkeeper.

Born at Mariano del Friuli in the north-east province of Gorizia on 28 February 1942, he developed with Udinese but had a severe baptism in the first team, conceding five goals in a 5-2 defeat away to Fiorentina when he was 19. It was not a happy period for the club. Zoff made four League appearances in that 1961-62 season, at the conclusion of which Udinese found themselves relegated.

In 1962-63 he was the regular choice and before the beginning of the following season, he moved on to Mantova who were in the First Division at the time. That season he played the first of three intermediate internationals for Italy.

However there was another set-back at the end of 1964-65 when Mantova were relegated. But they bounced back after just one term in Division Two and it was not until 1967 that Zoff switched clubs again. His destination was Napoli and in April 1968 he found himself capped for Italy at full level on his home ground in a European Championship game against Bulgaria, before an ecstatic crowd of 90,000.

His second international was in the semi-final of the same competition against USSR. Zoff remained unbeaten after extra time, with the Italians rather fortunately going through on the toss of a coin!

In the final in Rome, he was beaten for the first time in a 1-1 draw which also went to the extra period. But in the replay he kept the opposition out as Italy took the trophy in a 2-0 success. Before his debut in national colours, the Italians' first choice goalkeeper had been Enrico Albertosi. Now both players were tried on an alternate basis in the run up to the World Cup in Mexico. But after Zoff's tenth appearance in a 2-2 draw with Spain in Madrid, a match notable for the double own goal by Italy's Sandro Salvadore, Albertosi was made first choice.

Zoff's next outing was as second-half substitute against Switzerland in Berne in which he was not beaten in a 1-1 draw. Shortly afterwards he edged out Albertosi, and in 1972 was transferred to Juventus. The following year he finished runner-up in the European Footballer of the Year award.

It was the beginning of the goalkeeper's most rewarding period at club and country level. He was rarely absent from either the Juventus team or the national side. The club won five championships and two cups.

After conceding a goal to Yugoslavia 17 minutes from the end of a 3-1 win in September 1972 he was unbeaten in 12 entire matches. In the 13th, against Haiti in the 1974 World Cup, he finally conceded a goal a minute after half-time. His 1,143 minutes without letting the opposition score against him created a world record. It included two matches against England.

Noted for his agility, courage and anticipation, his reflexes were honed intensely by the defensive methods used in Italian football. In fact it often appeared far easier for him to deal with shots in international games where he often had more time to see the ball. However his prowess in the Italian League was such that he also established a record of 903 minutes without letting in a goal.

Zoff won his 64th cap in the opening World Cup game in Argentina in 1978. Having beaten the host nation to finish top of their group, the Italians went on to reach the semi-final and met Holland. In the second half, with Italy leading by an own goal, Zoff was twice beaten by

searing, long-range drives. He looked every part of his 36 years. His career seemed to be in the balance.

But it was not in jeopardy. He continued to be called upon by Italy even though other players were tried out for the day when Zoff would retire. The 1982 World Cup arrived with him poised to make his 100th appearance for Italy, and he marked the occasion with a clean sheet against Poland in a goalless draw.

Despite the Italians giving three low-key performances in the opening group matches, Zoff had kept his best for the second round tie with Brazil. He succeeded in keeping the Italians ahead when Brazil pressed desperately in the closing stages, trying to save the game. But Zoff remained cool, commanding and belied his age as he pulled out every morsel of know-how derived from 20 years in top class football.

In the World Cup final itself, Zoff again looked supreme. He collected the trophy after his 106th game for Italy, and went on to complete 112 appearances. His last international was against Sweden in May 1983 in a European Championship qualifying match in which he was beaten twice.

His 570 First Division matches included 332 consecutive appearances and with his two seasons in the Second Division added on, he had made a total of 644 League appearances. Upon retiring he took charge of the Italian Olympic team in 1988 and then assumed control of his favourite Juventus team.

Dino Zoff moves smartly to cut off the ball before it reaches Ray Wilkins. England beat Italy 2-0 at Wembley, but the Italians and Zoff qualified for the 1978 finals at the expense of the home side.
(HULTON)

GREECE

Greece have under-achieved greatly in international football and 1994 represents only their first appearance in the finals of the World Cup.

Entering the competition for the first time in 1934, Greece were somewhat unfortunate to be drawn against the hosts and eventual winners Italy for their qualifier and it was no surprise when they were defeated 4-0. The Greeks were on even more of a hiding to nothing four years later when having come through an eliminator against Palestine they faced Hungary for a place in the finals, only to find themselves on the end of an embarrassing 11-1 reverse.

Post-war results in the qualifying competitions were not especially encouraging although the Greeks did open their qualifying campaign for 1966 with two wins over Denmark and Wales. Unfortunately they could not sustain this form and lost their next three games. Then in 1970 they made a valiant effort in a competitive group and went into their final game in Rumania knowing that a win would take them through to the finals. Sadly they could only draw but the runners-up spot was achieved ahead of Switzerland and Portugal.

It proved a false dawn as Greece finished bottom of their group in the next two competitions, although in 1978 they again went into their last fixture in Hungary needing a victory to win the group. Qualification for the finals of the European Championships in 1980 provided new impetus but their home form then let them down in 1982 as they were unable to capitalise on winning in Denmark and drawing in Italy.

Nothing that followed hinted that qualification for America in 1994 might be a possibility, but Greece had the good fortune to be drawn in the group from which Yugoslavia were forced to withdraw. The crucial result for the Greeks came with a 1-0 win in Hungary and qualification for their first World Cup finals was clinched by a 1-1 draw in the next match away in Russia.

Greece celebrate the goal by Apostolakis which brought them a crucial victory in Hungary during the 1994 World Cup qualifying campaign (ALLSPORT/BEN RADFORD)

GREECE

Formed: *1926*
Joined FIFA: *1927*
Honours: *Nil*
Clubs: *4136*
Players: *201,000*
Division 1 clubs: *18*
Season: *September-June*
Colours: *White shirts, blue shorts, white stockings*

WORLD CUP RECORD

1930	*Did not enter*
1934	*Did not qualify*
1938	*Did not qualify*
1950	*Did not enter*
1954	*Did not qualify*
1958	*Did not qualify*
1962	*Did not qualify*
1966	*Did not qualify*
1970	*Did not qualify*
1974	*Did not qualify*
1978	*Did not qualify*
1982	*Did not qualify*
1986	*Did not qualify*
1990	*Did not qualify*

SWITZERLAND

Switzerland's qualification for the 1994 finals represented a welcome renaissance in their World Cup fortunes. Whilst never exactly a major force, the Swiss were useful competitors in the early World Cup competitions.

The country which is home to FIFA first entered the World Cup in 1934 and qualified for the finals in Italy where after beating Holland by the odd goal in five in Milan they then found themselves on the wrong end of the same 3-2 scoreline against the eventual finalists Czechoslovakia in Turin.

A 2-1 win over Portugal booked the Swiss a place in the 1938 finals where they excelled themselves in the first round, defeating a German side strengthened by its annexation of the best Austrian players. They triumphed 4-2 after a replay. In the quarter-finals Hungary proved too good for them, winning 2-0.

A third successive appearance in the finals in 1950 was marked only by a surprise 2-2 draw with the hosts Brazil, but when Switzerland hosted the finals themselves in 1954 they progressed to the quarter finals courtesy of a 4-1 victory over Italy in a play-off. It was the prelude to an amazing goal feast as the Swiss, having raced into a 3-0 lead against Austria, eventually lost 7-5 in a match in which they also missed a penalty!

These finals, though, proved something of a swansong. Although they qualified again in 1962 and 1966, on both occasions they lost all three matches in the finals. Four successive qualifying campaigns followed in which they were depressingly mediocre, catching the eye only in 1982 when they first beat England in Basle then threw them a lifeline with a shock win over Rumania in Bucharest.

The Swiss performed better when finishing third behind Denmark and the Soviet Union in 1986 but poorly in 1990, defeating only Luxembourg. Then in 1994 came success at last, the highlight of a triumphant qualifying campaign being the three points taken off Italy along the way.

SWITZERLAND	WORLD CUP RECORD	
Formed: *1895*	**1930**	*Did not enter*
Joined FIFA: *1904*	**1934**	*Quarter-finals*
Honours: *Nil*	**1938**	*Quarter-finals*
Clubs: *1473*	**1950**	*First Round*
Players: *189,255*	**1954**	*Quarter-finals*
Division 1 clubs: *12*	**1958**	*Did not qualify*
Season: *July-December; March-June*	**1962**	*First Round*
Colours: *Red shirts, white shorts,*	**1966**	*First Round*
red stockings	**1970**	*Did not qualify*
	1974	*Did not qualify*
	1978	*Did not qualify*
	1982	*Did not qualify*
	1986	*Did not qualify*
	1990	*Did not qualify*

The Swiss team line up for a World Cup qualifying tie during their successful bid to reach the 1994 finals (ALLSPORT)

ITALY

Italy equalled Brazil's record of three World Cup wins in 1982, having won their first two in 1934 and 1938, and had high hopes of a record-breaking fourth win in 1990 before losing on penalties to Argentina in the semi-finals.

In 1934 they beat the USA 7-1, Spain 1-0 after a 1-1 draw and Austria 1-0 to reach the final in which they defeated Czechoslovakia 2-1 after extra time. Four years on and Norway forced them to extra time before the Italians won 2-1 and then it was France, beaten 3-1, Brazil 2-1 and finally Hungary 4-2.

However in 1950 they had just two games: a 3-2 defeat against Sweden and a 2-0 win over Paraguay. More disappointment came in 1954 after losing 2-1 to Switzerland and beating Belgium 4-1; they lost a play-off 4-1 to the Swiss. After failing to qualify in 1958 they reached Chile to hold West Germany 0-0, lose 2-0 to the hosts and beat Switzerland 3-0 only to be knocked out. Worse, in 1966 after revenge against Chile by 2-0, they lost 1-0 to the USSR and humiliatingly 1-0 to North Korea.

There was better fortune in 1970. Sweden were beaten 1-0, Uruguay and Israel held 0-0. Mexico were defeated 4-1 and West Germany 4-3 after extra time before.the Italians finally lost 4-1 to Brazil. In 1974 Haiti were beaten 3-1, Argentina held 1-1 before they lost 2-1 to Poland.

In 1978 the tournament began with victories over France, Hungary and Argentina. West Germany were held 0-0 and Austria beaten 1-0, before the Italians lost 2-1 to Holland and 2-1 to Brazil in the game for third place.

More successfully in 1982 Italy won their third trophy. Beginning slowly with three draws, 0-0 with Poland, 1-1 with Peru and 1-1 with Cameroon, they survived to beat Argentina 2-1, Brazil 3-2, Poland 2-0 and West Germany 3-1 in the final. In 1986 there were further 1-1 draws with Bulgaria and Argentina before a 3-2 win over South Korea. Elimination came in the second round, 2-0 against France.

Not all Italians were behind manager Enzo Bearzot (left) when he selected Paolo Rossi for the 1982 World Cup squad. But his choice was vindicated when Rossi helped Italy to win the Cup for the third time.

ITALY	WORLD CUP RECORD	
Formed: *1898*	1930	*Did not enter*
Joined FIFA: *1905*	1934	*Winners*
Honours: *Winners 1934, 1938, 1982;*	1938	*Winners*
runners-up 1970; 3rd 1990; 4th 1978	1950	*First Round*
Clubs: *19,191*	1954	*First Round*
Players: *1,612,404*	1958	*Did not qualify*
Division I clubs: *18*	1962	*First Round*
Season: *September-June*	1966	*First Round*
Colours: *Blue shirts, white shorts,*	1970	*Runners-up*
blue stockings, white trim	1974	*First Round*
	1978	*4th*
	1982	*Winners*
	1986	*Second Round*
	1990	*3rd*

USA

The United States of America can claim to be one of a comparatively small number of countries to have entered every World Cup competition. Their most rewarding tournament came in 1930 and their best performance achieved in one game in 1950.

In 1930 they began impressively with 3-0 wins over Belgium and Paraguay to reach the semi-finals where they were beaten 6-1 by Argentina, but only after suffering several injuries. Four years later they made the long journey to Italy before playing a qualifying game with Mexico, winning 4-2 only to find themselves subsequently crushed 7-1 by the host nation. In 1938 they did enter but withdrew before playing.

They were required to play in a tournament in Mexico before qualifying in 1950. But they lost 3-1 to Spain in the opening match in the final series and were expected to finish well beaten against England. Instead they won 1-0 in arguably the most sensational result ever achieved in the World Cup. However they came down to earth in the next match, losing 5-2 to Chile.

Not having the benefit of any home matches in 1954 robbed them of any real chance of qualifying but they could not use this as an excuse four years later. There was similar disappointment in 1962 and 1966, though in the latter competition they were slightly handicapped by having to play both games with Honduras away and they did manage to hold Mexico to a 2-2 draw in Los Angeles.

They failed again in 1974 but in 1978 prospects slightly improved, as a better performance was ended only by defeat in a play-off against Canada. The US made little progress in 1982 or 1986 but finally reached the finals again in 1990 thanks to a dramatic win away to Trinidad and Tobago. In Italy, they were by no means disgraced.

Brian Bliss, one of the American squad which enabled his country to qualify for the finals for only the fourth time in their history in 1990.

USA	WORLD CUP RECORD	
Formed: 1913	**1930**	Semi-finals
Joined FIFA: 1913	**1934**	First Round
Honours: Nil	**1938**	Withdrew
Clubs: 6500	**1950**	First Round
Players: 1,700,000	**1954**	Did not qualify
Division I clubs: No national league,	**1958**	Did not qualify
ASL 10; WSL 9	**1962**	Did not qualify
Season: April-September	**1966**	Did not qualify
Colours: White shirts, blue shorts, red	**1970**	Did not qualify
stockings	**1974**	Did not qualify
	1978	Did not qualify
	1982	Did not qualify
	1986	Did not qualify
	1990	First Round

CAMEROON

Cameroon were unquestionably the sensation of the 1990 World Cup, defeating Argentina, Rumania and Colombia to reach the quarter-finals, where they were unlucky to lose 3-2 to England.

In 1966 they entered the competition for the first time but were among the mass exodus of African nations before a qualifying game was played. Four years later they were knocked out in the first match against Nigeria, but in 1974 forced a play-off with Zaire after being given a bye through a withdrawal in the first round. But Zaire won this game 2-0.

In 1978 Cameroon lost to the Congo but there was a transformation in their fortunes in 1982. In the first round, they beat Malawi 3-0 at home and then drew the return game 1-1 to progress into the next stage. Again they won on their own soil, beating Zimbabwe 2-0 and edged through into the third round despite losing the return match 1-0. But it looked bleak for them when Zaire won the first game by a single goal. However Cameroon swept through after winning 6-1 at home. This put them into the final round and they needed to beat Morocco for a place in the finals in Spain. They began well by winning 2-0 in Kenitra and eased through in Yaounde during their home clash with a 2-1 success.

Cameroon's group in Spain included Poland, Italy and Peru. In the opening game with the Peruvians in La Coruna they drew 0-0 and repeated the scoreline against Poland. They entered the last group game with Italy knowing that a win would put them into the second stage, but a draw would be of no use since the Italians had at least scored one goal. The outcome was a 1-1 draw. Cameroon were eliminated unbeaten and Italy went on to win the Cup.

Ebwere Bertin in action for the Cameroon in their final qualifying game against Tunisia in Tunis which clinched a place in Italy for the Africans.

CAMEROON

Formed: *1960*
Joined FIFA: *1962*
Honours: *Nil*
Clubs: *380*
Players: *18,578*
Division I clubs: *16*
Season: *October-August*
Colours: *Green shirts, red shorts, yellow stockings*

WORLD CUP RECORD

1930	*Not eligible*
1934	*Not eligible*
1938	*Not eligible*
1950	*Not eligible*
1954	*Not eligible*
1958	*Not eligible*
1962	*Not eligible*
1966	*Withdrew*
1970	*Did not qualify*
1974	*Did not qualify*
1978	*Did not qualify*
1982	*First Round*
1986	*Did not qualify*
1990	*Quarter-finals*

ARGENTINA

Having finished as runners-up in the initial tournament in 1930, Argentina had to wait until the 1970s before their first success but they have now appeared in three of the last four finals, losing to West Germany in 1990.

In 1930 they beat France 1-0, Mexico 6-3 and Chile 3-1 to reach the semi-finals where they defeated the USA 6-1. But they went down 4-2 to neighbouring Uruguay in the final. They did not enter in 1934, withdrew in 1938 and 1950 and did not enter in 1954. They qualified in 1958 only to find erratic form in Sweden, losing 3-1 to West Germany but beating Northern Ireland by the same score before crashing out 6-1 to Czechoslovakia.

In 1962 they edged out Bulgaria 1-0 but were beaten 3-1 by England and were held to a goalless draw by Hungary. However they began promisingly enough in 1966 with a 2-1 win over Spain, a goalless draw with West Germany and a 2-0 success over Switzerland. But it fell apart in the controversial quarter-final where they again lost to England by a single goal.

They did not qualify in 1970 but in 1974 reached the second round. After losing 3-2 to Poland, drawing 1-1 with Italy and beating Haiti 4-1, Holland beat them 4-0 as did Brazil by 2-1. The 1-1 draw with East Germany was of no assistance.

With home advantage in 1978 they made the most of it.

There were 2-1 wins over Hungary and France before a 1-0 defeat against Italy. In the second round they beat Poland 2-0, held Brazil to a 0-0 draw and took six goals off Peru without reply. In the final they beat Holland 3-1.

In 1982 a 1-0 defeat by Belgium was retrieved with a 4-1 win over Hungary and a 2-0 win over El Salvador. But then came a 2-1 defeat by Italy and a 3-1 reverse against Brazil. Yet in 1986 South Korea were despatched 3-1, Italy held 1-1 and Bulgaria beaten 2-0. Then Uruguay were beaten 1-0, England 2-1 and Belgium 2-0. In the final West Germany became their victims in a 3-2 success.

ARGENTINA

Formed: *1893*
Joined FIFA: *1912*
Honours: *Winners 1978, 1986; runners-up 1930, 1990*
Clubs: *3350*
Players: *307,000*
Division I clubs: *20*
Colours: *Blue and white shirts, black shorts, white stockings*

WORLD CUP RECORD

1930	*Runners-up*
1934	*Did not enter*
1938	*Withdrew*
1950	*Withdrew*
1954	*Did not enter*
1958	*Did not enter*
1962	*Did not enter*
1966	*Quarter-finals*
1970	*Did not qualify*
1974	*Second Round*
1978	*Winners*
1982	*Second Round*
1986	*Winners*
1990	*Runners-up*

Argentina fell at the quarter-final stage in 1966 after captain Antonio Rattin was sent off. England beat the ten-man South Americans 1-0. (POPPERFOTO)

RUSSIA

The USSR emerged from its post-war isolation to participate in the World Cup for the first time in the 1958 series. But fourth place in 1966 represented the Soviets' best performance and they never threatened to improve on that in 1990, as they failed to reach the second round.

However in 1958 they qualified at the first attempt in a group which included Poland and Finland. In Helsinki they beat the Finns 10-0 and dropped only two points, losing 2-1 to the Poles. In Sweden they began by drawing 2-2 with England, Austria were beaten 2-0 before the Soviets lost to the Brazilians by the same score. In the play-off for second place in the group, they beat England 1-0.

They lost 2-0 to Sweden in the quarter-finals and having qualified again in 1962 they began with another 2-0 victory over Yugoslavia. They were held 4-4 in an error-ridden game with Colombia before edging out Uruguay 2-1. But again the host nation knocked them out; Chile winning 2-1.

In 1966 they beat North Korea 3-0, the Italians by a single goal and gained revenge over Chile with a 2-1 win. The quarter-finals saw them defeat Hungary 2-1 at Roker Park, but West Germany beat them in the semi-finals and in the match for third place at Wembley, they lost 2-1 to Portugal.

In Mexico they opened the series with a goalless draw against the host nation, then defeated Belgium 4-1 and El Salvador 2-0 only to lose 1-0 to Uruguay in extra time in the quarter-finals.

After two failures the 1982 finals were reached. They recovered from a 2-1 defeat by Brazil to beat New Zealand 3-0 and then drew 2-2 with Scotland. In the second round they beat Belgium 1-0 but were held scoreless by Poland and eliminated. Four years later they were off to a fine start taking six goals off Hungary without reply. The Soviets then held France 1-1 and beat Canada 2-0. But in the second round they lost 4-3 to Belgium after extra time in Leon.

The Soviet Union were involved in a classic match in the 1986 finals in Mexico, eventually losing 4-3 to Belgium. Rinat Dasayev makes the catch (ALLSPORT)

RUSSIA (USSR)

Formed: 1912
Joined FIFA: 1946
Honours: 4th 1966
Clubs: 43,700
Players: 2,170,000
Division I clubs: 18
Season: March-October
Colours: White shirts, blue shorts, red stockings

WORLD CUP RECORD

1930	Not eligible
1934	Not eligible
1938	Not eligible
1950	Did not enter
1954	Did not enter
1958	Quarter-finals
1962	Quarter-finals
1966	4th
1970	Quarter-finals
1974	Did not qualify
1978	Did not qualify
1982	Second Round
1986	Second Round
1990	First Round

RUMANIA

One of the four European countries to enter the first tournament in 1930, they participated in all three of the pre-war series but have not carried on the tradition. 1990 saw only their second post-war appearance in the finals.

Rumania did make a useful start in Uruguay beating Peru 3-1 but then lost 4-0 to the hosts and eventual winners. But in 1934 they almost found themselves the first team to be disqualified from the World Cup. In the qualifying competition Switzerland complained that Rumania had fielded an ineligible player but the Rumanians were reinstated on appeal. Alas it proved a short-lived reprieve as Rumania lost by 2-1 to the eventual runners-up Czechoslovakia in the first round.

In 1938 the withdrawal of Egypt gave Rumania a free pass to the finals in France where they were surprised by Cuba who held them to a 3-3 draw. More shocks came in the replay when Cuba beat them 2-1. They did not enter in 1950 and failed to qualify in 1954 and 1958. In 1962 they withdrew and in 1966 again found themselves out of the finals despite winning all their home qualifying games. This was particularly disappointing for them.

At last in 1970 Rumania succeeded in emerging from the qualifying tournament to win a place in Mexico. But they found themselves in a strong group which included Brazil, England and Czechoslovakia who had been their initial opponents in 1934. Luck was against them.

England provided the first hurdle and Rumania lost 1-0. But revenge was obtained against the Czechs in a 2-1 win before Rumania faced the might of Brazil. Almost certain of reaching the knock-out stage, the Brazilians rested a couple of key players. Even so after a slow start, Rumania were not disgraced in their 3-2 defeat.

RUMANIA	WORLD CUP RECORD	
Formed: *1908*	1930	*First Round*
Joined FIFA: *1930*	1934	*First Round*
Honours: *Nil*	1938	*First Round*
Clubs: *5453*	1950	*Did not enter*
Players: *179,987*	1954	*Did not qualify*
Division I clubs: *18*	1958	*Did not qualify*
Season: *August-November; March-July*	1962	*Withdrew*
Colours: *Yellow shirts, blue shorts,*	1966	*Did not qualify*
red stockings	1970	*First Round*
	1974	*Did not qualify*
	1978	*Did not qualify*
	1982	*Did not qualify*
	1986	*Did not qualify*
	1990	*Second Round*

Marius Lacatus scored twice in Rumania's opening game of the 1990 finals, but suspension caused him to miss the crucial second round match against Ireland. Rumania were eliminated on penalties.

SAUDI ARABIA

Of the 24 finalists in 1994, Saudi Arabia are undoubtedly the youngest and least experienced as far as the World Cup is concerned.

The Saudis entered the World Cup for the first time as recently as 1978. It was not a particularly auspicious debut as in the qualifying competition they and Syria struggled to live with Iran, who easily won their group. In the next qualifying competition prior to the 1982 finals, the Saudis hosted the Middle East qualifying group matches and finished top, winning all four of their games. In the final round, however, they found the competition from the rest of FIFA's Asian region much stiffer, gaining just a single point from six matches.

They gave notice of their progress by winning the Asian Cup in 1984 and 1988 but were eliminated early in the qualifying rounds for the 1986 World Cup by another improving Gulf side, the United Arab Emirates. The Saudi bid to reach Italy in 1990 started well enough as they topped their first round group ahead of Syria and North Yemen, but once more they struggled to make an impression in the final round, losing out to South Korea and the UAE again.

The Saudis' qualifying campaign for 1994 received an immediate fillip in the opening match when they defeated Macao 6-0 in Malaysia, the venue for the first series of matches in their first round qualifying group. They then managed to draw with the hosts and with Kuwait to set themselves up for the return series of matches on home territory. They won all three games convincingly and were among the favourites going into the final qualifying group, staged in neighbouring Qatar. The Saudis were enthusiastically supported and emerged undefeated from their five games, including a match against Iraq which was heavy with political overtones following the 1991 Gulf war. They clinched their place in the finals with a 4-3 victory over Iran to finish top of the group.

Saeed Owairin (centre) in World Cup action for Saudi Arabia against Iraq in the final qualifying tournament for 1994 in Qatar (ALLSPORT/SHAUN BOTTERILL)

SAUDI ARABIA

Formed: *1959*
Joined FIFA: *1959*
Honours: *Nil*
Clubs: *173*
Players: *30,761*
Division I clubs: *12*
Season: *October-June*
Colours: *All-white*

WORLD CUP RECORD

1930	*Not eligible*
1934	*Not eligible*
1938	*Not eligible*
1950	*Not eligible*
1954	*Not eligible*
1958	*Not eligible*
1962	*Did not enter*
1966	*Did not enter*
1970	*Did not enter*
1974	*Did not enter*
1978	*Did not qualify*
1982	*Did not qualify*
1986	*Did not qualify*
1990	*Did not qualify*

BRAZIL

Brazil were the first country to win the World Cup three times and are the only one to have appeared in all the final competitions. They won the Jules Rimet Trophy outright in 1970 but have not reached the final since then, always falling short when looking like potential winners.

In 1930 they won one game and lost another; four years later they went out in the first round but improved in 1938. They edged out Poland 6-5 after extra time and beat Czechoslovakia 2-1 after a 1-1 draw, but then lost 2-1 to Italy in the semi-finals. Still they secured third place by beating Sweden 4-2.

In 1950 a 4-0 win over Mexico, a 2-2 draw with Switzerland and a 2-0 victory against Yugoslavia put them into the final pool where, after crushing Sweden 7-1 and Spain 6-1 they had to settle for runners-up spot, losing 2-1 to Uruguay.

Brazil were eliminated by Hungary in the quarter-finals in the 1954 series but impressed everyone in 1958. They beat Austria 3-0, drew 0-0 with England and beat the USSR 2-0, Wales 1-0 and France 5-2. In the final they also accounted for Sweden 5-2.

Retaining the cup in 1962 their victims were Mexico 2-0, Czechoslovakia held 0-0, Spain 2-1, England 3-1, Chile 4-2 and the Czechs finally overcome 3-1. But they were knocked out in the first stage in 1966.

Yet it was vintage Brazil in 1970. Czechoslovakia were beaten again this time 4-1, England 1-0, Rumania 3-2, Peru 4-2, Uruguay 3-1 and ultimately Italy 4-1. Even fourth place was disappointing in 1974. Brazil were third in 1978, thwarted by the vagaries of the schedule as much as anything else.

In 1982 defensive errors proved costly against Italy in the second stage and tragically they made a glorious exit after the lottery of a penalty shoot-out four years later, following a memorable game with France.

BRAZIL	WORLD CUP RECORD	
Formed: *1914*	**1930**	*First Round*
Joined FIFA: *1923*	**1934**	*First Round*
Honours: *Winners 1958, 1962, 1970; runners-up 1950; 3rd 1938, 1978; 4th 1974*	**1938**	*3rd*
	1950	*Runners-up*
Clubs: *12,890*	**1954**	*Quarter-finals*
Players: *552,000*	**1958**	*Winners*
Division I clubs: *National Championship: 22 clubs*	**1962**	*Winners*
	1966	*First Round*
Season: *January-December*	**1970**	*Winners*
Colours: *Yellow shirts, blue shorts, white stockings, green trim*	**1974**	*4th*
	1978	*3rd*
	1982	*Second Round*
	1986	*Quarter-finals*
	1990	*Second Round*

Brazil's captain in the 1970 World Cup was Carlos Alberto, the right-back; he managed to get himself on the score sheet in the final with the last goal of the game.
(SYNDICATION INTERNATIONAL)

BULGARIA

Bulgaria's unfortunate claim to fame rests in the fact that in five appearances in the World Cup finals prior to 1994 they failed to win a single match.

The Bulgarians took part in the World Cup qualifying tournament twice before the war but on each occasion found themselves out of their depth against powerful Central European opponents. In 1934 they suffered heavy defeats against Austria and Hungary and four years later crashed 6-0 against Czechoslovakia in Prague after holding them 1-1 in Sofia.

Bulgaria's post-war efforts began to take shape when they qualified for the finals in Chile in 1962 thanks to victory over France in a play-off. In this first of four consecutive appearances in the World Cup finals their only point came from a dull 0-0 draw with England. Another play-off win over Belgium won them a place in the 1966 finals but in a tough group which accounted even for the holders Brazil, it was no surprise that Bulgaria finished bottom without a single point.

Expectations were much greater four years later in Mexico, but although the Bulgarians played their part in a highly entertaining group, they lost to Peru and West Germany, and then failed to beat the group 'minnows' Morocco. They had a thoroughly disappointing tournament in 1974, overshadowed by the fine football of their group opponents Holland and Sweden, and once again failed to win a match.

Their fine sequence of qualifying for the finals was ended next time around by a rapidly improving France and in 1982 their failure to beat Austria in Sofia proved decisive. Their strange Mexican adventure in 1986 when they progressed to the second round despite not winning a match was followed by a disastrous qualifying competition in 1990 and they were not expected to qualify for America four years on. They succeeded, however, in the most dramatic fashion. Needing to win in Paris to eliminate France they did so with a stunning last-minute winner.

Bulgaria's Mladenov slides in during the opening game of the 1986 finals, a 1-1 draw with Italy
(ALLSPORT)

BULGARIA

Formed: *1923*
Joined FIFA: *1924*
Honours: *Nil*
Clubs: *4328*
Players: *441,300*
Division I clubs: *16*
Season: *August-May with mid-season break January-February*
Colours: *White shirts, green shorts, red stockings*

WORLD CUP RECORD

1930	*Did not enter*
1934	*Did not qualify*
1938	*Did not qualify*
1950	*Did not enter*
1954	*Did not qualify*
1958	*Did not qualify*
1962	*First Round*
1966	*First Round*
1970	*First Round*
1974	*First Round*
1978	*Did not qualify*
1982	*Did not qualify*
1986	*Second Round*
1990	*Did not qualify*

SWEDEN

Sweden's best performance came in 1958 when they finished runners-up to Brazil in the tournament held on their own territory. Apart from the initial competition, they have entered every series.

In 1934 they beat Argentina 3-2 before losing to Germany 2-1 and were given a first round bye in 1938 when Austria pulled out. They then took eight goals off Cuba without reply but were beaten 5-1 by Hungary in the semi-finals and 4-2 by Brazil in the match for third place. A 3-2 win over Italy and a 2-2 draw with Paraguay in 1950 put them in the final group where they were trounced 7-1 by Brazil, edged out 3-2 by Uruguay but ensured of third place by beating Spain 3-1.

Sweden did not qualify again until staging their own tournament in 1958. They beat Mexico 3-0, Hungary 2-1 and drew 0-0 with Wales. In the quarter-finals they overcame the Soviet Union 2-0 and West Germany 3-1 in the semi-finals. Against any other team but Brazil in the final, they might have caused an upset, but a 5-2 defeat was no disgrace.

They did not qualify again until 1970 where they were eliminated on goal difference after losing 1-0 to Italy and drawing 1-1 with Israel, because their 1-0 win over Uruguay was not enough. There was a better outcome in 1974, when after goalless draws with Bulgaria and Holland they again beat Uruguay 3-0 to reach the next stage. But they lost 1-0 to Poland and 4-2 to West Germany giving them merely the consolation of a 2-1 win over Yugoslavia.

Sweden managed a 1-1 draw with Brazil at the beginning of the 1978 final tournament but then lost by a single goal to both Austria and Spain. They did not qualify in either 1982 or 1986, and in 1990 must have wished they hadn't, as they lost all three matches in Italy.

Sweden's most successful World Cup was as hosts in 1958. Right-back Orvar Bergmark heads clear during a 2-1 win over Hungary

SWEDEN	WORLD CUP RECORD	
Formed: *1904*	1930	*Did not enter*
Joined FIFA: *1904*	1934	*Second Round*
Honours: *Runners-up 1958; 3rd 1950;*	1938	*4th*
4th 1938	1950	*3rd*
Clubs: *3400*	1954	*Did not qualify*
Players: *437,000*	1958	*Runners-up*
Division I clubs: *12*	1962	*Did not qualify*
Season: *April-October*	1966	*Did not qualify*
Colours: *Yellow shirts, blue shorts, yellow*	1970	*First Round*
and blue stockings	1974	*Second Round*
	1978	*First Round*
	1982	*Did not qualify*
	1986	*Did not qualify*
	1990	*First Round*

GERMANY

Only Brazil has a better record in terms of matches won in the World Cup than Germany but the Germans are catching up fast, and since they did not enter in 1930 and were not allowed back into FIFA until after the 1950 tournament, their record is even more impressive.

In 1934 they accounted for Belgium 5-2 and Sweden 2-1 before losing 3-1 to the eventual beaten finalists Czechoslovakia. They took third place beating Austria 3-2. Ironically the overrunning of Austria by Germany gave the Germans several Austrian players in the 1938 campaign in which they were surprisingly beaten 4-2 by Switzerland in a replay after a 1-1 draw.

In 1954, shrewd manipulation of the oddities of the system allowed them to qualify for the quarter-finals. They defeated Yugoslavia 2-0 and then trounced Austria 6-1 in the semi-finals to face the favourites Hungary in the final. Against all the odds they won 3-2.

They were far more cautious in 1958 but still reached the semi-finals where they lost 3-1 to Sweden and were well beaten 6-3 by France in the match for third place. But the quarter-final was their downfall in 1962 when Yugoslavia beat them by a single goal.

In 1966 a 2-1 semi-final win over the Soviet Union put them into the final against England which ended in their controversial 4-2 defeat in extra time. Although they took

revenge on England in the 1970 quarter-finals they had to settle for third after the exhausting 4-3 defeat by Italy.

Home advantage helped in 1974 and their disciplined performance in the final against Holland produced a worthy 2-1 win, but they lost in 1978 at the second stage, ironically beaten 3-2 by Austria. Since then they have not failed to reach the final. They lost disappointingly 3-1 to Italy in 1982 and 3-2 to Argentina in 1986 after clawing their way back into the match. But in 1990 they gained revenge by beating the South Americans 1-0.

The victorious German team of 1954 skippered by Fritz Walter (far left). Coal-scuttle helmeted soldiers are in attendance (JR).

GERMANY	WORLD CUP RECORD	
Formed: *1900*	1930	*Did not enter*
Joined FIFA: *1904-1945; 1950*	1934	*3rd*
Honours: *Winners 1954, 1974, 1990;*	1938	*First Round*
runners-up 1966, 1982, 1986; 3rd 1934, 1970;	1950	*Not eligible*
4th 1958	1954	*Winners*
Clubs: *26,162*	1958	*4th*
Players: *4,764,146*	1962	*Quarter-finals*
Division I clubs: *18*	1966	*Runners-up*
Season: *August-June*	1970	*3rd*
Colours: *White shirts, black shorts, white*	1974	*Winners*
stockings	1978	*Second Round*
	1982	*Runners-up*
	1986	*Runners-up*
	1990	*Winners*

COLOMBIA

Colombia's practical link with the World Cup dates back to the latter part of the post-war period. They had entered in 1938 but withdrew without playing a match. They did not enter in 1950 or 1954 and failed to reach the finals in 1958. However the Colombians made their bow in 1962 without causing too much concern to their opponents apart from the Soviet Union.

The first fixture was against fellow South Americans from Uruguay who beat them 2-1 in Arica. Then came the 4-4 draw with the Soviet Union and a 5-0 defeat by Yugoslavia. Finishing bottom of their qualifying group in 1966 and third out of four in 1970 was a disappointment in both instances. But there was an improvement in 1974 when they were only deprived of a place in the finals above Uruguay on goal difference.

In 1978 Colombia again finished bottom of their three-team qualifying group and four years later only succeeded in drawing their home matches 1-1 with Peru and Uruguay while losing both games away. In 1986 they were eliminated in a play-off with Paraguay, but four years later they finished top of their qualifying group and faced Israel in a play-off for a place in the finals. A 1-0 win in Bogota proved decisive.

They started the 1990 tournament with a 2-0 win against the United Arab Emirates, which meant that they needed just one more point to progress. But they lost 1-0 to Yugoslavia and looked to be going out when West Germany led 1-0 against them in the final minute. But a dramatic equaliser in injury time saw them reach the second round, only to lose 2-1 to Cameroon. They showed glimpses of Latin style and flair but were unable to impose themselves on the opposition.

COLOMBIA

Formed:	*1925*
Joined FIFA:	*1931*
Honours:	*Nil*
Clubs:	*3805*
Players:	*209,580*
Division I clubs:	*15*
Season:	*February-December*
Colours:	*Red shirts, blue shorts, tricolour stockings*

WORLD CUP RECORD

1930	*Not eligible*
1934	*Did not enter*
1938	*Withdrew*
1950	*Did not enter*
1954	*Did not enter*
1958	*Did not qualify*
1962	*First Round*
1966	*Did not qualify*
1970	*Did not qualify*
1974	*Did not qualify*
1978	*Did not qualify*
1982	*Did not qualify*
1986	*Did not qualify*
1990	*Second Round*

Carlos Valderrama played his club football in France for Montpellier before the 1990 finals. He was luckier than many of his Colombian colleagues, whose league fixtures were abandoned because of terrorist attacks organised by drug barons.

MOROCCO

It was Morocco who really signalled the arrival of Africa in the World Cup. The first African entry of significance in the qualifying tournament came in 1962 when Morocco eliminated Tunisia and Ghana to earn the right to play-off against Spain for a place in the finals in Chile. Over two legs the Spaniards were victorious but only by a single goal margin in each game.

By 1970 Africa for the first time was guaranteed a representative at the finals in Mexico. Morocco won through and memorably gave West Germany a fright in their opening game. They led 1-0 at half-time but lost out in the second period to goals from Seeler and Muller. A draw with Bulgaria crowned a highly successful debut in the finals.

Somewhat surprisingly Morocco failed to qualify for another World Cup until 1986 although they came close on two occasions. In 1978 they made a first round exit but only on penalties against Tunisia who went on to qualify. Then in 1982 having survived a penalty shoot-out against Zambia the Moroccans met Cameroon for a place in the finals but lost home and away to the rising stars of African football.

Then came qualification for Mexico in 1986 — conceding only one goal along the way — and it proved a truly memorable World Cup for Morocco. Starting off cautiously with a 0-0 draw against fancied Poland, they looked to be on the verge of a famous victory when England were reduced to ten men but then seemed to freeze. However, they made up for it with a stunning 3-1 win over Portugal to win the group and progress to meet West Germany in the second round, where they were defeated by a last-minute goal scored from a free-kick by Lothar Matthaus.

They performed poorly in qualification for 1990 but emerged to reach the United States in 1994 thanks to a 1-0 victory at home to a sadly weakened Zambia in their final match.

Moroccan defenders Masbahi and Naybet shadow Kalusha of Zambia during the match which saw the North Africans clinch a place in the 1994 finals (ALLSPORT/ ANTON WANT)

MOROCCO

Formed: *1955*
Joined FIFA: *1956*
Honours: *Nil*
Clubs: *1080*
Players: *62,000*
Division I clubs: *16*
Season: *September-June*
Colours: *All red*

WORLD CUP RECORD

1930	*Not eligible*
1934	*Not eligible*
1938	*Not eligible*
1950	*Not eligible*
1954	*Not eligible*
1958	*Did not enter*
1962	*Did not qualify*
1966	*Withdrew*
1970	*First Round*
1974	*Withdrew*
1978	*Did not qualify*
1982	*Did not qualify*
1986	*Second Round*
1990	*Did not qualify*

MEXICO

As befits a country which has hosted the World Cup finals twice, Mexico have a strong World Cup tradition. Qualification in 1994 secured a tenth World Cup finals appearance.

Mexico in fact took part in the very first World Cup match, a 4-1 defeat at the hands of France in 1930. Indeed they lost all three matches in Uruguay. Although the record shows that they failed to qualify for the 1934 finals in Italy, they did actually travel to Rome and played-off against the USA for a place in the tournament proper. They lost 4-2.

The Mexicans did not enter in 1938 but qualified easily for the first post-war tournament in Brazil, where they

were swept aside by the hosts in their first match and also lost to Yugoslavia and Switzerland. It was a repeat performance in 1954 as Mexico returned home without a point for their endeavours.

A draw with Wales in 1958 was a step in the right direction and in 1962 Mexico finally gained their first win in the World Cup finals, albeit against a Czech side who had already won through to the quarter-finals. Creditable draws with France and Uruguay in 1966 in goalkeeper Antonio Carbajal's record fifth and last World Cup was the prelude to Mexico hosting the finals in 1970. To the delight of the home crowd they progressed to the quarter-finals, only to lose 4-1 to the eventual runners-up Italy.

It was a shock when they failed to qualify for the finals in 1974 and an even greater one when they were defeated in the finals in 1978 by Tunisia. They failed to reach Spain in 1982 but were spared having to qualify when they replaced Colombia as hosts again in 1986. Again they progressed to the quarter-finals where their nerves seemed to fail them as they lost a penalty shoot-out to West Germany.

A FIFA suspension kept them out of Italia '90 but it was no surprise when they edged out Canada to qualify for the 1994 finals in the neighbouring United States.

MEXICO	WORLD CUP RECORD	
Formed: *1927*	1930	*First Round*
Joined FIFA: *1929*	1934	*Did not qualify*
Honours: *Nil*	1938	*Withdrew*
Clubs: *117*	1950	*First Round*
Players: *1,402,000*	1954	*First Round*
Division I clubs: *20*	1958	*First Round*
Season: *September-June*	1962	*First Round*
Colours: *Green shirts, white shorts,*	1966	*First Round*
red stockings	1970	*Quarter-finals*
	1974	*Did not qualify*
	1978	*First Round*
	1982	*Did not qualify*
	1986	*Quarter-finals*
	1990	*Suspended*

A spectacular goal from Negrete against Bulgaria helped Mexico progress to the World Cup quarter-finals on home territory in 1986 (ALLSPORT)

BELGIUM

Belgium were one of the four original European entries in 1930 and have since qualified for the finals seven times. Fourth place in 1986 remains their best performance, though they were possibly more impressive in 1990.

In 1930 they lost 3-0 to the United States and 1-0 to Paraguay, but after qualifying in 1934 lost 5-2 in the first round to Germany. There was similar first round disappointment in 1938 when France beat them 3-1, but they withdrew in 1950.

They succeeded in 1954 and began their programme by drawing 4-4 with England, but were well beaten 4-1 by the Italians. They failed to qualify in 1958 and 1962 but at least forced a play-off with Bulgaria in the 1966 version, before losing 2-1 in Florence.

However they played in Mexico in 1970 and started by beating El Salvador 3-0. The Belgians then lost 4-1 to the USSR and 1-0 to the host nation. Neighbours Holland edged them out of a place in 1974 and repeated the exercise in 1978. But the Belgians were able to turn the tables on the Dutch in the run-up to the 1982 finals. A 3-0 defeat in Holland did not prevent them qualifying along with France, thanks to an earlier 1-0 win over the Dutch.

El Salvador were again in Belgium's group, but it was Argentina who fell victims to the Belgians 1-0 in the opening match. A similar win was recorded over El Salvador and then came a 1-1 draw with Hungary. But they lost 3-0 to Poland and 1-0 to the USSR in the second stage.

Belgium qualified again in 1986 and it was back to Mexico where they started by losing 2-1 to the hosts once more. A 2-1 win over Iraq was followed by a 2-2 draw with Paraguay. However in the second round they surpassed themselves beating the USSR 4-3 after extra time and Spain 5-4 on penalties after a 1-1 draw in the quarter-finals. Argentina took revenge in the semi-final winning 2-0 and Belgium lost third place to France 4-2.

Wilfred Van Moer had over a decade as a midfield player with Belgium, dictating the course of many World Cup games during his era; he was still good enough in 1982 to be included in the Belgian squad for the finals.
(BELGIAN FA)

BELGIUM	WORLD CUP RECORD	
Formed: *1895*	1930	*First Round*
Joined FIFA: *1904*	1934	*First Round*
Honours: *4th 1986*	1938	*First Round*
Clubs: *3362*	1950	*Withdrew*
Players: *289,770*	1954	*First Round*
Division I clubs: *18*	1958	*Did not qualify*
Season: *July-June*	1962	*Did not qualify*
Colours: *Red shirts with tri-coloured trim,*	1966	*Did not qualify*
red shorts, red stockings with trim	1970	*First Round*
	1974	*Did not qualify*
	1978	*Did not qualify*
	1982	*Second Round*
	1986	*4th*
	1990	*Second Round*

SPAIN

Spain have never quite managed to live up to their reputation in the World Cup since finishing fourth in 1950 and they were disappointing again in the 1990 finals.

They began their World Cup challenge well enough in 1934, beating Brazil 3-1 but then lost 1-0 to the eventual winners Italy after a bruising 1-1 draw after extra time. In 1938 the civil war robbed them of any participation but in 1950 they showed something of their potential. They defeated the USA 3-1, Chile 2-0 and even England 1-0 to reach the last four. But after a 2-2 draw with Uruguay they were well beaten 6-1 by Brazil and 3-1 by Sweden.

In 1954 and 1958 they failed to qualify only to find themselves in a difficult group in Chile for the 1962 finals. They lost the opening game 1-0 to Czechoslovakia but managed to beat Mexico 1-0. However a narrow 2-1 reverse against Brazil eliminated them.

In 1966 the draw again did them no favours. Argentina beat them 2-1 before the Spaniards reversed the scoreline against Switzerland, but another 2-1 defeat by West Germany ended their interest. Again there were two competitions in which they missed out before qualifying again for the 1978 finals in Argentina. Yet they were beaten 2-1 by Austria in the first match and though they held Brazil to a goalless draw and defeated Sweden 1-0 they were still eliminated.

Staging the finals in 1982 seemed to provide Spain with the right platform to display their ability. But they just scraped into the second stage where they lost 2-1 to West Germany and were held 0-0 by England. However 1986 was much better. They were unfortunate to lose 1-0 to Brazil but impressively beat Denmark 5-1 before losing on penalty kicks to Belgium after a 1-1 draw.

SPAIN

Formed: *1913*
Joined FIFA: *1904*
Honours: *4th 1950*
Clubs: *30,920*
Players: *343,657*
Division I clubs: *20*
Season: *September-June*
Colours: *Red shirts, dark blue shorts, black stockings, yellow trim*

WORLD CUP RECORD

1930	*Did not enter*
1934	*Second Round*
1938	*Could not enter*
1950	*4th*
1954	*Did not qualify*
1958	*Did not qualify*
1962	*First Round*
1966	*First Round*
1970	*Did not qualify*
1974	*Did not qualify*
1978	*First Round*
1982	*Second Round*
1986	*Quarter-finals*
1990	*Second Round*

Emilio Butragueno (right), nicknamed 'The Vulture', swooped down on Denmark four times in a 5-1 win for Spain in 1986.

BOLIVIA

Bolivia qualified for only their third ever World Cup finals in 1994 when they edged out Uruguay to qualify as runners-up in their group behind Brazil. It was a fine achievement.

In the very first World Cup in 1930 Bolivia took up the invitation to compete in the finals despite having had a disastrous start to their international career in the South American Championships just a few years earlier. They were not disgraced in Montevideo although both matches against Brazil and Yugoslavia were lost 4-0 and they were left firmly at the bottom of the group.

When the World Cup returned to South America in 1950 the Bolivians qualified for the finals without playing a match as Argentina withdrew from their qualifying group. Then, thanks to European withdrawals, they found themselves in a first round group which consisted just of themselves and Uruguay. But with only one team qualifying from the group, further progress was never likely as a strong Uruguayan side defeated them 8-0 in Belo Horizonte.

Despite some respectable showings in between it was not until 1978 that Bolivia avenged these early defeats by eliminating Uruguay and finishing top of their qualifying group. This meant they now had to play off against Hungary for a place in the finals but they were

embarrassingly trounced 6-0 in Budapest and so did not make it to Argentina.

One of Bolivia's biggest advantages in international competition has traditionally been their home form in the high altitude of their capital city La Paz, and they finally made it count with four wins out of four in their home qualifying fixtures for 1994, including the notable scalps of both Brazil and Uruguay. A point in their final match, away in Ecuador, was then enough to take them through to the USA.

Milton Melsar (left) heads clear for Bolivia against Colombia during the 1993 Copa America (ALLSPORT/SHAUN BOTTERILL)

BOLIVIA

Formed: *1925*
Joined FIFA: *1926*
Honours: *Nil*
Clubs: *305*
Players: *15,200*
Division I clubs: *14*
Season: *May-December*
Colours: *Green shirts, white shorts, green stockings*

WORLD CUP RECORD

1930	*First Round*
1934	*Did not enter*
1938	*Did not enter*
1950	*First Round*
1954	*Did not enter*
1958	*Did not qualify*
1962	*Did not qualify*
1966	*Did not qualify*
1970	*Did not qualify*
1974	*Did not qualify*
1978	*Did not qualify*
1982	*Did not qualify*
1986	*Did not qualify*
1990	*Did not qualify*

SOUTH KOREA

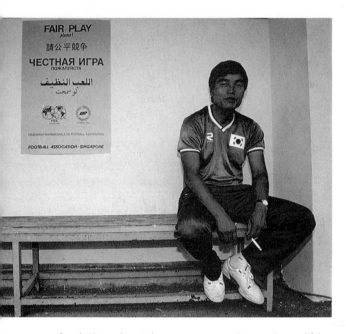

South Korea have shown some consistency in qualifying for recent finals, but progressing past the first round has proved beyond them.

Their initial achievement in reaching the 1954 tournament in Switzerland proved to be a chastening experience. Having overcome Japan to qualify, they were torn apart by the Hungarians in Zurich losing 9-0 and even lost 7-0 to Turkey.

They did not enter in 1958 but in 1962 again overcame Japan winning 2-1 in Seoul and 2-0 in Tokyo which meant they had to play Yugoslavia for a final place. In Belgrade they were beaten 5-1 and also lost at home 3-1.

They pulled out in 1966 and despite staging their sub-group in Seoul in 1970, failed to make any progress. But in 1974 they emerged from their initial matches to beat Israel 1-0 in the sub-group final and forced Australia to a play-off in the zone final before losing 1-0 in Hong Kong.

In 1978 they again negotiated the opening phase to finish second to Iran in the final round but were beaten 2-0 by Kuwait in a four-team group in 1982, though this was their only defeat in the tournament staged in Kuwait.

At last 1986 brought just reward. They beat Nepal 2-0 away and 4-0 at home, and after losing 1-0 in Malaysia, won the return game 2-0 to move on to the second round where they defeated Indonesia 2-0 and 4-1. In the final stage they beat Japan 2-1 in Tokyo and 1-0 in Seoul.

In Mexico their misfortune was to start the competition by playing Argentina. This 3-1 defeat was followed by holding Bulgaria to a 1-1 draw and they surprised Italy in the last group match before being edged out 3-2.

SOUTH KOREA	WORLD CUP RECORD	
Formed: *1928.*	**1930**	*Not eligible*
Joined FIFA: *1948*	**1934**	*Not eligible*
Honours: *Nil*	**1938**	*Not eligible*
Clubs: *476*	**1950**	*Did not enter*
Players: *2047*	**1954**	*First Round*
Division I clubs: *5*	**1958**	*Did not enter*
Season: *March-November*	**1962**	*Did not qualify*
Colours: *All red*	**1966**	*Withdrew*
	1970	*Did not qualify*
	1974	*Did not qualify*
	1978	*Did not qualify*
	1982	*Did not qualify*
	1986	*First Round*
	1990	*First Round*

A coach's life can be a lonely one; certainly this appears to be the case for Lee Hoe-Taik, South Korea's man in the hot seat as he takes time out to think tactics.

NIGERIA

Great things have for a while been expected of Nigeria in international football, due in part to some notable performances at junior level. In 1985 Nigeria defeated West Germany 2-0 in the final of the World Championships for Under-17s and two years later they lost out to the Soviet Union only on penalties in defence of their title.

Qualification for the United States in 1994, however, represented their first such success at senior level. They first entered the World Cup in 1962 when they fell at the first qualifying hurdle, beaten over two legs by Ghana. Following the African boycott of the 1966 competition Nigeria returned in 1970 and progressed to the final qualifying group at the expense of Cameroon and Ghana, but they finished runners-up behind Morocco.

In 1974 came disgrace as they were disqualified from the tournament by FIFA after crowd disturbances at their home fixture against Ghana led to the match being abandoned. A thumping 6-2 victory over Sierra Leone kicked off their next World Cup campaign but although they again reached the final qualifying group and made a bright start, they lost a crucial game at home to Tunisia and ultimately finished behind both the Tunisians and Egypt.

It was a defeat Nigeria avenged in the qualifying competition for 1982 when they eliminated Tunisia in the first round on penalties and progressed to a play-off over two legs against Algeria for a place in the finals. Sadly both matches were lost. Tunisia accounted for them again in 1986 in the third round, and they were unable to get past Cameroon in 1990 although they would have run them very close had it not been for an unexpected 2-1 reverse away to Gabon, who finished bottom of the group.

Nigeria's qualifying games in 1994 included an historic meeting with newly readmitted South Africa, and they clinched a place in the finals just ahead of African Nations Cup holders Ivory Coast with a 1-1 draw in Algeria.

The Nigerian team which secured their country's first ever World Cup finals place (ALLSPORT/CLIVE BRUNSKILL)

NIGERIA

Formed: *1945*
Joined FIFA: *1959*
Honours: *Nil*
Clubs: *521*
Players: *21,100*
Division I clubs: *14*
Season: *February-November*
Colours: *All green*

WORLD CUP RECORD

1930	*Not eligible*
1934	*Not eligible*
1938	*Not eligible*
1950	*Not eligible*
1954	*Not eligible*
1958	*Not eligible*
1962	*Did not qualify*
1966	*Withdrew*
1970	*Did not qualify*
1974	*Disqualified*
1978	*Did not qualify*
1982	*Did not qualify*
1986	*Did not qualify*
1990	*Did not qualify*

NORWAY

both Sweden and Switzerland were defeated in Oslo and Norway finished second in the group. In 1982 came a famous victory over England and a win in Berne against Switzerland, while in the next campaign Ireland were beaten in Oslo. Yet actual qualification still seemed a long way off.

The 1994 campaign, however, was triumph for the Norwegians. Given impetus by a 10-0 annihilation of San Marino, it gathered irresistible momentum as first Holland then Turkey, England and finally Poland all succumbed in Oslo, and a place in America was assured by an impressive 3-0 win in Chorzow.

Claiming the notable scalp of England in the process, Norway crowned their emergence as a force in European football by finishing top of their group and qualifying for the World Cup finals in 1994. It was the first time they had done so since the war.

The Norwegians had previously made an appearance in the finals in 1938, the first time they entered the competition. They qualified by defeating the Republic of Ireland in a high scoring tie over two legs and faced holders Italy in the first round in France. They forced extra time before a Silvio Piola goal spared the Italians' blushes.

When Norway re-entered the World Cup in 1954 it was very much as one of the weaker European nations, but despite their lack of overall success they were always capable of achieving a one-off result in Oslo. They defeated Hungary 2-1 in 1958 while losing 5-0 in the return, and beat Yugoslavia 3-0 in 1966 during what was their most successful qualifying campaign to date as they finished runners-up in the group behind France. They were to claim a notable success at the expense of the French in the 1970 qualifying competition with a 1-0 win in Strasbourg.

Norway reached a low point in their World Cup fortunes when they lost 9-0 in Holland four years later but this was followed by a better performance in 1978 when

Norway's keeper Erik Thorstvedt who has completed 80 international appearances (ALLSPORT/SHAUN BOTTERILL)

NORWAY		WORLD CUP RECORD	
Formed: 1902		**1930**	Did not enter
Joined FIFA: 1908		**1934**	Did not enter
Honours: Nil		**1938**	First Round
Clubs: 1810		**1950**	Did not enter
Players: 280,000		**1954**	Did not qualify
Division I clubs: 12		**1958**	Did not qualify
Season: April-October		**1962**	Did not qualify
Colours: Red shirts, white shorts,		**1966**	Did not qualify
blue stockings		**1970**	Did not qualify
		1974	Did not qualify
		1978	Did not qualify
		1982	Did not qualify
		1986	Did not qualify
		1990	Did not qualify

HOLLAND

Holland finished runners-up in successive finals in the 1970s when they were arguably the best team in Europe. But the 1990 finals perhaps came two years too late; the European Champions of 1988 were hugely disappointing.

There was a swift exit in 1934 when they lost 3-2 to Switzerland and though they forced extra time against Czechoslovakia four years later, they conceded three goals without reply. Holland did not enter in either 1950 or 1954 and failed to qualify in 1958. It was a similar story in 1962 and 1966 when the preliminaries proved too much for this still-then-emerging football country.

Still, there was a noticeable improvement in the 1970 qualifying competition, as they finished two places but only two points behind Bulgaria. But in 1974 there was an outstanding transformation. Holland qualified — if only just — on a vastly superior goal difference over neighbours Belgium, with both teams just dropping points to each other in goalless draws.

In the finals in West Germany they beat Uruguay 2-0, drew 0-0 with Sweden and then defeated Bulgaria 4-1. In the second round they took four goals off Argentina without reply, beat East Germany 2-0 and Brazil by the same score. In fact the only goal conceded had been by one of their own players. Alas the 2-1 final defeat by the West Germans was a huge anti-climax.

They were equally determined in 1978 beating Iran 3-0 and drawing 0-0 with Peru. But they were slack against Scotland and lost 3-2, although it did not prevent them reaching the second round where they beat Austria 5-1 and drew 2-2 with West Germany. Then a 2-1 success over Italy put them in the final where they lost again, this time 3-1 to Argentina after extra time.

Johan Neeskens (left, horizontal) one of the stars of the great Dutch side of 1974, in an aerial battle with Sweden's Ove Grahn in the 0-0 draw in Dortmund.

HOLLAND

Formed: *1889*
Joined FIFA: *1904*
Honours: *Runners-up 1974, 1978*
Clubs: *7912*
Players: *978,324*
Division I clubs: *18*
Season: *August-June*
Colours: *Orange shirts, white shorts, orange stockings*

WORLD CUP RECORD

1930	*Did not enter*
1934	*First Round*
1938	*First Round*
1950	*Did not enter*
1954	*Did not enter*
1958	*Did not qualify*
1962	*Did not qualify*
1966	*Did not qualify*
1970	*Did not qualify*
1974	*Runners-up*
1978	*Runners-up*
1982	*Did not qualify*
1986	*Did not qualify*
1990	*Second Round*

REPUBLIC OF IRELAND

The Republic of Ireland have been keen supporters of the World Cup but had never previously succeeded in reaching the finals until the 1990 tournament.

Their first attempt was in 1934 and they began by drawing 4-4 with Belgium in Dublin. But a 5-2 defeat in Holland ruled them out. In 1938 they lost 3-2 in Oslo to Norway and were held 3-3 in the return game.

In 1950 they had Scandinavian opposition in Sweden and Finland and after losing 3-1 in Stockholm to the former they beat Finland 3-0 in Dublin to record their first win in the tournament. They also drew 1-1 in Helsinki before losing 3-1 at home to Sweden.

In 1954 home and away wins against Luxembourg were cancelled out by losing twice to France. Four years later they put up a determined challenge beating Denmark 2-1 at home and 2-0 away, but lost 5-1 to England away and were held by them 1-1 in Dublin.

But 1962 was definitely a non-vintage performance. They failed to take a point against either Scotland or Czechoslovakia, yet forced Spain to a play-off in 1966 before losing that game 1-0 in Paris. In 1970 they were undistinguished in the company of Hungary, Czechoslovakia and Denmark and managed three points in 1974 when faced with the USSR and France, from whom they retrieved the trio. Moreover it was France who

stood in their way in 1978, though they had the satisfaction of beating them 1-0 in Dublin.

Incredibly it was France again who barred their way in 1982, but for the Republic it was unquestionably their best performance to date, finishing above Holland and losing out to France only on goal difference. They were disappointing in 1986 but reached the finals comfortably in 1990. In Italy they drew all three group matches, then defeated Rumania on penalties to reach the quarter-finals where they gave the host nation a fright despite losing 1-0, crowning a highly satisfactory debut in the finals.

REPUBLIC OF IRELAND	WORLD CUP RECORD	
Formed: *1921*	1930	*Did not enter*
Joined FIFA: *1923*	1934	*Did not qualify*
Honours: *Nil*	1938	*Did not qualify*
Clubs: *3503*	1950	*Did not qualify*
Players: *33,028*	1954	*Did not qualify*
Division I clubs: *12*	1958	*Did not qualify*
Season: *August-May*	1962	*Did not qualify*
Colours: *Green shirts, white shorts, green stockings*	1966	*Did not qualify*
	1970	*Did not qualify*
	1974	*Did not qualify*
	1978	*Did not qualify*
	1982	*Did not qualify*
	1986	*Did not qualify*
	1990	*Quarter-finals*

Tony Cascarino takes a determined swipe at the ball for the Republic of Ireland in their last World Cup qualifying game of the 1990 series against Malta. A 2-0 win clinched their place in the finals for the first time.

WORLD CUP RECORDS

COUNTRY BY COUNTRY RECORDS IN THE FINALS
1930-1990

	P	W	D	L	F	A
Brazil	66	44	11	11	148	65
*West Germany	68	39	15	14	145	90
Italy	54	31	12	11	89	54
Argentina	48	24	9	15	82	59
England	41	18	12	11	55	38
Uruguay	37	15	8	14	61	52
USSR	31	15	6	10	53	34
France	34	15	5	14	71	56
Yugoslavia	33	15	5	13	55	42
Hungary	32	15	3	14	87	57
Spain	32	13	7	12	43	38
Poland	25	13	5	7	39	29
Sweden	31	11	6	14	51	52
Czechoslovakia	30	11	5	14	44	45
Austria	26	12	2	12	40	43
Holland	20	8	6	6	35	23
Belgium	25	7	4	14	33	49
Mexico	29	6	6	17	27	64
Chile	21	7	3	11	26	32
Scotland	20	4	6	10	23	35
Portugal	9	6	0	3	19	12
Switzerland	18	5	2	11	28	44
Northern Ireland	13	3	5	5	13	23
Peru	15	4	3	8	19	31
Paraguay	11	3	4	4	16	25
Rumania	12	3	3	6	16	20
Cameroon	8	3	3	2	8	10
Denmark	4	3	0	1	10	6
East Germany	6	2	2	2	5	5
USA	10	3	0	7	14	29

	P	W	D	L	F	A
Bulgaria	16	0	6	10	11	35
Wales	5	1	3	1	4	4
Algeria	6	2	1	3	6	10
Morocco	7	1	3	3	5	8
Republic of Ireland	5	0	4	1	2	3
Costa Rica	4	2	0	2	4	6
Colombia	7	1	2	4	9	15
Tunisia	3	1	1	1	3	2
North Korea	4	1	1	2	5	9
Cuba	3	1	1	1	5	12
Turkey	3	1	0	2	10	11
Honduras	3	0	2	1	2	3
Israel	3	1	0	2	1	3
Egypt	4	0	2	2	3	6
Kuwait	3	0	1	2	2	6
Australia	3	0	1	2	0	5
Iran	3	0	1	2	2	8
South Korea	8	0	1	7	5	29
Norway	1	0	0	1	1	2
Dutch East Indies	1	0	0	1	0	6
Iraq	3	0	0	3	1	4
Canada	3	0	0	3	0	5
United Arab Emirates	3	0	0	3	2	11
New Zealand	3	0	0	3	2	12
Haiti	3	0	0	3	2	14
Zaire	3	0	0	3	0	14
Bolivia	3	0	0	3	0	16
El Salvador	6	0	0	6	1	22

*includes Germany 1930-38

Matches decided by penalty kicks are shown as drawn games

GOALS

GAMES	GOALS	AVERAGE	YEAR	LEADING GOALSCORER	GOALS
18	70	3.88	1930	Guillermo Stabile (Argentina)	8
17	70	4.11	1934	Angelo Schiavio (Italy) Oldrich Nejedly (Czechoslovakia) Edmund Cohen (Germany)	4
18	84	4.66	1938	Leonidas da Silva (Brazil)	8
22	88	4.00	1950	Ademir (Brazil)	9
26	140	5.38	1954	Sandor Kocsis (Hungary)	11
35	126	3.60	1958	Just Fontaine (France)	13
32	89	2.78	1962	Drazen Jerkovic (Yugoslavia)	5
32	89	2.78	1966	Eusebio (Portugal)	9
32	95	2.96	1970	Gerd Muller (West Germany)	10
38	97	2.55	1974	Grzegorz Lato (Poland)	7
38	102	2.68	1978	Mario Kempes (Argentina)	6
52	146	2.81	1982	Paolo Rossi (Italy)	6
52	132	2.53	1986	Gary Lineker (England)	6
52	115	2.21	1990	Salvatore Schillaci (Italy)	6

Six goals in Mexico made England's Gary Lineker (below) the 1986 tournament's top scorer.

Mario Zagalo, the serious Brazilian manager who managed one successful World Cup winning team after playing in two others.
(SYNDICATION INTERNATIONAL)

BOSSES

YEAR	WINNERS	MANAGER
1930	Uruguay	Alberto Supicci
1934	Italy	Vittorio Pozzo
1938	Italy	Vittorio Pozzo
1950	Uruguay	Juan Lopez
1954	West Germany	Sepp Herberger
1958	Brazil	Vicente Feola
1962	Brazil	Aymore Moreira
1966	England	Alf Ramsey
1970	Brazil	Mario Zagalo
1974	West Germany	Helmut Schoen
1978	Argentina	Cesar Luis Menotti
1982	Italy	Enzo Bearzot
1986	Argentina	Carlos Bilardo
1990	West Germany	Franz Beckenbauer

CROWDS

YEAR	VENUE	AGGREGATE ATTENDANCE	AVERAGE ATTENDANCE	GAMES
1930	Uruguay	434,500	24,139	18
1934	Italy	395,000	23,235	17
1938	France	483,000	26,833	18
1950	Brazil	1,337,000	60,772	22
1954	Switzerland	943,000	36,270	26
1958	Sweden	868,000	24,800	35
1962	Chile	776,000	24,250	32
1966	England	1,614,677	50,458	32
1970	Mexico	1,673,975	52,312	32
1974	West Germany	1,774,022	46,685	38
1978	Argentina	1,610,215	42,374	38
1982	Spain	1,766,277	33,967	52
1986	Mexico	2,401,480	46,182	52

WORLD CUP FINAL ATTENDANCES

YEAR	RESULT	VENUE	ATTENDANCE
1930	Uruguay 4 Argentina 2	Montevideo	90,000
1934	Italy 2 Czechoslovakia 1	Rome	50,000
1938	Italy 4 Hungary 2	Paris	45,000
1950	Uruguay 2 Brazil 1	Rio de Janeiro	199,854
1954	West Germany 3 Hungary 2	Berne	60,000
1958	Brazil 5 Sweden 2	Stockholm	49,737
1962	Brazil 3 Czechoslovakia 1	Santiago	68,679
1966	England 4 West Germany 2	Wembley	93,802
1970	Brazil 4 Italy 1	Mexico City	107,412
1974	West Germany 2 Holland 1	Munich	77,833
1978	Argentina 3 Holland 1	Buenos Aires	77,000
1982	Italy 3 West Germany 1	Madrid	90,080
1986	Argentina 3 West Germany 2	Mexico City	114,580

WORLD CUP

TRIVIA

The **record margin** of victory in a World Cup final tournament is nine goals: Hungary 10 El Salvador 1 (1982), Hungary 9 South Korea 0 (1954), Yugoslavia 9 Zaire 0 (1974). **Highest aggregate**: Austria 7 Switzerland 5 (1954). The **record scoreline** in any World Cup match is New Zealand 13 Fiji 0 in a qualifying match on 15 August 1981.

Just Fontaine (France) scored a **record 13 goals** in six matches of the 1958 World Cup finals. Jairzinho (Brazil) scored **seven in six games** in 1970. The only other player to score in **every match in a final series** is Alcide Ghiggia (Uruguay) with four goals in four games in 1950. Gerd Muller (West Germany) scored 10 goals in 1970 and four in 1974 for the **highest aggregate** of 14 goals. Muller scored 19 goals in the 1970 competition as a

whole, including nine in six qualifying games.

Pele is third highest scorer in World Cup final tournaments after Muller and Fontaine, having registered 12 goals: 1958 (6), 1962 (1), 1966 (1), 1970 (4).

Geoff Hurst (England) is the only player to have scored a **hat-trick in a World Cup Final**; he got three goals in their 4 - 2 win over West Germany in 1966.

The first player to score as many as **four goals in any World Cup match** was Paddy Moore who claimed all the Republic of Ireland's goals in the 4 - 4 draw with Belgium in Dublin during a World Cup qualifying match on 25 February 1934.

Robbie Rensenbrink (Holland) scored the **1000th goal** in World Cup finals when he

converted a penalty against Scotland in 1978.

The **first goal scored** in the World Cup was credited to Louis Laurent for France against Mexico on 13 July 1930 in Montevideo. France won 4 - 1. The news reached France on Bastille Day, 14 July.

The **fastest goal scored** in the World Cup finals was probably scored by Vaclav Masek for Czechoslovakia v Mexico in 1962, timed on film at 15 seconds. FIFA officially still regard Bryan Robson's goal in 27 seconds for England v France in 1982 as the quickest.

West Germany achieved the **highest scoring rate** for a winning World Cup side when in 1954 they scored 25 goals in six matches for an average of 4.16 per game. But the 14 goals they conceded was also a record!

Highest individual scorers in one match Finals- 4 goals:
Gustav Wetterstrom (Sweden v Cuba, 1938)
Leonidas da Silva (Brazil v Poland, 1938)
Ernest Willimowski (Poland v Brazil, 1938)
Ademir (Brazil v Sweden, 1950)
Juan Schiaffino (Uruguay v Bolivia, 1950)
Sandor Kocsis (Hungary v West Germany, 1954)
Just Fontaine (France v West Germany, 1958)
Eusebio (Portugal v North Korea, 1966)
Emilio Butragueno (Spain v Denmark, 1986)

The lowest attendance for a match in the World Cup finals was probably 300 for the Rumania v Peru game on 14 July 1930 in Montevideo, Uruguay. **The highest**: 205,000 for Brazil v Uruguay on 16 July 1950 in Rio de Janeiro, Brazil. Of this estimated figure 199,854 were officially recorded, 173,830 paid to enter.

The **first substitute** used in the World Cup finals was the Soviet player Anatoly Puzach at the beginning of the second half of the USSR v Mexico game in 1970. But on 11 October 1953 West Germany had used a substitute in a qualifying game with Saar, Horst Eckel replacing Richard Gottinger, and again in the return game on 28 March 1954 when Ottmar Walter took over from his brother Fritz.

The Brazilians were **unbeaten in 13 consecutive World Cup matches** between 1958 and 1966, winning 11 and drawing two. The run ended with a 3 - 1 defeat by Hungary at Goodison Park.

Brazil used **only 12 players** in the 1962 World Cup finals. Their one change came through injury to Pele, who was replaced by Amarildo after the second match.

Dino Zoff (Italy) became the **oldest player to win a World Cup winners medal** when he captained his country to their 1982 success at the age of 40. Apart from Zoff, only one other goalkeeper had captained a World Cup winning side. He was Giampiero Combi, the Italian goalkeeper in 1934.

Norman Whiteside (Northern Ireland) became the **youngest player**, at 17, to appear in the World Cup finals in 1982. His first team experience for Manchester United had consisted of just two appearances in their Division One side, one of them as substitute. He was 17 years 42 days old when he appeared against Yugoslavia on 17 June. Pele had been 17 years 237 days old in Sweden in 1958.

Quickest dismissal in a World Cup final tournament was directed at Uruguay's Jose Batista after 55 seconds of the match with Scotland in Mexico on 13 June 1986.

Pele is the only player to have played with **three World Cup winning teams,** though he missed the final in 1962 through injury. His 14 appearances came from: 1958 (4), 1962 (2), 1966 (2) and 1970 (6).

Vava (real name Edwaldo Isidio Neto) of Brazil is the only player to have **scored in successive World Cup Finals.** He did so against Sweden in 1958 (scoring twice) and against Czechoslovakia in 1962. Pele (Brazil) and Paul Breitner (West Germany) are the only others to have scored in two Finals. Pele scored two goals in 1958 and one in 1970; Breitner a penalty in 1974 and a goal in 1982.

Antonio Carbajal (Mexico) is the only player to have appeared in **five World Cup final tournaments.** He kept goal for Mexico in 1950, 1954, 1958, 1962 and 1966, with eleven appearances in all.

Only two men have **won a World Cup winners medal and managed a World Cup winning team.** Mario Zagalo played in the 1958 and 1962 World Cup winning teams of Brazil and was manager when they achieved their third success in 1970. Franz Beckenbauer led West Germany to victory as a player in 1974 and as manager in 1990. He was also a losing finalist both as a player in 1966 and as a manager in 1986.

Uwe Seeler (West Germany) established a record in World Cup final tournaments by making a total of **21 appearances**. This was equalled by Wladyslaw Zmuda (Poland). Seeler played in 1958, 1962, 1966 and 1970; Zmuda in 1974, 1978, 1982 and 1986.

The longest period that a **goalkeeper has remained unbeaten** in World Cup finals matches is 517 minutes. In 1990 Walter Zenga (Italy) did not concede a goal in three first round group matches against Austria, the United States and Czechoslovakia, and remained unbeaten throughout the second round match with Uruguay and the quarter-final against the Republic of Ireland. He was finally beaten in the 67th minute of the semi-final against Argentina by a header from Claudio Caniggia. Ironically he then conceded four from the penalty spot in the shoot-out which saw the Italians beaten 4 - 3 and knocked out of the competition. Previously the record had stood at 501 minutes, set by Peter Shilton (England) over two tournaments in 1982 and 1986. Shilton also played in the 1990 finals, where his longest unbeaten period was 381 minutes.

New Zealand established a record in the 1982 qualifying tournament by playing **15 matches.** During this period goalie Richard Wilson completed 15 hours 20 minutes without conceding a goal.

Edmond Delfour and Etienne Mattler (both Frenchmen) and the Belgian Bernard Voorhof, were the **first players to appear in three successive finals**: 1930, 1934 and 1938. Luisito Monti played in the 1930 tournament for Argentina and the 1934 series for Italy. Ferenc Puskas was in the Hungarian team during the 1954 finals and Spain's for the 1962 competition.

One factual analysis of the **1966 World Cup final** in which England beat West Germany 4 - 2 after extra time revealed the following statistics:
Goal attempts:
England 45 (four goals, one hit post, ten saved, six blocked, three deflected, 21 high or wide)
West Germany 37 (two goals, nine saved, nine blocked, five deflected, 12 high or wide)
Corners:
England 6
West Germany 12
Fouls:
England 22 (including three for hands)
West Germany 16 (including three for hands)
Offside:
England 1
West Germany 4
Goal-kicks:
England 16
West Germany 24
Throw-ins:
England 36
West Germany 19

In December 1983 a motion before FIFA's conference from the USA to equip goalkeepers with **helmets** was turned down.

Three managers have taken **different teams to World Cup final tournaments**. Rudolf Vytlacil, a Czechoslovakian, was in charge of his own country when they finished runners-up to Brazil in 1962 and four years later led Bulgaria in the competition. Blagoje Vidinic was the coach of Morocco in 1970 and Zaire in 1974. He was a Yugoslavian. Bora Milutinovic managed Mexico in 1986 and Costa Rica in 1990, and is in charge of a third team, the USA, for the 1994 finals.

The opening match of the 1966 finals at Wembley between England and Uruguay was nearly called off by Hungarian referee Istvan Zsolt. He discovered that seven England players had left their identity cards in the team hotel. Zsolt said: **No cards, no game.** A police motor cyclist was despatched to collect them.

The original **Jules Rimet trophy** had an eventful life. After being successfully hidden during World War Two, it was stolen while on display in a London stamp exhibition before the 1966 finals. It was discovered by a mongrel dog called Pickles, owned by David Corbett, a Norwood lighterman, from under a garden hedge. Handed to Brazil for permanent retainment in 1970 it was again stolen from a display box in Rio and never recovered.

Zaire became the **first black African country to reach the finals** in 1974. The country's president promised each member of the squad a house, car and free holiday for their families. The team lost all three games, failed to score a goal and conceded 14. The offer was withdrawn.

Friction which had existed throughout the post-war period between Honduras and El Salvador gradually became more intense in the late 1960s. The two countries met in a World Cup qualifying tie in June 1969. The first leg in Honduras on June 8 produced little or no trouble on the pitch, but the frustrations which had built up off it finally burst during the return game in San Salvador on June 15. Since both teams had won their home games, a third and deciding match was scheduled for Mexico City on June 27. Relations had deteriorated into open hostility, and **all-out war** lasted two weeks. Mercifully the play-off passed without any animosity between the players.

The first player banned by FIFA for **drug-taking** in a final series was the Haitian, Ernest Jean-Joseph in 1974. But his manager refused to send him home and he was extradited by security men sent from Haiti; he never played again. In 1978, Willie Johnston of Scotland was also sent home in disgrace after taking an illegal drug for medicinal purposes.

Pat Jennings (above) made his 119th appearance for Northern Ireland against Brazil during the 1986 World Cup, on his 41st birthday. (ALLSPORT)

Mo Johnston (above) set up a record for one of the four Home International countries by **scoring in each of five successive World Cup qualifying matches** in 1988-89; Norway (1 goal), Yugoslavia (1), Cyprus (1), France (2), Cyprus (1).

Brazil is the only country to have **appeared in all World Cup final tournaments**. They have also won the competition three times, a record shared with Italy and West Germany.

Before departing to Brazil to compete in the 1950 series, the England players **trained at Ascot**. Unfortunately they finished as also-rans.

The 1982 finals produced a number of **records**: the first hat-trick by a substitute, Laszlo Kiss (Hungary) v El Salvador; the fastest goal, in 27 seconds by Bryan Robson (England); the first penalty miss in Final, by Antonio Cabrini (Italy); a record score by one team, Hungary 10 El Salvador 1; and the first match to be decided by penalty kicks, West Germany beating France 5 - 4 after a 3 - 3 draw.

A total of **12.8 billion** television viewers watched the 1986 finals in Mexico. The final between Argentina and West Germany was seen by 580 million people in 160 countries.

Ernesto Mascheroni, the **last survivor** of the Uruguayan team which won the 1930 World Cup, died on 3 July 1984 at the age of 76.

Scotland's manager Andy Beattie **resigned** after the 1 - 0 defeat by Austria in the 1954 World Cup. Uruguay then beat the Scots 7 - 0.

Dino Zoff (Italy) was able to celebrate his 100th international appearance with a **goalless draw** against Poland in the 1982 tournament. But Polish international **Kazimierz Deyna** was not so fortunate on his 100th game in 1978. He **missed a penalty** against Argentina and the Poles lost 2 - 0.

A special **World Cup stamp**, approved by the Post Office and the Football Association, showing the flags of the 16 nations in the 1966 finals was banned by the Foreign Office because the British government did not recognise North Korea. The special commemorative issue was quickly changed to reveal footballers in action and became the first British stamps to feature sportsmen.

When Northern Ireland qualified for the 1958 finals in Sweden, their players were **ordered by the Irish FA not to play** in two of their three group matches as they fell on Sundays. But the team ignored the ruling.

The United States trainer ran on to the field to attend to one of his injured players in the semi-final against Argentina in 1930. He tripped, fell and broke a bottle of chloroform. The trainer was **carried off unconscious** while the player recovered without treatment.

The Argentine journalist Osvaldo Ardizzone established a **communication record** after his team qualified for the 1966 quarter-finals. His cable to Buenos Aires was 20,246 words long and took 5 hours and 40 minutes to transmit.

Refereeing can be a **monstrous undertaking**. In 1934 and 1937, two World Cup qualifying matches involving Hungary and Bulgaria and Lithuania and Latvia respectively, were controlled by Herr Frankenstein of Austria.

Sharp-eyed English referee Jack Taylor delayed the start of the 1974 World Cup Final between West Germany and Holland when he noticed that all the **flag-posts in midfield and at the corners were missing.**

Neither Argentina nor Uruguay could decide on **which ball to use** in the 1930 final. Belgian referee John Langenus decided to toss a coin. Argentina won and used their ball in the first half after which they led 2 - 1. Uruguay used theirs after the interval, and won 4 - 2.

Uruguay's goalkeeper in 1930 was Antonio Mazzali. He had played in the country's successful 1924 and 1928 Olympic teams but was destined not to appear in the first World Cup. The Uruguayan team had been isolated for almost eight weeks in a Montevideo hotel. One night Mazzali **sneaked out** to visit his family and was caught upon his return. He was sent home for good.

The two players with the **shortest last names** to have appeared in a World Cup final tournament are Cayetano Re (Paraguay) in 1958 and Francisco Sa (Argentina) in 1974.

INDEX

Errata

The publishers would like to acknowledge the following errata in sections reprinted from the 1990 edition:

Page 14 . . . 1934 Qualifying Group 3 should read Argentina qualified (Chile withdrew).

Page 103 . . . Referee for Cameroon v Rumania should read Silva (Chile).

Pages 158–79 . . . Statistics on domestic football in Italy, USA, Cameroon, Argentina, Rumania, Brazil, Sweden, Colombia, Belgium, Spain, South Korea, Holland and Republic of Ireland are for 1990.

Page 161 . . . Argentina's World Cup Record should read 1934 First Round.

Page 180 . . . Yugoslavia's record in the World Cup Finals should read W 14, D 7, L 12. Israel's record should read W 0, D 2, L 1.

Page 181 . . . Top scorer in 1950 Ademir's goals total should read 7.

Page 182 . . . Attendances for 1982 should read 2,064,364 (av. 38, 816); 1986 should read 2,441,731 (av. 46,956); 1990 should read 2,515,168 (av. 48,368).

Acknowledgements

World Cup (Brian Glanville/Jerry Weinstein) 1958
World Cup Digest (Jack Rollin) 1966
England's World Cup Triumph (Jack Rollin) 1966
A–Z of World Soccer (Norman Barrett) 1973
FIFA Technical Study 1970, 1974
Armada Book of the World Cup (Gordon Jeffrey) 1974
Official FIFA Report, World Cup Argentina 1978
Complete World Cup Guide (Jack Rollin) 1982
Chelsea Independent 1991
Guinness Record of World Soccer (Guy Oliver) 1992
BBC Television
FIFA News
Don Aldridge